REGNUM GLOBAL VOICES SOUTH KOREA

Maeul Ministry

The Missional Church in Urban Korea

Series Preface

The **Global Voices** series takes the missiological work of writers who have written in their own language and makes this accessible to the English-speaking world through translation and republishing. The key principle here is that the translated work reflects the context, experience and thinking of the local context. In so doing, Regnum Books seeks to amplify voices less easily heard outside their own contexts. Work of this nature will make a significant contribution to the development of 'polycentric missiology'; namely, mission thinking and practice that truly reflects the contexts, concerns and contributions of the global church in all its rich diversity.

REGNUM GLOBAL VOICES SOUTH KOREA

Maeul Ministry

The Missional Church in Urban Korea

Edited by

Eun-ha Cho & Kook-il Han

First published 2024 by Regnum Books International

Regnum is an imprint of the Oxford Centre for Mission Studies
St. Philip and St. James Church
Woodstock Road
Oxford, OX2 6HR, UK
www.regnumbooks.net

British Library Cataloguing in Publication Data
A catalogue record for this book is available from the British Library

ISBN: 979-8-8898-3879-1
eBook ISBN: 979-8-8898-3880-7

Typeset by Words by Design

Translated by Rebekah Hwajhin Lee

Distributed by Fortress Press in the US, Canada, India, and Brazil

Contents

Editor's Introduction
Maeul Ministry: Theological Reflections on Urban Churches

Eun-ha Cho

God has loved the world as to send God's only son. But today's world is in pieces due to war, poverty, sickness, and conflict. How will the church fulfill its calling as light and salt in this world? When only 20% of the South Korean public sees the Protestant church as credible, is there any hope for the church? To find answers to these questions, we turned to the churches in our communities, the *maeul.*[1] We discovered churches existing as community companions and friends. We listened to these ministry stories and studied the cases to confirm that the mission of God continues, each tiny seed growing, blooming, and bearing fruit wherever they are planted. This publication introduces six churches and one missions organization in urban settings, plus an analysis of each by seven scholars from their theological, pastoral, missional, and educational perspectives to explain their insights and implications on these ministry cases. May these stories encourage the ministers praying and struggling in the rapidly changing society, the church communities pursuing the vision of the kingdom of God, and others seeking to respond to God's calling in ministry.

Seong-won Park's "Pilgrimage Towards Life-Flourishing Culture and Community" examines the world and South Korean society today in terms of the flourishing of life. He critiques the dominant Western dualism from his ecological and holistic perspective, especially in today's climate crisis, and calls for a new theological and pastoral framework. He proposes cosmic ministry for the life-flourishing community, which requires an innovative transformation of existing theological and ministry themes to reflect the life-flourishing community movement.

Young-sang Ro recounts the state of the planet and the crisis of the church to add his reflections on the theology of life in "State of the 21st Century Global Village and Maeul Ministry's Focus on Communal Joy". He presents as the solution the maeul ministry that emphasizes love in action. The church is not a community that remains apart from the community but is present in the midst of it. Churches can perform their missional calling by presenting a variety of practical approaches and solutions to the neighbors' specific needs.

---

[1] Translator's Note: While the Korean term "maeul" traditionally means a small rural village, the term may name various units of local communities in rural or urban settings today. In this chapter and throughout the publication, unless otherwise noted, the term maeul is romanized and non-italicized in instances of adjectival usage (e.g., maeul ministry, maeul church). In nominal usage, they are variously translated as community, local community, neighborhood, village, or town.

Gongmyung Church is where hospitality and authenticity resonate. The church bears repeat visits and inspires inquiry behind its stories. It is co-pastored by Hung-young Baek (Seon-young Lee, spouse) and In-sung Hwang (So-yeon Bae, spouse). The two young ministers preparing for cross-cultural missions turned to Yangpyeong in South Korea as their mission field. They embarked on field research to find the town's needs and ways a church could meet them. They found a lone multi-household building at the end of a small path between rice paddies and started a church in 2018, confessing that "Transformation happens when the life of the triune God resounds in us and our lives, in turn, resound in others." The church has been like the water that primes the pump, inviting neighbors to gather, share their lives, and meet with God. Byung-ohk Lee explains that this was thanks to Gongmyung Church's healthy start as a missional church. The church's intention to resonate with God, with families, the community, the world, and even with nature spells for a bright future.

Seongam Church is the pride of Eunpyeong District in Seoul. Its residents mention the church as one of the district's positive aspects. How did the church become the neighborhood pride? When its pastor Joo-hee Cho was appointed to the church, he reflected on the public nature of the church and initiated an ecclesiological reorientation. For this purpose, he requested an external social scientific consultation, which raised the church's credibility in the community. Through the consultation, the church could systematically understand the town, and the pastor and the congregation could discuss the direction of the church based on a common understanding. This is how Seongam Church became the pride of Eunpyeong District, walking in step with the neighbors. In-sung Hwang assesses that this change in the church was made possible by the ecclesiological turn and the persistent communication between the congregation and others outside the church. When people truly listen to each other, consider their priorities, and humbly study the reign of God, the future will not be an object of fear but of hope.

Healthy church, proper ministry. Based on this principle, Hong-sun Kim who pastors Ansan Myungsung Church turned the once-derided church into a place the neighbors commend. Based on the pastor's balanced leadership and authentic love for the neighbors, the church at which people threw stones is now offered flowers. In 2014, when 304 young people about to bloom tragically drowned in the Sewol Ferry Disaster, the city of Ansan became a place of trauma and stigma. Based on the words of Romans 12:15 to weep with those who weep, Healing Center 0416 Rest and Renewal was established in a cooperative endeavor of Ansan Myungsung Church (operating institution), Seonbu General Social Service Center (project managing institution), and the Counseling and Coaching Support Center of Yonsei University (cooperating institution). The Center was a case of post-disaster care for healing and renewal that combined spirituality, local context, and expertise. Ansan Myungsung Church could holistically combine spirituality and professional expertise in its ministry to let the water of life flow beyond the power of death. This was possible thanks to the theological basis of ministry, the balanced core principles underlying the church structure, strong leadership and the congregants' volunteerism, communication between the church and town, and the holistic integrity of knowing and living.

Saerom Church in the town of Yakdae-dong in the city of Bucheon is known for its Kkobi Night Eatery. Kobi Eatery is a mobile restaurant providing meals to neighborhood youth three times a week. When grown-ups tell children to return home in the evenings, Kkobi Night Eatery invites those who stay in the streets and offers them a warm meal. The service became a friend of the youth. This was a project of three churches in Yakdae-dong, but it eventually grew into an integrated community care program for the younger generation. Saerom Church aims to provide integrated community care including healthcare, social welfare, caretaking, residential provision, and environmental protection. Its pastor Won-don Lee recounts Saerom Church and Yakdae-dong residents' recovery after the height of the Covid-19 pandemic to trace the movement of the Holy Spirit in their midst and the unexpected harvest. The powerful movement of the Holy Spirit and the experience of healing are described. Hong-eyoyl Hwang identifies Saerom Church's maeul ministry characteristics as the biblical and missional exegetical excellence of the pastor, continued development and expansion of terms and concepts, connecting with people and institutions in response to changes and challenges of the time, studying and applying the issues of the time before anyone else, identifying talented people through networking and inviting them to take responsibilities in missionary organizations or maeul ministry programs, presenting a good case of local ecumenism, good collaboration with the community service center, networking with the civil society in the city of Bucheon and contributing to their movement, locating their ministry in the larger trend of civilizational change, and the minister's excellent leadership.

Hannam Jeil Church is on Itaewon Street near the Seoul Central Mosque and where the 8th US Army Garrison used to be. This community has a culture distinct from any other location in South Korea. Chang-woo Oh was appointed as pastor in 1985 with the intention to do ministry like he would at a mission field. Telling himself "I am a missionary" he tried to understand the culture of Itaewon and pastor the congregation and the neighborhood. He intended for the church to be the center of the community, not an island, so naturally the churchyard was opened for neighborhood children to play. The maeul ministry that started this way developed through networking with local officials and studying the national social welfare policies. Programs were conducted not just for the community but with the community, which resulted in these efforts becoming life-giving ministries, and the church became the central heart of the community. Won-bum Chung comments that the church is not just for the church members but for the world and the local community. Chang-woo Oh's leadership of service and care for the whole community is based on missional ecclesiology and missional ministry philosophy.

Gwang-su An who pastors Suwonsung Church defines ministry as "all the tasks related to having non-believers believe in Jesus and have believers grow in faith to raise them as laborers for the kingdom of God in and out of the church." It would not be easy to define ministry more comprehensively than this. Suwonsung Church started with five households in 1982 and grew to have 5,000 members today. There is a balance between nurturing the people in the church toward maturity and actualizing the kingdom of God out in the world. The church especially started the social missionary system early on and is sponsoring civil society organizations such as Jubilee & Land Justice Association, Citizens' Action for Human Rights, Institute of Land and Liberty, and Christian Environmental Education Center to support others who do the work that the church may not be able to do directly. This shows integrated ministry pursuing both Christian identity and public citizenship. Bright Myeong-seok Lee explains that Suwonsung Church could be faithful as salt and light of the world for 40 years thanks to the tight-knit trust between the spiritual leader and the church community. This element enabled peaceful church operations and made the church capable of accepting continued change in response to the changing times and the needs of society. As Lee explains, Suwonsung Church has been weeping with those who weep and listening to those in pain to empathize with them. Such obedience to God's command and incarnational discipleship are what this generation and the world expect of the church.

Jeju Love Mission Society is a union of churches formed to revive local churches and evangelize the island of Jeju-do. From the missional perspective, the organization nurtured pastors' expertise and missional capacity by conducting intercessory prayer meetings, fellowship gatherings, and study groups. It grew to be a form of ecumenical movement starting from the grassroots. Kook-il Han and Sung-hwan Suh remark that the 20-year history of the organization shows the prophetic imagination and experimental courage of the young pastors in small churches. Their courage to pioneer the kingdom of God, and their noble vision and persistence to cooperate and unite with one another despite financial difficulties give hope for the Korean church. Ultimately, the most important thing in mission and ministry is people; together, we can overcome any obstacles.

Hearing the stories of such healthy churches near us was a joy. These stories challenge and inspire us. The pastors' commitment and dedication, the church communities' vision of the kingdom of God, their dialogue with the surrounding community and town, solidarity and cooperation with local government offices, and their faith in God's presence are what make the church be the church and the community be the community it is meant to be. And this is the evidence of the continuation of the mission of God.

I would especially like to mention that pastor Gwang-su An, the Director of Family, Church, and Maeul Institute, is in his last year before his retirement. The Institute has been in charge of planning and publishing this book. The providence of God to work through his life and Suwonsung Church he has pastored freshly inspires and challenges us. It is the oldest church to be introduced in this book, and has been one of the first churches to practice missional ministry. In the occasion of this publication, I would like to thank pastor An for leading many to the path of life, showing an exemplary life of faith to inspire many pastors and society leaders, and befriending the vulnerable in many corners of society.

Finally, I would like to express special thanks to Rebekah Hwajhin Lee for translating the works of various authors to be shared with the world church.

In great joy and excitement, I walk on the path of hope hand in hand with pastors who strive to minister well, these experts in the margins. As I share this excitement with all the readers, I hope these stories continue even to the third and fourth publications to connect the stories of the kingdom of God with the Korean church and the world church.

One sweltering summer day of July 2023,

Eun-ha Cho, Editor

Pilgrimage Towards Life-Flourishing Culture and Community

Seong-won Park

Song of Groaning

The song "Senzenina?"[1] which means "What have we done?" is a song of resistance against the Apartheid policy in South Africa. It was sung to oppose the injustice of division between the white and the black people. The song also calls out those who silently stand by and declare their culpability. The people of South Africa sang this song as they overturned the unjust and oppressive Apartheid policy.

Today, as all life is devastated and the groaning of creation reverberates into heaven, is this not the perfect song to sing over and over again like the wailing of our souls asking what have we done to the ecology? How grave was our violence and atrocity against nature? What has humanity done to the world of living things? Senzenina?

The Nicaraguan version of "Senzenina" is also shocking. The anonymous poet parodies the creation account in Genesis 1 in this accusatory confession called "Contra-Genesis." As the title hints, the poem progresses in reverse order of creation to charge human civilization for destroying God's creation.

Contra-Genesis

In the end, Humans destroyed the world called Earth.
Before the spirit of Humans swept over the face of the Earth
And destroyed everything, the Earth was beautiful.

Then Humans said, "Let there be darkness," and there was darkness.
Humans saw that the darkness was good.
Humans called the darkness Security.

Humans divided themselves by race, religion, and social status.
There was no evening, and there was no morning,
And it was the seventh day before everything finished.

Humans said, "Let there be a strong government to rule over our darkness.
To kill each other at our command
And effectively defend our darkness.
Let there be military.

We like the darkness.
So let us pursue those who speak truth to the end of the Earth and kill them," they said
And it was so.

---

[1] https://www.youtube.com/watch?v=SJP79Zon3Ek.

There was no evening, and there was no morning,
And it was the sixth day before everything finished.

Humans said,
"Let there be drugs and various ways of escape,"
And it was so.
This was to forget that
No matter how hard one tries to close one's eyes
Somewhere, there is a thing called truth
That nags at the conscience.
It was the fifth day before everything finished.

Humans said, "Let there be rockets and bombs
So we can kill a little more quickly
And more easily.
For a more efficient implementation of the task
Let there be gas chambers and furnaces."
And it was so.
It was the fourth day before everything finished.

Humans said,
"Let there be distinction between countries
So we can identify our enemies."
And it was so.
It was the third day before everything finished.

Finally, Humans said,
"Let us make god in our image
So that no other god can compete with us."
And it was so.
Let us have God think as we think
Hate as we hate
And kill as we kill.
It was the second day before everything finished.

On the final day
A giant storm covered the face of the Earth
A great flame erased the beautiful Earth.
Everything ended.
Only the deep stillness remained.

God said,
"What have Humans done?"
And in the deep silence that
Consumes even the smoky ruins
God was weeping.[2]

"Contra-Genesis" unmasks all the satanic facades of human systems through history. There may be other perspectives on the progress of human civilization, but what is clear is that the Earth's ecology is being irrevocably destroyed by humanity. This is evident in species extinction, disturbance of ecological order, climate change, genetic manipulation, emergence of new epidemics, and

---

[2] Translator's Note: Translated from Korean into English.

disintegration of communities. This is not just scientific data but our actual daily experience.

Today on Earth, not only the peace of humanity but also the life, justice, and peace of nature are violated. Without justice and peace in relation to nature, all life on Earth may be destroyed. Yet human violence against nature continues to intensify with the advancement of human civilization and technology.

Moreover, in the 21st century, there was the expectation that human life would become much more enriched thanks to economic growth and technological development. Today, humanity is facing multiple crises instead. Humanity has been suffering through regular waves of new epidemics such as Ebola, SARS, MERS, and Zika virus. Toward the end of 2019, the entire global system was halted by the unprecedented Covid-19 pandemic. It even stopped church services that not even wars in the past could halt. This new zoonotic disease emerged from nature, and its message is that without a drastic turn in human civilization, even more threatening diseases will continue to emerge.

The arrival of the Fourth Industrial Revolution predicted the age of super artificial superintelligence (ASI). By 2045 AI may develop to the point of singularity where it surpasses human intelligence. Then humans may become robotic, and robots be humanized to produce a new species of Homo-Deus. This may lead to a modern Tower of Babel where the entire creation order falls into confusion. Moreover, the disintegration of the community is accelerating due to smart technology, erosion of value systems, the pandemic, competition for natural resources, industrialization and urbanization, and family divisions. This erosion of community is impacting individuals, society, and the entire planetary community.

Meanwhile, South Korean society is facing the crisis of an aging population and low birth rate, culminating in the population cliff where the entire population steeply decreases. This spells the extinction of farming and fishery village communities. The world community is suffering from multiple issues beyond control, such as wars, economic inequality, ideological conflict and strife, energy crisis, monopoly and privatization of power, and fabrication and disinformation by politically partisan media. With the dawn of the age of AI, communities on all levels risk collapse, from the fragmentation of individual life between reality and virtual reality to the disintegration of the entire planetary community. Without a fundamental shift in human civilization, not only humanity but also the planetary community and the entirety of God's beautiful creation may collapse.

I identify the climate crisis, the beginning of the age of AI, the continued emergence of new epidemics, and the collapse of communities such as those in rural regions as the four crises facing this generation. And these four crises are directly and indirectly related to the human destruction of ecological order.

What can be done about human violence against nature? Is it possible to have peace on Earth without peace with Earth? Is it really possible to glorify God while destroying the works of the Creator? How will the church's theology respond? How will the church live out its missional vocation to proclaim the good news of eternal life?

Groaning of Creation

Today shocking data on the ecological crisis are reported one after another. According to John Van Klinken at the University of Groningen, for a century from 1850 to 1950, one species went extinct every year. By 1989, one species went extinct each day, and since 2000, a species is going extinct every hour. In the next 50 years, 25% of all Earth's species will go extinct. This is the repeated warning of the report by the United Nations International Panel on Climate Change (IPCC). IPCC predicts that by 2050, over one-fifth of the Earth's species will be gone. Even this report is known to have softened the blow due to lobbying by powerful nations and transnational corporations, so the reality can be assumed to be much more dire.

According to a report by the Lawrence Livermore National Laboratory, the ecological destruction in the present generation is commensurate to the one over three hundred million years. According to Alan T. Durning, for 50 years from 1950 to 2000, the amount of things humanity produced and consumed equals the amount of production and consumption over the entire human history before 1950.

Clara Deser of the National Center for Atmospheric Research in the United States said in 2008 that the amount of glaciers in the Arctic and the Antarctic that would have taken one or two decades melted in just one year in 2007. This meant the speed of climate change was accelerating by ten to twenty years. By 2050, 60% of Bangladesh may be underwater, which also means Dakar, Ho Chi Minh City, Shanghai, Mumbai, Bangkok, Guangzhou, and Kolkata will also be submerged. And they all happen to be cities in Asia. The IPCC warns that Asia will be most devasted by climate change.

The IPCC issued a special report called *Global Warming of 1.5 °C* ahead of the UN Climate Change Conference (COP 26) in Glasgow in November 2021. The report warned that if the Earth's temperature rises by two degrees Celsius above pre-industrial levels, there will be planetary devastation. The tipping point, or the point of no return, is the warming by 1.5 degrees Celsius. Some say that compared to this report three years ago, today, the deadline before the tipping point has drawn shorter by a decade. The report three years ago expected the tipping point to come between 2030 and 2052. The recent report expected it to be between 2021 and 2040. Average it out, and there is a high possibility of passing the 1.5-degree threshold by the year 2030. This means we only have seven or eight years until the Earth reaches the tipping point. The IPCC calculates that there is a 40% chance of reaching the tipping point within the next five years, and one of the years between 2021 and 2025 will have a 90% chance of being the record-breaking hottest year in modern history. To stop this trend, we have to achieve carbon zero by 2025, with only three years to go.

If we pass the tipping point, the arctic permafrost will melt to release an unprecedented amount of carbon, 28 times as much CO2. The thawing of the permafrost will release over 100 new kinds of virus that will put humanity under threat of new, never-before-seen diseases incomparable to Covid-19. Bill Gates had warned that after Covid-19, a completely new and different disease will appear that may kill 30 million people in six months. When the Earth's temperature rises up to the tipping point, all crops will burn, and farming will be impossible. This may cause the most serious crisis of all: a global food shortage that would lead to global violence and plunder.

Hans Blix, who was the Chairman of the UN Monitoring, Verification and Inspection Commission in Iraq, said the greatest threat to the world in the future is not the third and fourth world wars but global warming. The late Stephen Hawking also warned that climate change is more of a threat to humanity than terrorism. Global warming is as threatening as nuclear weapons, spelling the end of humanity. Some say the clock of judgment for the environmental apocalypse is pointing to 11:55 p.m.

The creation groans, not only due to climate change but also the pollution and devastation of all Earth's resources of water, air, and land; gene manipulation; ecological disruption due to rapid extinction of species; and advancement of bioengineering that enables human-machine fusion. Human civilization is roaring toward liberty until all limits are overcome, but the consequence is faster destruction of justice, peace, and connections with Earth and life.

What Makes the Creation Groan

Then what is making humanity and ecology groan? What actions of humanity have put the Earth, the source of life, in this mess? What has broken the peace of nature and peace with nature? We tend to think natural disasters arise from nature. However, the IPCC reports scientific research that shows that today's climate change and ecological crisis have human causes.

Multiple reasons for climate change and ecological crisis may be found at various angles. I would point to five elements of human civilizations as the Big Five factors behind today's ecological crisis. They are:

1. Capitalism in pursuit of unlimited growth
2. Hegemonic empire
3. Developmentalism
4. Anthropocentrism
5. Modernist ideas represented by dualism, dichotomist thinking, enlightenment, scientism, and technicism.

All five factors were initiated by Western civilization. I am not alone in this speculation. Western scholars themselves have criticized Western civilization for a long time. The German historian and philosopher Oswald Arnold Gottfried Spengler (1880-1936) already in 1918 published a book called *Der Untergang des Abendlandes,* The Decline of the West.

It is true that Western civilization has partly contributed to making human life more convenient. But not all of its achievements have been positive. Western civilization has brought many harms as well as benefits. Its impact on not only human society and culture but also on nature has been extremely destructive. In other words, human progress that made life convenient has broken the peace of nature, which in turn threatens the peace and life of humanity. Without elaborating on all the details in this essay, I would have to point out the three key elements of development – industrialization, urbanization, and modernization – as the main culprits of the ecological crisis.

Industrialization changed the human economic basis from agriculture to industries. But today it has resulted in the destruction of the agricultural basis that sustains human food production. For industrialization, labor had to be concentrated in one place, which caused urbanization. Urbanization along with industrialization accelerated the disintegration of the farming villages, and land's essential function of producing life was distorted to become capitalized. For the acceleration of industrialization, technology was modernized. Technology today has advanced to the point of manipulating even the wellspring of life through bioengineering and cloning. The capacity for mechanical manipulation means humans and their machines are encroaching on the sphere of divine creativity. With the Fourth Industrial Revolution, humans are welcoming the age where they are controlled by human-made AI. All this is breaking not only the peace with the land but also the peace between the Creator and the creation, between human and human, and between human and nature, as told in Genesis 3.

In this sweeping crisis of life, how will the church respond to the powers that make humanity and all God's creation groan?

Creation Yearning for Redemption

In this situation, two opposing movements are arising worldwide and in Korean society. On the one hand, there is still the pursuit of economic growth. Let alone the Park Chung Hee administration that prioritized national economic growth. Since the Lee Myung-bak administration, Korean citizens have thrown their support behind politicians who promise to revive the economy. As soon as the Lee Myung-bak administration came to power, policies on American beef import, marketization of education, privatization of public utilities, the Four Major Rivers Project that started with the Grand Korean Waterway, international relations using financial resources, pro-wealthy policies, and Korea-US FTA were passed one after another, almost all neoliberal, anti-ecological policies. But other administrations of Kim Young-sam, Kim Dae-jung, Roh Moo-hyun, Park Geun-hye, and Moon Jae-in, both left and right of the political spectrum, followed the neoliberal policies. The Yoon Suk Yeol administration, as ironic as the Donald Trump administration in the United States, is entirely ignorant as to have no idea what impact their policies will have; all their policies are anti-ecological and anti-peace. But this is not just the phenomenon in South Korea but in many other countries worldwide. Since the launch of the UN IPCC in 1988, the commitments at Rio 1992, Kyoto 1997, and Paris 2015 have yet to be followed through because governments have been dragging their feet in service of the capital.

While national policies and human civilization continue along the path of growth and developmentalism, there is an entirely different movement of the people at the lower levels of society. There is a velvet resistance against the basic exhaustion resulting from industrialization, urbanization, and modernization. The exhausted and burnt out but discerning citizens have decided to be no longer exploited of their life and soul to the neoliberal economic globalization. While mainstream society continues to follow the neoliberal economic trends, a minority of people with ecological and cultural awareness are mobilizing in various ways to return to farming and agriculture, live closer to nature, and conduct farming experience programs. These are movements that flow against industrialization, urbanization, and modernization.

During the Asian Financial Crisis in 1997 in South Korea, people began returning to the farmlands. However, the attempt at this time was unsuccessful because they tried to sustain an industrial lifestyle in the agricultural living space. But the recent return-to-farming and return-to-rural movements' purpose is not simply to move from the cities to the farming regions but to change the philosophy of life to be ecological. The number of people moving to the countryside in search of this sustainable alternative lifestyle is increasing yearly. In parallel, the alternative school and farming experience movements are also going strong. The television program "I am of Nature" that recently rose in popularity perhaps provides vicarious satisfaction for the unconscious yearning to resist civilizational progress and the desire to return to nature.

They say six out of ten people living in Seoul have this desire. Even the educated elites with stable jobs in their mid-30s are increasingly leaving everything for the farms. An elite in the early 30s who works in the parliament told me that while he can't make the move just yet, he will soon move to the farms. This trend is not just in South Korea. On organic produce, Japan is much farther ahead than South Korea. European countries that experienced industrialization, urbanization, and modernization much earlier than South Korea have nurtured their desire to return to nature for a long time.

European scholars have seen that the thought structures of Enlightenment rationalism and scientism have resulted in anthropocentric civilizational development and harmful consequences and are constructing a new thought structure to overcome them. Some have called for the need for humanity to consider again the extramundane. Quantum physics that transcends Newtonian mechanical physics explains that while the macrostructure of the universe is formed, there is even now the continued movement of life on the microscopic level of biology. Therefore, we must pay attention to the movement of life in the visible world.

Diarmuid O' Murchu, the Irish Catholic priest, asserted that modern humans need a spiritual homecoming to nature, a reconnection of the body to the Earth. To awaken from the stupor of obsession and work addiction in modernity, the way of silence and meditation should be charted by more creative use of rituals in our cultures.

Gyeongan Graduate University (GGU), where I serve, organized international symposia from 2017 to 2021 titled "Character and Spirituality in the Fourth Industrial Revolution" for five years. The symposium discussions also concluded that organic and relational epistemology and cosmic spirituality, which means spirituality that facilitates new recognition of the Earth and connection with the cosmos, are necessary in the Fourth Industrial Revolution.

Both the suggestion of O'Murchu and the symposia can be summarized to mean that in extreme harm to human thought and culture brought on by industrialization, urbanization, and modernization initiated by the West, we must discover alternatives in nature rather than human-made civilization.

While this solution has not yet proven itself to be the decisive answer, the increasingly urgent issues of climate change, job instability due to neoliberal market structure, and the epidemics of Ebola, SARS, MERS, Zika virus, and Covid-19 related to ecological disruption will continue to speed up. Considering the pursuit of natural lifestyles in the name of "well-being" by the urbanites, even in their neoliberal milieu, this trend will likely take a more concrete shape as a solution for the future.

Now, in response to finance-centered neoliberalism that may bring an end to ecology and capitalism, there is an increasing call for a community movement to harness life-supporting agriculture to ensure the protection of life and a sustainable future. This community movement has already been suggested by the pioneer of non-violent resistance, Mahatma Gandhi, in his movement against British industrialization and urbanization. He advocated for the Swaraj community movement to say that protecting agriculture and the village that forms the basis of life is the way for humanity to become self-reliant. The ecological community movements are also progressing in many other parts of the world.

From 2004, when I started teaching at Youngnam Theological University and Seminary, I consistently raised how the church may respond to this life-flourishing community movement. I started a course that joins physical experience with theological reflections by having students work on a vegetable garden on campus. Seeing the Presbyterian Church of Korea-Tonghap (PCK) General Assembly launch the Maeul Ministry Movement years later is a good sign.

Theological Reflection to Restore Peace of Creation and Peace with Creation

Among Christian theologians, many acknowledge how Western civilization and Christian theology have significantly contributed to ecological destruction today. Lukas Vischer of the Commission on Faith and Order in the World Council of Churches, who had for a long time led the ecumenical movement on mission and unity and theological response to ecological crisis, stated in his paper on the relationship between mission and ecological crisis that Christian mission has not proclaimed the flourishing of life to humanity and creation. Instead, it ultimately spread the message of Western civilization and human domination and control over nature, and Christianity must accept great responsibility for the ecological crisis today. In other words, Christianity is gravely responsible for breaking the peace of nature and breaking human peace with nature.

Dietrich Bonhoeffer pointed out that the spiritual and intellectual foundation of European and American civilizations historically identified by wars, industries, and machinery was formed by instrumentalizing nature under Western reign. Human domination over nature was the basic theme of European and American history. Later in prison, Bonhoeffer pointed out that the West's purpose is to be independent of nature, and they have made scientific instruments the human environment, customs, home, and universe. Western civilization has not only fragmented nature but also destroyed the nature-human community.

Historically, the destruction of ecology began and was accelerated by humanism and modernism.

Bonhoeffer's critique of Western civilization aligns with the thoughts of the anonymous Nicaraguan poet of "Contra-Genesis" and the opinions of many conscientious Western scholars such as Lukas Vischer. Critical scholars of the East point to the West's Enlightenment rationalism, scientism, technicism, anthropocentrism, historicism, dualism, essentialism, and the value of "liberty" that the West has enshrined have objectified nature and alienated humanity from nature. Professor Emeritus Larry Rasmussen of Union Theological Seminary in New York, whom I met when attending the Ecumenical Council on Mission and Ecology convening at John Knox Center in Geneva, said that Bonhoeffer's assertions seemed overstated. Now, not anymore.

Anthropocentric theology was also formed out of this epistemological structure. God created the world and continues to create today. God's theological scale includes not only human salvation and emancipation but also the redemption of all creation as stated in Romans. Yet Christian theology and mission have disregarded this immense scale of creation and salvation to divide everything and limit God's salvation to humanity, and that only to spiritual salvation.

Such a dualistic conception was structured after the bubonic plague that killed a third of the European population between 1347 and 1351. Having no knowledge of where the plague came from, there were two opposite responses. First was the religious response to call the plague God's judgment. The answer, then, should be to ask God for salvation. And for the people dying in misery, the religious response was to at least assure them of eternal life after death so they could die in peace. Following this trend, theology, spirituality, and ministry continued on the dualistic path of mysticism and emphasis on the afterlife. The trend later resulted in the 16th-century emphasis on original sin. Complete human depravity due to original sin was emphasized in mainstream theology. This was developed by the Dutch Catholic theologian Cornelius Jansen in Jansenism, and in Protestantism, it was underscored by the reformers such as John Calvin and later Puritans. This emphasis on spiritual salvation and primacy of after-life based on the church's dualistic response to the bubonic plague continues today in mainstream Christian theology.

The other response to the plague was secular. Scientific research was conducted on the cause of the plague. Immediate salvation did not come no matter how much one prayed to God, so humans sought solutions for themselves. This search for human solutions resulted in 16th-century humanism and the Renaissance. In the world of God-human-nature, in the Middle Ages, God was at the center, and humanity and nature were less important. Human capacity was also disregarded under the domination of the church. But after the plague, humanity started exploring human capacity in the ancient Greek and Roman cultures in the Renaissance. The Renaissance resulted in humanism, which developed rationalism and scientism and resulted in today's technological progress, from the discovery of bacteria, the invention of the microscope, the development of the steam engine, and the development of today's computers and artificial intelligence.

These two opposing responses to the bubonic plague resulted in religion's dualistic focus on spiritual salvation, pursuit of other-worldly faith, and rejection of materials and science as worldly values that should be distinguished from the sacred. On the other hand, science developed to consider religion an irrational and false superstition with no reasonable grounds.

A powerful dualism functions in both religion and secular society. Theology should have regarded God's creation, including human capacity and science, as the object of theology and ministry and provided pastoral care. Instead, it distinguished the world and its material and scientific realm and disregarded them as secular. This resulted in the rampant development of science and secularism. Humanism and science declared that only what is rational is true and what cannot be proven scientifically does not exist, and have ignored and denied the sphere of religion, faith, and the soul. Religion excluded science, and science rejected religion. The worst consequence of this dualism was the broken spiritual connection to the cosmos.

Recently, there has been much theological reflection on this issue. There is a move to expand the scope beyond soteriology to creation theology. Redemption must be holistic redemption of the soul and the material existence, of both humanity and other creation. New theological concepts and movements such as creation spirituality, eco-spirituality, and spiritual homecoming are appearing.

There are also efforts for more non-dual, holistic, and relational perceptions of the world. In August 2007, at Hanmaeul Community in Jangseong in South Jeolla Province of South Korea, the Council for World Mission of the World Council of Churches (WCC) co-organized the theological council on a new theological framework for the 21st century. Young theologians of the Global South agreed that the epistemological framework should first be changed from the West's dualistic, anthropocentric, and paternalistic framework to the holistic, relational, and organic one. On this framework, new theology must be constructed. Some holistic, relational, and organic epistemological alternatives were presented, such as *ubuntu* in Africa, *sangsaeng* (相生) in Asia, and *sumak kausai* in Latin America.

What Must be Done?

In this situation, we, especially the church, must seek alternative solutions. How will we curb uncontrolled human hubris that counters God's creation order so humanity can follow nature's ways and relate with God's creation? How will the 21st-century human oppressed under materialism and unlimited competition enjoy the beauty, peace, and flourishing of life in creation? How will we see the Western value systems that continue dominating our thought processes for 500 years with new eyes based on our Asian identity and values?

What should be the theology of the church? How can ministers be good shepherds in this crisis of life? Will our churches be operated based on capitalist consumerism? Will we become churches of the cities that suffocate us? Will our churches submit passively to the march of death? Or will we be ministers of life who fight against the power of exploitation, death, and destruction?

The church today must find a model for an alternative world. The problem is that heretical organizations are searching for alternative worlds in this crisis, while the traditional church has absolutely no interest in these matters. They are immersed in issues of the church with narrow scripture interpretations and narrow ministry philosophies that maintain the status quo. It is time to break out of these limitations.

Producing a New Theological Framework and a New Study of Ministry

When God created the world, all living beings, not just humans, were created. All life was to live together in harmony. Different ethnicities with their own ways of life were also meant to live together in harmony. The birds of the air, the fish in the sea, and the plants on land were made, each according to their kind, to live together in harmony. This is also true of humanity. All humans were made with their different histories and cultures to live together in harmony.

Traditionally, theology has been Christocentric in its interpretation of God's sovereignty over human history. But now, the theological framework must expand to embrace all of life in God's creation. God's sovereignty must not be limited to humanity and the spiritual dimension of humanity but expanded to all living communities that God created. In today's destructive crisis, theology must become the theology for the biological community.

Thus far, ministry meant ministry for congregations; in other words, ministry over people in the institution of the church. Now, we must think beyond this narrow definition. The minister today is called to minister to the people as well as the created world – wind, water, earth, society, economy, culture, arts – wherever the minister is located. The minister must be the theological coordinator or a pastoral coordinator so the creation can flourish and give glory to God.

The biblical imperative behind this process is given in the ministry vision for the new heaven and the new earth in Isaiah 65: 17-25. In Isaiah's ministry vision for life, justice, and peace, we find the theological discourse of cosmic ministry. Cosmic ministry is the comprehensive ministry for all God's creation as called for in this day and age.

In a deep reading of John 10:10, we can find the fundamental purpose of Christ's ministry. The verse says Jesus came to us to give life in fullness, and warns that the thief comes only to steal, kill, and destroy this life. In the dualistic and metaphysical framework, the thief was understood as the anti-Christ or Satan. In today's reality, who or what is the thief?

The thief that steals life today is the anthropocentrism that consumes all of life's resources, especially natural resources, for human benefit in the name of economic growth and development in neoliberal economic globalization. Rampant modernity that destroys all traditional values for the sake of survival in the 21st-century information society, Western philosophy that dichotomizes and antagonizes all organic relationships between spirit and body in the name of science, colonialism that legitimizes human over nature are stealing, killing, and destroying God-given life. Our theology and ministry must restore the life that had been stolen by these thieves.

Beginning a Theological Discussion on the Dilemma of Modern Civilization

If the flourishing of life is the prime goal of humanity today, it must start with the agricultural movement that forms the basis of life. We must seriously reconsider the ancient concept of *nongjacheonhajidaebon* (農者天下之大本), which means a country exists on the foundation of agriculture. Agriculture is not merely one economic sector but the foundation of all life. Unless this foundation remains firm, no life is possible.

In today's global crisis, scholars foresee that in 30 years, only the countries that have maintained their agricultural lands will be able to survive. There is even the claim that the Earth can only be preserved when 70% of land surface is set apart for agriculture. Agriculture is the work of laying the basis for life.

The two major British economists David Ricardo and Thomas Robert Malthus made opposite claims. Ricardo asserted that Great Britain can prosper through industrialization since food can be supplied from its colonies. Malthus maintained that agriculture is the basis of life and should not be neglected. Great Britain followed the Ricardian theory at first, but after encountering food insecurity in the First and Second World Wars, they accepted Malthus' warning to make policies restoring agriculture.

At the Agriculture and Earth Forum in Wonju, South Korea, in April 2004, the participants agreed that life-sustaining agriculture must be the solution to the dilemmas of modern civilization. The harms of industrialization, urbanization, and modernization must be overcome and healed through life-flourishing agriculture.

In the past, agricultural regions were also important in the church's mission. But back then, the effort progressed in the framework of rural enlightenment, a form of rural modernization. Today the rural villages and urban cities must be reconstructed together to become a sustainable garden of life, the living garden of God. Constructing this life-flourishing community should be the missional focus of today.

Thomas Barth, the grandson of Karl Barth, gave up studying at the University of Basel and enrolled in a technical school for farming to become a leading organic farmer in Switzerland. The leading practical theologian of Germany, Rudolf Boren, had said doing theology is akin to farming.

While teaching in Youngnam Theological University and Seminary, I taught a course called "The practice of theology of life and social transformation" to nurture future ministers. This was a course on theological practice to facilitate students to consider creative ministry paths in the face of life-threatening issues. The thrust was to explore new forms of ministry and life-flourishing theology based on agriculture. This was not the traditional ministry vision for rural churches. The ministry vision was to heal modern culture alienated from the ground of life that is agriculture and nature. This study of ministry pursues reconciliation, biological well-being, and the flourishing of culture and the arts for the 21st century. The course would discuss the development of prophetic and cosmic ministry to transform society and culture so that modern humans exhausted by industrialization, modernization, and urbanization can relate with God and nature to enjoy a flourishing life.

As the PCK General Assembly has recently attended to the Maeul Ministry Movement, the concept of maeul ministry is trending. But the ministers who have been practicing maeul ministry say it does not make sense for the church to claim to do ministry in a community. It is not the church leading or ministering to the community, but the church and the community together sharing, caring, and nurturing life. Moreover, in the face of ecological crisis, there is growing awareness that humans and all of God's creation must relate together. Therefore, for humanity to overcome today's crisis and properly actualize God's vision of creation, it must transition from industrial and post-industrial civilizations to life-flourishing cultures. Through this transition, the life-flourishing community must be built, and the church should commit ourselves to this cause.

In 2021, GGU in cooperation with the Institute on Family, Church, and Maeul, launched the Life-Flourishing Community School. In cooperation with Gyeongan Presbytery, ministers of Gyeongan and Youngju Presbyteries were offered basic and intensive courses. The faculty lectured on the theory and presented church cases in alternating weeks to weave theory and practice. The basic course was conducted online through distance learning, and the intensive course involved field visits to case churches. A course for church elders, *gwonsa*,[3] and ordained deacons was also launched. The participating ministers describe the impact of their learning as akin to "Columbus discovering the New World." They express that they have discovered a passion for a new kind of ministry midway through their ministry career. In leading the Life-Flourishing Community School, I felt a strong need for a comprehensive restructuring of theology and practice.

Concrete Suggestions for Cosmic Ministry for Life-Flourishing Community

Practical strategies are necessary to construct and lead a new paradigm for the life-flourishing community ministry. Below are a few such steps.

Establishing a Theology of Life-Flourishing Community

There must be a theological framework for proper theological treatment of the life-flourishing community. The framework may start with a new attempt to understand the God of the Trinity. Traditional theology and ecclesiology are focused on Christology. Jesus Christ is the decisive revelation, but Jesus Christ cannot be considered apart from God the creator and the Holy Spirit who brings renewal. The revelation of Jesus Christ has been understood as comprehensive but mainly historical. This is apparent in calling the Christ who came into the context of the Roman Empire the "Lord of Lords" and "King of Kings." This is the understanding of Christ who came into the existing human power structure to emphasize God's authority over the world's authority. The existence of Christ was also understood only in terms of soteriology.

---

[3] Translator's Note: Church office generally ordained to women in the Korean church and widely considered higher in status than deacons but lower than elders.

The ecumenical movement since the 1980s began to reflect on the Holy Spirit as the neglected member of the Trinity. The growth of the Pentecostal movement seriously challenged the traditional churches to rethink the Holy Spirit. This was the context of the Canberra Assembly of the WCC that discussed the Holy Spirit as its theme.

But today, in the face of ecological crisis, we must begin reflecting on God, the Creator. The Creator God is the foundation, yet our theological focus on Christology has neglected theological work on God the Creator. It is impossible to properly understand life's system, structure, purpose, and goal without proper theological reflection on the creator God. Meditation on God the Creator for a deeper and broader understanding is a prerequisite to any breakthrough in relationship with extra-ecclesial bodies for maeul ministry, communication with society, and interreligious conversation and cooperation.

Therefore, theologians and the church must create a fresh new theological framework to encourage discussion and study.

Understanding the Bible from the Perspective of Creation Theology

Traditionally, the church has understood the Bible as the history of redemption. At the same time, the Bible was read with a literary critical lens to understand it in its historical and cultural contexts. The study of the historical Jesus was also conducted in this framework. But now, we must read the Bible from the perspective of creation theology.

To perceive God's revelation in the cosmic web of life and not just in the history of the redemption of human soul, the Bible must be read from the perspective of creation theology alongside Christology and historical and literary criticism. The preaching of the Word should also be conducted on this basis.

Traditional theology focused on soteriology that begins in Genesis 3 up to Revelation 21. But this focuses on the aftermath of the original problem. Of course, this aspect is important. But God's original plan for the cosmos is in Genesis 1 and 2. This perfection of creation was marred by the fall of humanity in chapter 3, and God's act of redemption from this threat of destruction continues from there on and through the New Testament. Revelation 21 and 22 describe the completion of this redemption. Thus far, we have focused on the parts of the Bible from the fall to the redemption. Today, it is necessary to read the Bible to understand God's act of creation and the declaration that it was good, as well as its restoration in the creation of the new heaven and the new earth.

Ministry for the life-flourishing community involves producing new Bible study resources based on this perspective.

Cosmic Ministry of Life-Flourishing Community

Traditionally, the church has focused on ministry to people. The imperative was the salvation of souls, so the focus was only on the salvation of humanity and that only of the human soul. But actually, the purpose of ministry is the redemption of all created world. The basis is found in both the Old and the New Testament.

Isaiah 65:17-25 gives the vision of life, justice, and peace in the image of the new heaven and the new earth. This is the proclamation that humanity and all planetary communities are the objects of God's redemption, emancipation, and restoration.

As declared in Genesis 1, God created the world and saw that it was good. In other words, the task of preserving the creation made good in God's eyes is the church's responsibility. This is the goal of the missional church and the focus of ministry.

In that sense, the ministry of life-flourishing community must be cosmic. The minister is responsible for coordinating the blessing of the life-giving God so that all creation can have life in fullness. The human responsibility to be the steward of creation includes such scope.

Theology must not be one of many scholarly disciplines but one that communicates with all other disciplines. Ministry is not just one occupation among many but an occupation that provides comprehensive pastoral care to lead all other occupations and the life-flourishing community to align with God's will. So it is necessary to continue research and education to establish this study of life-flourishing ministry for continuing ministry education.

Life-Flourishing Farmland Ministers

Today, the rural population is rapidly decreasing. The youngest farmers are in their 50s, and those in their 60s lead the young people's association. Elementary schools in rural regions are closing down one after another, and more rural populations are moving to the cities where they still cannot find jobs.

In this desperate situation, the children of farmers aspire to move into the cities successfully. They witnessed their parents' hardships and do not want to return to the countryside. People who move back to the rural regions are those who have become disillusioned by city life.

In today's Korean economic structure, it will become increasingly more difficult to find a job in the city, and even the jobs acquired will be temporary, paying wages too low to support an urban life. The situation requires the government to socially and culturally restructure the rural economy with public resources to attract urban populations to the farmlands.

In today's social structure, the church is the only institution that can remain in the farmlands. Hospitals like obstetrician-gynecologist specialists and elementary schools have long shut down. But churches must stay in the countryside right to the end. The church is called to be the coordinator of life-flourishing society construction in rural communities.

Seminaries must train and produce ministers for these life-flourishing communities and then financially support their livelihood and agricultural activities for at least five years. If the ministers manage to settle as a farmer and a community coordinator in the five years, they will be able to persist longer for about ten years. By year 15, they will become specialists in this field. To revive the rural village and town communities and agriculture, these life-flourishing community ministers must be nurtured and institutionally supported by the church and its theological education.

Life-Flourishing Community Liturgical Calendar

Agriculture is aligned with the movement of the creation and the cosmos. Conventional agriculture has mechanically restructured the creation order, so even if agriculture flourishes in this method, it is only the agribusiness that succeeds, not the true life-flourishing agriculture.

Organic farming is proposed as a solution, but even organic farming has become industrialized these days, and the "organic" label cannot be trusted. So today, there must be attempts at natural farming, in other words, agriculture that follows the course of nature in its own process of life and creation. These attempts are being made in various agricultural sectors.

For this purpose, we must understand how the creation's rhythm of life takes effect in nature. Farmers know very well the decisive impact of the rhythm of the lunar calendar on farming. So the church, based on creation theology, must attempt to realign our rhythm of life from that of the industrial society to the ecological society.

The traditional liturgical calendar is aligned with soteriology. Alongside this soteriological church calendar, we also need to coordinate an agricultural church calendar based on creation theology.

The Eastern Orthodox Church and the WCC have jointly proposed that a Season of Creation be observed from September 1 to the second week of October. The season is today observed by churches worldwide. Worship should also be restructured based on this calendar.

Life-Flourishing Community Christian Education

Education is a key source of energy that enables a sustained flow of history. Church education so far has been based on soteriology, focusing on forming people with Christ-like character. While making people into honorable Christians is meaningful, this education has been limited in nurturing people to become subjects and agents of life.

Public education is in a more serious bind. Schools are already focused on producing the technical human. Under the impact of neoliberal economic globalization, education is forming the economic human with only the skills to make money. The market logic has consumed education itself.

To educate humans who ensure the birthing, protection, care, and flourishing of life, the agriculture-based perspective of life must be established. Education that trains one to discipline oneself to align with this agricultural rhythm of life is necessary.

Farming experience programs are already widely spread, but farming itself should be a part of education for life. Education in the church must be restructured from the perspective of creation theology, and the church must cooperate with public education institutions to nurture people to have respect for life. Life-flourishing spirituality can be grown in the life-flourishing garden of the church. Schools can teach farming skills as well. Farming can satisfy the scientific curiosities on how plants grow and teach the principles of cosmic creation and the preservation of life.

Life-Flourishing Community Mission and Service

Christian mission so far has focused on sharing and witnessing to Jesus Christ. Alongside this mission to share the redemption history of God in Jesus Christ, the mission of the church to share God's vision for the entire creation is necessary. Caring for all God's creation should be recognized as a part of the mission of God. The missional church must understand its mission to include this aspect.

Restoring life to the farmlands devastated by industrialization, urbanization, and modernization is the first task of the life-flourishing mission. Training workers and constructing a system of service for this mission is an urgent task.

To revive the farmlands to become flourishing communities, the church needs to raise up workers of at least four types. The first is the minister who ministers to the cosmos, the second is the people attempting new life-flourishing farming, the third is educators to train in this new farming technique, and the fourth is administrators coordinating these affairs.

To overcome the high youth unemployment rate today and attract more people to the rural regions in the long term, churches can raise young people for the mission and service of constructing life-flourishing farmlands.

Life-Flourishing Community World Mission

Traditionally, the church has been sending out cross-cultural missionaries to start churches. Now, we need life-flourishing community missionaries.

To build a new trend for life-flourishing culture, we must train missionaries in life-flourishing agriculture and life-flourishing community building and send them out to other parts of the world to teach and learn our respective lessons. Such mission sending and exchange should first be conducted with churches in Asia.

Mission-sending policies of churches with the vision for life-flourishing ministry should be reexamined so that they can gradually include life-flourishing agriculture and community mission programs alongside traditional world mission.

Life-Flourishing Community Art and Culture

Life without art and culture may degenerate the human into an instrument of labor devoid of leisure. This can produce doctrinaire humans and make re-creation impossible.

Life-flourishing art and culture can conduct the important function of restoring the original value of the currently industrialized arts and culture. Instead of sensationalizing artworks and modern culture providing cheap stimulation, a new culture and aesthetic to align our breath to the rhythm of life is necessary.

For example, the Western clothing we generally wear today is designed to oppress our bodies. For our bodily energy to flow naturally, our fashion must be changed. In that sense, Asian costumes are much more conducive to letting life's energy flow. Contemporary *hanbok* designs have already become widespread in

South Korea. The entire Earth community must work on this task to design clothing for the flourishing of life.

An urgent problem today is the degeneration of food culture. Food is now considered an aspect of culture, beyond something to be consumed for survival. Food culture connects humans to life and nature. Food culture must be rethought to overcome the crisis of the climate, the crisis of life, the crisis of health, the crisis of psychology, and the crisis of culture. This food culture must be restored as part of the life-flourishing culture.

Performance arts such as music, fine arts, theater, and cinema should be attempted by and for the life-flourishing community. Architecture and interior design should also be tried with life-flourishing culture in mind.

The church that conducts life-flourishing ministry must intentionally drive such initiatives for life-flourishing art and culture. Various programs, such as organic textile dyes, traditional games, environment-friendly interior design, earthen house construction, songs, plays, and pictures composed with nature as a subject, can be attempted.

Constructing a Life-Flourishing Garden and a Life-Flourishing Society

The vision of the new heaven and the new earth in Isaiah 65 must ultimately be lived out in our daily lives. Our nation must rebuild the social structure for the safety and flourishing of life. A new theory and vision must be proposed for a new social structure in a life-flourishing society, turning away from industrialization, urbanization, and modernization.

The church must propose a new comprehensive plan to construct this life-flourishing society. The plan must include strategies to heal the harmful effects of modern society, starting with ensuring the safety and flourishing of physical life.

For the church to be a model of such experimentation, we need go beyond planning church building construction and expansion for retreat centers, education halls, and service facilities, and expand our purview to make comprehensive rural community reconstruction plans.

For rural communities to enjoy comprehensive welfare, they need all four aspects of medicine, education, leisure, and culture. If these aspects of rural life are provided through social welfare, fewer people will leave the farmlands, and more people will move back to implement these welfare initiatives.

At the same time, the realities of today's agricultural structure make it difficult for everybody in the rural regions to participate in farming. Many people today have multiple jobs, but it is really the rural population who need multiple jobs to make ends meet. When the young, educated population comes to the countryside, they can bring their workloads to continue their tasks. They are free to move anywhere in the nation or the world.

The church can make the master plan for constructing this life-flourishing garden, gather its missional resources for this purpose, and implement the plan.

The Life-Flourishing Community School by GGU and the Institute for Family, Church, and Maeul have visited the case churches and found holistic practices of life-flourishing community ministry. Several types can be identified as follows.

- Life-flourishing nature community ministry – constructing a nature-friendly environment for maeul communities
- Life-flourishing cooperative community ministry – organizing cooperatives to provide supportive labor, such as Maeul Love Volunteers
- Life-flourishing welfare community ministry – making a system of total care (in cooperation with local government bodies)
- Life-flourishing education community ministry – cooperation with local schools, local school revitalization
- Life-flourishing culture community ministry – constructing cultural communities, operating cafes, organizing leisure activities
- Life-flourishing liberal arts community ministry – story-telling, writing, distributing, publishing (archival work)
- Life-flourishing dining table community ministry – organic produce, starting restaurants, sharing packed meals, joint meals
- Life-flourishing economic community ministry – building a direct distribution structure for agricultural produce
- Life-flourishing leisure community ministry – organizing, sponsoring, and conducting life-flourishing community celebrations
- Life-flourishing healing community ministry – rest, breathing, exercise, meditation, prayer

The key point is that while these types are categorized by their focus, a life-flourishing community requires all these comprehensive elements. They must be included and combined as the community requires. Because the church must care for, serve, and construct the whole of God's created world, this ministry for the life-flourishing community must become mainstream.

Bringing it All Together...

For the future of life and our spiritual journey, we must remember the covenant with God anew.

> "As for me, I am establishing my covenant with you and your descendants after you and with every living creature that is with you, the birds, the domestic animals, and every animal of the earth with you, as many as came out of the ark." (Genesis 9:9-10)

> We know that the whole creation has been groaning together as it suffers together the pains of labor, and not only the creation, but we ourselves, who have the first fruits of the Spirit, groan inwardly while we wait for adoption, the redemption of our bodies. (Romans 8:22-23)

> The thief comes only to steal and kill and destroy. I came that they may have life and have it abundantly. (John 10:10)

After the flood in the days of Noah, God made a covenant on perpetual salvation. This was the covenant with humanity, their descendants, and all life with them. It is not just humans who are parties to this covenant. There is an entire world of living things. And it goes beyond this generation to all the coming generations. Ourselves, our descendants, and all of creation on Earth are parties to this covenant.

The human violation of this covenant is a collective human sin. In the face of threats against life, the major task of the church is to consider how our ministry can understand and witness this groaning and redemption of creation. If the church is the witness to the good news of Jesus who came to give life in full, then it must struggle against the powers that steal, kill, and destroy the life of creation. It must respond to its vocation to fill the cosmos with the life of Christ who gives new life in the face of death and its power.

The church must transform human culture today to become a life-flourishing culture and start on the journey to build the life-flourishing community in which God's creation may enjoy life in all its fullness.

Introduction: State of the 21st Century Global Village and Maeul Ministry's Focus on Communal Joy

Young-sang Ro

The Earth Today and the Signs of the End Times

Today the entire planetary community faces a threat to our existence. Multiple disasters and crises are headed our way. The situations we face today have been foretold in various ways in the description of the end times in Matthew 24:3-14: deceptions, wars, plagues, natural disasters, multiple calamities, persecution, love growing cold, and lawlessness. If wars and disasters are physical signs, deceptions, lawlessness, and lack of love are spiritual and moral signs. Ultimately, humanity will not be able to escape destruction from wars and calamities, deception, injustice, and growing hatred, and they will have to face an entirely new world.

Rumors of war are one of the critical signs that signal the beginning of the end of the end. The Covid-19 pandemic impaired the global economy, resulting in a cloud of conflict covering the world. Along with regional wars such as the one between Ukraine and Russia, nuclear conflict, terrorism, and immigration are the crises waiting to be resolved. The threat of nuclear attack by North Korea is a particular issue confronting the Korean people.

It can be said that the 21st-century actually began not on January 1, 2000, but in early February 2020 when Covid-19 spread throughout the world. Abusive factory-style farms have pushed animals' immune systems to the limits, making animal-to-human disease transmission much more likely. 21st-century diseases like Ebola, SARS, MERS, Zika, and Covid-19 are caused by ecosystem destruction. Unless human civilization makes a turn, diseases of greater severity will continue to emerge.

This means we must cultivate a new culture that enhances ecological spirituality. Besides the pandemic, climate change is resulting in rising sea levels, more disastrous storms and tornadoes, abrupt weather anomalies, and lower crop harvests. Human selfishness and overconsumption are threatening the climate and our future. In the next ten years, humanity will be in dire trouble if the earth's temperature cannot be regulated to limit its rise by no more than 1.5 degrees Celsius compared to preindustrial times. The energy crisis, water shortage, famine, and various environmental catastrophes are unfolding before our eyes. Yet we fail to respond ethically and rush headlong to the end of the world.

Economic inequality must be mentioned as another dilemma that threaten humanity. Today, people who enjoy abundance cannot empathize with the people in poverty; they casually enjoy their exclusive economic privileges. We are a species who would stop at nothing to ensure my children and I prosper.

We are ruled in an anti-democratic society where the voices of the powerful fill the air and the voices of the weak are neglected. Differences in opinion are silenced and everyone is forced to conform in this hostile society. Such a selfish and egotistic way of life is increasing social conflict. Conflicts grow deep between regions and ethnicities, among people with different ideologies and religions, between people of different age and gender, between the rich and the poor, and between the employer and the employee, and the cost of such social conflict in South Korea is relatively greater than in other countries (Ephesians 2:12-22).

Societal Crisis, and the Church at the Brink

In South Korea overheated social competition and economic instability discourage marriage and childbearing. The extremely low birth rate and the growing proportion of the elderly in the "super-aging society" threaten the traditional family structure. Urbanization and the increase of single-person households are disintegrating communities. This phenomenon is even more severe in rural regions, culminating in a steep drop in population. In addition, with the collapse of stable families, confusion about gender identity and sexual promiscuity is making it even more difficult to defend family values. It is becoming more and more difficult to raise children in the safety of the home.

In addition, with the advancement of science, humanity is facing the Fourth Industrial Revolution. The progress is on the one hand improving our lives, but it is also bringing another kind of crisis. As society switched to remote work during the Covid-19 pandemic, ICT usage became more widespread, causing greater concerns about inequality and alienation. Advancements in ICT made life convenient, but it is also much easier to spread misinformation and fabrication for one to privatize and monopolize power. Also, irresponsible genetic manipulation through bioengineering may bring unforeseen risks, yet we continue on this path in defiance of the Creator.

Comet impact, the sun's expansion and explosion, and the arrival of alien substances are all planetary calamities that may end humanity. The universe may seem stable, but upon closer look, there is constant unpredictability. We must examine these circumstances and prepare for the threats to our planet.

Finally, many groups of people have been marginalized in the process of globalization, and progressive groups have criticized globalization's injustices. Globalization has brought greater wealth to humanity, but as criticized, it has not been fairly distributed. That is why the Korean church has been putting much effort into alleviating the fallouts of globalization. The Korean church's missional efforts in response to globalization have not only been in domestic missions to foreign migrants but also in alleviating economic inequalities, which resulted in much positive impact on our society today.

In this secular, post-religious society, the church is facing an existential crisis and the need to reform. In this storm of social change, we must decide on the direction of our ministry and reform our church character and structure accordingly. Our denomination of Presbyterian Church of Korea – Tonghap (PCK) and the General Assembly would do right to develop our expression of public theology and construct wholesome systems and policies on this basis. We cannot afford to shirk this duty.

The steep growth of the Korean church leveled, its societal influence is decreasing in the aftermath of the pandemic, and its public credibility is also on the downturn. The world is drifting further away from God and God's word, religion, and society are further divided, and clearly such anti-spirituality spells doom for our future. Such alarm bells in church and society tell us that if civilization does not make a revolutionary turn in the next decade, this world God created will fall into unprecedented disaster. Decisive steps must be taken to turn the tide.

Theological Repentance in Response to Today's Crisis of Extinction

In this comprehensive dilemma, we need to turn to the ultimate reason behind this existential crisis. We must examine what is behind Covid-19, the threat of nuclear war, climate crisis, extinction of species, food and energy crisis, economic inequality, anti-democratic politics, heightening social conflict, low birth rate and aging society, the disintegration of traditional family structure, side effects of technological advancements, and natural and cosmic disasters. These planetary crises may be called the threat of extinction. Numerous species are going extinct each day, and we cannot but ask if the human species will one day follow.

In this crisis we realize that egocentrism, ethnocentrism, and anthropocentrism are at the heart, growing like cancer. Due to the individualization of happiness, our communities have fragmented and our social values have been confounded and dismantled. Selfishness is taking all of humanity down the path of destruction.

1 Corinthians 12 emphasizes unity and communality. Scripture teaches that true life looks like organic unity in the body of Christ. A machine does not have life, but an organism does. 1 Corinthians 12 describes this state of a living organism in the repeated phrase "many parts, one body" and explains it in terms of interdependence, mutual care, and empathy. All living things are connected in a web, and the study of ecology tells us that creation is organically connected and related to their environment. The Gospel of John defines salvation as having eternal life through faith, and 1 Corinthians 12 describes true life as relational wholeness based on unity in diversity.

We rediscover that the many life-destroying problems of society and humanity come from the absence of communities united in love. Human selfishness brought about the climate and ecological crises. Individual and national self-interest blind us to march into war and conflict. This society's indifference to one another's welfare makes individuals see no other option than suicide. It is also causing many to give up on marriage and childbearing.

Scripture tells of the power of Jesus Christ, the power of the Holy Spirit and love, and the recovery of compassion through salvation that can unite disparate parts into one organic body. By strengthening such a web of relationships, we can overcome the extinction crisis today.

Therefore, to overcome the calamity we face today, we must strengthen communality. We must turn from grasping selfish benefits and prosperity and seek ways to coexist and prosper together with other humans and other species. For this purpose, the Presbyterian Church of Korea (PCK) Research Center studied *maeul* ministry to produce 24 publications. Maeul ministry may be characterized in various ways, but at its core, there is an emphasis on community.

Such communality is only possible in the power of love God has shown us. Therefore, maeul ministry may be defined as the ministry that embraces the maeul, the local community, and gives life to the world out of God's true love (John 3:16). Maeul ministry starts with the love of God. Love is the power that unites a community. By this love of God, we can build a communal maeul and the maeul church.

Maeul Ministry that Emphasizes Love in Action

John 3:16 speaks of God who loved the world so as to send God's only Son. If God only spoke of loving the world but never sent the Son to the world to die on the cross, then the love would have lacked substance, and the credibility of that love would be questioned. But God declared love for humanity and the world and sent Jesus Christ to be incarnated to the world as a demonstration of that love. Likewise, maeul ministry requires love in action. It is not abstract theology but incarnational and liturgical, and it must be concretely practiced in ministry.

Today, Korean Christianity is on a downward slope. But some churches still do dynamic ministry, and theologians gathered hundreds of cases from these churches, which became the study of maeul ministry. The ministry came first, and analysis and theorization followed. In that sense, maeul ministry is orthopraxis rather than orthodoxy. Theologians gathered countless stories of wholesome ministry which resulted in the concept of maeul ministry. The theory came from practice, and based on the theory, practice again emerged, which was reflected on to refine the theory.

Maeul Ministry: Cases and Theological Reflections I, II emerge from this context. The two-volume publication is structured first to present a case of maeul ministry, followed by a theological reflection on the case by a scholar. The case description and theological analysis form pairs throughout the book. In editing the publication series on maeul ministry for the PCK Research Center (24 total), I always worked to achieve a balance between books on theory and books on cases. Maeul ministry is a very practical theology of ministry. It is not an abstraction from an ivory tower but rooted in ministry practice.

Scripture attests that faith without action is dead. Faith that is not founded in action and practice goes stagnant. The gospel cannot be effectively delivered if listeners are only asked to believe the claim that God is love. For the listeners to realize this love and have faith, they must experience the actual love of God in Jesus Christ. When that love of God is communicated in the actions of the believers the gospel will be proclaimed with authority.

What Christians need the most today is this enactment of God's passionate love. When we love, we act. And when we act, we can sense the dynamism of the gospel. When, through such loving sacrifice, the despairing rejoice and the people on the road to destruction are saved, we will joyfully bear any hardship. Just as Jesus sacrificed his life until his blood was shed and his bones broken, there is no reason for us not to do so as well. Through such labor of love, the gospel will be spread even further and God will be even more glorified.

The Town as Church and the Residents as Congregants

John 3:16 says that God gave God's only son because God loves the *world.* God loves not only the ones who believe in Jesus, but the entire world, so whoever repents and believes can be saved. The God of love loves not just the church but all creation.

Maeul ministry highlights the image of Jesus Christ as the shepherd who leaves the ninety-nine to find the one lost sheep (Luke 15:4). God loves the church-going believers but is more interested in the people lost and wandering outside the church. Similarly, maeul ministry and the concept of the missional church are not about first having people outside the church repent, believe in Jesus, to ultimately have them become members of a church community. The order is reversed so that the church first becomes a part of the local community to form relationships with others. In that process, the community residents may come to believe in Jesus to become the people of God.

Romans 3:29 says, "Is God the God of Jews only? Is he not the God of Gentiles also? Yes, of Gentiles also". This is one of the foundational passages of maeul ministry. People in Paul's days considered YHWH one of the ethnic deities. But Paul recognized this God as not only the God of Israel but of all nations, and this is why he devoted himself to God's mission.

We must not contain the good news of Christianity to people in the church. A spirit of inclusion is needed, recognizing that people outside the church will also be saved if they only believe. Two millennia ago, the Apostle Paul broke down the walls of the Jews to open up Christianity to the world. Today, we must also attend to the maeul ministry methods that lovingly embrace people outside the church. Maeul ministry with this inclusivity will vitalize our churches.

We decided on the motto of maeul ministry as "the community as church, the residents as congregation". Many people misunderstand this motto as a growth-oriented message to mean that we intend to convert all town residents into church members. But that is not the intention. It means to embrace the local residents like we would church members and to consider them people beloved of God. It calls for the church to break out of its ghettoized community and go out to all corners of the town to visit and care for the residents. Our ministry must not stay within the church. When we go out to the local community and conduct ministries outside the church, we will be able to make more contact with people to lead them to salvation. In that sense, the motto "the community as church, the residents as congregation" may be clarified if revised as "considering the town as church and the residents as congregation".

Such ministry may be illustrated with the following examples.

First, half of the scholarships awarded to youth in the church may be awarded to youth who do not attend church.

Second, when Korean churches pickle kimchi together in the fall they generally share some with unchurched neighbors. The distribution process can be more effective if churches ask the heads of townships to distribute the kimchi to them.

Third, maeul ministry emphasizes town visitation. The purpose is to visit and encourage all the households with various difficulties. While the local governments are doing a lot of good to provide welfare for the residents, but there are still people out of sight and reach of the government system. Churches' small group leaders who are closer to the residents can fill the gap by approaching these households to provide appropriate care.

Today, people in and out of the church are experiencing hardships after the Covid-19 pandemic. In this situation, the church must lead in serving both its congregants and the unchurched, without discrimination. Just as God sent God's only Son because God loves all the people of the world, we also must care for the entire neighborhood. Ministry in the age of the pandemic must go beyond ministry for the church to become an inclusive ministry that embraces the entire town and its residents.

Maeul Ministry and Maeul Enterprise

Maeul ministry is interested in individual and communal happiness. This means maeul ministry emphasizes constructing the local community based on communal values (John 17:21-23). Maeul ministry analyzes the cause of our society's present crisis as rooted in an individualistic lifestyle. Therefore, the ministry strategy is to instill the Christian values of unity and communality based on love in all spheres of society, including the economy, education, welfare, environmental protection, and culture. Therefore, maeul ministry seeks to integrate based on community spirit the major institutions that constitute a town. It is an attempt to reconstruct all stakeholders from the perspective of maeul community. It is interested in building up active subjects who work for each other's happiness rather than prioritizing bottom-line profit.

If churches in a town collaborate to start a social enterprise to give work to the unemployed, then our towns will become much happier. This means to start and operate businesses for people in poverty. I would name such businesses maeul enterprises. These businesses would not operate with a profit motive but for the welfare of the local residents. This would also require job training to give people the capacity to do the necessary work.

For example, in a rural village that mainly produces strawberries, a farmers' cooperative may build a strawberry preserve factory. This would create jobs for the economically poor. The shelf life of soft strawberries is short, so processing them this way would also greatly help provide sustainable income for the village. By starting such maeul enterprises that are responsive to community needs, it would be possible to provide social welfare more effectively.

Once I traveled to Wēnzhōu, one of China's wealthiest regions. There were many good-sized underground Protestant churches there, and I remember seeing a lot of imported automobile brands. A local resident explained that many factories making small electrical parts were constructed here at one point. The local people operated these factories together, and the region became known for its specialty in electrical parts, which led to economic growth for the whole place. Likewise, businesses that fit the regional characteristics can closely relate to resident life. A woodwork and wood dish business in Namwon, a business preserving shrimp and other seafood in Gyeokpo, and a dairy factory in Anseong can be started as maeul businesses in the form of cooperatives where the residents work for the common good.

So, community care continues after giving bread to the hungry. People should be supported economically to prevent poverty, and in times of crisis, there should be a system to bring them out of the situation. This is the difference between community social welfare and individual acts of charity. Community welfare is closely related to such social enterprises and social economy movements today. Governments and churches should do their best to support these maeul enterprises. A good case of church involvement in maeul enterprise was the ministry of God's Will SoongEui Church. The church's *kimbap* restaurant and box factory as social enterprises expanded our imagination of what is possible. Korean churches in the past have worked with farming cooperatives to connect the church with the local community. This not only helped the community but also grew the church, giving more people the opportunity to encounter God's salvation.

Maeul Ministry and Maeul School

Maeul school is another example of an effort to raise community wellbeing. A few years ago, the term "*sampo* generation" trended. That meant a generation resigned never to enjoy dating, marriage, and childbearing. We know very well that South Korea's fertility rate is the lowest globally. If young people continue to avoid having children, then the nation will disappear off the face of the earth. There are many reasons why people give up on childbearing, but the biggest is economic. Once women give birth, they are pressured to give up their careers. At the same time, child rearing requires much more money, squeezing household finances. Society must do all it can to solve this issue, and one of the solutions is the maeul school approach to education.

We often think of what is best for our own children only. We raise and educate them selfishly. I often wonder if anything good can come of such schooling. It is no wonder we see rampant violence and bullying in school. It is time we learn to regard all the children as our own and raise them together as a community. The maeul school approach is how the community operates the local school and raises the children together.

Young parents these days have a hard time sending children to school. They lack the time and resources to care for their children properly. It is also difficult to form good parent-child relationships today, and many families are gripped by domestic violence. Regarding this situation, I thought of the boarding schools in England and the United States. Many boarding schools in the West provide K-12 education. Parents can entrust their children to these schools, including during vacations. The children can also come home on the weekends or commute daily. The point is that entrusting the children to the school is possible. Many boarding schools in other countries were started by churches and monasteries. I think it is necessary to encourage the operations of such mission schools and alternative schools. In recent years, close to half of the alternative schools in South Korea have been started by churches. If we develop such community education movements with a basis on maeul ministry, I believe they will significantly contribute to our church and society.

Suppose we train qualified teachers to entrust children's education fully. In that case, parents will have enough time to devote to economic activities and achieve career success, facilitating better relationships with their children. For this to happen, the school must be a safe space. Here, the cooperation of the government and education stakeholders is required. More than anything, children with violent tendencies need special attention, so stronger character education programs are needed, and more counselor teachers should be stationed. Schools should be more than a place for academic achievement.

At the same time, parents should be actively involved in local school matters. Parents who attained higher education and have extra time may volunteer to support school education and contribute to school improvements. Parents in the community may plan out meals and help with the cooking.

So I recommend the Ministry of Education to make one government-sponsored K-12 boarding school in each town. Boarding schools may be costly, but the government should increase the education budget for the sake of the students. The schools should teach not only Korean language, English, and Mathematics but also let students run freely in school yards and athletic facilities, teach them to play a musical instrument, take them on trips to local cultural and historical sites, and take them on camping trips to mountains and creeks. If the town cooperates to make the school a space of proper education, our children's lives will be enriched and happy. This is what I would call the maeul school. It is where all the community residents cooperate, and all the town resources are contributed to make a good school. There is nothing more urgent for Koreans today than such education service.

Maeul Ministry and Maeul Environment Guard

I earlier discussed issues of livelihood and education. An issue as important is the matter of protecting the natural and cultural environment. A community's natural environment greatly affects resident life. Air and water quality, distribution of green terrains and parks, preservation of historical structures, quality of residential neighborhoods, and the quality of available cultural activities are all elements that should be considered for our quality of life.

Recently, I saw many urban renewal and stream improvement projects as part of the community building movement considerably impacting residents' quality of life. Reports have shown that stream improvement and slum renewal projects in Japan and South Korea resulted in considerable outcome. As the residents participated in the efforts to beautify their neighborhoods, their quality of life improved, and the towns could also become tourist destinations.

In the past days of industrialization, we used to produce factories emitting toxins. The society may have achieved some economic development for a while, but people's quality of life deteriorated. As a healthy mind requires a healthy body, a clean natural environment greatly impacts our quality of life. We must devote effort to repairing old buildings to restore dilapidated neighborhoods and care for the natural environment.

Through industrialization we have come to realize the significance of natural and urban environments and that they cannot be maintained by individual effort alone. That is why an organization that may be called maeul environment guard is necessary. In the past I heard of a church in Seoul that with support from the district government planted flowers and made gardens by the side of the road. Such cooperative efforts to improve the town environment raise our quality of life.

If rubbish is strewn about in the streets and broken buildings are neglected here and there, the residents cannot be happy in such a town. There are lots of ways to improve the local environment without devoting much finances, and these little things can strengthen the residents' affection for the town. Especially projects to preserve green spaces and to make outdoor exercise facilities between high-rise apartments is a very important task the residents and the local government can work on together.

If a town's natural environment is well-preserved, it will also improve the resident relationships. Letting clean streams flow, caring for the town forest, repairing streets and houses, and inviting the birds to stop by can improve the residents' own character to make communal happiness possible. Nothing could be better than this. The love of God will transform and beautify not only humanity but also the natural environment.

Maeul Ministry and Maeul Clinic

I want to introduce the healthcare cooperatives being discussed today as a concept of local social welfare. In a healthcare cooperative, local residents cooperate with healthcare professionals to establish and operate a healthcare clinic. A healthcare cooperative exists not only to cure diseases but also to assist in public health and prevention. This is done by conducting programs such as lectures, exercise classes, hiking clubs, and workshops on nutrition through which the residents can take care of their health. If such community clinic introduces healthy food and educates on healthy diet, this will contribute to disease prevention and the construction of a healthy society. Health-related television shows are popular these days. Each broadcasting station is making more of such programs. Churches should also remind people that health is one of the blessings of God (III John 2).

Thanks to a good public health insurance system, Korean citizens receive high-quality care, resulting in a longer average lifespan. But the healthcare system is not without issues. The most problematic is the hospitals' temptation to overtreat based on profit motive.

In this situation, a healthcare cooperative for the public good will be a valuable public resource. On this issue, I suggest that such a healthcare cooperative be considered a maeul clinic. This emphasizes that healthcare institutions should function for the public good rather than private profit.

For this purpose, if local students are sent to medical schools to become excellent doctors and return to town to operate the maeul clinic in a cooperative, our society's healthcare system will improve. These clinics should go beyond treating diseases and become responsible for resident health. In addition to the maeul clinic, the town will greatly improve if the local church cooperates to operate a hospice center for end-of-life care. Here of course, I don't mean that the maeul clinic should be operated by the government. It should be a clinic of, by, and for the town residents. If such such maeul clinic cooperatives multiply, Korean citizen health would improve. Of course, for this purpose, the clinic's director and administrative staff should be conscientious in their operations, and this would only be possible based on social capital built over a long period of time.

In recent years, increasing numbers of hospitals have been established and operated by churches and church-related organizations. Their purpose is not to make a profit but to provide services to people who cannot afford the cost. While such medical institutions for social welfare is important, we should also consider developing clinics as cooperatives. As profit-making private hospitals and public clinics for the common good complement each other to fill the gaps, our healthcare system will surely improve.

Maeul Ministry and Maeul Bank

The Jubilee Law in Leviticus mentions a system of lending to people in the nation for low or no interest. The nation of Israel freed from slavery established such a system to support the poor to overcome their situation and achieve financial autonomy. Such a system of favorable interest rates for the poor will also benefit our society. Above all, such a system should understand the borrowers' situation and provide another chance to people whose businesses went bankrupt.

Grameen Bank in Bangladesh is a good example. This is a bank for the poor, lending to them for low-interest rates to assist their financial independence. Grameen in Bengali means "village", so Grameen Bank means maeul bank. It is similar to South Korea's Saemaeul Credit Cooperative. Grameen Bank leads in microfinancing, lending small amounts to low-income populations without requiring a security deposit. Muhammad Junus who started this bank was awarded the Nobel Peace Prize in 2006. He benefited more than a hundred million poor households. The story is told in Junus' book *Creating a World Without Poverty* that has also been translated into Korean. A similar leader in microfinancing in South Korea is the Happy Bank Microcredit Program by Happy World Foundation affiliated with Holy Light Kwangsung Church.

In South Korea, microfinancing similar to Junus' Grameen Bank has been operating as credit cooperatives. In the past, many Korean Protestant churches used to establish non-profit credit cooperatives, though in recent years, the number has vastly reduced. These cooperatives used to function as useful bank for the local poor. Today if we renew the effort with more stable operations church and society will see good results.

Our financial system today is very unfavorable to the poor. The wealthy are judged credible enough to lend from banks, but the poor have low credit scores so they are forced to lend on high interest. It is easier for the wealthy to amass more wealth while the poor lose the little they have. Wouldn't the opposite be more just? Such inequalities in lending need to be addressed. To support people who took out predatory lending, the Korean organization Lifeway Fund gives low-interest loans without requiring deposits. The program is alleviating a lot of people's suffering. I was told that the principal collection rate from the lenders in this organization is above average.

Networking and cooperation of schools, hospitals, banks, businesses, town offices, and churches to improve the town would alleviate suffering. An act of love for an individual is important, but if we work on the social structure to benefit many, we will see much more fruit of love. We must always remember that Jesus Christ took the sin and suffering and died on the cross not just for myself but the entire humanity.

Maeul Ministry and Maeul Center

The official name of the town-level government changed from town office to community service center and now is called administrative welfare center. It is an effort to make the government office more accessible to the residents, but a distance remains. The government should look after the residents so that they can at least prevent people from ending their lives due to financial pressures. To create such dynamic town offices and local government services, our perceptions need to undergo much change.

For a town office to be a true center of the community, more staff should be making rounds in town rather than sitting in their offices. To find the residents' actual needs, they must first go out to the streets and consistently communicate with the residents. Like a church pastor visits their members, the town office staff in South Korea should take the initiative to find out the needs of the residents.

For this purpose, I propose changing the name of the town office to maeul center. This requires the office to position itself as the center of the town rather than as a group of bureaucratic officials lording above the town residents. And the role of the maeul center should be more specified. They should provide welfare to the financially worse-off and listen to the town residents' different requests.

Recently, community self-governance centers have been formed in the town offices to educate the townspeople on different aspects. They provide culture classes, workshops on community self-governance, volunteer opportunities, and other ways to revitalize the town.

Community self-governance is a fundamental concept for advancing South Korea's democracy today. All the democracies in the West have active resident governance. Community self-governance means that the residents take ownership of town governance to find needs and meet them for themselves and that the local government branch is not the only one initiating town programs. Such a structure will strengthen the root of our country's democracy. To have the town residents take ownership and govern themselves, their governing capacity must be improved. Liberal arts education at community self-governance centers and Bible studies in churches will critically contribute to this purpose.

Churches can contribute to establishing such community self-governance in many ways. In addition to learning the scripture, the participants can discuss specific ways to understand their neighbors and improve their quality of life. Congregants and community residents can cooperate to submit proposals to public project financing contests. Churches can also collaborate with local governments on many programs to enrich the community.

There are increasing church associations such as Church-Town Councils for mutual cooperation in local administration. These developments should be promoted should be even more. There has been no political party or president in South Korean history that had not emphasized the importance of community self-governance. Nobody would deny that participatory self-governance of citizens has contributed to the blossoming of democracy in our nation. Community self-governance is the flower of democracy.

Local Community Welfare as Maeul Welfare

The client of local community welfare is not the individuals but the entire local community. The services should therefore be provided not by large public institutions or smaller private organizations alone but as an association of these actors that form the community. This is also to approach resident welfare not in terms of needy individuals but as the whole community. It is to assist in the welfare of an individual not just as isolated individuals but in relation to their community. It is good for an individual or an institution to support an individual in need, but local community service should aim to make the entire social structure function for the welfare of the individual.

What we most need today is to consider social services from the perspective of the local community. Indeed, the welfare of the entire town is raised as each individual's welfare is improved. But social services in respect to individuals and town as the whole are not the same. That is why I propose the concept of maeul welfare, in which the town is the agent of local community welfare. Recently another term, local community protection, is also used as part of local community welfare. A comprehensive approach by the local community to the local issues addressing the economy, education, healthcare, and psychosocial aspects should be further developed.

There are two models of local community welfare: the outcome-oriented model and the process-oriented model. While the outcome-oriented model assesses whether and how much the community's needs have been met, the process-oriented model is concerned with the kinds of effort necessary to meet the needs. In the process of local community welfare provision, we must encourage sustained interest and participation of community residents. For this purpose, resident capacity for self-governance and consensus building should be developed so that the residents themselves can tackle local issues. The community self-governance system should be organized, and various organizations should collaborate and participate in joint programs.

Churches can do many things in this process. The most crucial role of the church is to have people regard the community and its residents with compassion. Today we are too lost in individualistic self-fulfillment. We must develop the capacity to notice others' needs and empathize with them. Scripture often suggests ways to look beyond the self to care for others, so in studying the Bible to shift our perception, we can greatly contribute to local community welfare.

We still remember the tragic suicide of a mother and two daughters in Songpa District in Seoul in February 2014. The fact that a household was neglected in a relatively well-to-do district became a wake-up call for society. Despite the extensive social welfare provision system, the government cannot find all the people needing support. Local organizations such as churches should be attentive and be actively involved to intervene effectively. Churches have a tight web of relationships in town and may be welcomed by visited households. They are well-positioned to find people in need.

There is a saying that even a nation cannot solve the problem of poverty. If it cannot be solved by the nation alone, then churches, businesses, hospitals, schools, and local governments in the community can cooperate so that nobody will have to end their life because of financial troubles. In South Korea there is not enough tax revenue to sufficiently support needy people. If churches lead in providing social welfare, our society will improve.

Maeul Church at the Center of Maeul Ministry

A church must be deeply interested in the happiness of community residents. Traditionally, churches have been deeply involved in resident lives. When a child was born, they were baptized with the blessing of the residents. They were congratulated for their rites of passage. The town rejoiced together at weddings and mourned together at funerals. The church was there at every important moment of life. Such traditions have very much deteriorated in the church today. Weddings are performed in wedding halls and funerals in funeral homes. This should be an opportunity to deeply reconsider the role of the church in society. There might be specific ways for the community residents to cooperate in providing humble housing for the newlyweds or providing lifelong insurance for a child born in the community. Churches may participate in starting and supporting a hospice center for each town so that the town can be present at the deathbed to pray and mourn together.

What are some things the church can do? As I edited publications on maeul ministry in the past few years, I explored ways for the church to contribute to our communities' spiritual, psychosocial, and material wellness. Churches should first help the community residents notice their neighbors beyond their own individual concerns. Churches should enter the town's center rather than stay apart from it and should serve the town to become the maeul church.

Even a small church can act in love. If one small church can support an individual's livelihood and improve the person's life, then this is no small achievement. It is vital to commit to helping the poor for the long term. We may have little, but if we are constantly attuned to ways we can gather resources to help others, we will be truly fulfilled. Churches that are known as exemplars of maeul ministry tend to be smaller than larger. Maeul ministry does not require a big budget. We can do a lot with a small amount of resources.

Medieval towns in history had a town hall, an opera house, and a church at the center. These three institutions cooperated for the wellness of the town. A few years ago, I visited a town near Davos, Switzerland. I got out of my hotel and took a walk around town in the evening. Small quaint shops lined the street on the way to the town square. I remember how I sauntered into some shops and bought a little trinket on a whim. As expected, there was a large church in the town square. The church had a monastery where the monks spent their lives praying, studying, and making new products for town welfare. As I entered the church and looked around the several structures, I imagined a church placed at the center of a town and deeply invested in the matters of the town. Of course, such concentration of power on the church was a reason why the Medieval church became corrupt. But politics and religion are essentially related and function to check and balance each other. Today South Korea is on a downward path due to politicians' lack of imagination. Christianity must provide a new vision for the people. Humanity is on a crossroads. Are we to break through the dilemma and chart a new path based on God's word, or stay the course on the frustrating status quo?

Future of Maeul Ministry

Earlier I mentioned that I edited a series of twenty-four publications on maeul ministry as Director of the PCK Research Center. There have been doctoral dissertations on the subject of maeul ministry in South Korea and English presentations at overseas academic conferences. Maeul ministry is spreading worldwide. The PCK (Tonghap) first emphasized maeul ministry, and other denominations such as the Presbyterian Church in Korea (Hapdong), the Presbyterian Church in Korea (Baekseok), the Presbyterian Church in the Republic of Korea (Gijang), the Korean Methodist Church, the Koran Baptist Convention, and the Anglican Church of Korea are following suit. With further research, maeul ministry may contribute to world theology as an alternative method of ministry. Recently, I was invited to an Assembly of God of Korea's Busan Regional Presbytery to speak on maeul ministry. Some of the Assembly of God churches are also investing effort into these matters. As these initiatives grow, our ministry can become more practical and concrete.

I will end by introducing a case of a mid-sized church practicing maeul ministry. Myeongnyun Joongang Church is located across Sungkyunkwan University. Located in a college town, it has been operating a small student residence to let university students stay at low cost. For maeul ministry, the church decided to expand the student residence and devote more attention to it, resulting in a growing number of young people attending the church. Many churches today lack younger membership, but this church is distinct for its dynamic young adult ministry. The student residence was repaired, a library was built, and the old beds were exchanged for new ones. Once a month, elders take turns to treat students with fried chicken, and scholarships are also offered. The church was meeting the needs of the local students, and the outcome was flourishing young adult ministry.

Such a share-house system for young people is a small example of maeul ministry. There are countless other examples of ministry for the community, and they are expanding even more. The English term "sharing" in concepts like shared economy and shared housing may be translated into the Korean word *nanoom* to mean mutual partaking rather than public ownership. So rather than a publicly-owned economy, it can be better understood as a shared economy. Rather than a publicly owned residence, it is a shared residence and a shared space. The many government policies will not solve the real-estate dilemma in South Korea today. When we understand the residential space as the common good and share the space as the space of residence and relationship-building, much of today's real estate issues will be resolved. Unless the citizens of Korea change their value system to be willing to share their space with others left out in the cold, the real estate issue will not be solved. We must all have the community spirit armed with the love of God so that we can put love in action toward mutual coexistence.

Maeul Ministry Series Publications by the Presbyterian Church of Korea Research Center

PCK Research Center. *General Assembly Policy Resource Book. Maeul Ministry Manual.* Seoul: PCK Books, 2017.

Cho, Yong-hoon. *Maeul Community and Church Community. Presbyterian Church of Korea Research Center Maeul Ministry Monograph Series 1.* Seoul: Dongyeon, 2017.

Kim, Do-il. *Family, Church, and Maeul Happy Together as Education Community. Presbyterian Church of Korea Research Center Maeul Ministry Monograph Series 2.* Seoul: Dongyeon, 2018.

Sung, Seok-hwan. *New Challenges for the Church in the Local Community. Maeul Community and Church Community: Presbyterian Church of Korea Research Center Maeul Ministry Monograph Series 3.* Seoul: Nanum, 2018.

Ro, Young Sang, ed. *Maeul Church and Maeul Ministry (Theory). Presbyterian Church of Korea Research Center Maeul Ministry Series 1.* Seoul: PCK Books, 2018.

Ro, Young Sang, ed. *Maeul Church and Maeul Ministry (Practice). Presbyterian Church of Korea Research Center Maeul Ministry Series 2.* Seoul: PCK Books, 2018.

Kim, Do-il, ed. *Maeul Ministry for the Kingdom of God – With the Community, with the Lord: Bible Study Resource Book 1. Presbyterian Church of Korea Research Center Maeul Ministry Series 7.* Seoul: Dongyeon, 2018.

Han, Kook-il, ed. *Church that Stands with the Community – With the Community, with the Lord: Bible Study Resource Book 2. Presbyterian Church of Korea Research Center Maeul Ministry Series 8.* Seoul: Dongyeon, 2018.

Shin, Jeong ed. *Practicing Maeul Ministry with the Community Residents – With the Community, with the Lord: Bible Study Resource Book 3. Presbyterian Church of Korea Research Center Maeul Ministry Series 9.* Seoul: Dongyeon, 2018

Ro, Young Sang ed. *Maeul Ministry that Saves the World – With the Community, with the Lord: Bible Study Resource Book 4. Presbyterian Church of Korea Research Center Maeul Ministry Series 10.* Seoul: Dongyeon, 2018

Han, Gyeong-ho ed. *Community Cooperative Movement and Maeul Ministry. Presbyterian Church of Korea Research Center Maeul Ministry Series 11.* Seoul: Nanum, 2018.

Korea Academy of Christian Social Welfare, ed. *Maeul Ministry and Local Community Welfare. Presbyterian Church of Korea Research Center Maeul Ministry Series 12.* Seoul: Dongyeon, 2019.

Han, Gyeong-ho, ed. *Rural Churches that Grow the Community. Presbyterian Church of Korea Research Center Maeul Ministry Series 13.* Seoul: Dongyeon, 2019.

Ro, Young-sang, ed. *Introduction to Maeul Ministry. Presbyterian Church of Korea Research Center Maeul Ministry Series 14.* Seoul: Kingdom Books, 2020.

Oh Sang-cheol, ed. *Statistical Survey of the Korean Church on Social Service and Volunteering. Presbyterian Church of Korea Research Center Maeul Ministry Series 15.* Seoul: Nanum, 2020.

Song, Min-ho. *The Way to Missional Church: From Traditional to Missional Church. Presbyterian Church of Korea Research Center Maeul Ministry Series 16.* Seoul: Nanum, 2020.

Ro, Young-sang, ed. *Onnuri Community Church's Mission for a Better World. Rural Churches that Grow the Community Presbyterian Church of Korea Research Center Maeul Ministry Series 17.* Seoul: Kingdom Books, 2020.

Salim Christian Environmental Education Center, *Maeul Ministry for Flourishing of Life. Presbyterian Church of Korea Research Center Maeul Ministry Series 18.* Edited by the Research Center of the Presbyterian Church of Korea. Seoul: Nanum, 2020.

PCK Research Center, ed. *Maeul Ministry and Frontier Churches. Presbyterian Church of Korea Research Center Maeul Ministry Monograph Series 19.* Seoul: Qumran Publishing House, 2021.

Ro, Young-sang and Do-il Kim, ed. *Frontier Ministry that Embraces the Maeul and Saves the World. Presbyterian Church of Korea Research Center Maeul Ministry Series 20*. Seoul: Qumran Publishing House, 2021.

Ro, Young-sang, ed. Public Relevance of *Maeul Ministry and Church Building in the COVID-19 Pandemic. Presbyterian Church of Korea Research Center Maeul Ministry Series 21*. Seoul: Qumran Publishing House, 2021.

Kim, Do-il, et al. *Missional Church Education for All Ages. Presbyterian Church of Korea Research Center Maeul Ministry Series 22*. Seoul: Dongyeon, 2022.

PCK Research Center. *Stories of Maeul Ministry Published in Kidok Gongbo. Missional. Presbyterian Church of Korea Research Center Maeul Ministry Series 23*. Seoul: Dongyeon, 2022.

Lee, Won-don. *Web-of-Life Ministry and Community of Care in the Civilizational Transition of the COVID-19 Pandemic. Presbyterian Church of Korea Research Center Maeul Ministry Series 24*. Seoul: Nanum, 2022.

Resonance of Gongmyung Church

Hung-young Baek

Two Ministers Dreaming of Overseas Missions go to Yangpyeong

Our Calling

The name of the church we are serving is Gongmyung Church. It is a Korean word that means resonance. In a way, it fits our church's co-pastoring structure. Us two pastors and our spouses are from the same home church young adult group. Let me share how we both ended up pastoring together.

I, Hung-young Baek, had wanted to be a missionary to China. So I chose to major in Chinese literature and spent a year in China during undergrad for a short-term mission, after which I felt the confirmation to become a cross-cultural missionary. I had intended to be sent as a lay missionary immediately after graduation, but my home church pastor advised me to first graduate from a seminary and experience being an associate pastor in a Korean church, then go to the mission fields. So I obeyed and enrolled in a seminary. I did full-time ministry for ten years, and throughout the years I consistently met and talked with missionaries visiting back home. As I continued praying and considering the calling I heard in my youth, God inspired me with the message, "Your calling is not to go on missions to China but to build the kingdom of God wherever I tell you to go." You could say that South Korean households where faith is rarely passed down to the younger generation are also the "unevangelized tribes." I realized that answering my calling and living as a missionary does not require me to go to China, a specified place, but to raise the kingdom of God anywhere I am placed. I also often shared with my wife that if God is leading us to minister here in South Korea, we would like to form a small community where different families can share their daily lives.

As for pastor In-sung Hwang, as a freshman at the university he participated in a missions program of an organization called Nations Trust in England for two months, visiting England and North Africa. That is where he dedicated himself to missions. To keep the promise, he married as soon as he graduated and resided in Wales from January 2004 to 2010 as a lay missionary. Then after getting an M.Div. at the Presbyterian University and Theological Seminary, he continued to do a Th.M. and Ph.D. at the same institution. Once he got ordained in 2016, he had a chance to return to England for further studies and to do ministry. He was admitted to a doctoral program plus a guarantee of a full tuition scholarship. It was a great opportunity and could have been a way for him to function as a bridge between England and South Korea. But suddenly, the path to England was closed. There were many circumstances, but ultimately, he felt he was being called to Korea rather than Europe. He was compelled to plant a church in Korea just like he would have for missions in another country. So his family moved to Yangpyeong in February 2017 and then considered several ministry options.

The Co-pastors Meet

As the two families were preparing for to be sent for overseas missions, God led us to meet each other for the first time in June 2018. Pastor Hwang had planned to stay in Yangpyeong for two years to see if any path opens up, and he would locate elsewhere if no opportunity surfaces. At first, it was quite daunting to determine where to start, but after visiting a study group organized by a local church he started finding out about the town of Yangpyeong little by little. In the first months, the family attended Sunday services in other regions, held services at home as a family, or attended local church services. Around this time the two pastors met.

In June 2018, I was preparing for a summer trip to Europe with my eldest son who was getting homeschooled. I had known pastor Hwang from our home church young adult group, so I contacted him for some travel tips. As we caught up, our topic turned from the summer trip to starting a church together. And soon, our two families began planning to get together at Yangpyeong and plant a church. In December of that year, pastor I resigned from the church where I was serving as an associate pastor and moved to Yangpyeong to devote to church planting. Our distinct callings became our common calling through dialogue and collaboration, and in 2018, our co-pastorship started.

Figure 1: Co-ministry of pastors Hung-young Baek and In-seong Hwang

The Town as our Parish: Gongmyung Church Seeking Resonance

Ecclesiology

The South Korean church's soteriology, which commonly defines the world as an object of redemption, needs to be expanded based on the mission of the triune God. It follows that our ecclesiology should also progress to extend beyond the institution of the church and our church community to understand the church in more universal terms and to recognize our missional calling to participate in the church of God out in the world. So Gongmyung Church's foundation is on trinitarian theology based on *mission Dei*. The name of our church, Gongmyung, or resounding, originates from our mission statement that says, “Transformation happens when the life of the triune God resounds in us and our lives, in turn, resound in others.” In other words, when the life of God on a mission takes priority in churches and individuals, God resounds in them to then be able to resound in others.

Based on this ecclesiology, our weekday motto is to consider our town as our parish. That is why we focus on ministry in town through our bookshop *Chaekbogo Gagae.*[1] The space is not just for church members or Christians but is open to anyone who needs help regardless of religion or church membership. It is especially frequented by young parents who gather and share their stories at our hosted gatherings. Of course, our church does more than maeul ministry. Gongmyung Church members gather for weekday and weekend fellowship and service to pursue spiritual growth.

Vision

As the two pastors and our spouses began to meet, we wrestled with the questions “What kind of church does God desire?” and “How should we respond?” For about a year from the moment we first met until the first church service at the rented space in 2018, we discussed the church’s vision and core values. Our vision was articulated: "Just like the perfectly harmonious relationship in the triune God, when we dwell in God and God’s love to practice that love in action, our neighbors will naturally see the kingdom of God through us” (John 13:34-35[2]). We summarized this vision in the statement, “The mission of Gongmyung Church is to let the life of the triune God come and resound in us, then to let our lives resound in others to bring about transformation.”

Based on this mission statement, the following six core values were selected.

The first is wholesome daily life. This means to be authentic Christians, faithful in church and outside the church in our daily lives, striving to obey God’s word in action.

The second value is financial transparency. All share the rights and responsibilities for the finances, and all financial transactions are open to all.

The third is the priority of family. We help others to recognize the significance of the roles fulfilled by the father, the mother, and the children. They are all distinct callings that cannot be substituted. At the same time, we try to cultivate household cultures in which we can refer to God in daily conversations.

The fourth is service and participation in the neighborhood. We recognize that our calling and mission field is not somewhere far away but right here where we stand. We work to build a community in which we share our lives with our neighbors.

---

[1] Translator’s Note: The bookstore name is a pun that can mean both: Flip through a Book Shop, or Come Visit for a Read.

[2] I give you a new commandment, that you love one another. Just as I have loved you, you also should love one another. By this everyone will know that you are my disciples, if you have love for one another. (John 13:34-35 NRSV)

The fifth is the priority on relationship building rather than numerical growth. We pursue a community of caring fellowship where we are interest in each other's lives and where such interest is received with gratitude. We pursue depth of relationship rather than many shallow meetings.

Sixth is participation. This participation should be real. Rather than having one person decide on the direction for all, everyone in the community should have agency to come together to discuss, debate, accept, be convinced, and relent in this participatory, albeit slow, process.

Resounding Gongmyng Church and *Chaekbogo Gage*

Preparation

Field Research

To find out the needs in the town of Yangpyeong, we searched the Yangpyeong County website to use statistical data on the demographics of townships and villages. The search yielded several characteristics.

The first is that more outsiders are moving in than expected. Yangpyeong Station for the metro, train, and the KTX is nearby, so people can commute to Seoul while living in Yangpyeong with lower cost of housing and education. Of the 10,000 people residing in our small rural township of Gangsang-myun, 55% are young couples under 50 with children. Several such regions in Yangpyeong were notable.

The second characteristic is that despite the inflow of new young residents, there is a decided lack of cultural facilities. There was a lack of programs to meet the needs of young parents interested in children's education. Many of these families especially had their fathers commute to work in Seoul, and mothers were left to raise their children during weekdays. So we recognized the need to support the mothers as they adjust to the new town.

Determining the Location

We started looking for a church space. We were lacking in finances, but our goal was big and idealistic. We looked through various places in Yangpyeong for a few months as we considered the region's needs and the potential for us to share our vision. Finally, in March 2018 we found a place not far from downtown Yangpyeong where we could have worship services, operate a bookstore to serve the neighbors on the weekdays, and stay close to nature to experience God's creation. But our two families could not come up with the KRW 40 million deposit and remodeling cost. Fortunately, we could at least pay the 10% down payment when we gathered all our money. We were hoping for this offering to prime the pump. Then the property owner allowed us an additional two-month grace period. In the meantime, we experienced the amazing provision of God through many fellow ministers and churches to fill our financial needs. The finances and materials for remodeling could also be procured thanks to many people's contributions.

On June 6, 2018, the first Sunday worship service of Gongmyung Church was held, with a message preached by the Rev. Lee Jang-ho.[3] And on September 11 the bookshop began operations. On the weekdays the place serves as a library and bookstore to serve the neighbors; on Sundays it is a church sanctuary.

Trips to other Bookstores and Libraries

The reality is that simply making a church space would not allow us to meet with young families. We needed a space to serve as a community lounge, somewhere people can gather to talk and empathize together and where we can meet their needs. Churches often operate a small library. It's relatively easy to start, and once it has been in operation for a while, churches can get local government subsidies for the library. But long-term it is difficult to sustain the library as intended. Getting local government finance before the library and its community decide their identity results in the library programs being determined by the government agenda. After considerations, we decided to meet the residents as a bookstore rather than a library. But none of us were familiar with operating a bookshop, so the two families began visiting small bookstores nationwide for a year. We saw small shops that could take root in their communities and meet their neighbors through cultural events or reading groups.

Based on the several cases we saw, we decided that we should operate a small bookshop and a café for sustainability. Beyond being a place where people read or buy books, it should be a space of sharing and dialogue, where seminars, English classes, or literature lectures related to books can be organized. At the time, there was only one neighborhood bookshop in Yangpyeong County besides the public library, so there was a real need for more. After we decided to start a bookshop, we consistently met with an expert in children's literature to determine the character of our space with key concepts such as children's education and child-rearing through picture books. In addition, in an effort to be hospitable to the neighbors, we took lessons on hand-drip coffee brewing.

Figure 2: Preparations for Church Planting (Visits to Bookstores)

[3] Translator's Note: Senior Pastor of God's Will Kwangsung Church in Seoul, Korea.

Figure 3: Preparations for Church Planting (Coffee Brewing Class)

Chaekbogo Gage in the Local Community

Early Days

Space of Learning

The bookshop *Chaekbogo Gage* officially began on September 11, 2018. This neighborhood meeting space was designed to house a picture book library and books to sell, a small café space for people to have tea, and a small seminar room to conduct meetings. But simply having a space does not guarantee that people will come. We promoted the space in the local Mom Café[4] which resulted in more people stopping by than expected.

In the beginning, the two pastors and the spouses used our talents and our university majors to meet the residents through English and Chinese character lessons, photoshop tutorials, cross-stitching, and picture book reading. We especially used picture books to share Christian values. On the first Wednesday of each month in the morning hours, we had regular events introducing picture books on a select theme such as "How to Read a Picture Book," "Caldecott Award Winners," "Community", "Habit," "Peace," "Back to School," and "Nature." We discussed various themes and related them to Christian values in our daily lives.

On the last Friday of each month, we selected themes young parents may be interested in to organize evening lectures on child-rearing. Some lecture themes were "Touring through European Picture Books," "School Education 1 – Raising our Children Together," "School Education 2 – Raising a Child in England," "Childcare with Picture Books," "Restorative Justice – Belligerent Child, Reconciling Parent."

---

[4] Translator's Note: Moms' Cafés are web posting communities for young mothers in a region. Café members use the space to post questions, discuss life or share news in town.

Space of Play

On public holidays such as the March First Independence Movement Day, Children's Day, Parents' Day, and Hangul Day, we organized special bookstore program for the neighbors. On Hangul Day, there was a "Carpenter for a Day" event for dads and their children, on March First there was an event to reenact the Independence Movement. On Children's Day, there were events for the whole family to remember the value of family. These events reminded the participants of the purpose of education, and we could naturally share Christian values.

Especially on Christmas, after the service, we invited ten families to the "Christmas with Family" bookshop program to share a meal and celebrate with piano, guitar, dance, *daegeum*,[5] and handbell performances prepared by families. The participants could enjoy each other's company and recognize that we are all connected in the community. Only a few of the ten families were Christian, so we did not take time for official service or prayer. But at the end of the event, when we each lighted our candles, turned off all the lights, and sang "Silent Night" together, we were reminded of the meaning of Christmas and the value of togetherness.

Space of Connection

As we organized literature lectures in *Chaekbogo Gage,* several residents asked us what is distinct about the lectures organized by our bookshop. The answer was simple. At other places, once the event is over, people simply go back home. But in *Chaekbogo Gage* the real event is the fellowship after the lecture. In no time, the neighborhood residents made connections with each other. People began talking about the authenticity and natural relationship building in these events, which led to nearby Gaegun Elementary School contacting us two pastors to teach students about reading. People also started asking if small groups could rent out the space. Piano teachers wanted to hold recitals for their students, and a Japanese madame wanted to have a piano concert before she left Korea. Teachers of Yangpyeong Elementary School held a recorder concert, and homeschoolers of Yangpyeong rented the space for their gatherings. Gyeonggi School of Dreams[6] uses it for their regular meetups. With these events, the space naturally establishes its presence in the community. In addition, the county officials and township mayors also stopped by to suggest ways to collaborate. We also discovered that given the regional characteristics, many families are interested in alternatives to formal education; many have moved here partly because of it and are already homeschooling their children. So my family started a regular homeschooler gathering in Yangpyeong. I continue to meet with people asking for advice and connect them with other homeschooling families in town.

---

[5] Translator's Note: Traditional woodwind instrument of Korea.

[6] Translator's Note: This is a local education community building initiative in Gyeonggi Province that started in 2015 to subsidize student and community-initiated education programs.

Figure 4: Culture Lessons and Lectures

Ministry after Covid-19 – Taking a Step Closer

Extension of Cultural Lectures (Online)

After Covid-19 started in January 2020, the ministry of *Chaekbogo Gage* changed little by little. Due to government quarantine policy, it became difficult for people to freely visit for tea and conversation. We needed to make a big decision. To sustain the meetings, we made lectures available both online and offline. So since 2021, *Chaekbogo Gage* has been conducting 14 lectures during the summer and winter breaks and during the semesters on topics such as literature for adults and youth, picture book-play and picture books as literature, English language picture book and literature reading, cross stitching, nonviolent communication for children, arts and picture books, and classic picture books. The lectures halted for a bit toward the beginning of the pandemic but as we continued these lectures the bookshop is once again bustling. *Chaekbogo Gage* is becoming an *Adullam* (a shelter) for parents and children.

Chaekbogo Gage Radio

Previously we had Christmas events inviting neighbors to share the meaning of Christmas. In the pandemic it was difficult to meet in person, so we produced special radio programs to share the meaning of Christmas. For two seasons in 2021 and 2022, we uploaded the audio of *Chaekbogo Gage* Christmas program online. It was produced and hosted like an open studio welcoming anyone who visits the store, whether Christian or not. It helped the residents find solidarity and connection with others in the neighborhood, and significantly, we could also share the true meaning of Christmas.

Participation of Local Government

After a while us two pastors of *Chaekbogo Gage* and the visitors started small regular meetings with funding from Gyeonggi Province Resident-Organized Program. It became an unexpected opportunity for us to establish our presence deeper into the community. Pastor Hwang led the pro-environment gathering called "Zero Waste," and a church member and I led a gathering on peace movements called "Restorative Justice." Participants varied, from church members to bookstore visitors and others in the community we had never met. And their religions were all different as well. But we could confirm our connection through the common issues of ecology and justice, which made us recognize the need for solidarity. The fundamental purpose of these programs is to restore the world God has entrusted us according to the principles of justice and righteousness in the kingdom of God. The neighbors see this missional authenticity and are willing to participate and connect.

Resonance of Co-workers

The lectures at *Chaekbogo Gage* receive only a minimum participation fee. So it is quite difficult to invite speakers. But one or two people started contributing funding as they understood the purpose of *Chaekbogo Gage*. Moreover, some even came to give lectures for free. Of course, church communities were the first to contribute. The expert in English language picture books and literature, the guitarist Youtuber, the mother who majored in European art history and lectures at a university, the violinist keeping their career on hold to raise children, the mother in the community who loves to grow flowers are all contributing to teaching children and adults. Other outsiders have also contributed: the Director of the Letitia Research Center with picture book lectures and the former owner of the café *Namuwa In* with the carpentry program. They all resounded with the purpose of *Chaekbogo Gage* and are serving the residents.

Other co-workers are the neighbors. They are constantly concerned with the sustainability of the bookshop. They get a drink from our café and buy books from the shop out of love, even when it would have been faster and cheaper to buy books online. During busy hours, people tactfully give up their seats and even clean up the tables and chairs after themselves. They may as well be the honorary owners of the bookshop. We are trying even harder to make the shop sustainable for these visitors' sake. This is how we build a community where one life impacts another.

Gongmyung Church

Church Community

Church Membership

As mentioned, the first official worship service was on June 6, 2018. For the first year, only the two families gathered for worship. There were no other church members, but on the weekdays, we met people through *Chaekbogo Gage* as town residents, not as pastors and pastors' wives. We did not intend to keep our vocations secret, but slowly people naturally found out that the two bookshop owners were pastors. Once we formed relationships and built trust through the bookshop, the residents started asking about the church community and faith. Some said this is their first experience with a church and expressed interest in spiritual life with us. We also met other Canaan Saints[7] who used to go to church before but left the church disappointed. We also conducted Bible studies for about ten weeks with earnest religious seekers. All the church members today except one family are the neighboring residents we met through *Chaekbogo Gage*. They all have different stories. There is one who had attended Catholic mass for a bit before getting married and is now starting a religious life for the first time, the Canaan Saints who had not been attending church for a while, the people seeking a church near their new home, and others who had been searching for a wholesome church. The two pastors and their families did not set out on evangelism trips or emphasize church attendance. But people gathered as they saw how we Christians conduct our daily lives, and we became a community.

Figure 5: 2022 Thanksgiving Sunday

Three Key Concepts of Gongmyung Church

As we two pastors reviewed our ministry so far, we recognized three key concepts of Gongmyung Church: hospitality, authenticity, and resonance.

The first is hospitality. We are so busy in our daily lives that we do not welcome people, we just deal with them. To welcome people, it takes time, space, and heart. Gongmyung Church in the early days and *Chaekbogo Gage* has been consistently welcoming.

---

[7] Translator's Note: This is a Korean neologism for Christians who no longer attend the institutional church but continue to subscribe to the religion. It is a play on the Korean word *an-na-ga* which means "not going (to church)." When said backwards, it sounds like *ga-na-an*, or Canaan.

The second concept is authenticity. One of the reasons why the Korean church is derided by society is because they meet people with an ulterior purpose of proselytizing. Knowing this full well, from the beginning of doing church we kept the purpose of church as being a lifelong neighbor to others rather than making church members out of them. People naturally recognized this authenticity.

The third concept is resonance. The continuing co-pastorship structure is evidence of such resonance. Despite our different characters, personalities, and theological stances, we embrace and care for each other to achieve resonance. And this resonance seems to be resonating with the Sunday worshiping community and the weekday local community.

Community for the Next Generation

Intergenerational Service

While the younger adults form the majority of church membership, the age range of the second generation is varied from age 3 to young adults. In Gongmyung Church, we decided from the beginning to have intergenerational services. Intergenerational services are good ways for parents and children to build spiritual intimacy, and it is also amenable to families discussing and applying the sermon message together. Faith can be passed down only when directly experienced rather than heard from others. Of course, there are several challenges. Selecting music and tailoring the sermons for different age groups is difficult. Recently, we wanted to help mothers of infants who cannot focus on the service, so we started separate pre-school and lower-primary age children's gatherings during the preaching hour. Starting this year, the parents have been rotating weeks – 1 per week – to serve as Sunday school teachers.

Family Worship

Left alone, a family does not make a spiritual community. Parents must show by their actions how they worship and live out the word of God. To raise such spiritual communities, Gongmyung Church made a slogan *Hwamokhan Hwayoil* (Harmonious Tuesdays) to support families with family devotionals on Tuesdays, Thursdays, and Saturdays.

Fellowship in Daily Life

Day-to-day lifestyle was what we saw as most important when we started a church in Yangypyeong. Both of our families agreed that ministry one day of the week is not enough. So church members visit for various cultural lectures at the bookshop or simply come by to chat on the weekdays. Even during the pandemic, we continued men's gatherings and women's gatherings from time to time as quarantine measures allowed. If there was a family from whom we haven't heard for a while, we called them up to meet and catch up on their lives. We try to avoid obligatory pastoral visits, but we think personal contact and care in any form can function like these traditional visits.

Spiritual Formation

As more people became interested in becoming church members, we encountered several issues, and that was on the church members' spiritual growth. As mentioned before, the congregants' spiritual maturity and experience vary. We could not serve everyone with the same mold. Until the third year of doing church, we were happy to simply gather and worship together. But when the pandemic hit, we realized that our spirituality cannot be sustained and nurtured simply by being part of a community. So we started conducting spiritual training programs for the church members as necessary. Rather than making it one of the many church programs, we try to help each person find and experience God for themselves.

Tasks and Aims of Gongmyung Church

As Pastor Hwang and I started Gongmyung Church we had to face a realistic need to take up a second job. We had to earn a living for our own families, and we recognized all workplaces in the world as God's mission fields. The workplace where we make contact with the world and our neighbors would be our site of ministry. We did not want to take jobs only for our family finances but consider them a calling to participate in the mission of God for the world. But as contact with neighbors increased and the number of church members increased as well, we started encountering another issue. As our pastoral roles and callings in church increased, realistically we had to spend more time with ministry and formation for the congregation. In getting connected with many people, meeting with them all on weekdays and weekends became difficult. Even in the co-pastorship structure of Gongmyung church, this is not easy, so certainly it would be much more difficult for a single pastor. Even in a small church, the responsibility for ministry and care is on the pastor. And the church members also ask for such care. But as we committed to the bookshop on the weekdays it is also difficult to devote all our remaining time for church members. So as a co-pastor of Gongmyung Church, I wonder how long I can continue with the two jobs. We started a self-supporting ministry for practical purposes, but as the church is growing and we are seeing more needs of the church members, we will have to prioritize our energy. This is where our church is today. It seems we are back to square one on our thoughts on self-supporting ministry.

The second issue is our definition of community. We hope this community is more than a gathering where people find stability and a sense of belonging, but where people care for and encourage each other to live more God-centered lives. Today, as the number of church members is growing, the pastors cannot form personal relationships with everyone or hear their daily concerns. So the community and we the pastors are praying on this matter to prepare the next steps. At the same time, we are also discussing how we might become a community for the world rather than a community in the church.

Gongmyung Church, true to its name, started with two families that *resonated* with each other. The two pastors and their wives have been praying, planning, and walking in step with one another. We did not imitate any special system or pursue a new theological trend. We simply considered what kind of church would be wholesome in God's sight, and based on our discussions, we took steps toward our neighbors authentically in our day-to-day lives. Now we also want to continue walking in step with our Gongmyung Church members. At the same time, we want to step closer to the local neighbors, our "weekday church members," as well. We continue to dream of a community in which the life of the triune God continues to make contact with our lives and our lives contact with others to form a new us.

Missional Church Actualizing the Trinity as Communion

Byung-ohk Lee

Some may say it is nonsense to compare the missional church characteristics and maeul ministry of Gongmyung Church, which has yet to start its fifth year, on the same plane as other churches with 20 or 30-year history. Yet, despite its short history, from the missional perspective, Gongmyung Church is undoubtedly attractive and curious. Gongmyung Church was started based on missional ecclesiology, and its mission is based on understanding the Trinity as communion. The church is headed by two pastors and successfully operates a small bookshop called *Chaekbogo Gage.* Even more encouraging is that this church grew when most churches have seen decreasing membership during the Covid-19 pandemic. Except for one household, most of the church members are new Christians. Of course, churches are growing even today, but generally, they are filled with Christians moving from one church to another. In this context, Gongmyung Church's growth is an astonishing achievement. Gongmyung Church's missional and experimental move can be an endless source of inspiration and challenge for existing churches and pastors seeking to establish a new church.

Mission before Church: Missional Church

Gongmyung Church started with the mission of God. So the church exists for this mission. The simple sentence "Gongmyung Church started with the mission of God" is a historical description of the church's beginning and a very important theological proposition. This means the mission is before church. To understand this, before we discuss the beginning of Gongmyung Church, we must first review the beginning of the church in the Bible from the perspective of the mission of God.

The exact day the Christian church started is debatable. But at least by the time the four Gospels were written, the church already existed. The primary readers of the Gospels were communities in specific contexts. So already by that time it was impossible to discuss the gospel and the mission without the church. The gospel is the story of the life, passion, and resurrection of Jesus, and even if we say that the disciples started the church, it was Jesus who called, trained, and sent the disciples. Clearly, the gospel and Jesus came before the church.

The mission of God means God is the agent of mission. Theologians Stephen B. Bevans and Roger Schroeder powerfully asserted that the church began with the mission of the Holy Spirit, based on the Book of Acts. On the other end of the spectrum is the old ecclesiology and missiology of Christendom asserting that mission emerged out of the church and the church is the agent of mission. After the Edict of Milan by Emperor Constantine, the West became one big church or a Christian domain, and people born in this region naturally received infant baptism to become Christian. In this Christendom, the church became the agent of mission and mission was the work of the church from Christendom to non-Christendom. This ecclesiocentric missiology was shaken after World War II in the liberation of non-Western nations. China, for which the West exerted centuries of effort in mission, turning communist was another factor. In deep repentance of church-centered mission, at the International Missionary Conference in Willingen in 1952, the concept of *missio Dei* emerged. Salvation is not provided by the church but by the mission of God to send God's son to save the world. This recognition of the mission of the Triune God was a Copernican revolution of our understanding of salvation and mission. God is the one who is on a mission, and people or the church follow after God to participate in this mission. Therefore, God calls the church to send it out to the world.

From this perspective of the mission of God, Lesslie Newbigin firmly established that mission and the church cannot be understood apart from each other. Then the North American scholars of Gospel and Our Culture Network refined the missional church concept. Understanding the West to be in post-Christendom, there was a new recognition that Christians' spheres of daily life and the location where the church community is placed are the spaces of mission. There was a new recognition that the people of the early church were in similar situations. Like the early church, the missional church keeps the mission of God as the reason for its being, and its purpose is to participate in God's mission to actualize God's reign in their locale.

Examining Korea's Christian history from the mission of God perspective, God's mission came first, the missionaries followed to participate, and then the church was born, which also participated in God's mission. In this regard, the early Korean church appears to have some characteristics of the mission church. But it is hard to say that they entirely sought to be missional. The Christendom ecclesiology spread by Western missionaries greatly impacted the Korean church from the beginning. The scope of Christendom shrunk from the entire West (Roman Catholic) to individual states (Lutheran, Calvinist, Anglican, etc.). After the Enlightenment, when Christendom moved out of the West, it shrank even further to the level of individual churches, and this is true in Korea. This ecclesiocentric Christendom model continues to be the central paradigm. And as it had been in the West, over time, the Korean church gradually became the agent of mission and has been the master of it. The Korean church has neglected the fact that God started it for a mission, and it lost its identity as being in service of the mission of God. In other words, the church no longer resounded with the mission of God.

In this context, that Gongmyung Church was started with the mission of God takes on special significance in South Korea. The church's reason for being is to resonate with the mission of the Triune God. Many of the churches in Korea today mentioned in missional church discussions started without this theology of *missio Dei*. But Gongmyung Church was intentional about its missional ecclesiology at its start. If the existing churches emphasize Christology and are based on the more Father-centric theology of the Trinity modeled after the Western churches, then Gongmyung Church is based on the understanding of the

Trinity as communion, closer to the Eastern Orthodox Church. This point will be further discussed later. But here I will sum up that if most churches are built on Christology, Gongmyung Church was built on relational trinitarian theology. This point has profound implications for all aspects of Gongmyung Church.

Resonating with the Mission of God: Beginning of Gongmyung Church

The co-pastorship structure of Gongmyung Church is the most concrete evidence of its relational trinitarian theology. Hung-young Baek and In-sung Hwang cooperate in ministry leadership. They started the church together in Yangpyeong because they both had missionary experiences and hoped to devote themselves to it. Of course, in the beginning they understood the mission only in terms of overseas missions, but their understanding deepened through their lay missions experience and their theological studies. As they saw their plans delayed or overturned, they came to accept that God was leading them to another way, and that is how they came to understand Yangpyeong in South Korea as the mission field to start Gongmyung Church.

The two pastors were raised in Suwonseong Church, known for their zeal for mission, but they had never attended the church at the same time. Baek was planning on becoming a missionary to China and majored in Chinese literature. He was very active in campus ministry to the extent of becoming a leader of the university's chapter of Campus Crusade for Christ. He even took a year's leave from school to serve as a lay missionary in China. He planned to return to China after graduation, but at the advice of the pastor of Suwonseong Church, he enrolled in seminary. In the next decade he served as an assistant pastor in several churches. During this time, he continued to contact with overseas missionaries and moved on to graduate school to study Christian Education. He still plans to be sent to missions in China at the right time.

Hwang participated in a missions training program of Nations Trust in England during the summer break of his first year in university. That was when he committed himself to a life-long mission. After graduating from the university, he served as a lay missionary at a missionary organization called Wild Step in Wales for seven years. He felt the need for theological education, so he enrolled in the M.Div. program at Presbyterian University and Theological Seminary (PUTS), then continued with a Th.M. program in Missiology at the same school. He applied for a Ph.D. program in England to be accepted with a scholarship. However as unfortunate circumstances prevented his continued studies, he enrolled in a doctoral program at PUTS. This circumstance led him to rethink Korea as a mission field and to plan for ministry accordingly. He came to regard his own local region – Yangpyeong – as a mission field.

Around this time, the two families met each other and ended up starting a church. In conversation, Hwang mentioned the idea that they might start a church together, and Baek heard it as the voice of God. Baek's wife had been mentioning for a while how Korea is also a mission field and that they should consider starting a church here, but he had not seriously considered it until he heard Hwang's story. And Hwang's proposal to start a co-pastorship greatly resonated with Baek. So from June of 2017, the two families regularly met and traveled together to form a community. On December that year, Baek resigned from the church he was serving to start preparing for church planting full-time. The official first Sunday service of Gongmyung Church was in June 2018, but the two pastors both point back to the two-family worship and fellowship gatherings as the real beginning of the church. This was an understanding of missional ecclesiology in which the community, not a building, is a church. Plus, their identities as missionaries are reflected in church planting. In this process, they raised funding in the name of missions rather than church planting.

The two families' most profound discussions as they began the church were "What kind of church does God desire?" and "How should we respond?" In early 2018 the two families started meeting full time, and the church officially started in June, yet by the end of the year there were no church members except the two families. But rather than discussing ways to attract people to church, they discussed what kind of church God might most desire. In this process, Hwang shared his theological insights on the missional church from his doctoral training and Baek his practical ministry experience to debate and reach consensus. Another important discussion was to decide on the name of the church that displays the church's identity. After considering many options, the two pastors and their spouses agreed on "gongmyung" (共鳴) or resonance. In physics or engineering, resonance means that if a substance with a certain reverberation frequency regularly receives the same kind of reverberation on the same frequency, the reverberation and energy increase. Gongmyung in the native Korean language is *matoolim,* which means to echo together. This means Gongmyung Church aims to fulfill God's will, which is the mission of God, rather than its own.

Gongmyung Church: Being a Community

Gongmyung Church was started after critical reflection on the Korean church's soteriology, ecclesiology, and leadership. To be more precise, individualistic soteriology resulted in narrow ecclesiology making the church into the ark that saves from the flood. This church-centered ecclesiology naturally led to a pastor-centered or vertical structure. But in the light of trinitarian ecclesiology, Baek and Hwang subscribe to a soteriology beyond the individual, an ecclesiology of presence in the world, and a more horizontal leadership structure. This intention is well expressed in the church's mission statement: "The mission of Gongmyung Church is to let the life of the triune God come and resound in us then let our lives resound in others to bring about transformation of life."[1] This was then specified in their six vision statements: (1) wholesome daily life, (2)

---

[1] Gongmyung Church Blog, "Gongmyung Church Mission Statement." https://m.blog.naver.com/PostView.naver?blogId=gm-church&logNo=221238756383&navType=by [Accessed 25 January 2023].

financial transparency, (3) priority of family, (4) service and participation in the neighborhood, (5) pursuit of a small community, and (6) participation.[2]

The central principle of Gongmyung Church is *mat* (together) *oolim* (echo). The church blog explains togetherness and echoing in more detail. On togetherness, they explain:

> Gongmyung Church seeks to take after God's harmonious relationship of the Trinity in the Father, the Son, and the Holy Spirit and to have fellowship with God above all, then to take and share this harmonious relationship with our family, church community, and local community. We also seek to mature together in relationships of mutual respect, rather than in one-sided giving and receiving, to form a life-giving ecology.

Echoing is explained as the following:

> Gongmyung Church seeks not only to be present with God, people, and the local society but to be a church that echoes and resonates the life of Christ in this togetherness. In sharing the good news filled with God's creativity, Jesus Christ's gracious salvation, and the Holy Spirit's intimate fellowship, we refine each other to be trained to take this good news to all the created world.

Sunday Worship

Although the first official worship service of Gongmyung Church was on June 6, 2018, the two pastors both see the beginning of the church as the day the two families began to worship together. Even after that official first worship, only the two families were present for service for the first six months. Still, they say they were filled with joy and gratitude and would have been happy to worship like this for the rest of their lives. This tells a lot about Gongmyung Church. They value worship because they believe the church exists to worship God. This is absolutely basic, but more explanation is due. Baek, who had been ministering in traditional churches, asked many questions to Hwang, who was theologically trained on missions and the missional church, and one of the major topics was worship. They visited some of the churches in South Korea known to be missional. They saw many of them doing much work for the local community but being relatively negligent of worship service or even forgoing church ministry completely. They were critical of this tendency and naturally the two pastors wanted to emphasize the importance of worship.

In addition, the two families were inspired by their intergenerational worship with the children, which led to structure their services for the church in this way. Gongmyung Church seeks to have all ages together in worship, from infants to the elderly, so they can experience being one as a community. Moreover, "Intergenerational services are good ways for parents and children to build

---

[2] Gongmyung Church Blog, "Vision of Gongmyung Church" https://m.blog.naver.com/PostView.naver?blogId=gm-church&logNo=221238861781&navType=by [Accessed 25 January 2023]. These visions are closely interrelated. For example, spiritual life does not end with Sunday service but worship must extend into wholesome day to day life as life of worship. And the daily life consists of families and communities where families are located, so family and community are considered priority.

spiritual intimacy, and they are also amenable to families discussing and applying the sermon message together. Faith can be passed down only when directly experienced rather than heard from others."[3] For people of all ages to worship together they had to adjust the difficulty level of praise songs and sermons. They share the songs and the sermon script with the church members during weekdays for them to prepare in advance, and they also encourage individual devotional times using the same devotional guide (*Daily Bible*). Each Sunday the pastors take turns to preach based on the text of the day according to the guide. After the service, they have Bible study with the sermon message for in-depth study. Younger children may become passive in worship, so to encourage their active participation, elementary-age and older children were encouraged to participate by scripture reading or praise leading. During the pandemic, worship with children had to be changed. Then as more people attended services and were hungry for deeper spiritual reflections, they changed the order of worship to have preschool and elementary-age children listen to a brief message and then leave for Bible study on their own before proceeding with the rest of the sermon for the church, just as many churches do in the United States.

Family Worship

Family worship is an important part of Gongmyung Church efforts to make daily life be act of worship. Family worship is deeply related to the "vertical mission." Baek compares the vertical mission with the horizontal mission in his understanding of family worship.[4] The Korean church has so far emphasized the horizontal mission to other countries or regions, but not the vertical mission from parents to children. The result is that many children of Christian parents are not themselves Christian. Considering the South Korean crisis of rapid population decrease, the vertical mission is more urgent than ever before, perhaps even more than the horizontal mission. This is why intergenerational worship services are held on Sundays and family worship is encouraged on weekdays.

Families do not become spiritual communities overnight. Training and effort are necessary, and above all the parents must be model worshipers. Clearly the primary responsibility for the children's spiritual growth is on the family, not the church. Therefore, Gongmyung Church encourages family worship sessions every Tuesday, Thursday, and Saturday called *Hwamokhan Toyoil* (Harmonious Tuesdays). For the Tuesdays the ministers upload family worship guide videos incorporating a picture book. Thursday worship is structured around sharing one's experience of God in daily life and recording them in the Family History Book. Then on Saturdays, each family worships in preparation for Sunday worship. Especially the Thursday Family History Book sessions go beyond family worship to become a process of spiritual training and maturity. Gongmyung Church emphasizes the "three S's" – space, sharing, and sympathy – as principles for family worship. The principles are well demonstrated in the

---

[3] Hung-young Baek, "Kong-myŏng-kyo-hoe i-ya-ki — ch'aek-po-ko-ka-ke," [Story of gongmyung church – chaekbogo gage], *Educational Church* 486 (2019), 59.
[4] Interview with Hung-young Baek and In-sung Hwang on 1 November 2022.

Family History Book sessions.[5] Families need an intentional time and space to share about God. These sessions provide this intentional space for family members to share their personal lives and their spiritual journey. Through such sharing, they can sympathize with each other and pray more specifically for one another. Gongmyung Church uses the Family History Book for this purpose. A calendar is given to each family to record reasons to be grateful or to rejoice, or any encouragements, challenges, or changes in the family so that each person and the whole family can share specifically how they experienced the presence of God. On the last Sunday of each month, all the families in the church share their Family History Books to let these individual experiences become the church's experience. This naturally becomes a space where they share prayer requests with the church, pray together, and strengthen community ties.

Bible Study and Spiritual Formation Program

In the early days of Gongmyung Church, Sunday worship, family worship, and sharing individual devotionals were the entirety of church programming. As time passed and the church took on a more formal structure, other aspects that can be found in other churches also emerged. Gongmyung Church was started as an effort to go beyond the usual church model so its unique characteristics are maintained. But it has also been changing to adapt some of the spiritual training programs from traditional churches. It is not that the old church education programs are in and of themselves problematic. What matters is the kind of Christians and churches that are formed through these programs. With this in mind, Gongmyung Church is today conducting (1) Alpha Course, Gospel Sharing, and Man-to-Man Spiritual Training for new believers; (2) Inquiring after Theology (on systematic theology), Family Worship Training, and Literature Reading Groups for adults; (3) Mothers' Prayer Meeting and Mother Wise for mothers; and (4) Sunday worship (pre-school/ lower primary school age), weekday gatherings (upper primary/ secondary age), and family worships for the children and the youth.[6] For the new believers, the 12-week Alpha Course is conducted by the pastors visiting the home of the new church members to allow for more in-depth education and fellowship. The two pastors alternate the weeks in the spirit of co-pastorship and to enrich the training content. This may be considered an introduction to the missional church. The Inquiring After Theology gathering is unique in that this newly formed church is attempting to provide systematic theology education for the laity, which is not being attempted by even larger churches. The program is getting a good response, and attracting more men than other events. All these programs are subject to change to fit the church's shifting circumstances.

---

[5] Hung-young Baek (2019), 60-6.

[6] From Hung-young Baek's presentation of Gongmyung Church case at "Missional Church Plant Case Presentation" at the PCK Centennial Memorial Building on April 28, 2022.

Leadership Structure

One of the major concerns at the start of Gongmyung Church was that the most churches tend to revolve around the head pastor at the center and that their relationship with the laity is vertical rather than horizontal. So Gongmyung Church intentionally pursues a more horizontal and democratic leadership structure. The co-pastorship structure contributes to this aim. Both pastors conduct all the church gatherings (worship service or Bible studies), and the four people, the pastors and the spouses, make decisions on the programs together.[7] No action is taken until all four people agree. Important church decisions are made at the church community meeting held four times a year. Any church member who finished the newcomers' Alpha Course can participate in this meeting. The board of elders is not yet formed, so all decisions are made through direct democracy. The church members are also being trained to participate in more decision-making processes. As part of this effort, seasonal events and programs for 2022 were left to the lay church members to form planning committees and conduct the programs themselves. Not everyone is willing to participate in these decision-making processes, but the pastors encourage such involvement in the long term.

Chaekbogo Gage

Chaekbogo Gage is an attractive pun. *Gage* means a shop, meaning a place where books are sold, and *chaekbogo* is added in front to make the phrase sound like an invitation to visit. The bookshop was started by Gongmyung Church to be present in the local community, considering the town as the parish, based on trinitarian missiology and ecclesiology.[8] Gongmyung Church wanted to set up the space not just for Christians and the church members but for the local people who need support, especially for "he young parents raising children to share their situations and stories."[9] They hoped for the bookshop to become the town's community lounge.

Why a bookshop? Once the pastors decided on Yangpyeong as the town to plant the church they conducted different research on the region. With the public data made available by the Yangpyeong County Office, they checked the geographic spread of the population and their age. Local cultural events and civil society events also hinted at the region's needs. Considering the pastors' tight budget, they looked for a bookshop space in rural Gangsang Township. Compared to other places, this township had more residents who recently moved from Seoul. They were generally married couples under age 50 who were raising children and youth. For this demographic, Gangsang Township greatly lacked cultural facilities. And there was a dire lack of bookstores. In the whole of Yangpyeong County, there was only one library and a bookstore. Starting a

---

[7] Interview with Hung-young Baek and In-sung Hwang on November 1, 2022.

[8] In-sung Hwang, "Kong-myŏng-kyo-hoe i-ya-ki, kŭ tu-pŏn-tchae 'ch'aek-po-ko-ka-ke-t'-lŭl t'ong-han tae-an-chŏk sa-lye-pun-sŏk" [The second story of Gongmyung church: analysis of chaekbogo gage as alternative], Educational Church. 485 (2019), 68.

[9] Ibid.

library meant they could get public funding from the local government, but that risked the library operations and aims being determined by the government as well. So they decided to operate a bookshop, but only after taking a year to visit successful small neighborhood bookstores nationwide. As they saw these spaces operating cultural events and reading clubs and functioning as a community space for local conversations, the pastors drew up a plan that may be feasible with their own human, material, and geographic resources. They decided to make the bookshop the main business and operate a small library and a café on the side. While the bookshop was started in response to the local need, it was the two pastors who specified that the response would be in the form of a bookshop. As parents of young children, they could personally identify with other parents of similar age. They also loved reading and had their thoughts on the matter. The bookshop was also a feasible business within their budget. It was also a way to pay for the living costs of the two families. Given their experience as lay missionaries, they recognized the importance of financial independence, so they planned to receive a minimal salary from the church and remain financially independent with the profits from the bookshop. So Baek and Hwang may be addressed as pastors in church meetings, but they asked to be called bookshop owners when at the shop.

This is how *Chaekbogo Gage* started officially on September 11, 2018. They also operate *Matulim* Small Library in the bookshop as a children's picture book library. It operates from Tuesday to Saturday, 10 am to 6 pm, and the space is also rented for neighborhood meetings. The bookshop displays a various selection of picture books for children and grownups organized by themes, books on child rearing, and other literature. They also host picture book reading and discussion gatherings on the first Wednesday of each month on select themes, which are meant to share Christian values with the neighbors.[10] Along with these gatherings, various cultural events for children and adults, and seminars inviting speakers are also organized.

On the small sign board of *Chaekbogo Gage* there is a short description of the store: "Neighborhood bookshop where my life reaches your life". *Matulim* is the Korean word for *gongmyung*, or echoing together, and this spirit of resonance is expressed in the description. The spirit of the triune God is in this library and bookshop space. The triune God is the one who saves the world, but this God is also the one who created the world and is present in the books, the bookshop, and with the non-Christians. The pastors' blog post on August 18, 2018 promoting the bookshop well expresses their expectations and hopes as they launched the business. According to this post, *Chaekbogo Gage* is a small neighborhood bookshop "where you read books, buy books, and become more familiar with books." The shop description articulates their aims as follows:

> We hope this place will be where you get acquainted with books just as you would with another person. We hope this space can be a space of rest for some and where others can find new dreams and possibilities through encounters with books. Some of you might even nod in sympathy with others' stories. Where anyone can be

---

[10] Ibid.

> welcomed as they are… a precious space where you and I meet. Where you and the books meet. This is what we hope for.

Before Covid-19 *Chaekbogo Gage* functioned as a space of learning, a space of play, a space of meeting, and a space of connection.[11] As a space of learning, various lectures were conducted. It was a space of play through programs such as Christmas events and Maeul School,[12] and as a place of meeting for homeschooling families who moved to the region for alternative education. It was a space of connection, bringing the local mayor and government officials together with residents.

In the pandemic, in-person gatherings were restricted so they conducted online and offline meetings. This became the opportunity to increase the number of lectures. When they could not invite people to Christmas events, they set up an open radio studio at the bookshop to share the meaning of Christmas and allow the residents to feel a sense of solidarity and belonging. Around this time, the shop's pastors and visitors submitted proposals to Gyeonggi Province for funding for the Restorative Justice Program and the Zero Waste Program. Baek's Restorative Justice program on peace and Hwang's Zero Waste Program on environmental issues are for anyone who shares the concerns regardless of religion. These events allowed the pastors to meet a new group of people and expanded the reach of the bookshop. In addition, although *Chaekbogo Gage* aims for financial independence, they charge minimal fees for lectures to enable more people to attend. This means it is difficult for them to invite speakers. But as more people heard about the mission of *Chaekbogo Gage*, more residents and various experts have been volunteering their lectures for little or no charge. The people who visit the space volunteer to clean up after themselves, organize the books, or give up their space for others. They order coffee and buy books from the store to help the store stay in operation. All this is evidence of *Chaekbogo Gage* forming a community in town just as it had intended.

Theological Reflection

Church Resounding with the Mission of the Trinitarian God

Among many churches in South Korea known to be missional, there are not many that were started on the basis of missional ecclesiology. Churches planted with a holistic understanding of the Trinity that encompasses both Western and Eastern church theologies are even more rare. Perhaps Deobureosoop Dongsang Church in Bongdam in Gyeonggi Province may be the missional church with this holistic understanding of the mission of the triune God. But even in this

---

[11] Hung-young Baek, "I-us-kwa kong-myŏng-toe-nŭn kong-myŏng-kyo-hoe" [Gongmyung church that resonates with the neighbors], *Gidok Gongbo.* 2022 November 11. http://m.pckworld.com/article.php?aid=9574131654 [Accessed 2 February 2023.].

[12] Maeul School was a cultural learning program for children of church members as well as non-members that was conducted over the winter semester break of January and February in 2019. The program grew in capacity in the winter of 2020. Summer Maeul School also started in 2019, though all sessions were conducted as one-day-classes since the summer semester breaks are shorter.

church the trinitarian understanding does not seem organically reflected in all aspects of church identity and programming. In contrast, while Gongmyung Church's theology may seem simple, the trinitarian missiology and ecclesiology are organically incorporated into its identity, the leadership structure, and the ministry of *Chaekbogo Gage*.

As noted, the Western church's Father-centered trinitarian theology significantly contributed to the emergence of the concept of *missio Dei* in which God, not the church, is the agent of mission. But this theology that emphasizes oneness of the Trinity and the Father God tends to establish unilateral or vertical relationships between God and church, God and society, and church and society. Early discussions of the missional church were influenced by this Western church's trinitarian theology. The missional church concept emphasizes the importance of being before doing. Western trinitarian theology does not adequately explain this relationship of existence and action, but Eastern church's relational trinitarian theology explains the relationship much more adequately. In this trinitarian theology, the emphasis is on the relationship and communion within the Trinity, which is reflected in humans and earthly beings. This means all beings are connected to God and to each other. In relational trinitarian theology, just as the triune God exists in communion, to exist means to belong to a community.[13] In other words, to exist means to be connected to the community of the triune God, and in this context all beings are organically interconnected. Therefore, the church's existence as well as mission cannot be understood apart from its relationship with God, or its relationship with the world. What begins and enables and sustains this chain of relationships is the triune God. Therefore, from the perspective of relational trinitarian theology, being and doing are organically connected. Doing may be understood in terms of becoming and belonging. Humans shaped after the triune God seek to become more like the Trinity. This means a being is in the process of becoming more like the image of God as well as belonging more to the community of the Trinity. This is well demonstrated by Gongmyung Church in their concept of resonance and their emphasis on relationships. This understanding is also richly incorporated in *Chaekbogo Gage*. This is apparent in the way the visitors feel a sense of community, belonging, and solidarity at the shop.

This basis on relational trinitarian theology is naturally reflected in the church's cooperative leadership. It is not a vertical structure centered on one senior pastor but one based on a team of several people.[14] The leader of a missional church must foster a true church community that participates in God's mission by sharing their day-to-day life in the neighboring community.[15] The leader must make space for the church community feel a sense of belonging and are motivated to share their lives in action.

Gongmyung Church's co-pastorship is itself a reflection of the life and leadership of the relational Trinity. The pastors' family gatherings and trips even

[13] Craig Van Gelder and Dwight J. Zscheile, *The Missional Church in Perspective: Mapping Trends and Shaping the Conversation* (Grand Rapids, MI: Baker, 2011), 109.
[14] Ibid., 157.
[15] Ibid., 156.

before the official start of the church let them experience what it means to belong to this community. The pastors Baek and Hwang often had conversations late into the night, and the two couples often discussed the ministry. They encourage even the new church members to participate in community meetings, which shows their understanding of relational trinity. So as in the mission statement of Gongmyung Church, it seeks "to let the life of the triune God come and resound in us then let our lives resound in others to bring about transformation of life." In the same way, *Chaekbogo Gage* is the "neighborhood bookstore where my life reaches your life".

Chaekbogo Gage as Proximal Space: Functioning as a Community Lounge

From the perspective of the missional church, *Chaekbogo Gage* is a proximal space. A proximal space is not the church but a third space where it is possible to commune with non-Christians. In Christendom all space of the church and society were Christian. In the post-Christendom only the households of believers and the church are Christian spaces. Therefore, for meaningful interactions with non-Christians, a third space is necessary. The workplace can be such a place, but the church cannot employ everyone. So a proximal spaces are missional spaces, specifically, places and events where Christians and those who have yet to be Christians can have meaningful interactions.[16] Proximal spaces are generally formed in cafes, pubs, or restaurants located near heavy foot traffic. Korea never was a Christendom, but proximal spaces may also be identified as the contact points where Christians and non-Christians meet. The two pastors of Gongmyung often say they hope *Chaekbogo Gage* may become the town's community lounge. Historically, the community lounge, or *sarangbang*, was a proximal space in Korean missions history.

Many church historians and missiologists found that missionaries to Korea a century ago found the *sarangbang* functioning as the contact point or the missional space. The missionaries made good use of *sarangbang,* even making them missions headquarters. The *sarangbang* in those days

> Was a space for men. The location of *sarangbang* was far from the inner quarters where the homeowner resides and was by the gate through which one enters and exits the house. In the evenings, a passing traveler may visit a respectable-looking house, tell the homeowner of his situation, and stay a night at *sarangbang*. The traveler may even stay for several days. In the days when there was no mass media, people could hear news of the world from visitors in *sarangbang*. It was also where people shared village information or formed opinions on public matters.[17]

Based on this understanding of *sarangbang,* missionaries used this space as a contact point with Koreans. "*Sarangbang*" was where one could meet male spiritual seekers to have religious conversations, debates, and fellowship. It was also used to share the gospel, give spiritual instruction, perform direct

---

[16] Alan Hirsch, *The Forgotten Ways: Reactivating the Missional Church* (Grand Rapids: Brazos, 2006), 37-38.

[17] Hee-kuk Lim, *Ki-ta-lim-kwa sŏ-tu-lŭm-ŭi yŏk-sa: han-kuk chang-lo-kyo-hoe 130nyŏn* [History of Waiting and Hurrying: 130 Years of Korean Presbyterian Church]. (Seoul: PUTS Press, 2014), 43.

evangelism, as well as conduct Sunday services, Bible studies, and prayer meetings, or distribute evangelism tracts and literature."[18] Many churches started in a *sarangbang*. And "sarangbang was a natural contact point with residents, just as Apostle Paul made the synagogue the contact point to meet the Jews."[19] Later, sarangbang was made in the regional missions headquarters buildings or churches to function as a missional space. If the existing sarangbang space was discovered and used missionally in the beginning, later *sarangbang* was intentionally constructed as a missional space.

In this consideration, *Chaekbogo Gage* is a proximal space mentioned in the West's missional church discourse but also goes beyond it. It should instead be called a missional *sarangbang*. Rather than trying to convert visiting non-Christians, Chaekbogo Gage intends to be a community lounge where people can freely come and go to be together with others, just as Koreans used to come and go in *sarangbang*. Because the bookshop's primary purpose is relationship building and networking, the space does not make visitors uncomfortable by attempts at direct proselytization.

Tension and Harmony between Gathering and Sending Out

In Korea, missional churches are known to emphasize the outward dynamic over the inward. But most Korean churches pursuing growth and gathering for the past century cannot and will not immediately become churches that send people out. Before a missional church can send out, it must first gather. The problem is not in the gathering itself, but that the purpose of the gathering is on church growth. This also assumed the goals of worship and discipleship training were church growth. Missional ecclesiology does not intend to stop people from gathering in the church. The aim is to train the gathered Christians as missionaries and Christ's disciples out in the world. From the missional perspective, it is vital to establish this virtuous cycle of gathering and sending. But it seems this cycle of gathering and dispersion is not operating very well in many of the churches known to be missional. In other words, many of them relatively neglect the gathering process. While these churches look commendable today, their sustainability in the next generation is not guaranteed.

On this point, Gongmyung Church constructed this feedback loop comparatively well. At the risk of oversimplifying, Baek emphasizes gathering and Hwang sending out. If Baek prioritizes church ministry a little more, then Hwang tends to focus on maeul ministry at *Chaekbogo Gage*. In the first two years of Gongmyung Church, Baek learned of missional church and maeul ministry from Hwang with a degree in missiology. Hwang learned the importance of worship and spiritual formation from Baek. Based on a decade of ministry in traditional churches, Baek saw how Christians mature through worship and spiritual formation and has been emphasizing these factors in

[18] Chang Uk Byun, "The Missionary Methods and Educational Mission Policy of William Baird," *Korean Journal of Christian Studies* 74 (2011), 324.

[19] Yong-gyu Park, *Han-kuk kyo-hoe-wa min-chok-ŭl kkae-un p'yŏng-yang san-chŏng-hyŏn kyo-hoe* [Sanjeonghyeon church in Pyeongyang that awakened the Korean church and its people], (Seoul: Word of Life Press, 2006), 24.

intergenerational worship and family worship. As discussed earlier, missions today must be conducted horizontally and vertically. Faith is inherited within the family, so family worship and worship in daily life are critical. This perspective by Baek deepened and developed Hwang's trinitarian theology and missional church discourse. Today, the two pastors' differences in theology and practice are contributing to the health of the church. This is a strength not found in other missional churches.

Conclusion

There is not a lot of missional churches in South Korea that achieved growth through maeul ministry. Many community or town residents benefit from the church's ministry but rarely become church members. That is because these churches generally do not intend their ministries to result in people coming to church. However, the case of Gongmyung Church offers a different implication. 90% of current church members are new Christians who joined the church by visiting *Chaekbogo Gage*. They became committed to the church not simply because of the bookshop but also because there is a clear pastoral structure in the church. The excellent and surprising aspect of Gongmyung Church is that unlimited growth is not the purpose of the church. They are considering the most appropriate size for the church to enable fellowship. Once the number increases beyond this point, they intend to plant another church with a portion of the church members. They conduct ministry as they resonate with church members and townspeople. To avoid using the people for successful ministry or church growth, they pursued financial independence from the beginning and kept the church and the bookshop accounts separate. Today, as circumstances keep changing, they continue to seek ways to adapt and make spaces for the laity in the decision-making structure. In the long-term, this new church will face many obstacles in its journey as a missional church. But I am hopeful because it intends to resonate with God, families, the community, the world, and nature. I hope Gongmyung Church continues to show what it means to resonate with the mission of the triune God for the benefit of many other churches walking on the same path.

Bibliography

Baek, Hung-young. "Kong-myŏng-kyo-hoe i-ya-ki – ch'aek-po-ko-ka-ke" [Story of gongmyung church – chaekbogo gage]. *Educational Church* 486, 2019, 58-63.

_________. "I-us-kwa kong-myŏng-toe-nŭn kong-myŏng-kyo-hoe." [Gongmyung church that resonates with the neighbors], *Gidok Gongbo.* 11 November 2022. http://m.pckworld.com/article.php?aid=9574131654 [Accessed 2 February 2023].

Byun, Chang Uk. "The Missionary Methods and Educational Mission Policy of William Baird," *Korean Journal of Christian Studies* 74, 2011, 317-340.

Gongmyung Church Blog. "Vision of Gongmyung Church." https://m.blog.naver.com/PostView.naver?blogId=gm-

church&logNo=221238861781&navType=by [Accessed 25 January 2023].
Gongmyung Church Blog. “Gongmyung Church Mission Statement.” https://m.blog.naver.com/PostView.naver?blogId=gm-church&logNo=221238756383&navType=by [Accessed 25 January 2023].
Hirsch, Alan. *The Forgotten Ways: Reactivating the Missional Church.* Grand Rapids: Brazos, 2006.
Hwang, In-sung. “Kong-myŏng-kyo-hoe i-ya-ki, kŭ tu-pŏn-tchae 'ch'aek-po-ko-ka-ke-t'-lŭl t'ong-han tae-an-chŏk sa-lye-pun-sŏk.” [The second story of Gongmyung church: analysis of chaekbogo gage as alternative], Educational Church. 485 (2019), 71-74.
Lee, Byung-ohk. Interview with Hung-young Baek and In-sung Hwang, 1 November 2022.
Lim, Hee-kuk. *Ki-ta-lim-kwa sŏ-tu-lŭm-ŭi yŏk-sa: han-kuk chang-lo-kyo-hoe 130nyŏn.* [History of Waiting and Hurrying: 130 Years of Korean Presbyterian Church]. Seoul: PUTS Press, 2014.
Park, Yong-gyu, *Han-kuk kyo-hoe-wa min-chok-ŭl kkae-un p'yŏng-yang san-chŏng-hyŏn kyo-hoe* [Sanjeonghyeon church in Pyeongyang that awakened the Korean church and its people]. Seoul: Word of Life Press, 2006.
Van Gelder, Craig. and Dwight J. Zscheile. *The Missional Church in Perspective: Mapping Trends and Shaping the Conversation.* Grand Rapids, MI: Baker, 2011.

Ecclesiological Turn and Ministry Development of Seongam Church

Joo-hee Cho

The Situation at the Beginning

Way to Communicate

Church is a community. It is an interconnected, organic community. Scripture says the church is "the whole body, joined and knit together by every ligament with which it is equipped, as each part is working properly, promotes the body's growth in building itself up in love" (Ephesians 4:16). Church is a community intimately connected to and united with Jesus Christ and to each other. Therefore, only as church ministry is firmly based on communication can it fulfill its identity as Christ's "body, the fullness of him who fills all in all" (Ephesians 1:23).

What is notable here is that communication is different from organizational management. Most of the churches have complicated organizational structures. Organizational management can be one way to facilitate communication but is only part of it. Communication starts with the community leader's genuine desire to communicate. If a church is organized (i.e., a board of elders exists), then the path of communication starts to open when the pastor shares their thoughts with the elders who are closest to them organizationally. Sharing each person's thoughts about the direction of the church and then gathering these thoughts to produce one ministry is a process that takes practice.

Seongam Church has been devoted to this process. Each Sunday when the board of elders gather, we prepare for the service with a song and a prayer. We share the most mundane happenings of the church and share the common objective to look after the church members. We build up this framework of communication.

Church Resource

To take the first practical steps to communicate with the neighbors around Seongam Church, we decided to construct the Vision Center. We got to construct the building on a plot of land beside the church. But encountered a problem in the process of construction. We had a vague idea of using the place for the church and the neighbors, so the building was designed for this purpose. However there had not been sufficient examination of the building's utility, considering the substantial amount of financing going into the project. There were a few hasty plans but nothing concrete about the usage.

In this process, I found the church members caring and attentive to the neighboring community. The purpose of building construction was always meant to benefit the community beyond the church. Seongam Church congregation's compassion was the key element that shaped how this building would be used in the future.

Seeking Ways to Change

Decision to Seek Consultation

How can a church live alongside the local community? And what should be the first step? To answer these questions, we requested external consultation for an objective assessment of our church. Implementing the consultation method unfamiliar to the Korean church was not an easy task. There was an agreement that our church needed to clarify the purpose of the building in construction, but implementing the consultation method for this purpose required further persuading the church community. And the way to go about this process was, again, communication.

The already-worn path of communication with the board of elders was the key factor that lowered the resistance of the elders. Communicating only for a specific purpose is ineffective but consistent day-to-day communication can deepen our understanding of each other. This was evidence of the importance of daily contact and communication beyond instrumental communication.

As consultation started, instead of the board of elders persuading the rest of the church on the consultation plan in one session, the process was further subdivided. The board of elders first had to accept the plan, then other ordained church officers were persuaded, which laid the ground for all church officers to accept the plan. This means the board of elders was briefed on the consultation plan over three sessions and other ordained officers twice, giving them a basic understanding of what should be done before the consultation started. This became a key setting that enabled us to overcome several obstacles in the consultation process.

Role of the Pastor

A critical element in this process is the leadership of the senior pastor. The senior pastor must meet and negotiate with the consulting team multiple times. The pastor's failure to comprehend the consultation may lead to unintended outcomes.

A consulting team is an outsider group for the church. The basic language of consultation and the church may be different. On this point, the pastor must work to translate the language of the consulting team and the church to facilitate communication. This is the role of the pastor. The consulting team also does not have a detailed understanding of the church. Unlike a company, a church is much more influenced by affect and culture. It is easy for a consulting team to overlook this point, so it is essential to consider this when forming the consulting team, and the team should also consistently communicate with the pastor. The church may also have difficulty communicating its opinions to the consulting team because they are unfamiliar with the terminology or the protocol. So there must be someone in between to mediate the language of consultation as they are delivered to the church, and the pastor is in the most appropriate position to do so.

Another thing the senior pastor must do is assess the flow of the consultation at every moment of the process. The process requires a lot of committee meetings and the consulting team conducts the process without a complete understanding of each church. In that sense, when the pastor can sense the interactional dynamic between the consulting team and the church community, the pastor can mediate to overcome various challenges.

However when the pastor takes too much initiative, the direction of the consultation may be skewed. So the pastor must be a leader in the spirit of stewardship rather than intervention. The pastor should function as a fence or a net to facilitate the communication of the two groups unfamiliar with each other.

Ecclesiological Turn

Need for Change in Ecclesiology as seen in Ministry Practice

The Korean church started questioning traditional ecclesiology. The church exists in local society. Local residents become church members and the church exists because of their commitment and love. The church is a community of people with the vocation to call the unredeemed in the world to saved as people of God. So the church community exists in connection with the world.

Year / Religion	1985		1995			2005		
	Pop.	%	Pop.	%	% of increase	Pop.	%	% of increase
Total	17,203	42.5	22,598	50.7	-3.3	24,970	53	1.1
Buddhist	8,062	19.9	10,321	23.2	-12.1	10,726	22.8	1.04
Christian[1]	6,489	16.0	8,760	19.7	9.0	8,616	18.3	-1.8
Catholic	1,865	4.6	2,951	6.6	19.1	5,146	11	175
Other	791	2.0	566	1.3	-37.7	482	1	-15

Table 1: Religious population in South Korea: Numbers and Trends (thousands)

[1] Translator's Note: "Christian" in the official South Korean government census data denotes Protestant Christianity. Catholicism is counted separately.

At the time Seongam Church started our consultation the Korean Protestant church was beginning to show signs of serious trouble. The 2005 Population Census (Daejeon: KOSIS, 2006) reported in 2006 showed that in the decade between 1985 and 1995 the total population identifying as religious increased from 17.2 million (42.5% of the population) to 22.6 million, a 31.4% increase. From 1995 to 2005 the religious population increased 1.1% which is far below the growth rate of the previous decade. Specifically, Buddhists increased by 1.04% and Protestant Christianity by -1.8%, either stagnant or decreasing, while the Catholic population increased by 175%. Protestant Christianity was shunned by society.

The Korean church has not been negligent of society. Its role in providing social services should be credited. But the services were ultimately to conduct missions and increase the number of churchgoers, and this strong sense of purpose separated the church from society. As a result, the church was not able to respond appropriately to society and society grew to distrust the church. The church's exclusive religiosity eroded its public stature in the pluralized modern society and negatively impacted missions.

This phenomenon has gotten even worse in the recent years. The 2020 Social Credibility Survey of the Korean Church conducted by the Christian Ethics Movement of Korea and Ji&com Research reported in 2021 that 18.9% of the respondents said they regard Protestant Christianity as credible, which is a steep fall from 26.1% in 2009. An entire religion, not a consumer product or a company, has experienced a shocking fall in credibility.

But other results in the same study are contradictory. To the question, "Which religion's social service activities benefit society?" 32.9% responded Catholicism, 10.2% Buddhism, and 35.7% Protestantism. This unexpected result shows that Protestant Christianity's social credibility is inversely related to social recognition of its social services. Another set of numbers can explain this puzzling result. Regarding whether the Korean Protestant church is communicating well with society, 34% said very well, 61.6% not very well, and 3.8% answered they didn't know. The result shows that Protestant Christianity has a severe communication problem with society. This is related to the church's public character.

Ecclesiology and Public Character

Society's perception of the Korean church is derived from the church's reputation. Undeniably, one of the reasons why the Korean church's reputation fell is that the social service provision has not been central to the church's mission. There is a public aspect in the very existence of Christianity. The church community is responsible for the society where it is located. This means the church must put away its excessively church-centeredness. It must be aware of how society sees the church, not just how the church sees society. In other words, the church must regard the town as the church's town and must accept that the church is also the town's church.

Alan Hirsch in his book *The Forgotten Ways* (Grand Rapids: Brazos Press, 2008, 94-95, 97) used two figures to explain this. First is the traditional ecclesiology as shown in Figure 1.

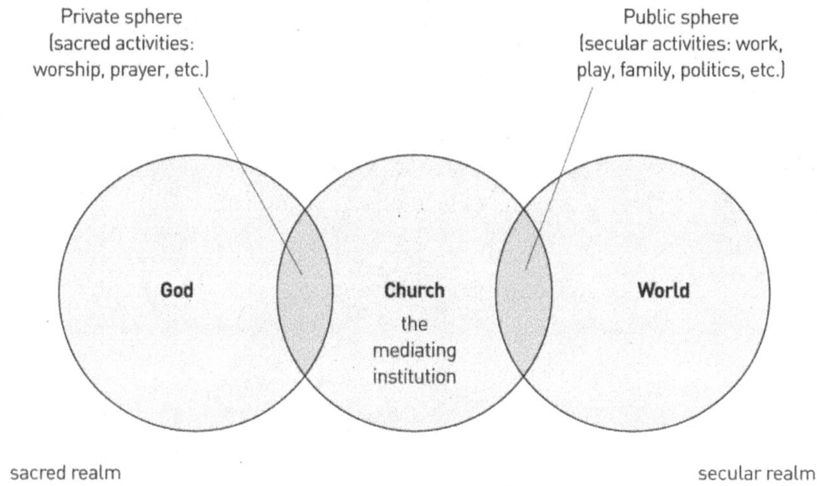

Figure 6: Dualistic Spirituality

This figure represents the view on the church and the world that was held by most of the Seongam Church members. This ecclesiology separates God and the world. And the church's role is to tell the world about God. So the overlapping plane where God and church meet is sacred, and the overlap between the church and the world is secular.

The problem with this figure is that God is shown to have no relations to the world without the mediation of the church. This even deviates from the traditional confession of Christian faith that God is Lord of all. This figure makes out the world to be Godless and perceives God and the world in dualistic terms.

Seongam Church also used to have this ecclesiology. Our prayers and ministries were based on the belief that the world only needs the salvation of Jesus Christ, and the church is called for this purpose. Even social service ministries were conducted to demonstrate God's love and as a charity by the saved on behalf of the unsaved. This perspective made relationship-building with the world difficult despite the church's consistent attention to the world.

But Hirsch presented a different model in Figure 2. This model shows God, the church, and the world interacting with one another.

In this model, the world is present between God and the church, and in the sphere between God and the world, the church is present. Of course, God is also present where the world and the church meet. The church views the world as not a Godless place but as connected to God, the sphere where God intervenes. This means the church does not separate God and the world but regards the world as the object of God's mission. In this view, the church's role is to unify God and the world. Jesus Christ reconciled the church with God and gave the church the task of reconciling the world with God (1 Corinthians 5:17-19).

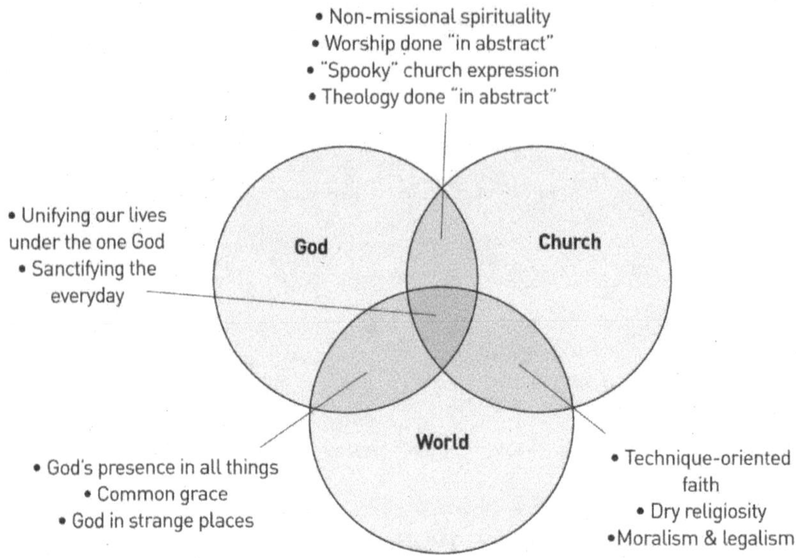

Figure 7: Nondualistic Spirituality

God and the world, God and the church, and the church and the world each have separate and distinct spheres of relationship. Yet the spheres are not self-contained and exclusive but open to sharing with others. Therefore, the church is in a unique position where it cannot understand the world without God nor understand God without the world. This must be at the center of the mission of the church, and this is the main reason why the church must have a public presence.

To make this ecclesiological turn, Seongam Church incorporated education as a key pillar of the consultation process. The church congregation and I focused on this aspect of education for 8 out of 14 total months of consultation.

Change in Understanding of Local Community

The transformation of Seongam Church started with this ecclesiological turn. This change in ecclesiology is never easy due to three factors. First is the need to turn away from the familiar ecclesiology. A church's ecclesiology is a complex outcome built through years of communal practice and reflection on spirituality, theology, culture, and history. The church has been existing and conducting ministry based on this ecclesiology. In other words, this old ecclesiology was the ground of the church's existence that enabled the church to bear fruit and motivated its commitment to God.

The second reason is that in the process of turning toward a new ecclesiology, the congregation may feel that its past existence and history are negated. As discussed earlier, although there are problems with the traditional ecclesiology, it should not be entirely denied. The traditional ecclesiology did provide the ground for the church's existence and served as the principle on which the church's mission could bear many fruits. An easy mistake in a church's transformation is to denounce or separate from the past. A church is built on top of the history of God's providence and the sacrificial commitment of the Christians who lived through their own day and age. So any new effort that negates or separates from the past is simply ignorant. This means we must not forget that the ecclesiological turn is a process of growth toward Christ.

The third is that the pastor and the church members must transform together. The pastor must first achieve one's own ecclesiological turn. Pastors are used to seeing themselves as teachers. Instead, pastors need to shift their self-perception to become a learner. We cannot expect the church members to change their ecclesiology without the pastor first going through the change. And the pastor must also remember that we tend to be more lenient on ourselves. When a church community is stagnant and needs change, pastors rarely find themselves to be the problem. So if a pastor wants to transform the church, they may take this as an opportunity first to reexamine their own ecclesiology. I see this as the crucial component.

In this way, the ecclesiological turn is a collaborative effort between the pastor and the congregation. The pastor and the church members must together change their perception of the local society. Therefore, such change takes time. It also takes the willingness to receive help from external sources that God already made available. Gathering support from trustworthy outside sources is an effective strategy.

Story of Seongam Church

Beginning of Change

Seongam Church sought consultation to seek change. This is the distinct element in Seongam Church's case. We recognized that we still lacked the preparation and capacity to truly encounter the local community, so we used the consultation method. Expert consultation is based on the social sciences, so it is also a strategic way to lend legitimacy to church programs. The whole of Korean society is built on specialized expertise. So the social scientific methodology was instrumental in the church earning public credibility in its communication on community development. This was also the factor that attracted the attention of local government offices, NGOs, and other social activists. The ministries developed through this process could naturally converge with the needs of the local society, and these needs could be responded to in cooperation with other experts and organizations. Through the process of education, data gathering through surveys, and pilot programming, professional, valid, measurable, and effective ministry programs could be developed.

Consultation Begins

Purpose and Aim of Consultation

The purpose and aim of the consultation are listed in Table 2 below.

Purpose	• Revitalize church social service program • Connect with local society and form positive relationships • Raise awareness of the presence of Seongam Church • Confirm the essence and identity of the Church in the congregation (education) • Recover public reputation of the church • Use of social service resources effectively
Aim	• Revitalize social service programming based on the assessment of Seongam Church's existing social service programs • Improve and update expertise of church social service program participants through education and training • Conduct general assessment of church social service programming • Conduct church social service pilot programs • Establish a comprehensive plan for social service programming

Table 2: Purpose and Aim of Consultation

Four Domains of Consultation

Data Gathering

For the church to meet with the local community it must first know the community. Data gathering is the minimum preparation for the church to encounter its neighbors authentically. Park Jong-sam, the first generation of Christian social service professionals in South Korea, criticized the church's lack of professionalism in his *Understanding and Practice of Church Social Service* (Human and Social Service, 2000). The main reason why the church is underestimated despite the massive amount of social service it provides is its lack of expertise. The church's own assessment of itself and its surrounding community is necessarily subjective. Employing social scientific tools to gather various data to read the local society accurately is important.

Data is gathered on two subjects. The first is the local community and the other is the church community. The church must be the object of study because while it has various self-assessment structures, they are always necessarily subjective. Seongam Church was no exception. Social scientific assessment of our church could be a good resource for objective self-assessment. This is a task as important as gathering data on the local community.

So two different methods were employed to study our church and local community. One was general information gathering from available data and statistics. For this purpose, we got hold of publicly available data reported on the state of the region and other data from local experts. On the church, we also gathered data on ministry, finances, and membership in the last five years for the consultants to analyze the data objectively.

The second method was surveys to objectively assess the church and society's current state. Surveys can gather information on participants' needs, educational achievement, economic status, perception and understanding of others, the congregation's spiritual characteristics and self-assessment. These surveys can directly determine ministry development.

General data gathering studies the foundations and the surveys determine ministry aims and contents. Analyzing the available data and the survey results directly impacted effective and biblical ministry programming and ensured the relevance and validity of Seongam Church's ministry development. Seongam Church's ministry programs were developed on this foundational research.

Education

As mentioned already, education is central to the consulting process. Meeting the local community without seeing changes in church leadership and congregation may make the encounter shallow or difficult. We set out eight months for three types of education. The first was through sermons. Preaching is the best opportunity for the pastor to meet with the entire church community. The pastor is in a unique place with two tasks in the consulting process. One is as a leader of the consultation process and the other as the subject of change through the consultation process. On this basis, the pastor must employ ministerial and spiritual terminology in sermons to persuade and guide the church members. The key is how.

The second type of education was workshops and training by outside experts. For about eight months Seongam Church conducted an education curriculum on Sunday afternoon services. We organized the curriculum into four general fields of theology, social service, culture, and liberal arts. We invited experts in each field to hear from them, and in some of the weeks we conducted trainings. In this process topics that had been neglected in the church community were brought to our attention. We could expand our thoughts and grow a desire for new kinds of ministries.

The third type was field visitations. In those visits, the congregation could try on the ministry visions of other churches on the same path and see what they had been doing with our own eyes. This activity allowed us to imagine our own future. We visited exemplary churches and local organizations, attended their lectures, and examined their ministries to ask them questions to get a taste of how their ministries look in practice.

Organization

The consultation was organized into three groups: the group of expert consultants, the church committee that represents the church in decision-making, and the regional committee composed of influential people in the local community.

Groups were organized to facilitate communication. Communication between the experts and the church committee, the church committee and the regional committee, and meetings of all three groups are key to a successful consultation process and result. Especially the regional committee was composed of influential local persons to allow for societal discourse to enter into the church and to let the church discussions flow out to the local community. For ministry in the church, a committee of congregants may be enough, but to do ministry in society, a church committee is not enough. A process of communication with society is a given. The three groups met regularly once a month, and two or three of the groups met as needed to communicate and facilitate the consultation process.

Forming a communication structure with the local society from the beginning is critical. The local society's participation at the stage of ministry development facilitates societal acceptance of the resulting programs. Non-church member participation in ministry programming invites the local residents to regard Seongam Church's social services ministries as "our programs" rather than "their programs."

Pilot Projects

Expertise is necessary for a church to conduct ministry in the neighboring community. Therefore, a process of confirming the expertise of the program through pilot projects is necessary. Short-term experimental projects were conducted to confirm their feasibility, identify points for improvement, and minimize risks. Evaluation of the pilot projects significantly allowed participants to reflect on their ministry and improve their professional capacity.

Resulting Ministry Programs

Four Main Programs

Seongam After-School Program

Seongam After-School Program was commissioned by the District Office. The district has many families where both parents work, so there was a societal need to provide childcare. Our consultation survey identified the same need, so our church decided to participate. There are four characteristics of Seongam After-School Program. First is that we provide a safe space. It is not easy to procure an appropriately safe space in the community, but our church has been in this neighborhood for a long time and already had the space. Community residents could trust the caretakers in the church to entrust their children's safety.

The second characteristic is the church's compassion. A church community knows the love of Jesus Christ. We can provide more than a safe but sterile space like public social service or education institutions. Seongam Church could ensure quality care and education while warmly embracing the children. The welcoming church community could provide an environment where children can make happy memories.

The third is our official processes to ensure the quality of care. Rather than setting up an organization and conducting the after-school program by our church alone, we chose to cooperate with the District Office to acquire public credibility.

The fourth is sustainability. Compared to public education institutions, there is less turnover of friends and teachers in after-school programs. Generally, once a child enrolls in a program they tend to stay until their family moves elsewhere. This ensures stable group of service recipients. Children may depend much more on our teachers who provide sustained care and attention than the teachers in school. So teachers who have built relationships with the children for a while can provide education that fits the needs of each child. The more time they share, the deeper the relationship and the richer the fruit.

Today in the 18th year of operation 40 elementary-aged children attend the program, divided into two classes. The program is firmly rooted in the local community. Five committed teachers warmly welcome the children; the program space is always filled with happy children's laughter.

Baobab Café

Baobab Café was started in response to the local people's desire for a community lounge. Baobab Café fulfills four functions. The first is as a community lounge for people to visit, and the second is to provide quality information to raise the residents' quality of life through liberal arts lectures. These lectures are conducted once or twice a year to provide quality information for self-development right in our town. The third function is to provide opportunities for the residents to volunteer. The café space allows the residents to share their time and leisure activities. The fourth function is to provide a cultural space. Living room concerts and poetry readings may be organized in the space.

The café is a space entirely for the residents. So, along with Five Beans Small Library (Beans is another word for five pieces of stones in children's play), the café name was picked among the submissions by the residents. We invited the residents to the launch celebrations of the café and the library to promote our intention to make them available for the residents. Both the library and the café have been in operation for 18 years.

To ensure the café is used for the common good, we decided on three rules. The first is to not use the café for church affairs. A café is just a café. We do not evangelize or push our religion here or try to promote church culture here. The second is to not change the café operations time and spatial arrangements for church matters. We cannot change the café operations time to hold church events in the space. The third rule is not to give special exceptions to the church. The church members and local residents have equal rights to the café space.

Operating based on these rules, the café is commended by the community residents. The space was selected as one of the shared spaces recognized by the city government of Seoul. It is a neighborhood-friendly space, a space that welcomes children and seniors, young and old.

Five Beans Small Library

Five Beans Small Library is a children's library. It was launched in response to resident needs as well. Libraries kept getting built and developed in the region, but there were very few children's libraries, which meant demand outstripped the supply. Today there are about 20,000 books and 1,500 library members.

Recently the library has been operated a little differently. The library's main function is to gather quality books and make them available for borrowing. But today many libraries are providing quality content in other ways as well.

So we are working on the library in three ways. First is to continue to provide quality books, second is to develop childcare and education programs, and the third is to ensure the safety of the facility and the environment. For this purpose, we absolutely need a professional librarian in addition to volunteers.

Five Beans is operated by a professional librarian and volunteers. The cost of operations is financed by the church, Eunpyeong District Office, and the city government of Seoul. We also have the cooperation of the Ministry of Culture, Sports, and Tourism, the Small Library Association, the Eunpyeong District Office, and related organizations in the region. The dedicated librarian develops the curriculum and guides the visitors.

Visitation Ministry

This ministry was organized in response to local needs as well. In our district, we have a high senior population and a large proportion of them are lower income. So despite various public social services available to them, there are people still beyond the reach of government welfare. The visitation ministry was launched to pay visits to seniors who live alone. We call the seniors by phone and ask about their health and other matters of well-being, and if they need help we connect them to relevant professionals. For this purpose, we organized a team to make phone calls, and the ministry grew to respond to growing needs.

Today the ministry developed to provide a week's worth of side dishes for the seniors who live alone. Each Tuesday a team gathers to deliver the food. We cooperate with the District Office, the Town Office, and the National Health Insurance Service in selecting people to support.

Regular and Intermittent Services

Community Youth Care

This care service basically happens in networking circumstances. A church-affiliated non-government organization called Good School Network submitted a program proposal to the Eunpyeong District Office and the District Office of Education (DOE). Once the program was selected, the DOE allowed the program to be promoted in schools. The District Office finances the operations, the NGO conducts the program, and the church provides the space, the volunteers, and snacks for the youth.

The school announces the program to the parents through their regular correspondence channels to encourage the youth to apply, and the program is held in the church space. This may seem like a complicated process, but there is an important reason why it should be this way. It conveys the message that child rearing is a responsibility of everyone and assures the DOE, the schools, the local government, and the local community that the church is capable of functioning as the central channel for such a program.

Churches are experienced educational communities. It is difficult to find other such educational systems besides schools and private institutes. This is one of the unique capacities of churches. So the church community can be an essential organization in these collaborative education programs and earn recognition as a relevant group in the society network.

These Saturday programs for youth are necessary because after-school programs for elementary children do not operate on weekends. On the weekends households must look after the children on their own, but if both parents must work through the weekend, this is a dilemma. So there was a local need for weekend programming for such households.

Community Youth Care program curriculum is generally on character development and creativity enhancement. It is conducted as extra-curricular activities that elementary children generally don't have access to. This program demonstrates that the local community seeks out collaboration with churches if only the churches have the professional capacity and are willing to meet the need.

Weekday Care

This program is basically is similar to Community Youth Care except that it happens on weekdays, and its emphasis is on education rather than care. We offer short-term programs organized by subjects such as science, languages, or culture.

But this program is also distinct from schools or private institutes in that the children learn through play and participatory learning. We help the children acquire skills for life through direct experience. The scheduling may change as necessary, but the programs are generally offered in the first and second half of the year and last ten to twelve weeks. So for about half of the year, we meet with the children once a week.

Through these programs the church can form relationships with children, volunteers, and parents. They can also become familiar with our church and our Sunday School. There is no question that missional opportunities open up through these ministries.

Gong Gam Camp

Unlike other ministry programs conducted through collaborative networks, the church conducts this summer program for neighboring children, though with the help of another specialist organization. Each year, 100 children participate in this day camp, half church members and half from the neighborhood. The church and the organization The Baeum collaborate to select the speakers.

We set up a few rules for this program. First, we appoint three teachers for each class. One of them must be a Sunday School teacher to facilitate the church children and unchurched children to form groups and get along with each other.

The second is concerning child management. We inform the parents when the children arrive and when they leave and communicate with them on whether they are safely participating in our programs. In addition, we send pictures of the children participating in pre-announced programs to assure them that the children are under good care and that this church program is legitimate.

The third is preparation and evaluation. We prepare the programs with professionals to ensure their quality. We conduct a general run-through of the program to raise the quality of church education and show that the church functions as an educational platform for the local children. Multifaceted evaluation is also conducted through satisfaction surveys of the teachers, the children who attend the program, and the parents who send the children to gather objective assessments and update our quality of education.

By conducting this program, our church could acquire a status as an educational institution in the community and increase missional contact with local children. Moreover, the teachers who participate in the program could enhance their educational capacity. Our Sunday School teachers can observe how education professionals conduct lessons and become aware of society's standard of education. These trained Sunday School teachers gain even more authority in the eyes of the children.

Seeing the Future of the Church in the Local Community

Church as the Space to Educate the Next Generation

The church is one of the few local institutions with permanent space. In Korean society, education is everyone's concern and a complex challenge nobody can answer. In this respect, there is a dire need for someone to vitalize education, support it, and share the burden.

One thing I find in Seongam Church's ministries for children is that the church's commitment to the next generation raises the church's credibility in the community and provides an opportunity for the church to communicate and relate with the community. This can be a God-given opportunity for the Korean church and a chance for the church to find a solution to its problem of declining church membership among the youth.

Rediscovery of Resource

God provides abundant resources. The Korean church has so far been doing ministry with only internal resources. Ministry for the church should use internal resources, but ministry for the society need not be limited. God has already provided many resources in the local community. If the church is willing to share, the government and civil society can provide valuable resources.

Beyond resource sharing, cooperation with these public agencies can be a way for the church to expand its scope and establish its presence in the local community.

Church's Participation in Public Sphere

The public sphere is waiting for the church to do its part. Recently there have been discussions on projects to share religious spaces with the local community. A religion by definition has a public status. The Korean Protestant church must first become aware of its public nature to recover this public status.

A positive recent trend is the increasing number of studies on the public nature of the gospel. Churches with traditional ecclesiology should also consider this trend with open minds. In this process, the church that declares the kingdom of God can effectively reap the fruit of social transformation.

Conclusion

The church must be attentive to the two-fold command of Jesus in the Bible on love: "He said to him, "'You shall love the Lord your God with all your heart and with all your soul and with all your mind.' This is the greatest and first commandment. And a second is like it: 'You shall love your neighbor as yourself.' On these two commandments hang all the Law and the Prophets." (Matthew 22:37-40). The church's dignified service to the community is not optional but most basic and essential. Our love for God is proven by our love of neighbors, and our love of neighbors by our love for God.

Therefore, the Korean church must be a neighbor to the society. To become a neighbor, the church must develop and conduct programs and network with society. The church must not forget that it is a community that shows the world the love of Jesus Christ and gives them a taste of the kingdom of God.

Seongam Church has been building a cooperative structure with educational organizations, administrative offices, public education institutions, local NGOs, social service organizations, and other churches in the region. Many ministry programs arose out of these collaborations. Now is the time for the Korean church communities to confess that Jesus Christ is not only the Lord of the church but also the Lord of the world and to approach society not in the way the church wants but in the way God wants. This is essential to the church's mission.

From Traditional to Missional Church: Case of Seongam Church

In-sung Hwang

Introduction

The philosopher of science Thomas Kuhn explained the paradigm shift of scientific theories in his *The Structure of Scientific Revolution*. The scientific theory is today applied to various fields beyond science. Kuhn basically asserts that a paradigm keeps getting proven and reformed. If there are more cases in the extraordinary that do not fit the existing paradigm, then the old paradigm ultimately collapses and a new paradigm that can explain the new cases appear. Kuhn calls this the scientific revolution. The same principle may be applied to the church and theological trends. The truth exists but the method of approaching and explaining the truth continues to change according to the age and circumstances, and at times they develop through a process of rupture.[1]

Through more than half a century, in the rapid change of industrialization and urbanization, the Korean church has grown in the industrial society's framework of mass production and institutionalization. But today in the new century and especially in the massive shift after the Covid-19 pandemic, there are cases that the old church paradigm cannot explain. We are at a point of a new paradigm shift.

In this, there are two types of change: the pioneer type for a completely new system, and the transitional type seeking ways for traditional churches to transition to a new paradigm. In the former, it is easier to apply a new ecclesiology but churches lack different resources. They must start from the very bottom. In the latter instance, churches have the traditions and resources but considerable time is required to shift to a new paradigm. In the Korean church today in need of a new paradigm, studies and strategies on these two types of change are necessary.

In this paper, I will examine the case of Seongam Church in Eunpyeong District on how a traditional church is serving the community as it shifts to the new missional church paradigm.

Basis of Change

Seongam Church belongs to Pyeongyang Presbytery in the Presbyterian Church of Korea -Tonghap denomination. It is located in Nokbeon-dong of Eunyeong District in Seoul. After its founding in 1977 in Eungam-dong, the church building was constructed where it is now in Nokbeon-dong in 1980. Senior

---

[1] Thomas S. Kuhn, *The Structure of the Scientific Revolutions*. Fourth edition (University of Chicago Press, 2012).

pastors stayed for two to three short years until the sixth pastor An Gi-hak ministered for 13 years until retirement. The current pastor Joo-hee Cho was appointed as the seventh pastor toward the end of 2002.

Nokbeon-dong where the church is located has one or two high-rise apartments but generally consists of low-rise townhouses. Most are small multiplex housings with basement stories, and the housing is generally cheaper compared to other areas in Seoul, which means most residents on the lower income bracket. Given this characteristic, there are lots of young couples with young children trying to settle down as a family. This is also primarily a residential area rather than populated by businesses, factories, or trade.

Seongam Church is located in this geographic area on a path off of the main street. Most of the church members live in this area. In recent years, the proportion of people who attend an urban church from another district or city is increasing due to rising cost of housing and education. But Seongam Church has grown over its 45 years as the town's church and its members share commonalities with the rest of the town. Today, Seongam Church is a mid-sized church with 650 adults and 220 children and youth.

The construction of Vision Center was a good start toward change, but the more important factor was the generally positive stance of the congregation to church community service initiatives. The senior pastor Joo-hee Cho also saw in his childhood how a church functions as the center of a town and the pastor as a respected elder of the community, and this formed the basis of his initiative to change. Cho had also done theoretical research on ecclesiology and church community service during his Doctor of Ministry course at Fuller Theological Seminary.[2]

Turning Point

The turning point was the church discussion on ways to make use of the Vision Center that was to be built on the former church parking lot. The construction was decided in 2007 and the work began in 2008. Cho and the church discussed how the center can function to serve society and not just the church. There were limits to their discussions and resources, so they commissioned a consultation with the Church and Social Service Research Institute composed of directors of various social welfare centers. During 14 months of consultation, surveys were conducted in the church and the neighborhood to assess their needs. For eight months the church was educated on the rationale behind their service to the community. Then they conducted several pilot projects which developed into the various ministry programs that continue today.

---

[2] In an interview Ju-hee Cho stated he experienced an ecclesiological reorientation based by reading *Forgotten Ways* by Alan Hirsch. Alan Hirsch, *The forgotten ways: Reactivating the missional church.* (Brazos Press, 2006).; Gidok Gongbo, "Kyo-hoe-lon ko-min-ŭl ham-kke-han nae in-saeng 3ka-chi ch'aek" [Three books that accompanied my contemplation of ecclesiology], (19 June 2019).

Content of Change

Aims of Missional Ecclesiology

North American theologians who had been considering the need for change in traditional churches recognized that Western society is no longer Christian but secular. They welcomed the missional approach of Lesslie Newbigin of England and tried for a long time to bring change in their ecclesiology. The result is the emergence of the term missional church in North America in the 1990s, which today is also well-known and often used in the Korean church. The definition of the term missional church is not static but has a characteristic of a movement and cannot be narrowed down to one definition and aims. Nevertheless, we know the general direction of change it aims for. Choi Dongkyu identifies the key ideas of the missional church as the usage of the concept of the kingdom of God as the redemptive reign of God, application of *missio Dei* as a key ecclesiological concept; emphasis on contextual aspects in the rediscovery of the local church; and the emphasis on public discipleship to overcome narrow individualistic faith.[3] Han Kuk-il has been collecting and studying the new types of ministry over several years to identify ten factors commonly found in missional churches. He explains that the missional church is a reform movement to return to the essence of the church rather than an emergence of a new ecclesiology.[4] Charles

---

[3] Dongkyu Choi, "A Critique from the Perspective of Church Growth on the GOCN's Missional Ecclesiology," *Theology of Mission* 25 (2010), 238-241.

[4] Kook-il Han, *Sŏn-kyo-chŏk kyo-hoe-ŭi i-lon-kwa sil-che* [Theory and practice of missional church], (Seoul: PUTS Press, 2016). 42-49. Han lists ten characteristics of the missional church as the following:

1. The missional church is a movement that aims for the kingdom of God, participating in the mission of the triune God on earth, and valuing the missional identity of the local church as the holy catholic church.
2. The missional church movement starts by grounding Christian identity and reason for existence on their calling and sending out to the world.
3. The missional church movement seeks to restore trust with the church's local community. By restoring the authenticity of faith and mission, the movement constructs missional infrastructures between the church and the world.
4. The missional church activities are based on day-to-day fellowship with local community residents. On this basis a wide array of missionary movements are conducted.
5. The missional church does not consider only the foreign countries as sites of mission as in the traditional missionary paradigm. The world is the mission field but it begins by accepting the local as the site of mission.
6. The missional church movement goes beyond the traditional pastor-centered paradigm to call and send all Christians to mission in their respective places. The movement is based on this theology of the laity, where the pastor and the laity are cooperate for in the kingdom of God.
7. The missional church movement is not about specified programs formed around a church, but considers all life and community circumstances to call the daily life the mission field.
8. The missional church movement seeks balance between the church's two

van Engen in explaining the missional church reinterprets the four marks of the church – one, holy, catholic, and apostolic – in the Nicaean Creed. These four marks are more than just adjectives that describe the static idea of the church, but "adverbs" that highlight the church's dynamism.[5] In the same context, Darrel Guder also asserts that the church should be regarded as a dynamic being called and sent out to be apostolic, catholic, holy, and united, in the reverse order.[6]

Bilingual Proficiency for Translation

The purpose of this essay is not to explain the definition and conceptualization of missional ecclesiology or to analyze it. Rather, I am more concerned with the question of how the Korean church, especially the traditional churches, can accept and embrace the concept of missional church to work toward gradual change. The missional church concept includes other concepts of *missio Dei*, intercultural interpretation, mission-shaped church, and the economics of Trinity. A bilingual proficiency is necessary to explain these ideas in everyday ministry. Instead of using difficult pedantic theological jargons and concepts a mode of education and communication is necessary to facilitate gradual change in a congregation's awareness and action.

Improvement rather than Negation

A common mistake in promoting the missional church is to be overly negative in criticizing the existing church structure. Of course, for a new paradigm to emerge, there must be reflection and criticism of the old. But when a pastor or a leader is trying to bring change in a traditional church's ecclesiology, the approach should be to suggest ways to improve rather than voicing a hard no. Is it truly possible for the Korean church to reform by starting from square one?[7] I am not saying that we should ignore the existing paradigm or negotiate on the matter of truth. I am only asserting the need for gradual change rather than an abrupt about-face in ecclesiology.

---

dynamics of gathering and dispersing.
9. The missional church movement avoids local church-centric growth but rather unites to cooperate with other local churches for community evangelization.
10. missional church movement recognizes the community as the mission field. It is the movement to lôcalize the kingdom of God and develop the community through the church.

[5] Charles van Engen, *God's Missionary People: Rethinking the Purpose of the Local Church* (Grand Rapids: Baker, 1991), 68.
"Maybe it is time we begin to see the four words of Nicea not as adjectives which modify a thing we know as the Church, but as adverbs which describe the missionary action of the Church's essential life in the world."

[6] Alan J. Roxburgh, Darrell L. Guder ed., *Missional Church: A Vision for the Sending of the Church in North America* (Grand Rapids, MI: Wm. B.Eardmans Publishing Co., 1998).

[7] Neil Cole who wrote *Organic Church* and Alan Hirsch who wrote *the Shaping of Things to Come* emphasize complete overturn and a qualitatively different newness. Neil Cole, *Organic church: Growing faith where life happens*. Vol. 16. John Wiley & Sons, 2005.; Michael Frost and Alan Hirsch. *The shaping of things to come: Innovation and mission for the 21st-century church.* (Grand Rapids, MI: Baker Books, 2013).

When attending lectures or discussing missional church, pastors of existing churches express difficulties with the oppositional board of elders or the operational committees that are reluctant to change. There is a vague fear that the new direction of the church may shake the church's identity and negatively impact church growth, or that it would decrease church officers' influence over the church. Kuhn also explained that people in the old paradigm characteristically reject cases and types that don't fit the existing paradigm.[8] That is why some younger pastors turn to church planting to conduct their own experiments in ecclesiology and ministry on a new foundation. Such pioneering of new types is necessary. But at the same time, the missional turn in existing churches must also be seriously studied. Seok-hwan Sung states that while the spirit of the missional church should be maintained, we can boldly give up the term "missional church."[9]

Even in new churches planted with new ecclesiology, most of the members have already been trained and educated in traditional ecclesiology from other churches. These may be new churches in form, but the congregation undeniably retains the older paradigm. So there is a need for gradual change in ecclesiology.

Gradual Change in Ecclesiology using Images

In this context, Joo-hee Cho' use of images to educate and communicate on the missional church in Seongam Church is notable. Cho specifically made use of Alan Hirsch's Venn diagrams to explain the change from the traditional dualism of church and society toward the framework of *missio Dei*.[10] Hirsch describes the traditional church's ecclesiological paradigm as based on the dualism between the sacred and the secular and that people in the dualistic spiritual paradigm see God as the divinity located in the church and the object of a very private religion.[11]

According to Hirsch this dualistic ecclesiology separates life in the church and in the world and shrinks God to stay within the realm of the church. He suggests a non-dualistic alternative in a new diagram that aptly explains how God is not separate from the world but reigns over all spheres of the world including the church.

---

[8] Thomas S. Kuhn, *The Structure of the Scientific Revolutions.* Fourth edition (University of Chicago Press, 2012).

[9] Seok-hwan Sung, *Chi-yŏk-kong-tong-ch'e-wa ham-kke-ha-nŭn kyo-hoe-ŭi sae-lo-un to-chŏn-tŭl* [New challenges of the church that stands with the local community], (Seoul: PCK Research Center, 2018), 83.

[10] This was also his main topic of study during his time in the D.Min. program at Fuller Theological Seminary.

[11] Alan Hirsch. *The forgotten ways: Reactivating the missional church.* (Grand Rapids, MI: Brazos Press, 2006).

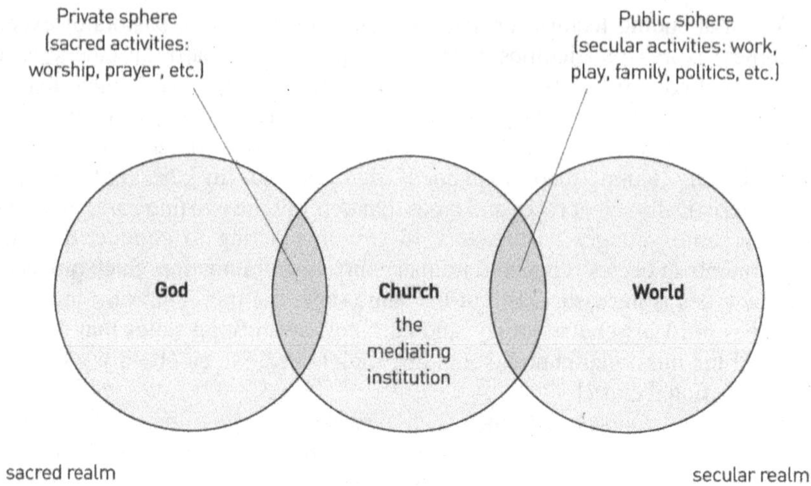

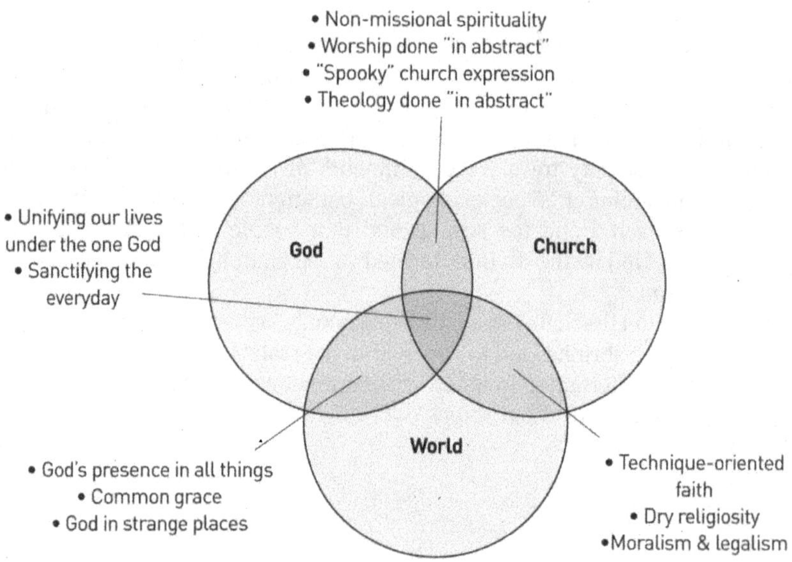

Figure 8: Alan Hirsch's Non-Dualistic Ecclesiology[12]

There are limits to explaining all the theological implications with a diagram. Hirsch's diagram of non-dualistic ecclesiology seems to show that there are spheres in which the reign of God does not reach. If I further develop Hirsch's perspective, then the diagram can be redrawn as below.

[12] Ibid., 191-192.

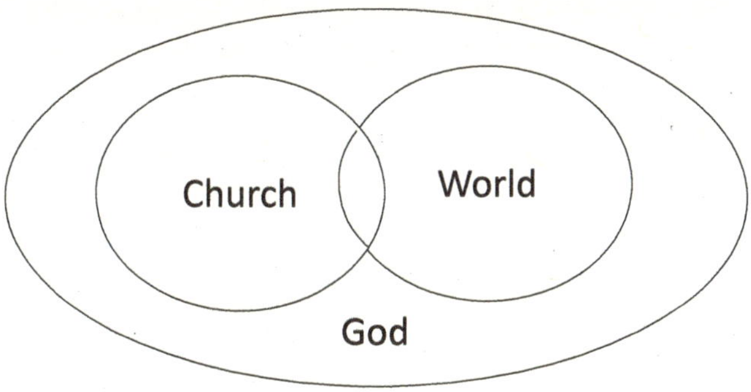

Figure 9: World and Church within the Reign of God

In Figure 2, the church and the world are completely within the realm of God and there are other realms that the church and the world have yet to grasp.

My point is that the responsibility to help the church understand difficult theological and ecclesiological concepts, perhaps using such diagrams, is on the pastor. The pastor must have a good grasp of ecclesiology and its implications, consistently study its application in different contexts, and communicate it to the church in simple terms. In practical application a simple visual explanation of the theory is necessary, and in the long term, consistent education is required. As Seongam Church received consultation from an external organization for 14 months, it spent eight months to educate the new ecclesiology.

Need for a Holistic Approach

The ecclesiological turn must first happen in the pastor. Based on the pastor's own ecclesiological conversion the other church leaders can be authentically persuaded and all church members can be consistently educated. If the church leaders are on different grounds and if the education curriculum or system does not support the pastor's points in their preaching, the church members will only be confused. A systematic and comprehensive education system is necessary. One or two seminar events will not change the congregation's perspective. A consistent process of repeated emphasis can help engrain the change. The same vision and perspective should be shared from the children in Sunday School to the adults. While using existing educational resources is appropriate, they must also be revised to fit each church's situation.

Seongam Church consistently educated and trained through preaching and Sunday afternoon lectures inviting specialists in theology, social service, culture, and the liberal arts. And they also arranged visits to other churches doing ministry based on this new ecclesiology.

When training the entire church, expecting everyone to understand or accept the change is unrealistic. Focusing on explaining and persuading a smaller group of more committed leaders is necessary. Alan J. Roxburgh explains the church's leadership structure by distinguishing between the boundary-defining group and the larger group of core-defining congregation. It is the boundary-defining group's commitment and motivation that make the church dynamic.[13]

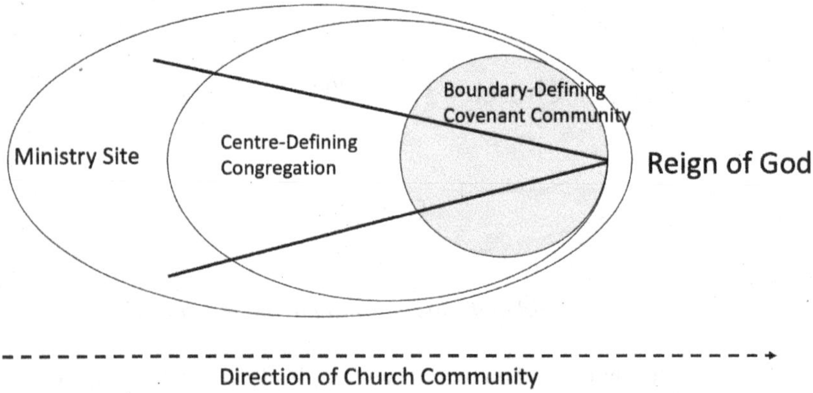

Figure 10: Missional Church Community[14]

So when trying to shift from the traditional way of doing church to a new church movement, ecclesiological change must come first. The pastor must first go through their own ecclesiological turn. Based on this authentic change, the central leadership and the rest of the congregation must be given comprehensive training through preaching, education, expert lectures, and field visits. Care should be taken to achieve gradual change while refraining from denying the church members' own experiences. Seongam Church managed to effectively achieve this by using Alan Hirsch's diagram of non-dualistic ecclesiology.

Changes in the Subjects of the Movement

Pastoral Leadership: From Manager to Facilitator

Kook-il Han names the minister-centric structure as a characteristic of Korea's traditional churches. This is intimately related to church-centric faith. As explained above, in a dualistic ecclesiology a good Christian is someone who actively participates and serves in church. The more this is emphasized the more they become dependent on the pastor. In the multi-faith South Korean society, Protestant Christianity more recently arrived proselytized more aggressively than other religions, which also fed into the dualistic ecclesiology. The pastor's

---

[13] Alan J. Roxburgh, Darrell L. Guder ed., *Missional Church: A Vision for the Sending of the Church in North America* (Grand Rapids, MI: Wm. B. Eardmans Publishing Co., 1998), 300-310.

[14] Ibid., 311.

role became decisive in the church-centric spiritual life, forming a hierarchical structure between the pastor and the laity.[15]

Han states that we need not regard this minister-centric structure negatively. It is an efficient structure where a pastor's personal change of ecclesiology can quickly spread to the rest of the church.[16] In other words, in a Korean church the pastor's role is decisive. They should not be authoritarian leaders ready with all the answers but someone who can bridge the church and the world so that church members can live as Christians in the world. The pastor is the mediator between God and people and the church and the world. For this process, the new ecclesiology must be at the basis. The role of the pastor and the congregation can change dramatically depending on how they regard God, the church, and the world. Pastors must be facilitators[17] rather than providing the answers, helping the community ask questions, contemplate, and seek solutions together. This does not mean that everything is relative. There must be a basic standard for approaching issues. This means the pastor's role is also distinct from those of coaches and facilitators.

Seongam Church went through a 14-month consultation process to turn a building on a former parking lot into a neighborhood community center. For the church members, the outside specialists are unfamiliar people. The consultants also do not have a good understanding of church circumstances. So the pastor's mediating role is critical. Joo-hee Cho acted as a caretaker rather than intervener, in other words, a facilitator. The pastor who already has the authority and trust in the church community can understand the language of the external experts and translate the message in the language more accessible to the congregation. This was a key element that led to effectiveness of external consultation.[18]

Cho mentioned the importance of objective self-assessment through outside consultation as a reason why there were hardly any tensions with the church members in the process of transition to become the missional church. In other words, the pastor and the church members were not oppositional to each other but in the same team asking how the church may change. The pastor stood with the church members as one of the learners receiving the consultation and discussing actions on that basis.[19]

---

[15] Kook-ill Han, "Missional Church in the viewpoint of the Korean Local Church." *Mission and Theology* 30 (2012). 90-96.

[16] Kook-il Han, "Missional Church's Practical Models and Principles: Missional Church that Learns from the Fields of Korean Church." *Theology of Mission* 36 (2014). 361.

[17] On the role of facilitators, see Seong-hong Moon, *Kyŏng-hŏm-hak-sŭp p'ŏ-sil-li-t'e-i-syŏn* [Experiential learning facilitation]. (Seoul: Real Learning, 2021).

[18] This is perhaps based on Joo-hee Cho's experience of having to temporarily fill the role of a senior pastor when he was officially an assistant pastor. It was a position with more responsibilities than authority, so he had to put down his pastoral sense of authoritativeness and served the congregation to see good results.

[19] From interview with Joo-hee Cho.

Integrated Missional Leadership

Pastors are at the center of complex relationships. They must disperse the authority formerly focused on one person while providing certain standards to determine the direction of change. Kim Gwang-geon states that both dispersive leadership and charismatic leadership must go together in integrated missional leadership. In the postmodern society, leadership is affected not only by the validity of the leader's suggestion but also by the leader's character and personality. In other words, it is the leadership of affect. Therefore, rather than the leader monopolizing all authority,[20] the leader can invite others to participate and solve issues as a group.[21] But Kim points out that the capacity of the individual leader is also important in dispersive leadership.

> The contemporary phenomenon of decentralizing leadership and authority does not result in the elimination or weakening of the community leader but paradoxically makes the leader's role more significant. This is because post-authority, dispersion of authority, and changes in the forms of authority all require a new model of leadership rather than an absence of one. In this regard, in a faith community, an individual's leadership becomes even more significant.[22]

Charismatic leadership must also be reinterpreted and applied as something inspired by the pastor's individual character rather than based on the non-personal pastoral office. Missional ecclesiology requires integrated leadership that combines charismatic leadership based on the leader's character and relationships, and dispersive leadership.

Seongam Church also showed dispersive leadership in the process of change. Various church members shouldered different responsibilities to participate. But at its root was the church pastor's capacity to meet and persuade different groups and consistently cast vision to people based on trust, enabling communal leadership to function. Cho Ju-hee calls this "empowering leadership."

Ownership of Church Members and Local Residents

The role of church members is significant in this process of change. They must mature to become more than church hands who support the pastor's philosophy, and as independent subjects who can themselves be leaders who actively participate, present opinions, and make changes.[23] In the church, a church member's role may be limited, but in other spheres of life they are each a subject. In this dynamic, the pastor turns into a supporter. The church members must be prepared to live as ministers and missionaries themselves. R. Paul Stevens refers

---

[20] Michael Frost & Alan Hirsch, *The shaping of things to come: Innovation and mission for the 21st-century church.* (Grand Rapids, MI: Baker Books, 2013).
[21] KwangKun Kim, "The Interdisciplinary Reflection upon Missional Leadership Model for Missional Church," *Koeran Journal of Christian Studies* 11(2020), 431-432.
[22] Ibid., 433.
[23] Jong-seok Bae, "Cho-chik-ch'e-lo-sŏ-ŭi kyo-hoe-wa chang-lo-ŭi yŏk-hal," [Role of the church and elders as institutional bodies] In Hyung-gee Lee, et al., *Kyo-hoe chik-che-lon: han-kuk kyo-hoe chik-che kae-sŏn-ŭl wi-han mo-saek* [Offices of the church: Strategies to improve the offices of the korean church]. (Seoul: Yeyoung, 2012), 240-248.

to Ephesians 4 to state that building up the church community as a body does not mean boosting the minister-centric structure but considering how each member's gifts fit into the whole. So the role of the pastor to raise and prepare the laity is once again essential.[24]

Taking this concept further, the community residents are also each subjects who should be invited into discussions on common issues. They may not give input into the church's aims and programming, but if the church is already acting in the social sphere, then the local residents may also be invited to the process of decision-making.

Seongam Church asked for an external consultation and formed a committee structure composed of the church committee, a group of external experts, and a group of local representatives whose members were recommended and selected from the local government, the resident council, and the women's society. The church could communicate with this regional committee on the church's intention to make the consultation and ministry program development a collaborative project. These interactions are possible only based on the expanded ecclesiology. The pastor is responsible to the church congregation and the community by forming good relationships in the local community and exchanging influence.

As a result of the consultation, the church could identify the community's needs. They saw the need for childcare, a community center for young parents, systematic care for those in economic need, and a communal cultural space. In response, Seongam Church established the Seongam After-School Program commissioned by Eunpyeong District. Baobab Café is operated as a neighborhood meeting place where church members and local residents can equally make use of the space. The visitation ministry to the seniors is more than just food delivery; it is a way to assess the needs of poor households and connect them to social welfare organizations. The church is also selecting quality books for local residents, organizing cultural events, and encouraging the residents to volunteer for this effort.

Dialogue as Tool for Change

Communication Method of Traditional Churches

Traditional churches must assess and improve their communication structure and develop missional leadership. Especially the younger generations may have various questions and critiques of church and faith a communication channel inviting such questions is missing in most churches.[25] Faith is reduced to something to be believed in and trusted rather than something to explore, and churches do not tolerate questions very well. Kang Young-an criticizes this

---

[24] R. Paul Stevens, *Liberating the Laity* (Vancouver, B.C.: Regent College Publishing, 1984).

[25] Jae-hyung Jung. *Kyo-hoe an-na-ka-nŭn kŭ-li-sŭ-to-in ka-na-an sŏng-to-lŭl ŏ-ttŏh-ke i-hae-hal kŏs-in-ka?* [How should we understand canaan saints who don't attend church?], (Seoul: IVP, 2015), 78.

tendency as anti-intellectualism.[26] In this lack of communication structure pastors proclaim messages behind the pulpit without taking questions, and in small group meetings and fellowships the congregants focus only on applying the given answers rather than conducting authentic and open discussions.[27] Church-centered mission programs are attuned to the numerical growth of the church, so they tend to focus on events that can produce results in the short-term, such as evangelism crusades or mega projects. Rather than long-term considerations and study of the essence of the church and the gospel, visible results are all-important.[28] To get results in the short-term, top-down implementation is much more efficient than collaboration and debate. Such a tendency is communicated through various church training programs. In catechism classes such as Bible studies and discipleship training as well, rather than attending to the learners' varied questions that do not fit into the Christian mold, faith is taught to instill a set of correct answers. The result is the formation of passive Christians. A gospel program already theorized and catechized by others was imposed on the learners without giving opportunities with deeper questions of life. Such training that separates faith and life cannot narrow the gap between Christians in the church and secular people in the world. The outcome is the mismatch between Christians' knowledge and life.[29] Bae Jong-seok, Yang Hyeok-seung, and Ryu Ji-seong identify the Korean church's problem as its irrational, vertical, and hierarchical structure that makes all church members including the pastor forget that they are all equal before God. Due to centralized authority and tensions around it, it is difficult for the laity to participate in church administration. When tensions arise among different departments there is no other department to mediate the tension.[30]

Open and Authentic Stance

Paulo Freire explains the concept of dialogue stating that dialogue starts when the teacher is in a position to learn. When both the teacher and the learner are ready to learn, they together go through a process of change. Dialogue is a process where teachers and learners both recognize problems, interact with each other, and become conscientized as a community.[31] Dialogue is a process of true listening. The speaker can sense when the listener is simply waiting for one's turn to speak. We must work hard to listen well and to accept that listening may require us to respond through change.

---

[26] Young-an Kang, "Kyo-hoe an-ŭi pan-chi-sŏng-chu-ŭi, ŏ-ttŏh-ke kŭk-pok-hal kŏs-in-ka?" [How should we overcome anti-intellectualism in the church?] In *Han-kuk kyo-hoe, kae-hyŏk-ŭi kil-ŭl mut-ta* [Korean Church, Path of Reform] (Seoul: Saemulgyeol Plus), 38-54.

[27] Jae-hyung Jung, 81-92.

[28] Kook Il Han, Missional Church in the viewpoint of the Korean Local Church," 96.

[29] Ibid., 97-99.

[30] Jong-seok Bae, et al, *Kŏn-kang-han-kyo-hoe, i-lŏh-ke se-un-ta* [Raising up a healthy church] (Seoul: IVP, 2008), 147.

[31] Paulo Freire, *Pedagogy of the oppressed (revised)." New York: Continuum* 356 (1996).

A perfect theological and ecclesiological concept will only result in negative outcomes if unilaterally imposed rather than communicated through persuasion. Cho Ju-hee defines this as purposive communication and everyday communication. If the board members and the congregation already have a relationship of trust through everyday communications, new challenging situations and issues can be approached and solutions found together as a community. This is communication not just to educate or persuade on pre-determined answers but relational communication through which all parties seek the answer together.

When Seongam Church commissioned a consultation, they primarily worked on communication and education. This needed to be more than a perfunctory communication, where the pastor and a small group of leaders try to persuade and impose on the rest of the church a pre-determined agenda. The church members, the local community residents, and the objective assessment of expert consultants were all collected to consider and debate together. The board of elders and other church officers met even more frequently to discuss the direction of change. Through this process, the church could recognize themselves as the subject of change, not the external consultants.

Sustained Communication

To achieve ecclesiological transformation and have the congregation and the local residents recognize that they are agents of change, conversing on shared interests in day-to-day life is necessary. Change does not happen at formal events such as weekly services and sermons or board meetings; communication at these meetings alone may cause misunderstandings. There must be ways to maximize both formal and informal contact. And the more detailed the conversation content, the better. Over-explaining is better than vague and unclear directives. Informational materials should be produced on paper if necessary to explain projects fully, and there must be time for questions and answers. Even after an event or project is terminated, there must be ways to gather opinions to improve the existing system.

In the case of Seongam Church its pilot projects are notable. Through consultation, several practical suggestions were given. But before the church implemented new permanent ministry programs, they conducted pilot projects on their library, café, and care programs. A pilot project allows for a trial run for a set amount of time to receive feedback, improve the program, and decide on the next step.[32] In other words, Seongam Church was open to feedback.

Sustained External Support and Encouragement

Getting an organization or outsider's objective assessment and encouragement on church ministry or campaigns is often necessary. At times, it is easy to focus so much on internal matters that we forget the value of ministry. Getting outside evaluation is also a good way to redirect internal tensions.

---

[32] Jang-ro Lee, Kyo-hoe-kyŏng-yŏng-hak [Study of church administration] (Seoul: PCK Book, 2016), 53-56.

Seongam Church approached the transition from a traditional to a missional church in the form of a project. In 14 months, they had an external organization gather data and conduct surveys to assess the distinct needs of the community and the status of the church in the community. Visible results in the aftermath led to the church being mentioned by other churches as well as local media as a model church. The positive feedback then functioned as a basis for other collaborative programs in a virtuous cycle. It led to collaborations with the Eunpyeong District Office, and the District Office of Education (DOE) for Town Youth Care. The district financed it, the DOE mobilized the youth, and the church planned the specific program to conduct the weekend program. For Gong Gam Camp, 100 children in the Sunday School and the community came to the event that a third-party organization managed. Sunday School teachers participated in the program, which could naturally instill in the church members that community service is also church service. It was also an opportunity to bridge between church and community. Feedback received at the program's end contributed to objectively updating and assessing the ministry.

Conclusion

With the case of Seongam Church we saw how a traditional church planted in the industrial era could transition to become a missional church. The change in ecclesiology was the most important factor needed to shift from the old to the new paradigm. This means more than theoretical change. It requires qualitative change that the pastor and the congregation can understand and live by. The pastor's role is very important in assisting the church members to understand the various theoretical concepts of missional ecclesiology. It does not happen through simple information relay but requires trust-building in everyday relationships. The pastor's leadership is also a key factor. Charismatic leadership can be reinterpreted to include dispersive leadership and efforts to listen to different groups and negotiate between them to lead everyone toward a certain direction. Such ecclesiology and pastoral leadership require the process of dialogue. Through authentic dialogue of mutual learning rather than purposive communication, the church can listen to the local community and commit to actual change.

Seongam Church's ministry programs and change process showcase the theories mentioned in this essay. The construction of Vision Center led them to commit to more assertive change. Months of consultation allowed the church to listen to the local community. The pastor used bilingual skills to approach new ecclesiology as something that supplements, not negates, the old. And the pastor sustained the dynamism for change through sensitive and frequent contact with different parties. He distributed the authority, but ultimately, he was rediscovered as the key leader in the process.

Circumstances will continue to change. Paradigms are not stagnant but dynamic. A paradigm that was once new will encounter unexplainable outliers and will have to undergo another reform. But if we listen to one another, contemplate the most important matters together, and continue to be humble in studying the reign of God, changes in the future will not be something to be feared but hoped for.

Bibliography

Bae, Jong-seok. "Cho-chik-ch'e-lo-sŏ-ŭi kyo-hoe-wa chang-lo-ŭi yŏk-hal," [Role of the church and elders as institutional bodies] In Hyung-gee Lee, et al., *Kyo-hoe chik-che-lon: han-kuk kyo-hoe chik-che kae-sŏn-ŭl wi-han mo-saek* [Offices of the church: Strategies to improve the offices of the korean church]. Seoul: Yeyoung, 2012, 240-248.

Bae, Jong-seok, et al. *Kŏn-kang-han-kyo-hoe, i-lŏh-ke se-un-ta* [Raising up a healthy church]. Seoul: IVP, 2008, 147.

Choi, Dongkyu. "A Critique from the Perspective of Church Growth on the GOCN's Missionl Ecclesiology." *Theology of Mission* 25 (2010), 238-241.

Freire, Paulo. "Pedagogy of the oppressed (revised)." *New York: Continuum* 356 (1996).

Frost, Michael, and Alan Hirsch. *The shaping of things to come: Innovation and mission for the 21st-century church.* Grand Rapids, MI: Baker Books, 2013.

Han, Kook-il. "Missional Church in the viewpoint of the Korean Local Church." *Mission and Theology* 30, 2012, 90-96.

________. "Missional Church's Practical Models and Principles: Missional Church that Learns from the Fields of Korean Church." *Theology of Mission* 36, 2014, 361.

________. *Sŏn-kyo-chŏk kyo-hoe-ŭi i-lon-kwa sil-che* [Theory and practice of missional church]. Seoul: PUTS Press, 2016.

Hirsch, Alan. *The forgotten ways: Reactivating the missional church.* Grand Rapids, MI: Brazos Press, 2006.

Jung, Jae-hyung. *Kyo-hoe an-na-ka-nŭn kŭ-li-sŭ-to-in ka-na-an sŏng-to-lŭl ŏ-ttŏh-ke i-hae-hal kŏs-in-ka?* [How should we understand canaan saints who don't attend church?]. Seoul: IVP, 2015.

Kang, Young-an. "Kyo-hoe an-ŭi pan-chi-sŏng-chu-ŭi, ŏ-ttŏh-ke kŭk-pok-hal kŏs-in-ka?" [How should we overcome anti-intellectualism in the church?] In *Han-kuk kyo-hoe, kae-hyŏk-ŭi kil-ŭl mut-ta* [Korean Church, Path of Reform]. Seoul: Saemulgyeol Plus, 38-54.

Kuhn, Thomas S. *The Structure of the Scientific Revolutions.* Fourth edition, University of Chicago Press, 2012.

Lee, Jang-ro. Kyo-hoe-kyŏng-yŏng-hak [Study of church administration].Seoul: PCK Book, 2016, 53-56.

Lee, Hyung-gee, et al., *Kyo-hoe chik-che-lon: han-kuk kyo-hoe chik-che kae-sŏn-ŭl wi-han mo-saek* [Offices of the church: Strategies to improve the offices of the korean church]. Seoul: Yeyoung, 2012.

Moon, Seong-hong. *Kyŏng-hŏm-hak-sŭp p'ŏ-sil-li-t'e-i-syŏn* [Experiential learning facilitation]. Seoul: Real Learning, 2021.

Roxburgh, Alan J. and Darrell L. Guder ed., *Missional Church: A Vision for the Sending of the Church in North America.* Grand Rapids, MI: Wm.

B.Eardmans Publishing Co., 1998, 300-310.

Stevens, R. Paul. *Liberating the Laity*. Vancouver, B.C.: Regent College Publishing, 1984.

Sung, Seok-hwan. *Chi-yŏk-kong-tong-ch'e-wa ham-kke-ha-nŭn kyo-hoe-ŭi sae-lo-un to-chŏn-tŭl* [New challenges of the church that stands with the local community]. Seoul: PCK Research Center, 2018.

Together with Neighbors beyond Church Walls

Hong-sun Kim

For Healthy Church and Proper Ministry (Matthew 16:18)

My Maeul Ministry Story

I started ministry the year I graduated from seminary in 1985. My first placement was in a rural town (Yanghwa Church in Jochiwon which today became Muldaendongsan Church in the city of Sejong) where I ministered for six years (1985-1990). Then I served as an assistant pastor of Ansan Myungsung Church for four years (1990-1993). Then I was the head pastor of Cheonghak Church in Youngdo located in Busan (which today became Seonhan Iut Church) for nine years (1993-2001), returning to Ansan Myungsung in 2001 as the 20th pastor. I had been here ever since. This is the 69th year of Ansan Myungsung Church's founding.

I am the 20th pastor so you could guess what the 69-year history of this church was like. Some pastors stayed two years, others one, and some did not even stay a year. The head pastor when I served as the assistant served for ten years before his retirement. As for myself if I add the four years as the assistant pastor and 22 as the head pastor, I have been in this church for 26 years, which is longer than any other pastor.

When I came back to this church it was in bad shape. Lots of people left because of internal strife, and people who stayed were deeply hurt. The most painful thing was that the church division made the people lose all trust in pastors. I even heard in the early days from other pastors in the region the shameful comments that Myungsung Church made it difficult to evangelize in Ansan.

Ansan Myungsung Church is the second oldest church in downtown Ansan. There is Seong Gwang Church nearby which is well over a hundred years old. Our church started when a fraction of congregants in Seong Gwang started a new church. There is also Ansan Jeil Church of the Presbyterian Church of Korea – Tonghap that started eight years after us. We three churches boast long history and tradition at the center of Ansan. But at the time I came as head pastor our church was not living up to its history and name, and was merely a nuisance and an offense that blocks evangelism.

So when I became the head pastor I shared a prayer request with the church. "God, please make amazing things happen in this church. Surprise the people who say 'what good can come of Myungsung Church'."

Since then the congregation and I discussed what kind of church we should be as we made sense of the chaos and built ourselves up, and discussed the kinds of things we must do for the society.

"Healthy church, proper ministry" has been my motto since the beginning of my ministry career in seminary. I tried my best to maintain the church's health, and I consistently tried to do ministry properly. Wherever I did ministry, from my first ministry placement in rural Yanghwa township to the metropolis of Busan, or the mid-sized city of Ansan where I am today, "Healthy church, proper ministry" continues to be my aim and calling.

Today many pastors and laypeople are at a crossroads in deciding whether to raise up a healthy church and do proper ministry. I think such wrestling is a holy endeavor. Of course, some pastors may be concerned with ways to grow the number of church members or ways to prepare for comfortable post-retirement years, but these concerns are only partial. Most of the right-thinking pastors are no doubt regarding the present state of the Korean church and asking, "How can the church become healthy?" and "How can pastors minister properly?"

Any healthy pastor must keep asking "What kind of minister should I be?", "What kind of ministry must be done?", "What kind of church should be nurtured?", and "Am I properly walking on the path of my calling?" Healthy ministry is also defined by its direction rather than speed. A pastor must always check on the direction rather than the speed of ministry.

Becoming a Well-rounded Pastor

The key to a healthy church is balance and the key to proper ministry is the spirit of Coram Deo. The pastor should be well-rounded in terms of spirituality, professionalism, and moral standards. There are many pastors who are said to be spiritual but are socially problematic. The reason is their moral failure. They are famous all over the world and hold crusades in Korea and other countries, but I see them falling overnight not for their lack of spirituality but due to immorality. That is why a pastor must recognize one's weaknesses to supplement them and achieve a balance. Being especially talented in one aspect may be beneficial but also risky. The World Health Organization defines health as a state of physical, mental, emotional, and social health. Being healthy only in the physical aspect cannot be assessed as healthy. In the same way, the pastor must be healthy in terms of spirituality, professionalism, and morality.

A church must also be well-rounded in aspects of prayer, knowledge of the Word, and praise. Some churches emphasize prayer alone, others only Bible study, and still others praise. But all three are key elements in being filled with the Holy Spirit, so all three elements must exist. A pastor is not a superman and cannot be great at all tasks, so the laypeople and other ministers must be entrusted with tasks the head pastor cannot do in order for the church to tend to all three aspects. This is the role of the pastor. Some leave a church because there is no prayer, though the preaching is good. Others leave because the preaching is shallow even if the prayers are deep. And other young people leave because there is only prayer and preaching, and the praise isn't exciting. Christians with unbalanced diet is a problem but the church must also strive to achieve balance in prayer, word, and praise,

In addition, the church must also be balanced externally in evangelism, service, and mission. Our church motto is "Redemption of the soul through evangelism, redemption of society through service, redemption of the world through mission." Evangelism, service, and mission must all be conducted depending on the church's capacity, whether much or little.

If such balance is the key to a healthy church, the key to proper ministry is the spirit of Coram Deo, meaning the pastor must always remember that they stand before God. Am I a pastor when no one is looking? Any pastor can act like one in the presence of another person. But am I really a pastor when I am alone? At a market when nobody knows what I do, when I am traveling, when I am driving, when I am alone, I must examine if I am living as a pastor. That is how ministry can be properly done.

Sharing as an Expression of Love for Neighbors

Love for neighbors should be practiced concretely, not just through words, slogans, or catchphrases. Churches should actively engage in sharing. Church resources should be used for minimal self-sustenance then the rest should be shared. Churches may gather and save resources perhaps in the short term for specific objectives, but they should not consider gathering real estate or financial wealth to amass money in the bank as a mark of successful ministry and favor of God.

The church's calling to love the neighbors must be practiced through sharing. Whether a church is large or small, located in the countryside or the city is not important. If a church shares even a little, it is closer to its essence. If a church is not sharing because it is still small, still cannot afford it, or is still getting financial assistance, then it is farther from the essence of the church. Whether large or small, a church must always share with others.

For this purpose, Ansan Myungsung Church aims to be "always a friendly neighbor." Through continued sharing since 2001, our church changed from an object of scorn to one of appreciation. That was not achieved by organized spirit-filled revival gatherings for ourselves, by speaking in tongues, or being full of joy all on our own. People outside the church have no idea about such things and have nothing to do with it. But as our church opened ourselves up to the local community and approached them diligently and authentically, one day, we came to be appreciated by the community. Things happened to surprise the people who said, "What good can come of Myungsung Church."

Ansan Myungsung Church grew in numbers, in maturity, and in spirituality not though traditional evangelism but through maeul ministry. We continue to be a church aiming for balanced and healthy church growth.

Our church formed a permanent organization called Community Service Center to participate in community welfare needs throughout the year. There are also several service programs that happen annually.

- New Year Celebration inviting the town head and other community leaders (January after the calendar new year)
- New Year Celebration inviting the elderly leaders (February after the Lunar New Year)
- Dedication Service inviting families with adopted children for adoption promotion (May)
- Festival for Local Seniors (May)
- Well-being Concert for local residents (July)

- Blood Donation Drive Sunday (April)
- Cheoncheon Solomon Scholarship Award (November)
- Thanksgiving Fruit Basket Delivery (November)
- Christmas Giving for Gojan-dong
- Organic Produce Market and Joint Worship Service of urban and rural churches (November)
- Sharing love with neighbors on holidays (New Year, Chuseok, Christmas, Easter, Feast of Weeks, Thanksgiving)
- Sharing love with neighbors every month (Santa's Gifts to Neighbors on the 24th of each month)
- Isaac's Well Program (Provided 242 wells in Cambodia, one well per village, under the slogan "Turning Killing Fields into Healing Fields.")

These social mission programs can be categorized into three.

The first category is social mission financed with our church's own resources. The human, material, and spiritual resources are used to operate the Community Service Center where Dasol Library, Elim Café, Shalom Senior Center, and Daniel Tutoring operate entirely on church resources.

The second category is programs financed with public funding. We are operating two service centers (Danwon District Senior Center, Seonbu General Social Service Center) with financing from the local government. There are about a hundred paid staff working at these two centers. Adding other annual financings from the government, the centers operate on a budget of KRW 6 billion. These are programs that our church cannot operate alone. With support from the local government, we are providing services to seniors, North Korean defectors, the lower-income population, and the children, from the cradle to the grave.

The third category of service is operated in collaboration with the local residents. A cooperative is an excellent method of missions for this age. In December 2012 the legal basis was laid to allow any five people to form a cooperative together. The Good Village Cooperative was started at this time. Social cooperatives are well suited to Christian values, Methodist theology, and the Wesleyan tradition of social mission. A church need not be big or have much capital to start one. Through various town cooperatives or social cooperatives a church can practice love for neighbors. Ansan Myungsung is operating a social cooperative café called Beautiful Lamp and Energy Market Branch 2 for the environment, commissioned by the city government of Ansan.

For these various social mission programs there are several ongoing prayer requests that I always remind our congregation.

- May our church lay paths rather than build fortresses
- May our church raise up workers rather than buildings
- May our church experience spiritual growth rather than numerical growth
- May there be more happy Christians than successful Christians in our church
- May our church share and disperse rather than gather and amass

- May our church have the power of holiness rather than the appearance of holiness
- May our church be full of labor of love rather than tongues of angels
- May our congregation be people who believe well and live well

As we aim to become a healthy church doing proper ministry, we remember the words of Jesus who builds his church and the gates of Hades will not prevail against it (Matthew 16:18). Myungsung Church (教會) can be redefined as (交會).[1] A church is more a fellowship of service and friendship through worship and liturgy, rather than a group of people teaching and learning. So the church is 交會, a combination of communion and the community that communicates, a diakoinonia that combines diakonia and koinonia.

Weep with those who Weep (Romans 12:15): Lest we Forget and Witness another Shipwreck

On April 16, 2014, 304 people aboard Sewol Ferry en route to the beautiful and peaceful island of Jeju drowned in an absurd tragedy, the majority of them Danwon High School students on a school trip. The drowning surfaced the shameful reality of South Korea. The Sewol Ferry Disaster became a trauma for all citizens who lost the sense of security and a stigma for the nation that did not protect its people.

Ansan 安山 had always been a peaceful town, but no longer. Our church decided to make a space for rest and renewal to heal the trauma and erase the stigma. That is how Healing Center 0416 Rest and Renewal was set up. The purpose of this center was healing for the victims and renewal for the community in obedience to the Word to weep with those who weep. The intention was to make space for those who mourned the loss of their loved ones and give them space to rest.

On September 15, five months after the tragedy, our church cooperated with Seonbu General Social Service Center (Director Hwang In-deuk) – the oldest social service center in Ansan – and Counseling and Coaching Support Center of Yonsei University (Dr. Kwon Su-young) – a university established on Christian aims – to make space for healing from the Sewol Ferry Disaster and renewal for the local community. Our church proposed the need for a permanent space for psychological support after the disaster, improvement of quality of life, and community building for residents in Gojan-il-dong, Gojan-sam-dong, and Wa-dong where most families affected by the tragedy live. At this center, we would operate programs to restore the city and the town community and to promote the value of life and safety.

[1] Translator's Note: The Korean word for church is *gyohwe*, where *gyo*'s root *Hanja* character is 教 (teaching) and *hwe* is 會 (gathering). Hence *gyohwe* 交會 may be understood as a gathering where teaching and learning happens. 交會 is also read as *gyohwe*, but the character for *gyo* has been substituted with 交 (fellowship).

Myungsung Church at the center of Ansan has been a church in the area for about 60 years, so we wanted to do our part to be with those who mourn and support the vulnerable. So we provided the space and the financial resources to serve the community residents in their healing and renewal and for the restoration of the local community.

Seonbu General Social Service Center which our church is commissioned by the city of Ansan to operate has also been fulfilling its mission and social responsibility to conduct recovery programs and manage affected households. Also as an organization that operates local cultural and social service programs, it operates a Recovery Center to support the local residents and disaster victims in sharing their stories and grief in structured, professional, and sustainable settings. As a valued heritage of the Korean church, Yonsei University is an institution that aims to serve society, the nation, the people, and humanity. Its Counseling and Coaching Support Center in the United Graduate School of Theology sent counseling specialists to support traumatized residents as they recover psychological and emotional health. The cooperation of this influential educational institution added social capital to our endeavor, and the program also contributed to university efforts at social responsibility.

In addition, a network was formed among Ansan On Maeum Center constructed by the Ministry of Health and Social Service for psychological counseling, Ansan Medical Service Social Cooperative for physical recovery, and Dail Community for spiritual wellness as the Healing Chain Memorandum of Understanding was signed. For the recovery of the community, we also formed cooperative relationships with Ansan Volunteers Center and Gojan-dong Resident Self-Governance Center to construct a local healing and recovery system.

Local church response to Sewol Ferry Disaster had to be more than a one-time service event but professional, systematic, and sustainable. So Healing Center 0416 Rest and Renewal was the platform through which we conducted various programs.

After the disaster an invisible wall was erected between those who lost their loved ones and the other residents. Because it was impossible to break down the wall directly, we tried to make a path to confront the present, remember the past, and expect the future. We paved a walkway from the Sewol Ferry Memorial to Danwon High School by Ansan Myungsung Church and named it Precious Path of Life – Danwon Path of Renewal. People walking from one end to another could reflect on the value of life and safety, and as the more people visited the path, gradually the wall was broken down.

In this unspeakable disaster, to redirect the grief and mourning into sustainable healing and recovery, the residents of affected towns formed the Family Orchestra and the Senior Choir to conduct an annual memorial concert to gather the affected households and their neighbors together to promote solidarity. For three years from 2015 to 2017 this neighborhood memorial concert called *Eungwon* (meaning encouragement) was organized. Our church's Sewol Ferry Memorial Sunday where we invite families of victims has continued for the past nine years.

The Counseling and Coaching Program that was conducted for three years now turned into a service for various other needs. The professional counseling program for various individual and communal experiences and circumstances receives highly favorable feedback. More people have been seeking help by word of mouth, from families of victims, to friends, and to other neighbors. Programs such as the Parental Education and Coaching Program, Couples Therapy, Movement Therapy for Youth, Group Play Therapy for Children, and Senior Coaching Program have helped people transition from their crisis state to normality. Movement Therapy for Youth for the Danwon High School students was highly effective in supporting the youth through the grieving process after the disaster.

In April each year, the residents gather for the Neighborhood Memorial Flower Shop to make bouquets or potted plants out of donated flowers to share with families that lost their loved ones and their neighbors to show neighborly love as we remember together. Also, through "Let's Grab a Bite" the affected families and their neighbors had meals together on the Community Service Center rooftop to interact and try to bridge any gaps in perspectives, resulting in stronger relationships.

For Man Gae Neighborhood Workshop, families of victims with handicraft skills taught residents to make creative artworks to put on exhibitions and sales. In this program, the parents of the youth who passed away were more than somebody's mother but teachers. And as teachers they could recover their sense of self.

Healing Center 0416 Rest and Renewal which has been conducting these programs has been cited as an exemplary case of a program supporting disaster recovery that combined spirituality, local context, and expertise. In an age when a disaster can happen to anyone at any time, this is an innovative example of civil society recovery effort applicable elsewhere in the nation. When a disaster happens, the religious organization in the area can cooperate with the local social service organization and the specializing higher education institution to provide a private sector recovery effort that is entirely distinct from the public sector.

For three years after 2014, Ansan Myungsung Church spent KRW 537 million to operate Healing Center 0416 Rest and Renewal for recovery from Sewol Ferry Disaster without receiving any funding from the government or the denomination, financing it entirely by church donations and other project funding. In 2018 it was restructured as Gojan-dong Cultural Social Service Center Rest and Healing for local renewal and community building. Programs for healing, restoration, and memorial continue as our church fulfills our role as a neighborhood church. The neighborhood church, the social service center, and the university counseling center together laid the stones and the willing support of many sparked the fire around which the victims of disaster could gather for rest and renewal. Everything worked out for good by the grace of God.

On the day of the disaster Sewol Ferry disappeared under water. But by the ninth year since the disaster, we know that the 304 victims are somewhere in heaven comforting us and reminding us of the value of life and safety. Now the neighborhood and the church must be the healers. The grief and the pain should be redirected for solidarity and encouragement for the precious people to live another day in a new land. Remember lest we witness shipwreck again. And heal. Weep with those who weep (Romans 12:15).

Conclusion: Essence of Maeul Ministry and its Evaluation

Approach to Maeul Ministry

Ansan Myungsung Church aims to be a church that stands with the community, in the community, and among the community. There are a few requirements in maeul ministry.

The first is to know the town. The church must know the history of the town and the characteristics of the population – their gender, age, type of residence, and income level. Then the church must also know the present state of the town in terms of the local government, educational institutions, religious institutions, business facilities, and public facilities.

The second requirement is to know the church itself. The church must accurately assess the human, material, and spiritual resources it has and can gather. The church leaders' awareness of and motivation for maeul ministry should also be assessed. Is the church open to others or closed? Does it tend toward gathering people or sending them out to the world? Does the church have a presence in the community, and does the laity have a firm ecclesiology? Are they aware of the church's social responsibility to fulfill its public function? Assessing these matters will be key to preventing obstacles at later stages.

Third, for a church to conduct maeul ministry it must let people see that it is a church that laid down its authority and is actively approaching people first to share resources. This is done through active and frequent contact with the residents in daily life. The church should be present in community celebrations and tragedies and get involved in issues and long-term projects with material and human resources. The church can practice sharing out of available resources and assess to what extent the church is willing.

Fourth, the congregation should be raised up to be town volunteers rather than volunteering only in the church. They should be encouraged to participate in the township, the town, the resident association, and the women's association as members or to run for elections so that they can bridge between the church and the town.

Fifth, church space and facilities, after the Sunday service is done, shouldn't be left empty during the weekdays but be made available for public use. The church building, facilities, parking lot, various programs and tools can be happily lent as shared resources for local community events. This can be helpful to starting a maeul ministry.

Community Confessions for Maeul Ministry

Maeul ministry requires endless self-evaluation and reflection by the pastor and the laity. Is this ministry appropriate for our faith? Is it theologically, socially, or publicly sound? Then the community must ask the following questions.

1. Does our church have an authentic calling and mission for maeul ministry?
2. Does our church approach maeul ministry as a matter of social responsibility and confession of faith?
3. Does our church have a strategy to conduct maeul ministry professionally, systematically, and sustainably?
4. Is the maeul ministry of our church aiming to provide public good rather than simply operating as a tool for conversion and church growth?
5. Does our church confess that the ultimate goal of maeul ministry is love of neighbor in action reaching beyond boundaries?

Finally, I end this essay with excerpts that give a sense of outsider assessment of Ansan Myungsung Church's maeul ministry. They are a press interview I gave and the associated article, and a letter to the church from a mother of a victim of the Sewol Ferry disaster who is herself a practicing Buddhist.

Assessment of Maeul Ministry for
Healing Restoration from Sewol Ferry Disaster

Interview: Hong-sun Kim, pastor of Ansan Myungsung Church "Don't forget the lesson of Sewol Ferry" (Issue Time Correspondence. 2017.9.18. Yoon Young-seon. Web Edition)

I will continue to work for the recovery of our community.

It has been three years since the Sewol Ferry Disaster. But the truth of what happened has yet to be clarified. Some say there has been enough talk about it already and that we should move on. But pastor Hong-sun Kim of Ansan Myungsung Church says the Sewol Ferry Disaster is something we all must not forget, a pain we should remember throughout our lives.

Q: Six of the youth who died in the Sewol Ferry were Ansan Myungsung Church members. This must have been painful for you.
A: The Seweol Ferry Disaster was the most shocking incident of my life. Today even in the fourth year I haven't gone through a day without remembering it. The shock and the pain continue today. Myungsung Church is located right by Danwon High School, and some of our church members lost their loved ones. For me, everything about the disaster has permeated my daily life. The disaster does not leave my mind or my life.

Q: Were you also affected by the trauma?
A: Of course not to the degree of the families whose loved ones died, or the families whose loved ones' bodies have yet to be found. But for me as well, I think there is second-hand trauma. In the early days after the disaster, I did had some physical symptoms like feeling claustrophobic in a car. Now I don't feel it physically anymore, but the issue of Sewol Ferry remains large in my life.

Q: Did you seek out help for the trauma?
A: I did not. A pastor is in a position of constantly facing other people's trauma. I hear from my church members things that regular people rarely hear. If I had

severe physical symptoms from the Sewol Ferry Disaster I might have sought medical help. But after listening to so many stories, I think I became numb to it, so I haven't sought help for myself.

Q: I understand that immediately after the disaster you went down to the port. What was it like at the time?
A: What I saw when I first stepped foot into the gym at Jindo [where the families were waiting] was more shocking than anything in my life. What most stuck with me was the parents wailing in grief of losing their children. When you watch a documentary or a film, or read a novel about animals, the mother cries out when the cub is in danger or missing. It was like that. How could anyone talk sense when you don't know your child is dead or alive? It was not one but hundreds of parents screaming and wailing in grief, and others who were so exhausted they couldn't make a sound, all at the same time.

Q: The town must have been grieving as well.
A: Of the 304 people who died in the disaster, 250 of them were Danwon High School students. I visited the high school for the funeral of every single one of the students except the several whose bodies haven't been found. For five straight days, 250 funeral buses drove by the church. Everyone in town must have seen that funeral procession. The town is usually very welcoming and lively, but at the time it was just very dark and silent. Everyone was swallowing their tears in silence as they said goodbye to the children in their prime.

Q: Healing Center 0416 Rest and Renewal was established beside the church. What led to this development?
A: We defined healing as cure and recovery. The target populations are two groups, the families who lost their loved ones and the neighbors in town who had been indirectly affected. When things like this happen, we never had practice or experience on ways to support the victims. So it leads to misunderstanding on both sides. The neighbors are careful to avoid saying something insensitive and hurtful so they are wary of speaking up. But the families also desperately need someone to listen to their stories. The families of the victims in the beginning were going to Gwanghwamun, Yeoido [National Assembly], and Paengmok Port, but they eventually had to return home. And I figured there should be a space where they can find someone to comfort them and cry with them once they return.

Q: You mean the healing and recovery space was made in preparation for the families to return home?
A: That's right. Think of it as kind of like turning up the heater before people come in. If the heater is turned on after coming home on a cold day, it's still cold for some time. But if you set a timer to turn on the heater beforehand, the house is warm by the time you return home. Healing Center 0416 Rest and Renewal is like that. We are pre-heating the town ahead of the families who return after facing the cold winds.

Q: Please describe the specific programs conducted at Healing Center 0416 Rest and Renewal.
A: The programs can be generally divided into counseling and community recovery. For counseling that's exactly what is done, counseling people. And for community recovery, we try to comfort the town residents with cultural content. There is the Family Orchestra, the Healing Dance Youth Musical, and the Cheongchoon Song Class. The Cheongchoon Song Class is for the seniors. The elderly who lost their grandchildren and had to watch their children grieving their loss were comparatively neglected. This program helped them to process their grief and pain.

Q: I understand that when the Healing Center was established the plan was to operate it for three years, maximum. What will happen to it now?
A: The Healing Center building was constructed a year before the Sewol Ferry Disaster for the purpose of community service. So it will return to its original function of being the community center for social service and cultural programming. But the operations will not completely change. The community recovery programs will continue on. We plan to keep working to share the joys and pains of the neighbors so that the disaster trauma can be healed.

Q: What is one last thing you would like to say to the readers?
A: The Sewol Ferry Disaster is a major disaster of our time. But there is one lesson we can learn, and that is the value of life and safety of the citizens. I hope we don't forget this lesson of the Sewol Ferry Disaster. Also, the yellow ribbons or the yellow ribbon badges are really healing and supportive for the affected families. So I hope we continue to stand with them in this way. That way our society's capacity to empathize will grow, and ultimately our society will grow to become a thriving place.

Accompanying News Article: Closing Service for the Sewol Ferry Disaster Healing and Recovery Space: Healing Center 0416 Rest and Renewal (Christian Today 2017.9.18. Kim Shin-ui)

Healing Center 0416 Rest and Renewal (hereafter Rest and Renewal) was established after the Sewol Ferry Disaster to comfort the families of victims and the neighbors and to support their lives in the aftermath. The three-year program has now ended and is looking to a new start.

On April 16, 2014, the Sewol Ferry sank in the sea off the coast of Jindo resulting in over 300 dead and missing. Especially painful for the whole nation was that aboard the ship were hundreds of Danwon High School students in their youthful prime on the way to a school field trip.

On the 150th day after the disaster on September 15, Healing Center 0416 Rest and Renewal began operations at Elim House by Danwon High School in Gojan-dong. It was a collaboration among the Counseling and Coaching Support Center of Yonsei University (Soo-young Kwon, Director), Ansan Myungsung Church of the United Methodist Church (Hong-sun Kim, Pastor), and Seonbu General Social Service Center (In-deuk Hwang, Director).

Rest and Renewal did four types of work in conducting 31 creative and innovative programs, networking, mobilization, and space rental. 19,377 residents of Gojan-dong and the city of Ansan participated.

Programs in Rest and Renewal showed a successful model of civil society collaboration. The local social service center, a religious organization, and a counseling institution cooperated to meet the needs of the local residents and work for communal recovery. It is evaluated as having reached the stated goal.

Last Sunday, on the 17th at the sanctuary of Ansan Myungsung Church a thanksgiving service was held to appreciate the achievements of the past three years and declare the center's rebirth as a cultural and social service community center of Gojan-dong. Professor Soo-young Kwon of Yonsei University who was a board member of Rest and Renewal delivered the sermon, and the staff of Seonbu General Social Service Center gave a special musical performance. Plaquettes of appreciation were awarded to Korean Christian Counseling Association for their sustained financial support and to the Counseling and Coaching Support Center of Yonsei University. The mother of Soojin who was a second-year student in class number 9 of Danwon High School represented the families of the victims to express gratitude for Rest and Renewal that had consistently comforted and supported them for the past three years.

Soo-young Kwon, a professor at the United Theological Graduate School of Yonsei University highly assessed the program, stating, "The general service offered by the collaboration of the local church, the university, and the local community service center was a new experiment that showed the potential for public ministry to support the local community's healing and recovery. The church willingly opened itself up to become the inviting fireplace for the entire town."

Hong-sun Kim, the pastor of Ansan Myungseong Church stated that the ministry of Rest and Renewal is at a point of new start. He promised that the church will continue to do its best for this place to be a sacred space commemorating the value of life and safety for Gojan-dong as well as the entire city of Ansan.

While Rest and Renewal ended its three-year disaster recovery support service on September 15 as planned, there is a continued need for the center to try new programs to build resident capacity for local community recovery. It will continue to be operated as Gojan's cultural and community service center.

Letter from Hoseong's Mom

I never knew.

I really never dreamt I would lose my all like this. That I would end up like this!

I didn't have the courage to keep living in this town where my son is no more.

As a parent who couldn't protect her child, I couldn't handle the sympathetic glances of the neighbors

Or the reality that my son is no longer living.

As a mother who lost her son, not knowing what else to do, I went from place to place, from Ansan most affected by the Sewol Ferry Disaster, to Paengmok

Port, to Gwanghwamun Square, to Yeoido, and I didn't have the wherewithal to think about my neighbors. After a while when I returned to Ansan I noticed the hostile stares of Ansan residents, and that really hurt.

Lots of people were believing all the false information reported by the media.

I worried how I might meet with the people.

That was when Myungsung Church set out a time during their Sunday service for us to meet with the neighbors. The church consistently stood by our children.

At the Healing Center 416 Rest and Renewal, the 416 Workshop mother-teachers could have space to meet with Gojan-dong residents.

And we could converse with them in our cross-stitching, quilting, organic make-up, sock knitting, and woodcraft classes.

Through that opportunity, the mother-teachers of 416 Workshop continue to be active in Ansan.

I remember it all. Thank you, Myungsung Church and the staff of Rest and Renewal who welcomed us warmly.

The city of Ansan my son used to love, Gojan-dong where my son was born.

In hopes that Ansan may no longer be a city of pain but a city of hope…

Bu-ja Jung, mother of Hoseong, member of Mothers' Workshop,
Director of Memorial Division of 416 Family Association

"A Good Church": Maeul Ministry of Ansan Myungsung Church

Eun-ha Cho

For Maeul Ministry

The American educationist and social activist Parker J. Palmer in his *The Courage to Teach* identifies "disconnected life" as a modern cultural characteristic. People live in the structure of separation because disconnection protects us from the fears deep within us. The fears within are the following.

The first is the fear of encountering the other. It is the fear of having to accept ideas and facts we do not like. We want relationships in which our own ideas are accepted and the result of the encounter is under our control. So today when we are connected through social media 24 hours a day, we are living at a time when true connection has become most difficult. We live in an age of information explosion, but it is an age of chaos and it is difficult to discern facts and truths.

The second is the fear of diversity. We live in a pluralized world, but we fear that our own perspectives, experiences, and methods are not the only ways. Bias and intolerance are bound to increase in the age of artificial intelligence and big data analysis.

Thirdly, there is the fear of losing our identity. People mistake their thoughts to be their identity. When people's ideas are challenged through encounters, they feel their identity is threatened. That is why many encounters remain only competitive or shallow, and we continue to live in this structure of separation. It is difficult to experience empathy, understanding, and care in this age of alienation.[1]

"I am because we are. Ubuntu!"

This is a common greeting in Bantu language in Africa. I am because you are, and I am because we are. It highlights the communal spirit, and became well-known thanks to Nelson Mandela. The following is a story about ubuntu.[2]

A man who was studying an African tribe gathered the children and suggested they play a game. He brought a fresh basket of sweet fruits and said whoever finishes a race first will win the fruit basket. Surprisingly the children did not try to outrun each other but held each other's hands through the race to get to the fruit basket together. They all received the prize and happily shared the fruit among themselves. The man asked the children, "The winner could have taken all the fruit. Why did hold each other's hands?" The children responded in

---

[1] Parker J. Palmer, *The courage to teach: Exploring the inner landscape of a teacher's life*. (San Francisco, CA: John Wiley & Sons, 2007).

[2] Won-hyuk Lee, "Ubuntu, I exist because you exist". *Pressian.* 20 February 2010. https://www.pressian.com/pages/articles/99518, Accessed 25 March 2024.

unison, “Ubuntu!” And one of them laughed and said, “How can I be happy when everyone else is sad?”

Likewise, can the church be happy when the world is sad? Not so. The church exists for the world. It is not the ark of salvation for the believers alone. It exists for the world for which God so loved to send God’s only son.

A community is a specific, lived context of the people whom God loves, and Jesus also did his ministry in a community. During Jesus’ time on earth, he went from town to town to proclaim the kingdom of God and sent his disciples to the towns as well. Jesus’ ministry responded to the specific issues of daily life in the towns. The church must go beyond missions and ministry to laugh, cry, and live together as a part of the town. The church must be the light and salt of the world, being the first to reach out to the most unfortunate in town.

But what is the state of our churches today? What is the world saying to the church? We must ask foundational questions. What is the role of the church in the world?[3]

Fresh consideration of the church’s role changes the target of ministry from people in the church to the town. The town that had been the object of service and mission becomes the subject of fellowship and friendship, and the church becomes actively involved in the town’s affairs. The church is no longer the ark but the companion of God’s love, and this awareness of the missional church changes the aim of ministry. More and more churches are doing maeul ministry based on missional ecclesiology. A ministry that laughs, cries, and walks together with the town is the one that follows in the steps of Jesus.

Jesus said, “Weep with those who weep.” A major command from the Bible is to care for those who are at their ends and be with those who have collapsed under hardships and difficulties.[4] Jesus incarnated into the mundane context of people’s daily lives. This is the faith of the Emmanuel.

One of the most tragic events in South Korean history was the Sewol Ferry Disaster. On April 16, 2014 the ferry of Cheonghaejin Haeun on the way to Jeju Island from Incheon capsized in the seas (Maengol Sudo) near Gwanmaedo of Jindo District in South Jeolla Province. Of the passengers, 299 died and 5 are still missing. This tragedy showed the bare face of social chaos and apathy in matters of public safety. Most of the dead (90%) belonged to Danwon High School on their way to a school field trip, and 83% of them were minors, students in the second year of high school.[5] Ansan Myungsung Methodist Church is right next to this Danwon High School.

---

[3] Eun-ha Cho, “Ma-ŭl-kwa ham-kke ha-nŭn mok-hoe-ŭi ta-yang-han sa-lye” [Various cases of ministry with the community], *Christian Thought* (Seoul: CLSK, 2020), 45-46.

[4] Bless those who persecute you; bless and do not curse them. Rejoice with those who rejoice; weep with those who weep. Live in harmony with one another; do not be arrogant, but associate with the lowly; do not claim to be wiser than you are. Do not repay anyone evil for evil, but take thought for what is noble in the sight of all. (Romans 12: 14-17).

[5]Namu Wiki, “Cheonghaejin Shipping Sewol Ferry Sinking Accident” https://namu.wiki/w/%EC%B2%AD%ED%95%B4%EC%A7%84%ED%95%B4%EC%9A%B4%20%EC%84%B8%EC%9B%94%ED%98%B8%20%EC%B9%A8%EB%AA%B0%20%EC%82%AC%EA%B3%A0, Accessed 25 March 2024.

Ansan Myungsung Church had been conducting various ministries for the community before the disaster, but with the Sewol Ferry Disaster the city of Ansan was declared a special disaster region. The whole town was in pain and despair mourning the dead. Myungsung Church walked with the town through the process of healing toward recovery and hope. How could Ansan Myungsung Church become their friend and be known as "a very good church"? I will examine several factors based on the church's pastor Hong-sun Kim's explanation of the church, my own experience of the church, interviews with church members, and analysis of the sermons and the church structure.

Missional Characteristics of Ansan Myungsung Church's Maeul Ministry

Methodist Church that Practices Wesleyan Social Gospel

John Wesley who started the Methodist Church recorded the General Rules of the Methodist Society in 1743. All who desired admission to the society had to first "do no harm", second "do good", and third "attend upon all the ordinances of God" "to evidence their desire of salvation". The Holy Club of the Methodists started in 1729 as a gathering for reading, discussions, and prayer, but eventually they participated in charity and service. They gathered the poor to educate them, visited the sick and the poor, and visited prisons as well. They practiced piety, mercy, and practical holiness. Wesley called himself a Bible Christian, which means to strictly live in accordance with the Bible. Wesley's effort to achieve the perfection of Christianity challenges our spirituality today.

> Is the love of God shed abroad in your heart Can you cry out, "My God, and my All?" Do you desire nothing but him? Are you happy in God? Is he your glory, your delight, your crown of rejoicing? And is this commandment written in your heart, "That he who loveth God love his brother also?" Do you then love your neighbour as yourself? Do you love every man, even your enemies, even the enemies of God, as your own soul as Christ loved you?[6]

Wesley calls "almost Christian" those people who have the form of piety but lost its power, those who speak of grace and faith but have no love for God and neighbors. For one to be a true Christian one must have both the love of God and the love of neighbors as oneself evidenced in action. That is why Wesley so emphasized salvation, faith, and justification. We are sanctified in action. It means to actively do good, beyond passively avoiding evil deeds. Ansan Myungsung Church is a methodist church that is based on Wesleyan spirituality and tradition.

> The British historian W. E. H. Lecky said that Methodists saved Great Britain from the potential for a violent revolution in the late 18th and the early 19th century. There is no question that the Methodist society actively practiced spiritual and lifestyle reform alongside religious training, and worked for the social respect for human

---

[6] John Wesley, "I-lŭm-ppun-in kŭ-li-sŭ-to-in" [Christian in name only], Edited by Ad Fontes Wesley. *Kŭ kil: we-sŭl-li p'yo-chun-sŏl-kyo ilk-ki*], (Seoul: CLSK, 2021).

dignity. There are critiques by some historians that the conservatism of Wesleyan social activism fundamentally limited the extent to which they could achieve social change. In practice they provided genuine support to the poor laboring class that made up 80% of the British population at the time for their self-sufficiency, which is remarkable and phenomenal.[7]

The systematic theologian Theodore Runyon interprets Wesley's soteriology as new creation and actualization of hope. For Wesley, salvation meant the societal recovery of the image of God. Therefore the problems of human society today such as human rights, economic justice, poverty, gender rights, the environment, and church unity can be approached by the church through the Wesleyan method.[8]

In this context Ansan Myungsung Church is squarely within the Wesleyan tradition. They go beyond taking the form of piety read the times, listen to the needs of their town, live alongside the neighbors, and seek out the dark corners to restore human dignity. On the way to the pulpit in Myungsung Church there is a small door through which one must stoop with humility. This ritual every Sunday symbolizes the humility with which the preacher must stand before God and approach the world. Myungsung Church's actions to comfort the distressed victims of the Sewol Ferry Disaster and their Healing Center to support them is one aspect of Wesleyan spirituality in action. The church is also concerned with issues of economic justice, poverty, and the environment, always considering how the church may respond to these issues in cooperation with the town.

Community of the People of God –
Missional Church Participating in the Mission of God

One theological revolution of the 20th century is the theology of *missio Dei* at the 1968 Uppsala Assembly of the World Council of Churches. The theology of *missio Dei* credits God as the agent of mission, and the world became the mission field. The church is the object of God's mission and love, as well as a partner in mission to the world. The church is no longer Noah's Ark with exclusive hold on salvation but a witnessing community between God and the world. This missiological structure shifted the role of Protestant churches to be world-oriented and mission-oriented, holding significant implications for church practice. There was an effort by the Roman Catholic and Protestant Churches to turn from clericalism and sacerdotalism to what the church was in its early days. It was to turn from a pastor-centered church structure and mission to become a community of the people of God.[9]

Dietrich Bonhoeffer said we live in the community of Christ and in love. The church is only the church when it exists for others. Therefore, the church exists in the world.[10] According to missional church discourse, the church exists in the

---

[7] Jin-du Kim, *We-sŭl-li-ŭi sil-ch'ŏn-sin-hak* [John Wesley's Practical Theology], (Seoul: KMC, 2010), 50-53.

[8] Ibid., 47-48.

[9] Joon-gwan Eun, *Sil-ch'ŏn-chŏk kyo-hoe-lon* [Practical ecclesiology], (Seoul: CLSK, 1998), 28-29.

[10] Stephen J. Nichols, *Bonhoeffer on the Christian Life: From the Cross, for the World.* Translated by Kim Gwang-nam. Seoul: Abba Publisher, 2014, 60-63.

world. and mission is the essence of the church. The church was established for a mission. The essence of the church is to recognize ourselves as clergy and laity sent by the triune God and to participate in the mission of God in everyday life. The concept of the mission of God starts with the existential understanding of the church and Christians. In other words, Christians are called to live in the world and are called for a mission. So a Christian living with Christian values is itself doing missions, and the essence of the missional church is to be salt and light of the world (Matthew 5:13-16) in daily life.[11] Therefore a missional church must expand its ministry sphere beyond the church to the town and to the world. It is to go beyond pastor-centered ministry to encourage laity participation and have the laity live Christian lives in all spheres of life.[12]

If mission is the essence of the church and Christians are called for mission, then mission is the process of actualizing the gospel values through life of service and coexistence. A missional church integrates action and existential understanding, integrates abstract concepts with the mundane, and is not led by a special few people but is participated by all Christians. At the basis are the principles of coexistence, openness, communication, participation, and change between church and society. If in the past the church presented itself in the local community in the form of service and evangelism, now it must present itself in terms of coexistence.[13]

Ansan Myungsung Church exists in the community. It is a church that participates in the mission of God in the world. For the New Years the first thing they do is to invite the town leader who knows the town in and out to share their concerns and cooperate for the renewal and development of the town. The church space is more than a place for worship service; it is open for the people in town to share and use. The congregants are actively involved in various town committees, and community residents and church members cooperate to win public funding for creative town programs.

These ministries are conducted not by the pastor's initiative but by the church community as the people of God. This stance led to the church's actions after the Sewol Ferry Disaster devasted the town. The church led in the healing and recovery of the townspeople. Moreover, they set up a walkway symbolizing resurrection of life to facilitate the sublimation of death into life and despair into hope.

Working to Integrate Religious Values and Social Values

The neo-Orthodox theologian Lewis Sherril explained that the Hebrew community thrived thanks to their effort to connect their religious and social values. For example, the commandments to protect the socially vulnerable in Deuteronomy was a spiritual law in the people's relationship with God, but it

---

[11] Kook Il Han, *Sŏn-kyo-chŏk kyo-hoe-ŭi i-lon-kwa sil-che* [Theory and practice of missional church], (Seoul: PUTS Press, 2016), 120.

[12] Ibid., 118-119.

[13] Eun-ha Cho, "Village Education Community and Christian Adult Education: Focusing on Middle Ages" *Theology and Praxis* (Anyang: Diacon, 2021), 520-523.

was also how the community could sustain its well-being.[14] The Hebrew community taught both the religious ordinances and social values. A tenth of the harvest had to be left for the orphans, the widows, and the sojourners to help the socially marginalized to coexist in society. Such religious ordinances were thus connected to social laws. Ansan Myungsung Church allows for moral and ethical norms of society to be naturally embodied by way of religious rituals.

An example is how Myungsung Church emphasizes filial piety as a universal human and a religious value. The church operates Shalom Filial Piety Center, inviting the seniors in town for a New Year celebration. The pastor and his wife give a traditional Korean bow in respect to the town elders. The seniors do not stand in line for the meal, but the tables are set to provide a proper meal. Before the Covid-19 pandemic, seniors were invited for a meal every Saturday, and programs were conducted to support their healthy and happy lifestyles. The fifth of the Ten Commandments tells us to honor our parents. The first four commands are about human relationships with God, and the latter six are about relationships with humans. The first command on human relationships tells us to "honor your father and your mother, so that your days may be long in the land that the Lord your God is giving you" (Acts 20:12). This is the most basic virtue of human society, an unchanging ethical and moral standard. This is also the value and ordinance of Christianity.

This church continues to practice filial piety as an annual religious ritual where the head pastor leads by example. In May, commonly celebrated in Korea as the month for families, filial piety is emphasized by hearing testimonies from children and their parents on how they practice honoring their parents in daily life.

Standing with the Town by Sharing Religious and Social Space

Paul Tillich said the church building is another theological language, a theology and a sermon written in stone.[15] The church is an architecture made of stone and a space that expresses faith and devotion. Moreover, the church is a construction in a town and a space that symbolizes important rituals and community in that town. The architect Jung Shi-hoon said that after Emperor Constantine established Christendom there were three traditions of church construction. The first tradition was the church as domus Dei, or the house of God. The second is domus ecclesiae, or the meeting place of the people of God, and the third is a preaching hall to declare the Word and evangelize. These traditions emphasize the church space's ritualistic transcendence, the people's fellowship, and the Word's centrality, but these concepts separate the church from outsiders. To respond to the church's call for the common good in our new age, the church must develop its public aspect for all people.[16]

---

[14] Lewis J. Sherrill, *The Rise of Christian Education* (NewYork: The Macmilan Company, 1943), 32.

[15] Ho-hyeon Son, et al., *Han-kuk-kyo-hoe kŏn-ch'uk-kwa kong-kong-sŏng* [Korean church buildings and their public nature], (Seoul: Dongyeon, 2015), 11.

[16] Ibid., 36.

For a church building to have a public character, it must be assessed in terms of openness, accessibility, convenience, relationality, and location.[17] In maeul ministry, relationality is about how the church and the local community relate to each other as the building space is shared for community development. The church must adequately consider the geographic and historical context of the place. Ansan Myungsung Church space is more than a place for religious service and ministry to its congregation. It became a space for healing, education, and dialogue with the townspeople.

After the Sewol Ferry Disaster, the church set up the Healing Center and the rooftop space that overlooks Danwon High School as a place to remember the lost. It was named Lamp Garden, and it is sometimes called Onyu's Field to remember a teenager Yang On-yu who gave up her life to save her friend. Today, it is called "Scenes of the Healing Garden" set up as a space to meditate on human desire, life, death, mourning, and hope. In these ways, the church is open to the town as a space to contemplate worship and life, the sacred and the mundane, and life and death, and to learn, meditate, take action, and form relationships together. The church space is also where the community gathers for discussions, debates, and education. It is an open meeting space for all in Danwon District. People can feel free to come and go and find healing and reason to hope. It is a ministry for the entire town.

Seonbu General Social Service Center uses the first floor of Ansan Myungsung Church as educational facility on the weekdays. Sharing the space in this way enables the church to coexist with the local community and raise the quality of life of local residents. Ansan Myungsung Church's website introduces this purpose as the following.

> Myungsung 教會 (church) is Myungsung 交會 (gathering).
> The church is less a place of teaching and learning,
> More a place of relating with God through worship and communion
> And forming friendships with others through fellowship and service.
> So the church is a 交會 (gathering).[18]

Integrating Historicity and Spirituality

Ansan Myungsung Church inspires Christians with their duty to the nation and the people. The church reminds people of transcendence in pursuit of the kingdom of God while also reminding them that they are mortal, history-bound beings.

The last day of each month is the day of fasting and prayer for national reconciliation and reunification. An offering is gathered for the same purpose. Reminding the church that an average North Korean consumes 100 grams of

---

[17] Hye-jin Chung, "To-si kŏn-ch'uk-ŭi kong-kong-sŏng-e kwan-han non-ŭi" [Discussion on the public nature of urban construction]. Ho-hyeon Son, et al. ed. *Han-kuk-kyo-hoe kŏn-ch'uk-kwa kong-kong-sŏng* [Korean church buildings and their public nature], (Seoul: Dongyeon, 2015), 388-392.

[18] Ansan Myungsung Church http://www.ms21.kr/, Accessed 25 March 2024.

food a day while South Koreans throw out 430 grams, the church proposes concrete actions for patriotic Christians to heal the national division.

The Korean church has historically stood with the nation. Especially under the Japanese occupation they led in the March First Independence Movement. Of course, some missionaries were apathetic and Korean church leaders were passive, but despite these shortcomings the church played a considerable role.

The church was where the sense of justice and the desire for national independence were expressed in language. Through the church's domestic and international networks, the cruelties of Japanese rule were exposed to appeal to the world's conscience. Through the church, the independence uprising was declared. The church had raised the torch of history, and Christians' faith in God led them to refuse to bow to Shinto Shrines despite persecution. It was a resistance against the divinized human emperor. The church historian Min Gyeong-bae explains this as the outer and inner aspects of faith.[19] Keeping the faith and striving to live by the word of God can be a form of resistance to injustice. In other words, this is the integration of historicity and spirituality. The pastor of Ansan Myungsung Church, Hong-sun Kim preached on February 26, 2023, ahead of the March First Independence Movement Day saying the following.

> When the nation is in trouble are you willing to fast and pray, wrestling with God about the realities of this country? Jesus also watched Jerusalem about to be destroyed and mourned its demise saying, "Daughters of Jerusalem, weep not for me but for you and your children who will face destruction and judgment." Brothers and sisters. We talk about inheriting the spirit of March First. But that means more than organizing a memorial event. We must first bring back the tears for our country.... There are countless reasons to weep and pray for our country.[20]

Beyond political progressive and conservative, left and right, before heading to the squares and the streets, the church must head to an attic and pray to the God who is sovereign over our country's fate and let prayers ring out. In an age of divisions between political parties, between different age groups, and between employers and laborers, this is how national unity can be achieved, according to the sermon. Topics are introduced for the congregation to consider, discern, and pray for the nation before God who reigns over history while also helping them bracket their previous experience or political opinions.

The spirituality of Ansan Myungsung Church is the power to respond to the historical challenges and to take responsibility for the nation. The church raises its members to live as disciples of Jesus Christ and as responsible citizens in society. But the power that makes this possible comes from spirituality.

---

[19] Gyeong-bae Min, "Kae-sin-kyo-ŭi pal-chŏn-kwa kŭ hyŏng-sik" [Development of Protestantism and its Form], Religious Textbook Compilation Committee ed. *Sŏng-sŏ-wa ki-tok-kyo* [Bible and Christianity], (Seoul: Yonsei Univ Press, 1985), 379-381.

[20] Hong Sun Kim, "It's time we shed tears for the nation" from Sunday sermon at Ansan Myungsung Church 26 Feburary 2023.

Raising Women and Lay Leaders

In his book *Principle-Centered Leadership*, the management expert Stephen Covey explains the following three concepts. The first concept is to control oneself rather than controlling others. The second idea is that leadership is possible when one adheres to principles. Third, there are two types of greatness in leadership, which are incidental and essential. Incidental leadership refers to the leader's academic achievement, wealth, appearance, or position, while essential leadership refers to the leader's mature character. Maturity means to be patient, compassionate, discerning, forward-thinking, empathetic, and decisive.[21]

Leadership in Ansan Myungsung Church is a prime example of principle-centered leadership. In appointing leaders, they have principles on raising women and lay leaders, cooperating with the senior pastor, and drawing out the participation of the church community. They have three slots of Sunday services. In the earliest time slot, the deacons (who may or may not be ordained) say the congregational prayer, and for the third time slot, the *gwonsas* (woman leaders in the Korean church) take turns. People also take turns in alphabetical order. Half of the church administrative committee are women, and the heads of the education department and church environment department are women. In all departments, women and men participated equally.

When I visited Myungsung Church in Ansan to speak at their teacher training seminar, the topic was "Sermons by Teachers." It was to build teachers' capacity to preach to their students. It was impressive evidence of how the education department and other departments raise up lay leaders rather than having ministers leading at the helm. Before the seminar, the teachers came early to prepare, and most of them were attentive to the topic and asked various questions to discuss ways to develop their departments, showing initiative and commitment.

Life-giving Ministry in the Age of Climate Crisis

The biggest issue in society these days is the climate crisis. Covids-19 that started in 2019 and continues to affect our lives today is deeply related to disruption in the ecology. The virus was first found in Wuhan, China, but what made this mutation possible was the disruptions in the ecology. A virus needs a host to survive. Covid-19 was transmitted from animals to humans because humans encroached on animals' natural habits.[22]

The outbreaks of pandemics such as MERS, SARS, and now Covid-19 are becoming more frequent, showing the acceleration of ecological destruction and chaos. Global warming is expanding the geographic area where disease-carrying animals travel, raising the frequency of contagious diseases in temperate regions.[23] In response, Choi Jae-cheon talks about the ecological vaccine.

---

[21] Stephen R. Covey, *Principle-centered Leadership.* (New York: Free Press, 1992), 57-66.

[22] Jae Chun Choe, et al, *K'o-lo-na sa-p'i-ŏn-sŭ* [Covid Sapiens], (Seoul: Influential, 2020), 14-44.

[23] Ibid., 28.

Ecological vaccine means reflecting on human lifestyle, caring for nature, and responding to climate change with a sense of urgency. The age of the post-pandemic "New Normal" indicates the shifting norm to fit the multifaceted changes of our time. The "Old Normal" is the age of rapid global economic growth after World War II through unlimited competition, consumption, and production. Now is the age of the New Normal. It is time to reconsider the global economy that led to overconsumption and environmental destruction on the way to growth.[24] Covid-19 is a medical issue but also something that requires rethinking of human lifestyle. It requires prioritizing the ecology, establishing new norms, and living according to them.[25]

The issue of climate change is closely related to Christian faith. The theologian Leonardo Boff proposes the recovery of creation theology. Humans were created with divine dynamism to be with and among the creation. Creation theology helps to rediscover the meaning of soteriology. In the destruction of the creation and divisions of humanity, we experience redemption. The church community is part of this human community and the cosmic community.[26]

Soteriological spirituality sets humans apart from rest of creation in a dualistic structure of subject and object. Creation spirituality rediscovers the blessing of creation that preexisted salvation. It is holistic and relational, requiring humans to recognize themselves and act as one creation among many and responsible stewards of creation. Ansan Myungsung Church is taking leadership on this global issue of ecological preservation. The church agreed to cooperate with Salim, the Christian environmental education center as a Green Church, or an environmentally conscious church. They have special morning prayer services for the whole church that accompanies carbon fasting.[27]

Recognized in Town as "A Good Church"

Whether a church is benefiting the town by its presence and is beloved by the town can be accurately gauged by listening to the townspeople themselves rather than people in the church. The associate pastor of Ansan Myungsung Church, Hong Ung-gi, told a story of what he heard not long after he came to this church.

> For the first three months of working in this church, my family had to stay at our old place. So I stayed at a temporary lodging and had my clothing dry cleaned. Since I will become a regular customer at the dry cleaners, I greeted the owners and told them I am new at Ansan Myungsung Church. The dry cleaner told me that the church is a very good church. He told me the church is known about town as a good church. He added that the church is doing a lot of good for the town seniors. Our church had been inviting seniors for a meal every Saturday before the pandemic.

---

[24] Ibid, 36.

[25] From Eun-ha Cho, "Ki-hu-wi-ki si-tae saeng-t'ae-kam-su-sŏng hyŏng-sŏng-ŭl wi-han hwan-kyŏng-kyo-yuk" [Environmental education for ecological awareness in the age of climate crisis], *Theology and Context.* (Daejon: Mokwon University Theological Institute, 2020), 119-126.

[26] Leonardo Boff, *Ecology and Liberation.* Translated by Kim Hyang-seop (Seoul: Catholic Book, 1966), 53-55.

[27] Ansan Myungsung Church bulletin on 19 February 2023.

According to a recent report on a survey by Christian Ethics Movement Korea (CEMK), 21% of the participants said they trust the Protestant church and 74% said they do not. The social credibility of Protestant Christianity fell. On Protestant Christians' words and actions, 20.6% saw them as credible while 75.2% did not. On religious familiarity as well, Protestant Christianity was lower (19.6%) than Buddhism (23.2%) or Catholicism (19.9%). Especially the public image of Protestant social services fell 15.1% from the 2020 survey, down to 20.5%. According to CEMK analysis, it is not that the Protestant church had not been active in social services but that the public does not give credit for them. When asked to identify the religion that contributes positively to society, people without religion chose Catholic Christianity (23.6%), and Buddhism (14.6%), with Protestant Christianity trailing far behind at 5.1%.

On the Protestant church's contribution to social development in the future, 69.9% responded pessimistically and 25.2% optimistic. For the Protestant church to recover its credibility, the respondents said churches must become less selfish (34.2%), church leaders should live moral and pure lives (19.6%), church finances should be transparent (17.9%), and the Christians should be more tolerant of other religions (17.3%). On Protestant participation in politics, the absolute majority (83.2%) responded negatively and only 13.2% were favorable. Among them, 90.2% of the non-religious respondents said are negative about Protestant church involvement in politics. On these results, Jung Jae-young remarked that the Korean Protestant church needs internal reflections if it is to recover its public presence.

When such negative perception is prevalent, providing good social service programs is not enough to be known as a good church. As in the survey, non-religious people do not recognize church social service as having much positive impact on society. That Ansan Myungsung Church to be known to the non-religious dry cleaner as a very good church is evidence of how it has been relating to the town with authenticity.

How Ansan Myungsung Church became known as "a Very Good Church"

Ansan Myungsung Church which was once despised became known as a good church in the local community due to three factors. The first was the pastor's ministry principle, the second was the participation of the church community in the pastor's principle, and the third was the ministry system that enabled sustained development.

Pastor Hong-sun Kim's ministry motto of "healthy church, proper ministry" indicates his emphasis on direction rather than speed and genuine revival rather than numerical growth. For this purpose, he conversed with the church members on the kind of church it should be and worked toward the goal. This process was the important factor enabling the church to recover from its chaotic state at the beginning of Kim's ministry to become a church that is commended. Such ministry principle is not established by the pastor alone but in dialogue with the church members. It is not a top-down implementation of ministry programs but programs that emerge out of asking questions and finding answers together.

Ansan Myungsung Church has three types of maeul ministry structure that actualizes their love of neighbors. The first type of ministry is entirely financed by the church. These are Dasol Library and Healing Center 0416 Rest and Renewal. The second type is ministry programs conducted in collaboration with public agencies getting financing from local governments. These are operations of the social service center, children's daycare, and the local children's center. The third type of ministry is community movement of the congregants and the local residents through the Good Village Cooperative Café.

Along with the organizational structure, there is also the priority structure. This is about priorities and focus in ministry. In 2014 the entire city of Ansan was in shock and pain because the majority of the victims were Danwon High School students located in Ansan. When I visited Ansan at the time, every taxi had a yellow ribbon remembering the victims, and they transported visitors for free to the school gym where the victims were memorialized. Banners remembering the victims hung one after another in the streets. Waiting in the long line for two hours to pay respects to the dead, hardly anybody was flipping through their smartphone or chatting with each other. There were people pushing a baby stroller, others bent over their cane, all of them grieving as they waited their turn. Grief was pressing down on the entire town. Six of Ansan Myungsung Church's own teenagers were among the dead. The church sought out what they should do, and providing professional counseling, and organized a group of volunteers to respond to this emergency.

To respond proactively to this disaster the church set up Healing Center 0416 Rest and Renewal to care for the grieving families. The ministry was extensive. It involved opening up space for the mothers of the victims to operate a handicraft workshop where they can meet community residents and break down invisible walls of misunderstanding. They set up a path to memorialize the path the students used to walk. The local residents served as docents in this walkway to help meditate on death, life, and healing.

Ansan Myungsung Church, therefore, is a church open to the town and coexists with the town. Rather than building fortresses it makes paths, and rather than teaching it listens. It is a welcoming meeting place that comforts and empowers.[28]

For Proper Ministry and Healthy Church

In *What Makes a Healthy Church* written by the management experts Yang Hyeok-seung, Ryu Ji-seong, and Bae Jong-seok, there are eight factors that makes a healthy church. A church can be defined as a community and as an organization. As a community, it must have authentic worship, united membership, healthy individuals, and the character of service. As an

[28] Eun-ha Cho, "Ma-ŭl-kwa ham-kke ha-nŭn mok-hoe-ŭi ta-yang-han sa-lye" [Various cases of ministry with the community], *Christian Thought*. Seoul: CLSK, 2020, 45-55.

organization, a healthy church must be true to its purpose, the leadership must empower, church offices must be restored, and it must operate based on foundational principles.

When I visited Ansan Myungsung Church in 2016, I saw the concrete examples of its ministry that seemed an excellent example of a church that integrates spirituality and expertise. That impression has not changed. The pastor's motto "proper ministry, healthy church" is not only true to theology but is the principle at the basis of its operations. The church has strong pastoral leadership yet lay leaders are empowered to participate in the community. The church continues to work toward healthy spiritual growth of its members and for the integration of the daily and the sacred, the church and the town, knowing and doing. The missional nature of Ansan Myungsung Church is not only positively impacting the town but is also witnessing the kingdom of God as a very good church of our time.

Bibliography

Ansan Myungsung Church Website: http://www.ms21.kr/. Accessed 25 March 2024.

Boff, Leonardo. *Ecology and Liberation.* Translated by Hyang-seop Kim. Seoul: Catholic Book, 1966.

Cho, Eun-ha. "Ma-ŭl-kwa ham-kke ha-nŭn mok-hoe-ŭi ta-yang-han sa-lye" [Various cases of ministry with the community], *Christian Thought.* Seoul: CLSK, 2020 January.

_________, "Village Education Community and Christian Adult Education: Focusing on Middle Ages" *Theology and Praxis*, 2021.

_________. "Ki-hu-wi-ki si-tae saeng-t'ae-kam-su-sŏng hyŏng-sŏng-ŭl wi-han hwan-kyŏng-kyo-yuk" [Environmental education for ecological awareness in the age of climate crisis]. *Theology and Field.* 2021.

Choe, Jae Chun, et al. *K'o-lo-na sa-p'i-ŏn-sŭ* [Covid Sapiens]. Seoul: Influential, 2020

Chung, Hye-jin. "To-si kŏn-ch'uk-ŭi kong-kong-sŏng-e kwan-han non-ŭi" [Discussion on the public nature of urban construction]. Edited by Ho-hyeon Son, et al. *Han-kuk-kyo-hoe kŏn-ch'uk-kwa kong-kong-sŏng* [Korean church buildings and their public nature]. Seoul: Dongyeon, 2015, 388-392.

Covey, Stephen R. *Principle-Centered Leadership.* New York: Free Press, 1992.

Eun, Joon-gwan. *Sil-ch'ŏn-chŏk kyo-hoe-lon* [Practical ecclesiology]. Seoul: CLSK, 1998.

Han, Kook-il. *Sŏn-kyo-chŏk kyo-hoe-ŭi i-lon-kwa sil-che* [Theory and practice of missional church]. Seoul: PUTS Press, 2016.

Kim, Jin-du. *We-sŭl-li-ŭi sil-ch'ŏn-sin-hak* [John Wesley's Practical Theology]. Seoul: KMC, 2010.

Lee, Won-hyuk. "Ubuntu, I exist because you exist." https://www.pressian.com/pages/articles/99518. Accessed 25 March 2024.

Min, Gyeong-bae. "Kae-sin-kyo-ŭi pal-chŏn-kwa kŭ hyŏng-sik" [Development of Protestantism and its Form]. In Religious Textbook Compilation Committee ed. *Sŏng-sŏ-wa ki-tok-kyo* [Bible and Christianity]. Seoul: Yonsei Univ Press, 1985, 379-381.

Namu Wiki. "Cheonghaejin Shipping Sewol Ferry Sinking Accident"

https://namu.wiki/w/%EC%B2%AD%ED%95%B4%EC%A7%84%ED%95%B4%EC%9A%B4%20%EC%84%B8%EC%9B%94%ED%98%B8%20%EC%B9%A8%EB%AA%B0%20%EC%82%AC%EA%B3%A0. Accessed 25 March 2024.

Nichols, Stephen J. *Bonhoeffer on the Christian Life: From the Cross, for the World.* Translated by Gwang-nam Kim. Seoul: Abba Publisher, 2014.

Palmer, Parker J. *The courage to teach: Exploring the inner landscape of a teacher's life*. San Francisco, CA: John Wiley & Sons, 2007.

Religious Textbook Compilation Committee. *Sŏng-sŏ-wa ki-tok-kyo* [Bible and Christianity]. Seoul: Yonsei Univ Press, 1985.

Sherrill, Lewis J. *The Rise of Christian Education.* NewYork: The Macmilan Company, 1943.

Son, Ho-hyeon, et al. *Han-kuk-kyo-hoe kŏn-ch'uk-kwa kong-kong-sŏng* [Korean church buildings and their public nature]. Seoul: Dongyeon, 2015.

Wesley, John. "I-lŭm-ppun-in kŭ-li-sŭ-to-in" [Christian in name only], Edited by Ad Fontes Wesley. *Kŭ kil: we-sŭl-li p'yo-chun-sŏl-kyo ilk-ki* [The way: Reading John Wesley's Standard Sermons]. Seoul: CLSK, 2021.

Unexpected Harvest of the Holy Spirit in Small Church during the Pandemic

Won-don Lee

Becoming a Town Providing Integrated Community Care after Covid-19

Yakdae-dong in Wonmi District of the city of Bucheon had a town library and a children's center since the 1990s. In 2013, Kkopsari Town Film Festival and a café cooperative were organized to add to the dynamic ecology of learning, culture, and social service. Especially in 2018, Yakdae-dong Care Community Association was organized to set up a system of care in the town. In 2019 the urban farmers in the town voluntarily organized to farm small plots of land to grow their own produce in response to the climate crisis. Since June 25, 2021, Saerom Family Support Center's Silver Wings program and the Bucheon Healthcare Society Cooperative have been conducting Yakdae-dong Healthcare Leader Workshops. By September 3, 2023 they had conducted nine workshops via Zoom and in person to award certifications to participants. This program not only provided the basis for mission to the town of Yakdae-dong during the pandemic, but also networked with town nurses and healthcare leaders to provide holistic care through visitations. This was an integration of home visits by both medical doctors and church pastors, combining physical and spiritual care. This is also serving as the basis of preparation for the age of integrated care combining aspects of medicine, social service, caretaking, human habitation, and the environment.[1]

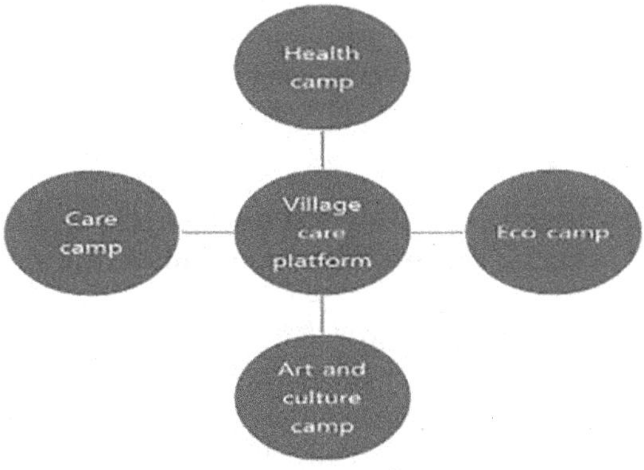

Figure 11: Yakdae-dong Care Platform

[1] After experiencing the COVID-19 pandemic, local communities now have no choice but to organize a system of care and mutual support. That is why we are discussing ways to set up a community of care through projects such as shared community kitchen.

Starting in 2022, Environmental Education Workshops were also conducted to provide certifications for participants. In this process of conducting trainings for leaders of health care and environmental education, a significant event occurred.

Saerom Children's Daycare was established as the first all-day care center in Bucheon in 1986 providing social services for children. In 2021 due to the pandemic and the general decrease in Korea's younger populations, the decision was made to close the center. The first two floors of Saerom Church building that was used for daycare were vacated to turn it into Yakdae-dong Ecology, Culture, and Care Center. The first floor was turned into a shared kitchen for the town and a health care lounge for the town seniors. The second-floor space would be used for cultural events and education. The church rooftop space was turned into farming plots for the town. So essentially it was decided that the entire church building be used to provide social service and cultural events for the town.

In October of that year, the renovation for Saedae Gonggam Center was finished to allow for the activities of healthcare leaders, cultural leaders, and urban farmers (environmental leaders) starting in November. Today in this space Korean language lessons, music lessons, health care classes, and midnight snack programs are conducted. As originally planned, town festivals, healthcare leader workshops, and various programs for small groups of town residents are conducted here. On the weekday other social service, education, environmental, and cultural programs for town seniors, youth, and other residents are happening in this space.

This is how Saerom Church's maeul ministry and mission programs have been networking to construct an ecology of social service, healthcare, and cultural development. I believe this is the path we small town churches must take after the pandemic. In this essay, I will recount how Saerom Church and Yakdae-dong have been cultivating an ecology of the heart (social sciences of the heart)[2] after the height of the Covid-19 pandemic. I will recount the process of how a small town church faced our challenges and rose from it, and how the Holy Spirit moved in our midst to result in an unexpected harvest.

Age of the Pandemic, De-growth, Post-Church, and Climate Crisis: Ecology of the Heart at a Small Church

Age of De-growth and Post-Church: Ecology of the Heart for a Small Town Church[3]

Today after the height of the pandemic there are still Christians who have not fully recovered physically and mentally. It was expected that there would be a

---

[2] Hong-joong Kim, *Social Sciences of the Heart" (*Munhakdongne Publishing Group: Seoul, 2009).

[3] Seongbo Sim, *K'o-lo-na si-tae, ma-ŭl-kyo-yuk-kong-tong-ch'e-un-tong-kwa saeng-t'ae-chŏk kyo-yuk-hak* [Age of Covid-19, Maeul education community movement and ecological education] *Salimteo,* 28 February.

20 to 30% decrease in regular church attendance after the pandemic, and there indeed are people who have not returned. There are people who were financially hard hit by the pandemic and no longer have the time or the mental space to continue their spiritual life, others who are undergoing a spiritual identity crisis, and others who are in survival mode and no longer feel like they have the capacity to look around for neighbors in need.

In the pandemic, the Korean church's seasoned spiritual leaders and believers no longer seem to be courageously taking up the cross for their neighbors and their community. The entire church rather seems to have fallen into immature narcissism, still holding onto the milk bottle. This immaturity disables the church from taking up the cross for this generation again, and this is the major reason why the church has forgotten its calling to be the salt and light of the world and is getting despised by the society.[4] In this context, Kim Hong-joong's book *Social Sciences of the Heart* gives considerable implications.

In this book, Kim identifies the 1987 era as the time of authenticity. It was a time of mass authentic effort to awaken human dignity by way of self-reflection and social participation. But unlike the post-war 1968 generation of Europe, such a period in Korean society was cut short. Only a decade after the 1987 era of authenticity the Asian Financial Crisis of 1997 hit to take Korean society into a new age of neoliberal survivalism. By this time, Korean society had already moved on from self-reflection and social participation and was drowning in competition, meritocracy, and individualistic survivalism. The key point is that after 1997, even the older generation that had fought for and achieved democracy through civil disobedience in 1987 was steeped in competition, meritocracy, and achievement mentality while maintaining the appearance of democratic authenticity. The now middle-aged leaders of democratization, in ways they educate their own children or amass wealth through real estate, have become the ones responsible for the state of South Korea today with its high economic inequality and real estate speculation.

Kim Hong-joong identifies three phases of modern South Korea – industrialization, democratization, globalization – as the "big dreams" that have driven our society. But today we have awakened from the dreams and cannot find a replacement. He says what we are now experiencing is a rude awakening from our dreams, and are watching these dreams collapse in horror. He calls this experience de-imagination, or the opposite of imagination. De-imagination is the experience of awakening from the dream that had hold over us, and the negation of our existential foundation that had been rooted in that dream. But Kim explains that this experience of brokenness can be sublimated through moral, cognitive, and religious capacity, and this capacity is called de-imaginability. In this sense, de-imaginability can be positive. De-imaginability is the power to

[4] These churches must remember what it means to grow up. An adult is nothing more than someone who carries their own luggage. A spiritual infant does not take up their cross which results in others carrying the cross for them. In Korean society and church today countless people have abandoned their own cross which forces the few to carry the crosses up the Golgotha.

deconstruct the structure of dream and desire, the underlying conviction, and the systems that arose out of that conviction. Kim calls on the readers to stand at this site of de-imagination of dreams that controlled society and to go beyond sympathy to share in the pains of others. This requires letting go of the self to feel the entirety of others' pain.

As I conduct maeul ministry in a town of lower economic class residents, I often see church members whose socioeconomic status rose to leave our town and move to middle-class high-rise apartments expressing spiritual numbness as they lost a sense of community. Their sense of community fades as they participate less in community gatherings. They tend to devote more energy to building their own fortress for narcissistic survival rather than cultivating communal and spiritual solidarity and cooperation. As I watch these church members in our post-pandemic era, I deeply understand the need for the empathy that goes beyond sympathy, and de-imagination beyond imagination Kim Hong-joong explained.

After the pandemic many people and communities in churches and towns have their hearts broken. We see people revert to seeking only earthly salvation based on worldly values, or revert to immature spirituality that can't look beyond the church toward the kingdom of God. In addition, with Covid-19 and subsequent seasonal natural disasters, many are exhausted and without the energy to share with their family and neighbors. What must be done?

"Power of the Air" Faced by a Small Town Church:
"Put on the whole armor of God" (Ephesians 6:10-17)

> "You were dead through the trespasses and sins in which you once walked, following the course of this world, following the ruler of the power of the air, the spirit that is now at work among those who are disobedient." (Ephesians 1:1-2)

In today's age of transition, there is severe conflict between the old and the new. A truly gospel-centered church must be able to create a sacred culture in resistance against the world. Spiritual and cultural conflict is inevitable. The letter to the church in Ephesus gives clues on the severity of this spiritual battle in the early church, and how the old Hellenism and new Christian culture clashed. In this context, the Apostle Paul admonishes the church to arm themselves with the complete armor of God. In Ephesus, Paul battled against the "power of the air" (individualistic survival, meritocracy, justification of greed) and idolatry (faith in and dissemination of falsehood) as he was spreading the gospel.

There were people who have been saying of Paul, "These people who have been turning the world upside down have come here" (Acts 17:6), "there is danger… that this trade of ours may come into disrepute" (Acts 19:27), "You also see and hear that not only in Ephesus but in almost the whole of Asia this Paul has persuaded and drawn away a considerable number of people by saying that gods made with hands are not gods" (Acts 19:26). Facing these public criticisms and opposition, Paul spent two years focusing on discipleship training at Tyrannus.

What is the "power of the air"? It is the force that nudges confused and aimless people toward narcissism, survivalism, meritocracy, and selfish greed. When such power infiltrates the community, the community becomes jaded by greed and cynicism. The community then lowers its resistance to selfishness, tamed by the greed that rules over our age until we become blind to how society has become so shameless.

There are many stories of how Jesus fought against the power of the air, healing the sick and driving out evil spirits caused by the empire's violent oppression that caused sickness, chaos, and disorder. Jesus did not simply heal physical sickness but liberated them from the power of the air.[5] Stories of Jesus' healing show how the sick people's social context is involved. Jesus knew that without healing the larger structure of the time, it is impossible to arrive at physical and psychological healing. That is why he not only healed the sick but fought against the norms and systems of the time such as Phariseeism. Beyond healing individual sickness or the social structure, the time's spirit, atmosphere, cultural norms, and institutions, in other words, the power that rules over the age or the air, had to be fought. In rereading the scripture in the pandemic, the call to fight against the spiritual power of the air beyond the individual and structural evils (Ephesians 6:12) is ever more clear.[6]

The body of the church community is spiritual. The body is a community, and this body communicates with the world with language (the Word). Here a pastor's role is to maintain the health of the body or the community. We are happy when in nature, when communities of people are formed, and people are in harmony with God. Humans are fallible creatures who are constantly tempted by the evil spirit (power of the air). The power of the air is the dominant values of the world today that constantly lie to us through the mass media saying happiness of the body can be bought with Mammon, material currently and capital.

In this way the language in the air today functions as the medium through which the neoliberalism of the empire and the Mammon infiltrate. The power of the air today spreads information and stories through global connections, controlling the minds of our congregations and town residents, imposing the

---

[5] But churches have a tendency to understand physical and psychological healing on only individual terms. So they have believed that healing comes from personal mystical encounters with Jesus.

[6] Seung-seop Kim, *A-p'ŭm-i kil-i toe-lyŏ-myŏn* [To make a way out of the pain], (Seoul: Dong Asia Books, 2017). In medicine the concept of the power of the air may be translated as epidemiology. Epidemiology studies the disease transmissions in a group and traces the causes. Traditional epidemiological research traced person to person contact, but in recent years there are more efforts to find sociological causes. This is what the study of public healthcare is about. Hate speech, discrimination against the unemployed, temporary employment, disasters… how do social wounds make our bodies sick? The healthcare specialist Kim Seung-seop wrote a book of personal essays on tracing the sociological causes of disease.

worldview of consumer capitalism and winner-take-all competition to alienate us from one another. Churches and church leaders must clearly understand that town residents and church members living in this age of Mammon cannot help but be selfish, divided, and alienated.[7]

The health and happiness of our bodily community can be achieved not by money and capital but through nature and interaction with other people. The Holy Spirit enables such holistic interaction of the body and the Word (language) to from a healthy body and to communicate with the world in constructing the kingdom of God. In spirit and in truth the church community can reconcile the spirit and the body of the neighbors.

Therefore, we must put on the new helmet of salvation, go beyond the empire's Mammonic survivalist individualism of the power of the air, and declare the salvation of our neighbors, society, and the creation. We must also shield ourselves with the shield of faith against the temptation of money, capital, and consumerism of neoliberalism. With the sword of the Spirit, we must be the new media that shares the good news of the gospel in resistance against disinformation. Pastors must deeply study the body, the mind, the language, and the spirit of divided communities. They must facilitate the community to discard what is of the flesh, in other words, the Mammonic pursuit of individual salvation and survival, and to be resurrected into a faithful community that cares for the creation. For this purpose, we must first correctly assess the church and the town community's ecology of the heart that was broken in the pandemic. The Korean church must now look after the heart of the Christians and residents and form a solidarity of care for the church and the local community in each town and region. Ministers and church members now have the new task of joining the church and the town into a new missional community and of connecting the hearts of the church members and townspeople in a new ecology of the heart for the town. For this purpose we must first examine the current state of the hearts of the church and the town and consider ways to connect the family, the church, and the town to have them resurrected in a Holy Spirit-filled ecology.

New Ecology of Heart to Connect Family, Church, and Town to Face the Power of the Air

In the post-pandemic era, Christians must be transformed from consumers of religion to committed believers. Rather than seeking to be served, Christians must serve. In this change, there is an essential element, and that is the fact that each person is a church. We must be sure to remember this. In the framework of consumerism in the age of industrialization, we talk about "going to church," but in the new spiritual framework

---

[7] Jin-kwan Kwon, "Min-chung-sin-hak-kwa ma-ŭl-mok-hoe" [Minjung theology and maeul ministry] (Lecture, Youndong Church, Seoul, Maeul Ministry Theology Academy, October 18, 2023).

of maeul ministry we must speak of "being the church" and "being through the church." In the former consumeristic paradigm, we say "The pastor is someone who fills my need and I go to church to fill my need." I am the consumer who sits back with arms folded, watching and judging the quality of the church's service to me. A believer in this era of transition who participates in maul ministry would confess, "I am the church." They are players on the field participating in missions, evangelism, visitation, and counseling. The laity in the town church in the era of maeul ministry are themselves the church trained to take the lead. The learning objective of maeul ministry is to turn spectators into participants, and consumers into owners. We do not go to church, because we are the church.

Saerom Church could witness how on top of this confession the Holy Spirit has been connecting our families, our church, and our town to construct a new ecology of the heart. Our church in Yakdae-dong had the special opportunity to be sensitized to the mystical and detailed movements of the perichoretic God who knits the web of life in the universe and in our town, knitting the web of life and ecology in our individual lives, the church community, and the town community, mutually indwelling, mutually permeating, and mutually dependent. The Spirit of life was present in us individuals, the church, and the town to form the web of life. As we believed and participated in this mystical movement we saw unexpected movement in Yakdae-dong, saw paths open up, and gathered harvests. This is the story I am about to share.

Holy Spirit Leading a Small Town Church on Unexpected Paths

What happened in Yakdae-dong during the Pandemic?

Figure 12: Yakdae-dong Summer School

In 2022, Yakdae-dong Summer School returned to Saedae Gonggam after two years of hiatus in the pandemic. The theme was "Play at Yakdae-dong Media Square." Yakdae-dong Summer School began in 2008 for church members and local residents of all ages. At the teacher training workshop that was conducted before the Summer School, it was decided that each small group would take pictures or make short films on town programs. These would be gathered on August 21 to be edited by each group with the coaching of a professional video producer and be uploaded to a new account on Yakdae-dong Culture and Arts School website.

The films showed how Yakdae-dong Family Library, Local Children's Center, Yakdae-dong Culture and Arts School, Kkobi Restaurant, and Maeul Film Production Workshop continued through the two years of the pandemic. Seeing these productions made me think of the title, "What happened in Yakdae-dong during the pandemic?" We were individually despairing and despondent but clearly, things have always been moving in Yakdae-dong.

What the Holy Spirit did during the Pandemic:
October 4 Literacy Class and Singing Class for Generational Interaction

Figure 13: Direction of community spiritual training after COVID-19

The following excerpt was written by Kim Hyun-ja, a *Kkumteo* Group Leader, describing the Literacy Class and Singing Class (called Saerom Silver Wings) on October 4, 2022.

> "Today marks the end of book six. Next, we will start book seven~ Remember how Ms. Cho Gyeong-ju said our silver-winged seniors are all refined and intelligent!!

Singing class~~! Clap your hands and move your body~~ You're getting better at singing and reading."

On October 4, we had a special luncheon with Yakdae-dong Saedae Gonggam Literacy Class and Singing Class.[8] Bucheon Citizens' ICOOP sponsored the gathering with rice and pollack soup meal kits. We joyfully cooked and served the meal, and everyone ate their fill appreciating a good meal when they hadn't had an appetite lately. Before the singing class began the instructor also brought pizza so everyone had a piece and even took another home. The Director of the Board of ICOOP also came by to teach us how to cook rice with mushrooms. And we also introduced the nurse Lee Mi-sook as Yakdae-dong healthcare leader. The healthcare leader is critical in the post-pandemic age of integrated care when each town must have their own system to take care of the residents.

Yakdae-dong Wednesday Bible Study Class

The following is another description of one Wednesday Bible Study Class written by a congregant.

> For the Wednesday Bible Study Class, we read Acts 4 where the apostles Peter and John witnessed to Jesus' resurrection before the Council. They said "Whether it is right in God's sight to listen to you rather than God, you must judge; for we cannot keep from speaking about what we have seen and heard" (Acts 4:19-20). Deacon Jung Seong-hoe shared that the days of the scripture must have been similar to today, everyone narcissistic and focused on their own survival. The apostles were also the products of the age. Deacon Jung marveled at how the apostles who had betrayed Jesus and fled just a few days ago had such a sudden turnaround to speak of resurrection. This was impossible without receiving the Holy Spirit. Ms. Jung So-young also shared what she learned in her training at Saerom Local Children's Center. She read how the early *minjung* church in Korea devoted to social services for children, and was moved that she is able to see the continuation of that in our church and town. Ms. Kim Hyun-ja who came a bit late shared how Deacon Jeon Yong-sam visited his home in Chungju, and the good news that Ms. Lin who is a foreign national married to a Korean man happily agreed to come to the Yakdae-dong Care Culture Fest on October 16, 2022.

Yakdae-dong Thanksgiving Celebration and Fall Care Culture Fest

Just as it was expected that 20 to 30% of church members will not return after the pandemic, there are people who haven't returned to Saerom Church, and others who haven't yet recovered from the physical and emotional aftermath of Covid-19. Even when the pandemic died down to allow for on-site services around the fall of 2022, people still hesitated to attend service or join the choir. So one of the woman leaders suggested that we should have a Thanksgiving Worship Service two weeks after the Chuseok Holidays. The members of Regional Group 1 volunteered to join the choir to fill the seats.

Every summer there is a big event called Kkopsari Film Festival in Yakdae-dong, but no events in the fall. During the pandemic the Yakdae-dong Culture and Arts School and Healthcare Leaders really developed. I thought of a fall festival to integrate the two groups and came up with the title Care Culture Fest.

I also happened to get acquainted with the youth welfare program called Tree Frog Bus as I was participating in the Bucheon Maeul Ministry Cooperative. So we put all these factors together for Sunday October 16, 2022. There was to be the Thanksgiving Service at 11 am in Saerom Church that marks the return to on-site worship service, followed by the Yakdae-dong Care Culture Fest at 3 pm on the front yard of Saerom Church where the Tree Frog Bus would be parked. We started early in the morning to help park the bus in front of the church. The bus and the churchyard formed a grand square to make this great event with artists and healthcare leaders possible.

For the Thanksgiving Service, Saerom Choir and Regional Group 1 collaborated for the special praise. For the Fest, the people from the Culture and Arts School, the Tree Frog Eatery, the seniors of Yakdae-dong who come to Saedae Gonggam Literacy and Singing Classes, and the Bucheon Maeul Ministry Cooperative all gathered at the church yard to mark the beginning of the festival (led by Seon Yi-jeong, the Director of the Culture and Arts School). In the bus, Sin Sil, the director of "I am a Mother Library" was in charge of the performances, followed by the stand-up comedy gig by the town artist Choi Dong-seok (Cheongma Yoo Chi-hwan Poetry and Theater Award Winner). The event then moved to the Saedae Gonggma space on the first floor of the church to be led by the town singer Lee Mi-seon (the instructor for the Literacy and Singing Class) and seniors performed their songs and other talents. We all saw that day that town festivals don't necessarily have to be large scale. The Fest that started in the Saerom Church yard will travel on the Tree Frog Bus to be organized in five other towns in Bucheon connected through the Bucheon Maeul Ministry Cooperative.

Yakdae-dong Care Walk (Town Visitation) with the Town Nurse and the Healthcare Leaders

The following exerpt is again the record of Ms. Kim Hyeon-ja expressing her gladness for the Yakdae-dong Healthcare Class and the town visitation program that became the Yakdae-dong Care Walk.

> At the Yaekdae Culture and Arts School space, the health care class [began], led by the town nurse Ms. Lee Mi-sook. This monthly class will provide healthcare information to town seniors and check their blood pressure and blood sugar. Today they learned about our bodily organs and their functions. These programs are meant to support the seniors to take care of their health. On an autumn day as the leaves turn red, the class was to start at half past ten in the morning, but people started coming in a little after ten. The oldest ladies in their 90s were here first, and another trio of ladies were in a hurry to visit the senior center next where they were offering a dementia diagnostic test. The seniors' blood pressure and blood sugar levels were checked as they came. Ms. Lee explained the body by first drawing an outline of a person then drawing in the organs one by one to explain their function. Today one out of four elderly are affected by dementia. Other seniors In-soon, Yang-geum, and Sang-yeong came late so they listened to the lecture first and then got their check-ups later.

I wrote the next excerpt as a reflection after the first Yakdae-dong Care Walk.

> Yakdae-dong Care Walk took its first step! Ms. Kim Hyun-ja who knows the stories of each and every senior and where they live in town led the visitation. As I participated in the first session of the walk, I realized that this is exactly the path that the church must walk. I asked for much prayer and encouragement from Ms. Cho Min-ja, the president of Yakdae-dong Women's Association who joined us, and from Ms. Jeong So-young who came to a maeul ministry event for the first time and has promised to visit the Literacy Class on Tuesday. We prepared a simple gift for each senior we visited. Ms. Kim tells me these gifts were made possible by three of the brothers of our church Jeong Sang-hoon, Kim Jong-gyu, Han Sang-gi, and I would like to thank them as well. The Care Walk will continue for the next three weeks. I dearly pray that we all encourage them, pray for them, and work together for the good of all.

The Rationale Behind the Maeul Ministry Cooperative

On September 16, 2022, in Yakdae-dong of Bucheon a preparatory seminar was conducted to begin the the Bucheon Maeul Ministry Cooperative. Professor Lim Jong-han who is a member of the preparatory committee (Dean of the Medical School of Inha University, Elder of Yakdae Methodist Church) put up the following message on the purpose of the cooperative in our maeul ministry group chatroom after the seminar.

> Bucheon is a city where the civil society movement developed very early. Small libraries, local children's centers, and local produce consumption movements developed in many places in the city led by churches and civil society organizations. In this process, cooperatives on education, social service, and the environment (renewable energy production) naturally developed. Pastors of small churches who are familiar with cooperatives decided to start a Maeul Ministry Cooperative (on 19 October 2022), and held a preparatory seminar at Saerom Church this evening from 6:30 to 8:30 pm. We discussed how the 1970s to the 1990s age of *minjung* theology was followed by the age of Small Church Movement in the 1990s to 2017, and how today in 2022 we are marking the beginning of the age of maeul ministry and maeul theology. This age under the shadow of industrialization and threats to ecology and community can be identified as the age of civilizational turn. Maeul communities must form new communities in this age of new civilization. The plan is to set up the Maeul Ministry Cooperatives at each of the 240 districts in the city to conduct programs. Please start your own Maeul Ministry Cooperative in the district or the city where you are, in Daegu, Gwangju, Jeonju, and Seoul. This will start a chain of cooperative formation on education, social service, health care, and the environment. This is how we can cast new visions on Korean society and the church.

Pastor Lim Jin-cheol (President of Direct Democracy Republic of Maeul All-Citizens Association) who was inspired by this message on the purpose of the cooperative suggested that we make chat rooms for people in other cities interested in maeul ministry to continue the conversation. Today thousands of seminary graduates are wandering without a ministry placement. Add the small church pastors who take second jobs as platform workers or construction workers to sustain their ministry and that makes about ten thousand pastors. The Maeul Ministry Cooperative intends to train the seminary graduates and pastors in setting up social economies (e.g. cooperatives, social enterprises, town enterprises) on education, culture, integrated social service, and health care.

Conclusion: Holy Spirit Leading us on a New Path – Unexpected Thanksgiving during Exile

In witnessing all the developments in Yakdae-dong as we emerge from the pandemic, I must confess that these are unexpected harvests of the Holy Spirit in an unlikely place. One of the unexpected fruits of the Holy Spirit in our town and church history is the summer event called Kkopsari Film Festival. The Fall Care Culture Fest in 2022 is the event that continues the tradition. The second fruit is how the spring season visitations to church members developed into a second round of visitations to the town seniors in the fall. This Healthcare Class and Care Walk is the outcome of the work of the Holy Spirit. Finally, the Day for the Laity and Travel Worship was a creative event that started in the fall of 2022. I will end this essay with the congregational prayer and an excerpt from of the sermon preached for Travel Worship on the Day of the Laity. The event was on November 6, 2022, the Sunday after the Itaewon Disaster where many died in a crowd crush.

Congregational Prayer at Travel Worship, a new Adventure of Imagination (Jeremiah 29:5-7)

Leader: Lord, we thank you this morning for allowing us to survive three years of pandemic and welcome a day of peace. Thank you for helping us conquer the hardships we faced in each of our families.

Congregation: You allowed us to achieve generational empathy through a big church building renovation, and the space is being shared by many different communities for social service, arts, exercise, and film production.

Leader: As we see seniors and children mingling in the space Saerom Church made for Yakdae-dong, we taste true freedom. Lord, at this moment we confess that our hearts are for the town. We pray that we may all mature in this Yakdae-dong space. (Deacon Kim Jeong-seop)

Congregation: Lord! Last week the Tree Frog Bus arrived at Yakdae-dong to organize the Care Culture Fest and give us joy and inspiration. Last week, there was the first special praise offering in a long while. Thank you for the chance to glorify you through song.

Leader: The Bucheon Maeul Ministry Cooperative was formed. May this be the first step for the church and the local community to cooperate for the good of all. We will also start the visitations.

Congregation: Saerom Church wants to expand the church and town visitations to be accompanied by the town nurse and healthcare leaders. Thank you, Lord, for the chance to meet the real needs of the people.

Leader: Be with pastor Lee Seung-hoon who leads Kkobi Youth Eatery, the volunteers, our youth and their families. Be with Ms. Lee Mi-seon who leads the singing class and the participating seniors, Ms. Gong Mi-ran who leads the Literacy class and the seniors who participate in that class, and *Gwonsa* Kim Hyun-ja and Deacon Seon Yi-jeong who coordinate all these classes…

Congregation: Bless the minister Eom Cheol-yong and Ms. Oh Soo-jeong of Family Library and the families who visit the library, *Gwonsa* Kim Gyeong-hee, Deacon Park Hye-jeong, the teachers, the children, and the families of Saerom Children's Center.

Leader: Let the regional group leaders and members care and support each other who are physically and emotionally ill. Remember *Gwonsa* Lee who is caring for her sick husband and give peace to the family. They want to overcome the sickness and return to normalcy. Comfort Deacon Park who must care for her mother each weekend. Provide for her mother so she can live in peace and safety, and comfort the family who is anxious and worried. (Ms. Oh Sye-hyang)

Congregation: Lord! The Thanksgiving Service on the 16th was the best offering we could give in this time of difficulty. The festival with the Tree Frog Bus that afternoon was a chance to promote the Saedae Gonggam space. It was a festival in your favor as the town and the church could rejoice together regardless of denomination. We also deeply thank you that the Sunday October 30 Regional Group Travel Worship was led and accompanied by you, Father (*Gwonsa* Kim Hyun-ja of the intercessory prayer team)

Leader: Lord! In a time of crisis may we look to you who will do new things. At the time of Babylonian exile, you said through the prophet Jeremiah, "Take wives and have sons and daughters; take wives for your sons, and give your daughters in marriage, that they may bear sons and daughters; multiply there, and do not decrease" (Jeremiah 29:5-7).

Congregation: In a time of exile, God, you lead us on a completely unexpected path. Faith, prayer, and prophesy come not from what is already in the world, but from you who make all things new. May our prayers be no longer passive and weak, seeking only what the world tells us is possible. We want to expect a new gift from the Lord that the world cannot imagine.

Together: Be with Saerom Church that is today expecting a new gift from you as we start this new imaginative adventure called Travel. Hear our prayer and answer us. Amen.

"Gospel of Life that Saves us from the Power of Death" (Romans 7:19-25). Excerpt from sermon on November 6

Today we remember the young people who had been suppressed by the aggressive pandemic prevention measures in the past three years and were unfortunately crushed to death in the small alleyway of Itaewon. It is a reminder that each city and town needs wholesome town festivals for the youth. It made me remember the commitment and leadership of our church's regional group directors who worked on our Fall Care Culture Fest and the Traveling Worship.

To prevent another disaster like this, rather than irresponsibly blaming the young people for going to a haunted festival, we need to promote wholesome festivals in each city and town, such as Yakdae-dong's Kkopsari Film Festival, the Fall Care Culture Fest, and the Care Walk where the young and the old are welcome. This can be a chance to mobilize local resident self-governance that makes such events possible. In this context, our fall Travel Worship on the Day of the Laity is the combination of our love of nature and travel, the laity's needs and their leadership....

On the week of the Itaewon disaster, there was a seminar of Christian theologians and social scientists titled "Arrival of the Post-pandemic Society: A Glimpse into the Changes in the Future." The Old Testament scholar Kim Hoe-gwon (Soongsil University) stated that the Korean church must show kingly and priestly leadership at our time in history. In his presentation, "Locating Theology and Church in the Post-Pandemic Age: Church as the Kingly Priest for the Earth Creation Community," he said that the church has a role as a civil society group with common resources. He said the Korean church must respond with creative liturgy in the face of the pandemic. This means the church must be the kingly high priest for the human community and care for all creation. Dr. Lee Jae-yeol (Professor of Sociology in Seoul National University) presented that the pandemic revealed how the issues of the society are also present in the churches, which is the issue of weak public sphere. He pointed out that we are facing the crisis of low birth rate and aging population, in our super-connected platform society. He also advised that the church should move away from church-centeredness and initiate change in society. The church should mobilize its collective social impact to promote empathy. Just like Dr. Kim spoke of the priestly church as the civil society organization with common public resources, and Dr. Lee of the "collective impact" the church can make as the town square and platform, I myself had the chance to lecture at the Presbyterian University and Theological Seminary and the Graduate School of Practical Theology in the last two weeks. I proposed that after the pandemic each church in town must display cooperative leadership to do ministry not as individual church units but in cooperation with the entire city.

The Bucheon Maeul Ministry Cooperative made events like the Fall Care Culture Fest, Tree Frog Youth Eatery, and Haebit Generator possible that couldn't have been done as a single church. Cooperation on the city level allowed these programs to bless many people. Above all, I could see the potential for the church as the ecclesia that Apostle Paul dreamed of. In the recently published Abingdon Commentary on the Letter to the Corinthians, the New Testament Scholar Hoesler wrote that Paul called the community he started the "ekklesia." It does not mean simply church, but a council. The council was a kind of discursive gathering representing the citizens, and this council included resident aliens. The scholar reminds us that Paul intended for his movement to become an alternative city council. We are connected to become the body of the resurrected Jesus Christ to network and interact with the city and the town community and form a grassroots *ecclesia* (church) movement. The Bucheon Maeul Ministry Cooperative also aims to become that city council of *ecclesia* Paul dreamed of.

To become such this grassroots *ecclesia*, we need two kinds of change. The first is for Saerom Church to become the *ecclesia* church for the town just like the early church that let go of circumcision and the law and welcomed the gentiles. We need to discard the old faith of the hypocritical Jewish synagogues that build walls of privilege called circumcision and the laws to exclude the uncircumcised. Our town church must lower our barrier and welcome all who would enter to cooperate and accompany us. We must become such a city council for the town.

Secondly, the worship of the *Sophia* wisdom by the group that formed around Apollo was based on the belief that individuals can achieve a highly spiritual state to the point of acquiring hidden spiritual knowledge and immortality. They claimed to have achieved a state of spiritual nobility and sought to achieve salvation by reaching a state of spiritual transcendence. But this sense of nobility is what brought chaos and divided the church of Corinth. To achieve the *ecclesia* of the early church that was like the city council, we must discard the self-centered faith that seeks individual well-being and nobility to form a communal body of the resurrected Jesus Christ. I believe this is the new age when such grassroots *ecclesia* (church) movement must be raised up in our Yakdae-dong and our city of Bucheon. Amen!!

Bibliography

Kim, Hong-joong. *Social Sciences of the Heart.* Seoul: Munhakdongne Publishing Group, 2009.

Kim, Seung-seop. *A-p'ŭm-i kil-i toe-lyŏ-myŏn* [To make a way out of the pain]. Seoul: Dong Asia Books, 2017.

Kwon, Jin-kwan. "Min-chung-sin-hak-kwa ma-ŭl-mok-hoe" [Minjung theology and maeul ministry]. Lecture, Youndong Church, Seoul, Maeul Ministry Theology Academy, October 18, 2023.

Sim, Seongbo. *K'o-lo-na si-tae, ma-ŭl-kyo-yuk-kong-tong-ch'e-un-tong-kwa saeng-t'ae-chŏk kyo-yukhak*

[Age of Covid-19, maeul education community movement and ecological education]. *Salimteo*, 28 February 2021.

Understanding Maeul Ministry of Saerom Church

Hong-eyoyl Hwang

Introduction

It has been three years since Covid-19 became a global pandemic. The virus has not been eradicated but social distancing is now over, and we are not required to wear masks indoors except in certain places. Church gatherings were once prohibited but now we are on the road to recovery. But as predicted, in most churches 20 to 30% of the members have not returned to on-site worship. The Korean church is experiencing a continued decrease in membership. In such circumstances, churches doing maeul ministry are not experiencing such serious hardship and are even starting new programs. So for this paper, I would like to present a new path for the future of the Korean church in maeul ministry.

I will examine the maeul ministry of Saerom Church in Bucheon. In part 2, I outline the 35-year history of Saerom Church from local community mission, to maeul formation, and to maeul ministry. Part 3 is an effort to understand Saerom Church's maeul ministry based on missional ecclesiology. I apply the concept of missional church as I understand it to Saerom Church's maeul ministry. Here I make the point that maeul ministry is not a unique phenomenon of the Korean church but has considerable overlaps with the missional church concept of North America. But in this examination, I will also draw out the differences between the Korean church's maeul ministry and the missional church concept. In part 4 I analyze Saerom Church's maeul ministry based on several different types of maeul ministries. Identifying the type of maeul ministry helps to better understand this case. Part 5 brings together all these discussions to identify the characteristics of Saerom Church's maeul ministry and its remaining tasks.

From Local Community Mission to Maeul Ministry

Won-don Lee, the pastor of Saerom Church divides the 36-year history of the church's mission into three periods. The first is the 1980s local community missions operating a children's daycare center and a study room. It was followed by the period of the Asian Financial Crisis when the church worked on caring for families in crisis. That was also a time of learning from the civil society and cooperating with them on projects such as the Small Library Movement. From 2013 until present, the local community mission, local social services, and maeul formation programs were integrated into the maeul ministry. In the post-pandemic age that requires integrated care (community care), maeul ministry is about knitting a web of care in the community.[1]

---

[1] Won-don Lee, "K'o-lo-na-mun-myŏng chŏn-hwan-ki, yak-tae-tong t'ong-hap tol-pom-

Previously I examined the maeul ministries of Hannam Jeil Church, Ssangsaem Jayeon Church, and Gogi Church based on missional ecclesiology.[2] Hannam Jeil Church and Ssangsaem Jayeon Church had a clearly marked transition period from local community mission to the maeul ministry framework. The period is not so clear at Gogi Church. At Saerom Church, 2013 is marked as the time of transition from local community mission to maeul ministry, but there is still overlap between the two. Pastor Won-don Lee stated in 2013 that the important point of transition is to "change the focus of church ministry and mission from the church to the town."[3]

Saerom Church's Local Community Mission (1986-1996): Ministry to Local Community and Children

Local Community Mission Programs

Yakdae-dong is a marginal town in the city of Bucheon. Its residents are older populations who had been living there their entire life and young families in their 20s and 30s, both parents working to pay for their housing rental. In the spirit of Jesus who started his ministry in the marginalized town of Galilee, Lee started Saerom Church in Yakdae-dong answering the call to share the gospel with financially hard-pressed young couples and their children. So Saerom Children's Daycare Center began operations on April 5, 1986, ahead of the founding of the church on June 8 of the same year. The daycare center cared for and educated preschool children from 8 am to 6 pm. Saerom Study Room was started at the request of local residents and working parents whose children graduated from the daycare center. It started in January 1990 in a building named Saerom House of Meeting by the church. As these local community mission programs for the town children progressed, a deacon in the church sold their private property to give an offering to purchase five thousand books. That began the town library called Yakdae Geulbang in February 1989. In this marginal town of Bucheon near an industrial complex, it is easy to fall into overconsumption and pleasure-seeking. The library, therefore aimed to spread healthy citizenship and Christian culture by encouraging communal reading and information sharing. On April 28,

---

ma-ŭl ka-nŭn kil" [The Road to Yakdae-dong Integrated Community Care in the Civilizational Transition of the Pandemic]. Co-authored by Won-don Lee, Seung-hyun Chung, Dongkyu Choi, Kook-il Han, Hong Eyoyl Hwang, *Sŏn-kyo-chŏk mok-hoe kil-chap-i: sŏn-kyo mok-hoe-lo-pu-t'ŏ ma-ŭl-mok-hoe-kka-chi* [A Guide to Missional Ministry: from Missional Ministry to Maeul Ministry], (Seoul: Dongyeon, 2022), 139-144.

[2] Hong-eyoyl Hwang, "Sŏn-kyo-chŏk kyo-hoe-lon-e-sŏ pon ma-ŭl-mok-hoe" [Maeul ministry based on missional ecclesiology] Co-authored by Won-don Lee, Seung-hyun Chung, Dongkyu Choi, Kook-il Han, Hong-eyoyl Hwang, *Sŏn-kyo-chŏk mok-hoe kil-chap-i: sŏn-kyo mok-hoe-lo-pu-t'ŏ ma-ŭl-mok-hoe-kka-chi* [A Guide to Missional Ministry: from Missional Ministry to Maeul Ministry], (Seoul: Dongyeon, 2022), 187-230.

[3] Won-don Lee, *K'o-lo-na-1-9 mun-myŏng chŏn-hwan-ki-ŭi saeng-myŏng-mang mok-hoe-wa tol-pom-ma-ŭl* [Ministry of the Web of Life and Community Care in Post-Pandemic Transition], (Seoul: Nanum, 2022), 23.

1990, Saerom Church Officer's Meeting combined Saerom Children's Daycare, Saerom House of Meeting, and Yakdae Geulbang to be handled by the church's local community mission committee. To raise the quality of these services and share the good news of the Kingdom of God to the neighbors and the community, the pastor and the program staff and volunteers started meeting once a month to pray and study.[4] The church's pastor Lee from the time of the founding of the church considered Jesus the "King of Festivities." He sought to form a community of Jesus in Yakdae-dong that is similar to Galilee, and to organize parties and festivals like Jesus did.[5] This intention is apparent in the three-step plan of local community mission.

Three-Step Plan of Local Community Mission

Won-don Lee understood Jesus' mission in Galilee in three steps.[6] The first step is befriending and fellowship. The first thing Jesus did in Galilee where the community was in shambles was to make a community that gathered for meals. Jesus was called "a glutton and a drunkard, a friend of tax collectors and sinners" (Luke 7:34). Jesus' first strategy was to recover the community of table fellowship. This community would later share Jesus' body together at the communion table. Jesus told parables of the kingdom of God describing it as a feast. Among different parts of the body, befriending and fellowship, making and sharing bread, are primarily the work of the hands. Secondly, out of the fellowship, trust builds naturally. This trust or faith is what the scripture says leads to forgiveness of sin. The poor were always called sinful and ill. But the people who met Jesus and formed a new community had the faith to identify themselves as both sinners and the citizens of the kingdom of God. As this faith spread like a virus, the new faith community liberated from the chains of law began spreading throughout Galilee. When Jesus said *Ephphatha, Talitha kum*, "the deaf and mute spirit come out", the blind could see, the deaf could hear, and the mute could speak. Thirdly, the people whose eyes, mouths, and ears were opened began to move. A woman believed that touching Jesus' cloak could heal her and that is what happened (Luke 8:40-48). The paralyzed man and his friends scaled the walls, made a hole in the roof and approached Jesus to be healed (Mark 2:1-12). This third step may be described as the work of the feet. Jesus never stayed in one town for long but moved to other towns. The declaration that the poor own the kingdom of God must now be spread to other towns. The gospel of the kingdom of God must be shared beyond all self-righteousness, taboo, and division.

Saerom Church found the wounds and sicknesses of the poor in the process of local community mission in Yakdae-dong. There weren't physical lepers we read about in the Bible but people had leprosy of the heart that similarly alienated them from the world. In the story of the paralyzed man, the friends used

---

[4] Won-don Lee, *Ma-ŭl-i kkum-ŭl kku-myŏn to-si-ka ch'um-ŭl ch'un-ta* [When a Town Dreams the City Dances], (Seoul: Donggyeon, 2011), 27-28.

[5] Ibid., 8.

[6] Ibid., 51-52.

collective wisdom to cooperate and open up the roof to take the patient over the crowds that stood between him and Jesus. Like the paralyzed man's body could get up and walk again, through local community mission Saerom Church aimed to raise up the community as the relational body and the body of Christ. A local community mission must serve the local residents and have its basis among the residents to be rooted in the community. This is the missional strategy to prepare for the 21st-century age of decentralization and local autonomy. Secondly, to raise up a faith community in a poor town like Yakdae-dong, a ministry of healing by faith is required. There are residents who do not have the mental, temporal, or economic capacity to participate in religious activities. Others are wrapped up in personal temptations, idols, and illusions. What they need is the good news of the faith that can fight against mistaken value systems and falsities. The healing that results from such faith was required of Yakdae-dong residents. Thirdly, Saerom Church needed the faith of the poor as it was to conduct local community missions to serve the poor. In the 21st century, the church must be poor in spirit. Rather than imitating the growth patterns of megachurches, exaggerations, ornaments, and hypocrisies must be discarded to devote all energy to the church's essential call to share and serve. A church that is poor in spirit that serves (*diakonia*) others is the one that will shine.[7]

Saerom Church's Mission in the Age of Economic Crisis and Local Governance (1997-2012): Ministry to Families and Town

The first local assembly election was held in 1991 and the first local government elections in 1995 to begin the age of decentralized governance. Saerom Church had to adjust to this new age of local governance. Also around 1994, the nearby towns of Sang-dong and of Joong-dong in Bucheon were redeveloped to host new business districts. Saerom church's local community mission in Yakdae-dong also required a change. But with the Asian Financial Crisis that hit South Korea in 1997, unemployment rose steeply and families were splitting. This was the urgent matter that Saerom Church had to face. 2012 was the International Year of Cooperatives. Saerom Church also turned its attention to social cooperatives and social enterprises. Ten years of local community mission by Saerom Church in Yakdae-dong led to the rediscovery of the maeul, or maeul/community-building, as the key missional task.

Social Service Mission in Response to Financial Crisis

In response to the Asian Financial Crisis, Saerom Church began the Exciting House Program on Thanksgiving Sunday of 1998 (October 18) for children who go to school without lunch. This was the first unemployment response program since the founding of the Bucheon branch of the Citizens' Movement to Overcome Unemployment. It was to provide a safe space and meals for children and teenagers. This is also proof of civil society's recognition of Saerom Church's education and social service programs for children and teenagers in the past decade. Saerom Church then combined Saerom Daycare Center, Yakdae Geulbang, Saerom Study Room, and Saerom Exciting House programs under

[7] Ibid., 53-55.

Saerom Family Support Center in 2000 to connect the different programs together and work to prevent family separations.[8] Director Oh Sye-hyang of the Family Support Center remarked on the rationale behind the center, "What we realized based on our programs for the children in this community is that this is only a band aid solution. A simple education or social service program won't solve the fundamental problem of the community. The issue of children is not just about the children but about the family structure. We must recognize and respond to the whole family system." She continued to explain the purpose of the center as "supporting and encouraging the lower-income families who are bearing the brunt of the social dilemma of family separation and educational collapse."[9]

Maeul/Community-Building

Background

Around this time maeul/community-building or community-building became a key missional task of Saerom Church. Before explaining maeul/community-building I will first point to how it is related to missions in the age of decentralization. Local community mission is a church-centered terminology. But "maeul-building" is related to the change in the urban administration paradigm in response to social issues that arose in industrialization, urbanization, and modernization. It is an effort to turn from development-centered urban administration toward resident participation for self-governance.[10] In this case, Saerom Church was responding specifically to the local changes and needs following urban redevelopment near the church. Maeul-building is complex and comprehensive. It is a local resident community that forms neighborhood networks in the process of responding to everyday needs. The movement aims to build "the kind of town needed in the 21st-century Korean society that responds with alternative education to educational collapse and college entrance competition, an alternative economy that harmonizes mutual benefit, redistribution, and exchange, an alternative culture that strengthens personal identity and forms communities, an ecological town that regards and reconstructs individual persons and communities within the wider ecology, and life politics that aim for human happiness."[11]

Saerom Church's Internal Factors toward Maeul/Community-Building

For Saerom Church, Maeul-making was the product of a decade of local community mission. The church aimed to build strong communities through the mission, but the residents wanted to earn enough money to move to a better area.

---

[8] Ibid., 56-74.

[9] Ibid., 68-69.

[10] Hong-eyoyl Hwang, ""Ma-ŭl man-tŭl-ki, ma-ŭl-mok-hoe-wa ma-ŭl-mok-hoe-ŭi sin-hak-chŏk kŭn-kŏ" [Maeul-building, maeul ministry and its theological basis], edited by Seong-yeol Kang, Myeong-gi Baek, *Han-kuk-kyo-hoe-ŭi mi-lae-wa ma-ŭl-mok-hoe* [Future of the Korean church and maeul ministry], (Seoul: Handeul, 2016), 135.

[11] Ibid., 136-138.

The ones who succeeded left and the poor families often broke up and also left town. So the church realized that unless the town changes, the church's ministry, mission, and evangelism are all for nothing. In the first period, Saerom Church considered the local community of Yakdae-dong as the object of mission, but in this second phase, the focus expanded to consider the church, families, and the entire town as the object of ministry. Saerom church discovered the maeul as they met and learned from the civil society of Bucheon.[12]

The other factor that led to Saerom Church considering maeul/community-building as a missional task is that over the decade of local community mission, many residents made use of the church programs but rarely joined the faith community. This issue was analyzed in the following ways. The first reason is that the residents are supported by the church's local community mission programs during weekdays, but on the weekends they attend extravagant megachurches out of their aspiration to a middle-class lifestyle. It seems that small Saerom Church reminds them of their own humbleness. The community residents were not willing to become a faith community that serves others in the local community. This is in line with the image of the middle and upper class constructed by the Korean church. People are under the illusion that if they attend a middle-class church, they will also become middle-class. Secondly, the first generation of church members (majority of church officers) were devoted to work and child rearing and did not have the time and the capacity to participate in local community missions. They gradually withdrew into their private spheres and could not lead the new Christians and the second generation of church members in missions. If even the officers of the church are captive to deception, idolatry, and fantasy then it would be impossible to free the unchurched neighbors from these things and provide spiritual comfort and encouragement. Despite these challenges, there was hope in the second generation of church members who were actively participating in mission and service. Yakdae-dong maeul-building was the product of such ministerial dilemma. A poor town of Yakdae-dong may be the very place where hope for education and social service can grow. The church calmly assessed the state of the town and constructed a model of maeul/community-building for the environment, education, and social services.[13]

Process of Maeul/Community-building

Saerom Church began planning maeulcommunity-building for Yakdae-dong in 1998. The maeul/community-building movement started with the adoption of Agenda 21 which was declared at the 1992 United Nations Conference on Environment and Development in Rio de Janeiro.[14] To implement Agenda 21, the city of Bucheon and civil society organizations formed an operational committee on November 10, 1999, and established Green Bucheon: Agenda 21 Implementation Council on January 8, 2000. The Council organized subcommittees on the environment, urban planning, transportation, economy,

[12] Won-don Lee, *When a Town Dreams the City Dances*, 9-10.

[13] Ibid., 84-86.

[14] Ibid., 88.

administration, social service, society, education, culture, women, youth, and citizen action. The Council consisted of 130 members representing citizens, civil society organizations, labor unions, businesses, universities, city assemblies, the news media, and government workers. Each subcommittee of 20 to 30 members met over 25 times for discussions, conducted field visits and surveys, and established the aim, purpose, and action strategies. They organized a public hearing to commit to the action strategy and declared Green Bucheon 21 in December 2000.[15] Maeul/community-building was a subcommittee under Green Bucheon 21, and a regional gathering of Yakdae-dong maeul/community-building was launched declaring the "Making a Beautiful Maeul of Yakdae-dong" on June 10, 2001 at Saerom Church, inviting the residents, members of the municipal assembly, local government personnel and civil society representatives. Saerom Church led Yakdae-dong maeul/community-building to encourage maeul/community formation through self-motivated resident participation and agreement, spread awareness of community connection to education, the environment, and social service, and promote cooperation between private, public, and civil society organizations.[16]

Green Bucheon 21 and Yakdae-dong Maeul/Community-Building

Saerom Church's Yakdae-dong maeul/community-building was part of Green Bucheon 21 which was a localization of the global Agenda 21. It was conducted through the cooperation of the Local Government of Bucheon and Yakdae-dong Community Self-Governance Center, and the gathering and cooperation of various civil society organizations and residents. Bucheon Small Library Network of Green Bucheon 21 decided to build a small library in Bucheon. This resulted in establishing Yakdae Family Library on December 24, 2002, on the third floor of the Yakdae-dong Community Self-Governance Center that was started on July 13, 2000.[17] Saerom Church's Saturday Faith Class became Saturday Culture Class, then Yakdae-dong Weekend School. The School began on September 11, 2004 to teach writing, singing, film production, Korean traditional percussion quartet, and environmental care, and organized field visits or weekend family trips.[18] Afterwards, Saerom Study Room joined the Association of After-School Study Rooms in Bucheon. In 2004 the revised Child Welfare Act legally recognize local children's centers (what used to be called "study rooms") as children's welfare facilities. Study rooms that started as a social movement thus became part of the public social welfare system to be called local children's centers. The same happened with Saerom Study Room as Bucheon's Local Children's Center Association was launched. In the years after the financial crisis, the children's center was provided comprehensive services for learning assistance, social welfare, and meals. Saerom Church also participated in establishing the Ordinance on School Meals in Bucheon and the

---

[15] Ibid., 97-98,

[16] Ibid., 90.

[17] Ibid., 98-107. For more on the Small Library Movement in Bucheon, see pp. 129-160 in the same book.

[18] Ibid., 95-96.

Bucheon School Meal Network to provide healthy school lunches.[19] In July 2001, the Korea-Japan Joint Workshop on maeul/community-building was organized in Yakdae-dong. The maeul-making team from the sister city of Kawasaki, Japan attended this event. Director Oh Sye-hyang of Yakdae-dong Family Support Center heard of the Human Rights Ordinance in Kawasaki so she visited the city in August to observe and learn from Japan's maeul/community-building and their children's rights ordinance. On November 28, 2003, the Children's Rights Network subcommittee of Green Bucheon 21 organized the Forum on Establishing an Ordinance on Children's Rights in Bucheon. Saerom Daycare Center and Saerom Church participated in these movements to improve the city children's welfare.[20]

Weaving the Web of Social Service, Education, and Culture

But maeul/community-building is not just about constructing a town space but about paying attention to the community and promoting the communication of people. Won-don Lee wanted to make a town where new time, space, and stories are birthed. Here the main characters are the town's children, mothers, immigrants, and seniors. In such a town, there must be festivals, because the festivals are what best mark the passage of time and display vitality. The people who make and participate in festivals are the central characters of the town. The children, the mothers, the residents, the immigrants, and the seniors seek out the town library, study room, and community center and their stories are collected to make the town open and dynamic. Like Lee's book title *When a Town Dreams the City Dances*, the town and the city must have the capacity for them to dream and imagine. Libraries, field trips, and the arts are the ways and spaces where the young and old can dream. In the era of low birth rates and an aging population, in the growing inequality, education, welfare, and culture must achieve local integration and networking to construct a comprehensive mode of delivery. So the most important task in maeul/community-building was to form an ecosystem that connects the study room, the library, the welfare center, the community self-governance center, the church, and the civil society groups. To construct such an ecosystem, Saedom Church proposed making a Lifelong Learning initiative for Maeul/Community-Building in the Yakdae-dong Lifelong Learning Center. It was to make a learning environment in town through the study of the liberal arts. Saerom Church worked to connect the small libraries together, launched the Wednesday Liberal Arts Café, and organized the Global Village Festival with the foreign migrants.[21]

Forming the Maeul Ministry and Integrated Care Network of Saerom Church (2013-Present): Life and Cooperation

With residents of Yakdae-dong, Saerom church established the cooperative Rabbit on the Moon that began operating a town café. Then about the time

---

[19] Ibid., 113-128.
[20] Ibid., 161-173.
[21] Ibid., 174-215.

Bucheon Film Festival was held, the Kkopsari[22] Film Festival was also organized to share the stories of the town, and these programs really began efforts in maeul ministry.[23] But as mentioned, maeul/community-building in Bucheon already started in December 2000 with the declaration of Green Bucheon 21, and the Yakdae-dong maeul/community-building initiative was declared in June 2001. So it could be said that Saerom Church's maeul ministry started before 2013. Back in 2007, Won-don Lee himself also divided the periods as the one on the local community and the children (1986-1997), the family and the maeul (1997-2000), and life and the global village (2000-2007).[24] But 2013 can be considered the key year that started maeul ministry because the year was when the town's ecosystem of learning, culture, and social service began to be constructed with programs such as the cooperative café and the film festival. In 2018, the Yakdae Care Community Council was started to set up care networks in each community. Starting in 2019, urban farmers organized to raise crops in response to the climate crisis. In 2021 Silver Wings of Saerom Family Support Center and Bucheon Healthcare Society Cooperative joined to conduct Yakdae-dong Healthcare Leaders Workshops in nine sessions to train people to care for the town in the age of integrated community care.[25]

Saerom Church's maeul ministry aims to weave an integrated web of care in Yakdae-dong. For the education and learning environment, Yakdae-dong Daycare, Local Children's Center, Family Library, Maeul Choir, Kkobi Broadcasting Station, Kkobi Night Eatery and its Kkobtels Friends, and the seniors of the Senior Center combined their efforts to organize the 2016 Town Summer School. The program was the outcome of the idea that the entire town is a place of learning, or a school. The town choir was made up of the youth and the seniors at the Senior Center who learned Korean traditional singing plus Saerom Church Choir. The town's Family Library, the Rabbit on the Moon Cooperative, the Unlimited Refill Club, and Kkobi Night Eatery joined the choir afterwards to compete in the Bucheon Unification Concert on August 15, 2016 to win second place. These efforts were about building the cultural environment. Saerom Church makes home visits to church members in the spring and to the hard-pressed residents in town in the fall to pray for them. The intercessory prayer team in the church prays for the community and the people for whom missions committees request special prayers. Home visits for town residents happen in cooperation between the intercessory prayer team and the local missions organizations, and this is the ecosystem of spiritual care.

When Kkobsari Film Festival was organized in Yakdae-dong in 2013 the residents made the fictional character Kkobi. Kkobi Night Eatery which provides free dinner to youth every Friday began operations in March 2016. Each week about a hundred youths visit the eatery where the food is prepared by three

[22] Kkopsari in Korean means to tag along.

[23] Won-don Lee, "The Road to Yakdae-dong Integrated Community Care in the Civilizational Transition of the Pandemic," 144.

[24] Won-don Lee, *When a Town Dreams the City Dances*, 174.

[25] Won-don Lee, "Unexpected Harvest of the Holy Spirit in a Small Church during the Pandemic". This publication.

churches (Saerom Church of the Presbyterian Church of Korea (Tonghap), Yakdae Joongang Church of the Presbyterian Church in Korea (Hapdong), and Yakdae Methodist Church that take turns to volunteer to shop, cook, and serve the meal. Kkobi Night Eatery is related to building the environment of social service and is a model case of ecumenical cooperation with other local churches. The three churches collaborated to conduct a six-week course called "Finding Hope in Maeul Community" and are promoting the Community Care Movement. In 2017 the Saerom Church youths who volunteer at the Kkobi Eatery met with young activists of the Tree Frog Eatery which provides meals for youth in the city of Bucheon. They agreed to grow crops together on the rooftop of the church. Another issue was that a system was needed for doctors to visit the elderly rather than having the elderly come to the hospitals. A time had come for the town to take care of their own through an integrated network for disease prevention and healthcare, and Saerom Church needed to play a part in establishing such a network. Around that time in 2021 the children's daycare center that operated for 35 years was closing down. After prayers and considerations, it was decided that the church building's first and second floors would be turned into spaces for the town's culture, healthcare, and environmental activities. On the first floor are the shared maeul kitchen and the seniors' café, and on the second floor are spaces for education and cultural events. The entire rooftop would also be turned into a maeul garden for ecological healing. The nine people who became certified healthcare leaders of the maeul in 2021 would take responsibility for operating these spaces.[26] These developments mean that Saerom Church's maeul ministry is expanding to include environmental programs and medical/healthcare services.

Understanding Saerom Church's Maeul Ministry based on Missional Ecclesiology[27]

Theological Conversion and Theological Direction

Theological Conversion

Missional ecclesiology starts with a conversion in one's understanding of mission. It requires overcoming the dualism between the mission and church, going beyond the attractional, church-centered understanding of mission to the eschatological perspective of the kingdom of God in the already and the not yet.[28]

---

[26] Won-don Lee, "The Road to Yakdae-dong Integrated Community Care in the Civilizational Transition of the Pandemic," 144-158.

[27] This section was composed based on Hong-eyoyl Hwang, "Korean Minjung church from the perspective of the missional ecclesiology" in the Korean Society of Mission Studies (ed.), *Missional Ecclesiology and Korean Church* (Seoul: Christian Literature Society of Korea, 2015), 415-30.

[28] Darrell L. Guder (ed.), *Missional Church: A Vision for the Sending of the Church in North America,* trans. by Sung-hyun Chung (Incheon: Juan International University Press, 2013), 28; Craig van Gelder & Dwight J. Zscheile, *The Missional Church in*

During his undergraduate years Won-don Lee participated in a class on ecclesiology in Yeondong Church. Then he led the Saerom Church's undergraduate group and went through a theological conversion. As Lee was an active member of the Korea Student Christian Fellowship he played a key role in the publication of *Scripture and Practice 1* (Seoul: Minjungsa, 1987) and *Scripture and Practice 2* (Seoul: Minjungsa, 1989).[29] Lee applied the outcome of his theological conversion to these Bible study texts.

Theological Direction

A missional church participates in the mission of God for the kingdom of God, based on the theology of the Trinity.[30] Saerom Church is participating in the mission of God to build the kingdom of God in Yakdae-dong. As shown in the three types of local community missions, the first step is about friendship and fellowship with the residents the church meets through mission programs and sharing meals. This parallels Jesus' likening of the kingdom of God to a house of feast. The second step is for the residents to join the celebrations to realize and believe that they are both sinners and citizens of the kingdom of God. The third step is to discard the self-righteousness, taboo, and separation, and to evangelize and declare to others that the poor belong to the kingdom of God.

Three-fold Conversation of Culture, Gospel, and the Church

Understanding the Culture

The concept of missional church in North America attempted a new understanding of the gospel and the church through a conversation between the gospel, culture, and church. There was a crisis of disconnection between church and culture, and that the church was submissive to the culture at large in North America.[31] Maeul ministry opposes the culture standing against the reign of God and seeks an alternative community and lifestyle. Won-don Lee describes the cultural difference between the age of industrialization and the 21st century as that of mass production of a single product (hardware/male/muscle) and limited production of multiple products (software/female/knowledge creation), between the analogue (big, powerful, foolish) and the digital (small, but smart and creative), between the megachurch (Goliath paradigm) and the small but influential and innovative church (David paradigm).[32] The maeul ministry of Saerom Church presents the kingdom of God's value of service, sharing, and celebration of the kingdom of God to the world of consumerism, individualism, capitalism, and survivalism. Through these values of the kingdom of God the

---

*Perspective: Mapping Trends and Shaping the Conversation (*Grand Rapids: Baker Academic, 2011), 18-25.

29 Interview with pastor Won-don Lee (25 August 2022)

30 Craig van Gelder & Dwight J. Zscheile, *The Missional Church in Perspective,* 26-27, 30-31.

31 Alan J. Roxburgh & M. Scott Boren, *Introducing the Missional Church: What it is, Why it Matters, How to Become One (*Grand Rapids: Baker Books, 2009), 72.

32 Won-don Lee, *When a Town Dreams the City Dances*, 232.

church is constructing the ecology of learning and education, the ecosystem of welfare, the ecosystem of culture, the ecosystem of spiritual care, the ecosystem of environmental conservation, and the ecosystem of integrated community care.

Understanding the Maeul and the Pastor's Self-awareness

The Bible tells the church to exist in the world but not be of it (John 17:11, 14). It means to refuse the value system of the world. But the North American church belonged to the Christendom of the past and did not wrestle with the present culture of the world. The advocates of the missional church reflected on this point.[33] Maeul ministry responds against industrialization and capitalism that broke down the maeul community to restore it through life politics, maeul economy/enterprise, maeul school, maeul culture, and the ecological maeul.[34] To restore the maeul the church must first be restored as a faith community. The community's constituents must not only have a common purpose but also koinonia/communication and participation among them. The koinonia in the church must similarly be constructed between the maeul residents and the church. In other words, maeul ministry is about how the faith community that gathers around the kingdom of God communicates with maeul residents to solve town issues. In this process, the pastor has the two-fold responsibility of constructing the faith community through scripture narratives and contributing to restoring the maeul community with the stories of the maeul. The pastor must also develop a biblical and missiological exegetical method to connect the scripture narratives to stories about the maeul.

Saerom Church made a new discovery after a decade of local community mission. Yakdae-dong residents wanted to earn enough money to move out of the maeul, and some of the families were broken down. And the residents were supported by the church's social service but on Sundays they went to larger churches attended by the middle class. Seeing this, Won-don Lee of Saerom Church transitioned to maeul ministry. Just as it takes a village to raise a child, the church realized that it takes the whole village to restore a family. With this realization, Saerom Church participated in maeul/community-building since 2000, and devoted itself to maeul ministry since 2013.

An example of Won-don Lee's missional exegesis is in his sermon, "Encountering Jesus in the Maeul" on the passage on Jesus healing Peter's mother-in-law (Mark 1:29-34).[35] Lee understands Jesus as someone who loved the maeul and the region, and that the ministry in Galilee is the model of evangelism and mission in maeul ministry. Lee explains the biblical basis of maeul ministry as the following: "Jesus came out of the synagogue and healed various sicknesses at the house of Peter's mother-in-law. He made the place the

---

[33] Craig van Gelder & Dwight J. Zscheile, *The Missional Church in Perspective,* 61.

[34] Hong-eyoyl Hwang, "Maeul/community-building, maeul ministry and its theological basis," 135-155.

[35] Won-don Lee, "Ma-ŭl-e-sŏ man-nan ye-su" [Jesus I met in town], Jeong Shin ed. *Practicing Maeul Ministry with the Community Residents – With the Community, with the Lord: Bible Study Resource Book 3. Research Center of the Presbyterian Church of Korea Maeul Ministry Series 9 (*Seoul: Dongyeon, 2018), 37-49.

basecamp for mission to the maeul. At Alphaeus' house, he formed a community of table fellowship with sinners and tax collectors, and healed a leper who was discriminated, alienated, and excluded from the society. This is how Jesus' new kingdom of God maeul movement started."[36] If the source of pain for the leper was alienation and discrimination, healing came from contact and relationship formation as Jesus put his hands on the person (Mark 1:41). Jesus' healing of the paralyzed man (Mark 2:1-5) is a demonstration of how "only through cooperation and solidarity of friends could they get to Jesus the healer by boring a hole on the roof to go past the crowd surrounding Jesus."[37] Lee explains that for maeul ministry the church and Christians must form a lifelong learning ecosystem, a social service ecosystem, and a narrative community for the maeul. Lee is gifted in connecting new issues or challenges facing maeul ministry to stories of the Bible. He also has a strong internal motivation to bring festivities to maeul community. Lee confessed that inside, there was a conflict between two modes of education. One is the oppressive modern and Western-style education focused on university entrance. The other was a totally different kind of education in that children should first and foremost be healthy and happy, which was Lee experienced in his childhood. His inclination to maeul ministry and festivals can be understood against this background.[38]

Missional Local Church's Theology and Mission Activities

Constitutive Factors of Missional Local Church

Missional ecclesiology is embodied in the local church. These churches may be identified as the missional local church. The constitutive elements of a missional church are mystery, memory, and mission. The element of mystery refers to the church leaders' obedience to God's election and authority rather than controlling the neighboring community for themselves. It also takes remembering how God chose God's people and acted on their behalf, in order for them to sustain their identity and work toward the future. Mission is not the action of the church but the process in which the church is formed through the mystery of God and the church's remembrance of its calling. A missional church is a church changed through remembrance and mission.[39] Won-don Lee sees the congregation as the family of God in obedience to God's election and mystery, rather than objects of control and ministry, and coworkers in maeul ministry (mystery). The people in charge of the missions departments of Saerom Church are faithful coworkers for Lee. Lee trusts that God who encountered him would also encounter the church members and maeul residents. He remembers such redemptive events in the faith community and the maeul, witnesses its present continuation and hopes for them in the future (memory). The church members and the residents who participate in this mystery and memory become the Saerom Church that conducts maeul ministry of community care, knitting a web of flourishing (mission). In other

---

[36] Ibid., 40.
[37] Ibid., 43.
[38] Interview with pastor Won-don Lee (25 August 2022)
[39] Alan J. Roxburgh & M. Scott Boren, *Introducing the Missional Church*, 39-45.

words, Saerom Church and town residents participate in the mission of God for the kingdom of God, and are the objects of the mission of God at the same time.

Missional Local Church Doing Theology

The ones who are doing theology in a missional local church are the congregation. This faith community attends to God's action in the local community. This means theology in a missional local church takes the form of community theology, prophetic theology, and outsiders' theology. Prophets are those who challenge the deviation of a community's theology from scripture. Outsiders' voices and their theology are necessary to prevent the missional local church's theology from becoming too narrow-minded in its attention to local society.[40] Won-don Lee's sermons and Bible exegesis reflect the experiences and issues of church members and maeul residents. For example, his book *When a Town Dreams the City Dances*, there are interviews with a teacher (Kim Gyeong-hee) in the Study Room and with the Director (Oh Sye-hyang) of Saerom Family Support Center, and an essay by a child in the church Sunday School.[41] But Lee also conducts a prophetic function of the maeul pastor by presenting the way of the gospel of the kingdom of God. Maeul ministry is the solution for a flourishing community, and the framework of integrated community care is presented to the church members falling in the way of self-centered survivalism in the neoliberal society. And to prevent the church's maeul ministry from being trapped in provincial matters, he opened up to outsiders' theology by inviting sociologists, philosophers, and theologians' inputs for self-reflection and self-criticism. Lee is striving to turn the attention of the church beyond the local issues to locate it in the macroscopic transition from capitalist industrialism to ecological renewal. This is evident in the new book on Saerom Church's maeul ministry, *Ministry of the Web of Life and Community Care in Post-Pandemic Transition* (2022). The book details the church's efforts to move beyond the status quo to tackle new challenges.

Missional Local Church's Missions Activities

The missional local church is an alternative community that works for the kingdom of God rather than gathering people to the church. It prophetically challenges the society's dominant patterns and fulfills its prophetic calling through its community structure. The missional local church notices the mission of the Holy Spirit working beyond existing borders and walls between the church and local community and participates in it. The missional local church manifests the presence of God in missional activities. It is a community where forgiveness occurs, vulnerabilities are accepted, and love is put into action. When the church conducts its mission through these ways of presence and love, neighbors also participate.[42] Saerom Church's maeul ministry has fulfilled the prophetic task of healing, building up, and connecting through sharing and service in a world of disconnection, separation, alienation, and oppression. Lee and the church

---

[40] Ibid., 91-93.

[41] Won-don Lee, *When a Town Dreams the City Dances,* 41-46, 68-69, 29.

[42] Alan J. Roxburgh & M. Scott Boren, *Introducing the Missional Church:* 108-11.

members as well as maeul residents have participated in maeul ministry to answer the prophetic call. Since the pandemic, Lee especially characterizes the new ministries as the maeul ministry of community care knitting the web of life. The whole armor of the Holy Spirit is necessary to resist the force of evil in the conflict between the old capitalist industrialism and the new ecological framework. The church must be laity-centered rather than clergy-centered, and the congregation should not be religious consumers but religious devotees wearing the armor of the Holy Spirit and chewing substantial food. Such laity is leading the programs such as the community Healthcare Leaders and Care Walks as the Holy Spirit works to form the spiritual ecosystem connecting the family, the church, and the town.[43] This is an important confession identifying the work of the Holy Spirit in the work of the missional local church. In the pandemic that felt like the Israelite exilic period, God did new things in Saerom Church's maeul ministry.

Missional Local Church's Faith Community Formation

Modern, North American culture emphasizes the autonomous self, allowing for ahistorical, individual, practical, and abstract actions in the process of building a faith community. But the missional local church forms itself through historical, communal, experiential, and dynamic action. The faith community matures only when it participates in mission.[44] Saerom church members have been participating in local community missions and maeul ministry, seeing the lives of the local residents change. They see the formation of cultural, educational, spiritual, and pro-environment ecosystem, and the construction of community care, and experience changes in ways they read the scripture and the ways they mature in faith. Saerom faith community matures as a missional local church through these missions activities.

Missional Minister's Leadership

Missional leadership that forms the missional church and declares the kingdom of God is nurtured by the Holy Spirit and the revelation of Jesus Christ who confronted the powers in obedience to God. The people of God and the leaders are imperfect, but the Holy Spirit leads them to an eschatological future. Missional leadership raises up people to declare God's plan for creation. Won-don Lee's maeul ministry in Saerom Church goes beyond cooperation with civil society organizations and cooperative governance with the city government and the maeul community center, knowing that the culture of the reign of God conflicts with the dominant culture and worldview. The situation requires the armor of the Holy Spirit in opposition against the power of the air (Ephesians 6:10-17). Forming a spiritual ecosystem on top of other ecologies is critical, and this is practiced in the church's maeul visitation ministry.

---

[43] Won-don Lee, "Unexpected Harvest of the Holy Spirit in a Small Church during the Pandemic", This publication.

[44] Darrell L. Guder (ed.), *Missional Church*, 226-36.

Won-don Lee and the Saerom Church faith community are fallible and may misinterpret the signs of the times as they work for the kingdom of God. Nevertheless, they confess that the Holy Spirit is leading them toward the eschatological future. Even during the pandemic new things were happening, such as the Yakdae-dong Healthcare Leaders Workshop to prepare them for the integrated care system, and the Fall Care Culture Fest in cooperation between the healthcare leaders and the literacy class. Members of the Wednesday Bible Study Class confessed that their mission is the work of the Holy Spirit. The Care Walk to community residents selected by the mission subcommittee among request submissions, and the founding of the Maeul Ministry Cooperative are the unexpected harvests of the Holy Spirit. In this process Lee trained healthcare leaders to visit the community and declare God's plans for the creation. Lee's leadership excels in connecting scripture narratives with maeul ministry. When maeul ministry must advance to the next step he makes he presents his biblical and missional hermeneutics for the next step. Lee connects church members with local residents, programs with programs, the church with other organizations and groups, trains leaders and places them in organizations as workers or leaders, and empowers their capacity. This leadership is based on his experience participating in the bible study curriculum development in the 1980s, his participation in the Korean Christian Student Association and Students for Social Development, his two-year training in inner city missions at the Social Mission Council, participation in Asia Christian Youth Training by the Christian Council of Asia, and on the theory of *minjung* education by Heo Byung-seop explained in his book *Let them Speak for themselves*.[45]

Understanding Saerom Church's Maeul Ministry among the Types of Maeul Ministry

I previously categorized different maeul ministries into types: community (Poolmoo School and Hongseong Local community, Wild Flower Maeul), church (Saeam Church, Jang Shin Farming Cooperative, Jageun Church), church-community (Baekwoon Church and Hanmaeum Community, Still Waters Church and Small Christ Community, Hanbeot Church and Ye Sa Rang Community, Multicultural Church and Borderless Village), non-government organization (Yeongdeungpo Urban Industrial Mission Cooperative, Bongcheon-dong House of Sharing Self-Rehabilitation Center in Gwanak District of Seoul), and social enterprise (Ulsan East District Social Enterprise Council). Maeul/community-building, can be categorized as efforts to vitalize the life to children and schools, maeul economy/enterprise that supports the maeul economy, culture that vitalizes community, transition to ecological community, life politics that saves the maeul, and the integration of these elements.[46] The authors of *Maeul Ministry that Saves the World* published by the Presbyterian Church of Korea Research Center similarly categorized types as

[45] Interview with pastor Won-don Lee (25 August 2022).

[46] Hong-eyoyl l Hwang, "Maeul/community-building, maeul ministry and its theological basis," 159-176, 138-150.

maeul ministry for ecological renewal, together making a welfare community of hope, maeul ministry and economic community, making a beautiful environmental community, forming a healthy maeul learning community, and maeul ministry and cultural community.[47] Saerom Church's maeul ministry can include ecosystems of education, economy, culture, environment, social service, and politics.

Saerom Church has been constructing the educational ecosystem in its local children's center, the Wednesday Bible Study, the Liberal Arts Class, and the Yakdae-dong Summer School. The cultural ecosystem refers to the Korean traditional music class, maeul choir, Kkopsari Film Festival, Kkobi Broadcasting Station, and the Family Library. For the social service ecosystem, they operated the daycare center, Kkobi Night Eatery for the teenagers, Silver Wings, and the Family Support Center. For the economic ecosystem, they operate the Rabbit on the Moon Cooperative and its café. Urban farming on the church building contributes to environmental renewal. On constructing the ecosystem of life politics they participated in the movement to write the Children's Rights Ordinance and the Bucheon School Lunch Ordinance. In terms of type, Saerom Church's maeul ministry has the three pillars of education, social service, and culture, while the economic and political aspects are relatively weak. Recently the environmental issue has been highlighted by urban farming efforts. The construction of the integrated community care system through visitations by healthcare leaders is an example of an integrated type that combines different aspects. It is remarkable that such a new type of maeul ministry could be added even during the pandemic. That is why Lee calls this the harvest of the Holy Spirit. Overall, Saerom Church's maeul ministry is the integrated type of maeul ministry devoted to social service, culture, and education, with less emphasis on economy and politics, and a recent addition of environmental issues and community care.

In the future there is a need to expand the economic and political aspects. The economic aspect is critical for a maeul's renewal. There are different realms of economy – market economy, national (public) economy, social economy, and household economy. One of the economic issues today is that the national economy that should prioritize the public good is modeled after the market economy prioritizing private interests. There is a need for the national economy to recover its purpose. If social economy takes up 20% of the entire economy, it will greatly alleviate economic inequality. Redistribution of resources is done through politics, and this is why maeul ministry must renew its efforts in politics as well.

The strength of Saerom Church's educational maeul ministry is that the pastor and the church members are the first to learn. I suggest that the church attend to and participate in peace education to practice restorative justice arising as a

[47] Young-sang Ro ed. *Maeul Ministry that Saves the World* (Seoul: Dongyeon, 2018).

solution to school violence, and apply it to other social relationships.[48] This will result in expanding and deepening the educational sphere.

Characteristics of Saerom Church's Maeul Ministry and Remaining Tasks

Characteristics of Saerom Church's Maeul Ministry

First, the pastor's biblical and missional hermeneutics of scripture narratives teaches how the mission of Jesus of Galilee and the mission of Saerom Church connect and apply to issues in its maeul ministry. Local community mission started with the three phases of Jesus' mission in Galilee. Maeul ministry is conducted through the method presented in Lee's sermon "Encountering Jesus in Town." The Christological exegesis on local community mission and maeul ministry then turned into pneumatological exegesis through the crisis of the Covid-19 pandemic.

Second, the terms and concepts in the church's maeul ministry continue to expand and develop. The local community mission of the early days turned into participation in maeul/community-building, then shifted to maeul ministry in the past decade. Recently they are advancing the Maeul Ministry Cooperative. This progression is also evident in the change from the study room to the children's social service center and to family support center. Visitations also changed from visiting only the church members to include other community residents an renaming it Care Walk.

Third, the terms and concepts continued to develop because the church tried to build connections between people, between programs, and with the maeul, and responded to social changes. In response to the Asian Financial Crisis the daycare center and the study room were integrated to form the Family Support Center. Church member visitations were expanded to include the maeul because the local community missions committee and the intercessory prayer team collaborated. Training Yakdae-dong Healthcare Leaders was made possible by the collaboration between Silver Wings and the Bucheon Healthcare Societ Cooperative. In the age of exclusion, discrimination, alienation, and oppression, connecting people, organizations, programs, churches, and maeuls for communication and relationship building is the life-giving logic.

Fourth, Won-don Lee appointed the talented residents and church members he met in maeul ministries as staff or directors of programs, trained them, and gave them authority and responsibilities.

---

[48] For more on restorative justice and peace education, see Hong Eyoyl Hwang, "Hak-kyo-p'ok-lyŏk-ŭ-lo-pu-t'ŏ p'yŏng-hwa-lo-un hak-kyo man-tŭl-ki-lŭl wi-han kyo-hoe-ŭi sŏn-kyo-kwa-che- choh-ŭn-kyo-sa-un-tong-ŭi hoe-pok-chŏk saeng-hwal-kyo-yuk-ŭl chung-sim-ŭ-lo" [Church's missional task to bring peace against school violence: restorative life education of the good teacher movement]. Edited by Hong Eyoyl Hwang, Co-authored by Eun-su Kim, Chang-hyeon Park, Hwan-cheol Yoon, Jun-hyeong Lee, Jong-hwa Lim, Hee-mo Lim, Yoon-gyeong Hong, Hong Eyoyl Hwang, '*Hel-cho-sŏn'-e ŭng-tap-ha-nŭn han-kuk-kyo-hoe kae-hyŏk* [Korean church reform in response to 'hell chosun'], (Seoul, Dongyeon, 2018), 159-202.

Fifth, Saerom Church has been actively studying and implementing cutting-edge movements of the age such as decentralization, collaborative governance, social economy, cooperatives, maeul/community-building, flourishing of life, networking, and integrated community care before any other organization. This is also the reason why their concepts and terms continued to evolve.

Sixth, as apparent in the Kkobi Night Eatery for the teenagers, the church has been participating in local ecumenism with other churches of different denominations.

Seventh, the church not only contributed to forming the civil society organization (CSO) collaborative called Green Bucheon 21, but has also played important roles in efforts such as the Children's Rights Ordinance writing movement and the Small Library Movement.

Eighth, as apparent in the formation of the Exciting Family Library on the third floor of the Community Service Center, the church has been a model of collaborative governance with the local government. It was astonishing to see Saerom Church's maeul ministry materials displayed at the entrance of Yakdae-dong Community Service Center when I visited the church eight years ago.

Ninth, Saerom Church's maeul ministry does not rest content in collaborations with other churches or CSOs, but connects with the larger shift from capitalist industrialism to ecological civilization. In this process, they are charting a new path. In the period of transition, the church is collaborating with other local churches toward ecological flourishing, living in a new spiritual lifestyle of interdependence between humanity and nature. They are working to build a caring community that shares the good news of the new civilization according to values of cooperation, communication, care, empathy, and sharing through the lifelong learning structure, the maeul enterprise, and the ecological maeul festivals (Maeul Ministry Declaration, September 26, 2022). This is how Saerom Church weaves the web of care. Their theme for the year 2023 is "A church abundant with life and care rather than material."

Tenth, all these characteristics of maeul ministry in Saerom Church are related to the pastoral leadership. Lee studies the issues and challenges of the time before any of the church members and wrestles to apply them to Bible study, mission, and maeul ministry. Along with the congregation and other maeul ministry pastors he continues to study and debate to learn from others in preparation for new programs and ministries.

Challenges for Saerom Church's Maeul Ministry

First, Saerom Church's maeul ministry has emphasized education, social service, and culture, less on economy and politics, and has recently added environmental concerns and integrated community care. In the age of climate crisis there is a greater need to emphasize environmental concerns. The ministry can also present a model of a comprehensive care system in the age of integrated community care. The political and economic aspects of maeul ministry should also be expanded.

Second, there is a move by the maeul's Community Service Center to erase Saerom Church's seven-year involvement in the decade-long history of Kkobsari Film Festival. Despite the church's decisive role in Yakdae-dong and maeul/community-building, there is widespread anti-church and anti-Christian sentiments in the society because of the familial succession of pastorship and sexual assaults by other pastors making the headlines, and due to selfish Christian individuals that people meet in their lives. No doubt Saerom Church is also encountering envious sabotage by various groups as well. Overcoming these challenges is a major task for the church.

Third, while the church has been leading in cooperation with CSOs and local governments, there is also a need to cooperate with other religions in maeul/community-building and integrated community care.

Fourth, there is a need to resolve existing gaps between the pastoral leadership and some church members. Some of the first-generation church members have become middle class and some have not returned to on-site service after the pandemic. Some may refuse to learn about the challenges and changes of the times, and others may simply not see the need for it. Some church members may take on key leadership roles in maeul ministry for their own aggrandizement.

Fifth, Saerom Church's maeul ministry is essentially a fight against the power of the air, so it is critical to put on the whole armor of God. But among the armor, the sword of the Holy Spirit is the only offensive tool. The belt of truth, the breastplate of righteousness, the gospel of peace, the shield of faith, the helmet of salvation are all defensive. This is a reminder that the Christian and the church must above all guard their identity as they fight to usher in the kingdom of God. While constructing the spiritual ecosystem in the maeul through the Care Walk, it is important to support Christian identity in the faith community. Aloisius Piris saw the essence of Christian identity as the two-fold fight on behalf of the poor and the fight to become the poor. There are two biblical axioms according to Pieris. The first is the irreconciliability of God and mammon, Second is the irreversible covenant between God and the poor in which Jesus himself is the covenant. In Jesus, God and the poor form an alliance against the common enemy of mammon.[49]

Conclusion

The discussions can be summarized as follows.

First, Saerom Church's maeul ministry started as local community mission in 1986. They participated in maeul-building in 2000, then conducted maeul ministry starting in 2013.

Second, based on missional ecclesiology, Saerom Church's maeul ministry can be commented on in terms of the following aspects. The theological basis was formed through theological conversion and the three-phase local community mission Won-don Lee experienced in his youth at Yeondong Church. The ministry is characterized by serving and sharing as an alternative to the world's culture and constructing a system of integrated community care to encourage residents to stay in town. The constitutive elements of the church have been the mystery of seeing the church members as coworkers in maeul ministry, hoping

---

[49] Aloysius Pieris SJ, An Asian Theology of Liberation (New York: Orbis Books, 1988), 15.

for the town based on the memory of the past event of God's salvation, and the mission for change in the church and the residents in the process of maeul ministry. The three theologies employed are community theology of the church members and the residents, prophetic theology that looks beyond town issues, and openness to outsiders' theology. The church's prophetic challenges, their recognition of the mission of the Holy Spirit, and ministry development through Lee's pastoral leadership are also key elements.

Third, Saerom Church's maeul ministry is the integrated type of ministry that centers around education, culture, and social service while economy and politics are secondary.

Fourth, the characteristics of Saerom Church's maeul ministry are the pastor's exegetical excellence, evolution and expansion of terminology and concepts, response to current issues and connection of people and organizations, study and implementation of latest trends, recognition and training of talented individuals to make them responsible for organizations and committees, regional ecumenism, collaboration with local community service center, connection with Bucheon's CSOs and contribution to civil society movements, situating these efforts in the macroscopic trend of civilizational transition, and excellent pastoral leadership.

Fifth, Saeom Church continues to face the following challenges: need for more emphasis on politics and economy, overcoming hostilities against churches and Protestant Christians, cooperation with other religions, overcoming the gap between pastoral leadership and the perception of some church members, holding on to Christian and church identity while achieving harmony between the struggle to become the poor and the struggle for the poor.

Bibliography

Gelder, Craig Van & Dwight J. Zscheile, *The Missional Church in Perspective: Mapping Trends and Shaping the Conversation,* Grand Rapids: Baker Academic, 2011.

Guder, Darrell L. (ed.), *Missional Church: A Vision for the Sending of the Church in North America,* trans. by Sung-hyun Chung, Incheon: Juan International University Press, 2013.

Hwang, Hong-eyoyl. "Hak-kyo-p'ok-lyŏk-ŭ-lo-pu-t'ŏ p'yŏng-hwa-lo-un hak-kyo man-tŭl-ki-lŭl wi-han kyo-hoe-ŭi sŏn-kyo-kwa-che- choh-ŭn-kyo-sa-un-tong-ŭi hoe-pok-chŏk saeng-hwal-kyo-yuk-ŭl chung-sim-ŭ-lo" [From school biolence to building peaceful school as missionary tasks of church: focusing on the restorative life education of the good teacher]. Edited by Hong-ryeol Hwang, Co-authored by Eun-su Kim, Chang-hyeon Park, Hwan-cheol Yoon, Jun-hyeong Lee, Jong-hwa Lim, Hee-mo Lim, Yoon-gyeong Hong, Hong-ryeol Hwang, *'Hel-cho-sŏn'-e ŭng-tap-ha-nŭn han-kuk-kyo-hoe kae-hyŏk* [Korean church reform in response to 'hell chosun']. Seoul, Dongyeon, 2018, 159-202.

_________. "Ma-ŭl man-tŭl-ki, ma-ŭl-mok-hoe-wa ma-ŭl-mok-hoe-ŭi sin-hak-chŏk kŭn-kŏ" [Maeul/community-building, maeul ministry and its theological basis], edited by Seong-yeol Kang, Myeong-gi Baek. *Han-kuk-kyo-hoe-ŭi mi-lae-wa ma-ŭl-mok-hoe* [Future of the Korean church and maeul ministry]. Seoul: Handeul, 2016, 133-211.

_________, "Sŏn-kyo-chŏk kyo-hoe-lon-e-sŏ pon ma-ŭl-mok-hoe" [Maeul ministry from the perspective of missional ecclesiology] Co-authored by Won-don Lee, Seung-hyun Chung, Dongkyu Choi, Kook-il Han, Hong-ryeol Hwang, *Sŏn-kyo-chŏk mok-hoe kil-chap-i: sŏn-kyo mok-hoe-lo-pu-t'ŏ ma-ŭl-mok-hoe-kka-chi.* [A guide to missional ministry: from missional ministry to maeul ministry] Seoul: Dongyeon, 2022, 187-230

Lee, Won-don. "K'o-lo-na-mun-myŏng chŏn-hwan-ki, yak-tae-tong t'ong-hap tol-pom-ma-ŭl ka-nŭn kil" [The Road to Yakdae-dong Integrated Community Care in the Civilizational Transition of the Pandemic]. Co-authored by Won-don Lee, Seung-hyun Chung, Dongkyu Choi, Kook-il Han, Hong-ryeol Hwang, *Sŏn-kyo-chŏk mok-hoe kil-chap-i: sŏn-kyo mok-hoe-lo-pu-t'ŏ ma-ŭl-mok-hoe-kka-chi.* [A guide to missional ministry: from missional ministry to maeul ministry] Seoul: Dongyeon, 2022, 139-144.

_________. *K'o-lo-na-1-9 mun-myŏng chŏn-hwan-ki-ŭi saeng-myŏng-mang mok-hoe-wa tol-pom-ma-ŭl* [Ministry of the Web of Life and Community Care in Post-Pandemic Transition] Seoul: Nanum, 2022.

_________. "Ma-ŭl-e-sŏ man-nan ye-su" [Jesus I met in town], Jeong Shin ed. *Practicing Maeul Ministry with the Community Residents – With the Community, with the Lord: Bible Study Resource Book 3. Presbyterian Church of Korea Research Center Maeul Ministry Series 9.* Seoul: Dongyeon, 2018, 37-49.

_________. *Ma-ŭl-i kkum-ŭl kku-myŏn to-si-ka ch'um-ŭl ch'un-ta* [When a Town Dreams the City Dances] Seoul: Donggyeon, 2011.

_________. "Unexpected Harvest of the Holy Spirit in a Small Church during the Pandemic". This publication

Pieris, Aloysius SJ. *An Asian Theology of Liberation.* New York: Orbis Books, 1988.

Ro, Young-sang ed. *Maeul Ministry that Saves the World – With the Community, with the Lord: Bible Study Resource Book 4. Presbyterian Church of Korea Research Center Maeul Ministry Series 10.* Seoul: Dongyeon, 2018

Roxburgh, Alan J. & M. Scott Boren, *Introducing the Missional Church: What it is, Why it Matters, How to Become One,* Grand Rapids: Baker Books, 2009.

Interview with Won-don Lee. 25 August 2022.

Hannam Jeil Church: Missional Ministry and Leadership

Chang-woo Oh

The Pastor's Story: In the form of an Interview Conducted by Dr. Won-bum Chung

Is there anything you would like to mention about your upbringing?

I experienced two churches in my youth. One was a large church, which was Youngnak Presbyterian Church, and the other was the mid-sized Euljiro Church. Youngnak Church, was the church my father chose when he moved south from North Korea in the Korean War. The church was initially mostly composed of North Korean refugees, and many second and third-generations are still attending the church. Then when Euljiro Church was founded near our house, my father started attending at the church's request. He served as a Sunday School teacher there until he turned 70. I still remember my father was very committed to evangelizing to the children. He always kept evangelism tracts, candies, and pencils in his leather briefcase. Today there are elders in Euljiro Church who came to church thanks to my father's evangelism. The elders there remember and appreciate my father's dedication to Sunday School. I remember attending Youngnak Church's early Sunday service with my father and then again attending Sunday School at Euljiro. The timing worked out. My father told me to listen carefully to pastor Han Kyung-chik's sermons. My own sermons, the tone of my voice, the easy expressions I use, and scripture-centered messages are all influenced by pastor Han. Thanks to this upbringing, I served as a pastoral intern at Youngnak Church after graduating from seminary. My father was pleased. Youngnak and pastor Han did much social service work, such as running an orphanage, a women's shelter, and a nursing home. Today in Hannam Jeil Church, we also operate a nursing home, a study room for elementary children (Kium Center), and a daycare. I see this as the result of my experience with pastor Han.

I attended Euljiro Church since I was little. I remember the tatami-style room we had to take our shoes off to enter for worship. I only attended Youngnak until middle school and mostly attended Euljiro Church. Euljiro Church was small but really dynamic; even middle schoolers went on summer camps all the way to Maepo in North Chungcheong Province. That was 1967, so this was ahead of time. The interesting thing is that the students ourselves planned these retreats. We went to Seoul Station and booked tickets for an entire train car. And each Sunday we made our own Sunday service bulletins. We placed grease paper on a wooden board and engraved the letters with an iron pen. Then we stamped the bulletins using a duplicating machine. My handwriting was good, so I usually made the bulletins. During summer breaks, we even made zines over 100 pages. It was a remarkable experience.

What led you to study theology?

My father dedicated my life to ministry. I grew up hearing about this so I naturally assumed I should become a pastor. That's also why my father had me listen to pastor Han's sermons in Youngnak Church. God's work is mysterious. I attended Soongsil High School which is a mission school. It was founded by a missionary in Pyeongyang in North Korea, but the school moved down South in the war. We studied the Bible and had chapel service once a week with messages by invited speakers. This experience made me want to become a school chaplain and ended up becoming one at Youngak High School. I was about to decide on a university in the last year of high school when the chaplain called me and asked to see my father. The chaplain advised my father to send me to Presbyterian University and Theological Seminary (PUTS). So I enrolled in PUTS and majored in Christian Education. Then I graduated to become ordained. Of course, I also have a personal experience of calling to study theology. In the second year of high school, I was diagnosed with second-stage tuberculosis. I was afraid I might die so I promised God that I would become a pastor if I could live. Then in the second year of seminary, my liver really flared up so I went to the hospital. They told me they couldn't treat the liver and the tuberculosis at the same time, so there was nothing to do but wait for my death. Then my father tossed me into the Haneol Mountain Prayer Center. He told me I could choose whether to live or die but I must do it in prayer. I got an answer to my prayer and returned home to humbly continue ministry to this day. Speaking of Haneol Mountain Prayer Center, every Sunday afternoon my father made our family attend the revival service by Pastor Lee Cheon-seok who was the director of the prayer center. Then on Sunday evenings we went to the Euljiro Church service. So since I was young, Pastor Lee Cheon-seok laid hands on me to bless me. He was really happy to see me get ordained. I have quite a Pentecostal spirituality.

What kind of minister did you aspire to be? Who was your ministry influence?

Of course, my ideal image of a minister was formed based on pastor Han Kyung-chik. That was also my father's wish. As I told you, I imitated pastor Han's sermons and was interested in his social service work. Pastor Han had really wished to found a hospital. As a child, I used to play in Youngnak Churchyard. When pastor Han saw us children on his way back from visiting the church members, he would approach us and pat our heads. It felt like the love of Jesus himself. My own practice of opening up the churchyard for children to play or preparing bread or cookies for them was also because of this memory of pastor Han. In any case, there is no denying that pastor Han is big influence. Then there's Pastor Lee Choon-seop of Euljiro Church. Pastor Lee was a great preacher, and his sermons for children were especially engaging. I heard these sermons as I served as a Sunday School teacher in my middle school years and also as I served as a pastoral intern there. My gestures, content, and expressions in my children's sermons are taken from Pastor Lee's example in many respects. In my middle and high school years, pastor Lee also took us caroling on

Christmas morning to the slums on Ttukseom Island on Hangang River. We made rice cake sticks with donated rice and gifted them to the households we visited. In the summer we visited churches in rural regions to conduct Vacation Bible Schools for the children, repair the church buildings, and clear out walking paths. There was also the affection of pastor Kim Seong-eok of Geumho Church where I served as a Sunday School director, and the advice of the pastor and chaplain Ji Jong-ho of Soongsil High School for me to enter into seminary. There are also seminary seniors, pastors Ha Yong-jo, Kim Gi-hong, Baek Do-woong, and pastors Park Wi-geun and Park Jong-soon of Seoul Presbytery. I'd also mention elder Kim Yong-deok and pastor Yoo Jong-man who worked with me to establish Yeongil Church and Bongsoo Church for China and North Korea mission.

Missional Church and Maeul Ministry in a City

Hannam Jeil Church changed from the traditional church-centered orientation to become a church in the community meeting community needs. I think the essence of the church as the body of the Christ who left the glory of heaven to come on earth is to live in the community as part of the community. This is also the way to become more sustainable and overcome the church's crisis of societal irrelevance and decreasing membership. But given our church's location in a city, the majority of church members live a distance away, so they lack interest in the neighborhood where the church is located. So as the pastor of Hannam Jeil Church, I proposed a community-related vision for the church members: to define ourselves as a community gathered in Hannam-dong to conduct mission in this town.

As a pastor, I directly and indirectly emphasize to the congregation their role in the local community. The church has grown to recognize the significance of the community and became interested in community missions. The process required the congregation to adopt our distinct spiritual and ministerial characteristics unlike other Korean churches prioritizing numerical growth. This is apparent in the congregation's input in the process of building a new sanctuary.

Our church is writing our own story of missional ministry with the catchphrase, "The most local church is the most global church." I will now tell the story of maeul ministry by this missional church located on the northern end of Hannam-dong in Yongsan District of Seoul characterized by the Itaewon night culture and poor neighborhoods on a hill.

Itaewon's Heterogeneity

Hannam Jeil Church on Itaewon Street is near Seoul Central Mosque and where the 8th US Army used to be. The church is surrounded by bars, clubs, brothels, and businesses for the LGBTQ that tend to form around US Army bases. So naturally, some of the church members work in these businesses. One day, an elder came to me with an envelope of a tithe offering, protesting against accepting it. It was an offering of the people in the sex industry. Back in the day when business was booming in Itaewon, ten or so crossdressers, gays, and transgender people attended our church. There were people whose spouse was a US military service person. People were also employed in bars and clubs or selling foodstuff for these businesses. Also, with the mosque nearby, meeting people from the Middle East, Southeast Asia, and Africa in the streets was easy. Given such heterogeneity some people suggested that we devote ourselves to specialized ministry. But I realized when I met them that they don't want special treatment and prefer to be treated as just another person. Today there are more bars and clubs that operate 24 hours a day in other districts, but back in the 1980s, Itaewon was the only area in Korea and Seoul that formed such entertainment district, so countless young people came. Today, many foreigners are in Korea nationwide for employment, but at the time, Itaewon was the place to find foreigners. Itaewon's distinct culture made it feel like a completely foreign country. In this setting it occurred to me that I should do ministry as if I were a cross-cultural missionary. Whenever I was shocked by the completely unexpected culture of Itaewon, I reminded myself that I was a missionary and that I am here to serve the community, not just the church members.

This heterogenous culture of Itaewon is closely related to our nation's history. Itaewon (梨泰院) can be rewritten as 異胎院, which means a place where people who birthed children of other nations live. When Korea was invaded by Japan in 1592 and by China in 1636, women who birthed children with foreign soldiers or were taken as slaves to other countries eventually returned to be met with hostile glances as if they had committed adultery. These women and children were disowned and alienated by their families and communities so the king's court allowed them to stay in Itaewon area. Then after the Korean War in 1950, the US Army was stationed here and entertainment businesses followed to make the Itaewon of today. Hannam Jeil Church is at the center of this foreign and heterogeneous culture. This might not be an ideal location for church growth, yet our church has persisted and is recognized as the town's center because of our missional ministry.

Personal Experience in an Urban Church

Another reason why I could initiate missional ministry here was thanks to my experience at my home church, Euljiro Church, which is at the center of Seoul near the most populous region of Myeongdong. And I served as a pastoral intern, an associate pastor, and now as the senior pastor, all in the city of Seoul. I was born and raised in this city and experienced nothing else, so I was always interested in urban issues and phenomena. Significantly, the churches I experienced, especially Euljiro Church where I spent my youth, can be said to have been doing missional ministry from the early days. I can never forget how all the middle and high school-aged youth brought a bag of rice to church on Christmas Eve to make rice cake sticks together. We celebrated after the Christmas Eve Service, then by early next morning the rice cakes became nice and firm for us carry them on our shoulders, 20 kilograms each. We took the first bus in the morning, bus number 65, to the shanty town of Ttukseom Island. We visited their homes caroling and handing out the rice cakes. My wife had a similar experience going around to police stations and fire stations with her friends on Christmas to hand out gifts and cook ramen noodles for them. This is amazing even for today's standard. Also, in the summer we went on summer retreats. The students did everything ourselves, booking a whole train car for transportation to and from the retreat center, planning the meals, buying the ingredients and cooking the meals, researching to plan the retreat activities, and preparing a bonfire. It was a special experience the church gifted us to mature us and make us feel capable. That is why I could naturally implement maeul ministry and the missional church concept of today to let the church experience a healthy culture that can change society.

I am also a son of a a war refugee. My father was from Pyeongyang. He escaped the battlegrounds alone during the Retreat of January 4, 1951, and never returned since. My grandmother was evangelized by a foreign missionary and taught the faith to my father, so I am a third-generation Christian. I now have my own grandchildren, so Christianity has been passed down to the fifth generation. My younger brother and I never missed a day of Sunday School for 13 years from kindergarten to high school. That is how much my life revolved around the church. I studied with the writing utensils the Sunday School handed out to us, and I attended on church scholarship. Naturally, I went to seminary to get ordained, and my brother became an elder in Euljiro Church. It would not be an overstatement to say the church is my entire life. My wife's spirituality is also centered on the church. She was born into a Buddhist family and encountered much opposition to attending church. But she continued to go to Sunday School alone and enrolled in a mission school thanks to God's providence. We met as friends in Euljiro Church and ended up getting married. So from my personal experience, I know that church life and culture have much to offer. I believe our hope is in the church and church-centered spiritual life, and that the church should also be at the center of the local community.

Maeul Ministry Efforts

Planning the Church Construction as the Center of the Local Community

The first thing I did when I became the senior pastor of Hannam Jeil Church was to remove the outer walls and the gate. I wanted the church to be the center and an essential part of the community, not an island to itself. The community residents naturally began using our restrooms and the children played in our yard. Once the 1988 Seoul Olympic Games ended, we planned to construct a new sanctuary. Buying the plot of land beside our church became difficult, so in prayer, we decided to rebuild our existing sanctuary to add more stories. We planned for the basement to be the sanctuary/concert hall, a parking lot and funeral home on the first floor, preschool classes and nursery on the second floor, children's ministry and a study room for the children on the third, youth ministry and a study room for the youth on the fourth floor, young adult ministry and missions associations offices on the fifth, guesthouses for missionaries and local community residents on the sixth, the parsonage on the seventh, and a garden and an outdoor concert hall on the rooftop. We drew up the blueprint and prayed for it, but the plan never materialized due to financial reasons. Today in 2022, we are finally working on this reconstruction so that the church can be the center of the town.

Getting a Doctor of Ministry Degree on the Contact Point between Church and Society in the Local Community

In my doctoral thesis, "Contact between Church and Society in the Local Community" I wrote about our church reconstruction blueprint to establish ourselves as the center of the town. A church is not a physical temple but the body of Christ, and we take part in the liturgy of the breaking of this body. I wrote about how the church layout was planned to house the departments and divide the sections at each level to serve the community. Later, the Hannam-dong Community Service Center and Hannam-dong Public Parking Lot were built around our church to actually make our church the physical center of the town.

Maeul Ministry as the Church Growth Strategy for the 21st Century

At the start of the 21st century, the strategic plan for future ministry was set for maeul ministry. Around that time, there was an awareness that the Korean church can no longer grow as it had in the previous decades. The future was uncertain, and the congregation requested a vision statement for the future. The church agreed to the strategic plan I presented. The church vision for the 21st century was articulated as "the community of Jesus that transforms the local community and conducts missions by the gospel." The phrase consists of key principles – local community, gospel, mission, and community of Jesus. On the principle of local community, at a time when Korean churches are becoming gated communities, our church should have a presence in the community and meet people's needs. Therefore, the phrase "The most local church is the most global church" is closely related to this idea. Practically, this means operating facilities and cultural programs such as a nursing home, a daycare, and after-school childcare. The second principle is transformation by the gospel. The church must be a faith community distinct from the world. We wanted to avoid assuming that a church, just as in other organizations, needs monetary and human resources to get anything done. It is by the gospel that is the power of salvation of Jesus that the world will be saved. So sermon messages are generally on the power of the gospel. Third, to be a community of Jesus that conducts missions means that we are called to the local community where the church is located. It also implies that Jesus is the master of our community and that we aspire to be like the church in Antioch where the laity led in ministry. Our church members agreed to this new vision's direction and content to participate in practice.

But it should be noted that the congregation expected a strategic plan similar to the five-year economic development plans in the age of President Park Chung-hee, which meant including numerical church growth goals, such as reaching 500 members in 10 years and 3,000 members in 20 years to become a megachurch. But as a minister, I conducted maeul ministry believing that the church belongs to God and God will do what God wills. I endlessly emphasized through my sermons that it is God who empowers us to do ministry, not the number of volunteers or the amount of offerings. That is why the gospel that is the power of God's salvation is emphasized in the strategic vision. Rather than emphasizing that certain ministry programs should be conducted, I emphasized the power of faith in God who makes all things possible. Ultimately, new ministry programs were implemented to operate a nursing home, a daycare, and the after-school care center while also expanding the horizon of evangelical ministry. And recently we could start the reconstruction of the church sanctuary with over 6,500 square meters of floor space. Having the gospel as the engine, our church could do much more ministry than our capacity.

Joint Church Programs

For maeul ministry based in the local community, the churches in the neighborhood needed to cooperated. The churches in Yongsan District were gathered and with the district office we expanded the existing Yongsan Church-District Council. In all 16 towns of Yongsan District as well, Church-Town Councils were launched to conduct programs in their spheres. The Church-District Councils have two major events each year. One is the New Years Service of all the churches at the District Office Auditorium. About 1,300 people attend to have the service at 7:30 in the morning. In the fall there is a charity concert to support the Yongsan District Food Bank & Market to help low-income households. A Christian association was set up for the district office staff. A service is held at the office once a month open to the staff, and the district pastors take turns to lead and give a message. Other joint programs have been Prayer and Fast on the Day of the Korean War and street demonstrations against a racecourse construction in Yongsan.

Scenes of Missional Ministry

First and Foremost, Breaking Down Walls

The first thing I did when I came to this church was get rid of the tall outer walls. At the time the church tried to stop people from loitering by making the walls and the gate taller. They were so high it reminded me of a penitentiary. So the first thing to do was break down the walls and remove the gate to allow people in. Naturally, the neighbors started using church facilities such as the restrooms, the children played in the yard, and people in the community were happy. Once, a young drunk person entered the sanctuary and set the curtains which burnt down a stack of Bibles. A passer-by noticed the fire, put it out, then contacted the church. Also when we worked on the churchyard to make it wider, the neighbors supported the construction and encouraged us to make it even wider, and did not complain about the noise and the dust. Later we set up a café on the first floor of our church to allow neighbors to conduct meetings. It became the regular meeting place for town residents. Our Education Hall is also open for community-initiated programs such as guitar lessons, Fathers' Choir practices, Hannam-dong Orchestra practices, and flute lessons. We also opened up the Education Hall garden as space for the residents and were even awarded by the Seoul city government for this contribution.

Next, Seeking out and Persuading

Most of the programs for the community were implemented after seeking out the district and town offices to discuss local needs. People in the church did not always welcome these community service programs, however. They asked whether it would help grow the church, and were concerned that church members' commitments would be divided. It was difficult for the board of elders to reach a consensus and for the entire church to agree. For example, our church needed more space for meetings before and after the Sunday service, so I thought of asking the café in front of the church if we can rent the space. This meant we needed a volunteer staff to operate the café so that we could pay for the cost of operating the café while we rented the space. But then I encountered opposition from the church members questioning why the church should pay for people to drink coffee. Still, I believed this was a necessary step so I negotiated with the café owner to share the cost of discount tickets for coffee. For a cup of coffee that costs KRW 3,500, church members could get discounts to pay only 1,500. After almost a year passed, the board of elders recognized the necessity of the café space and agreed that the church would pay for our congregation and have them use the café space freely. Such things also happened with preaching and education. Church members have different political inclinations, so they tend to be sensitive to liberation theology or anything that hints at Communism. That is why I tend to be careful with theological expressions related to local community ministry. It took much thought and patience to accomplish these ministries.

Currently Operating Ministry Programs in Town

Commissioned Management

District Nursing Home

Yongsan District built a nursing home in our town of Hannam-dong, and we took up the operational responsibilities. This also meant partially funding the nursing home. But since this was already a part of our church's Strategic Plan, we took up the task more readily than expected. Today, 80 staff members are taking care of 80 in-house seniors and 20 seniors who come for daycare. On Wednesdays and Sundays, we have services for the seniors and their families. The youth ministry also goes to volunteer. Other churches in the region also come to volunteer, showing a good example of missionary cooperation.

District Seniors Daycare

A daycare center for seniors is similar to a kindergarten. Seniors who need assistance at home can come to the daycare to stay from morning until evening. We operate various programs, and seniors with dementia and Alzheimer's are also attending. The Seoul city government has given the facility an excellence rating. Today, six caretakers look after 20 seniors, and we are discussing possibilities for expansion.

District Children's Daycare

This is the Yongsan District daycare center for children. Since it was built in our community and it was part of the Strategic Plan, our church took up the responsibility. Today there are four classes and 25 teachers. The teachers are committed to the work based on their Christian faith nurtured in teachers' prayer meetings.

Dream Afterschool Care (Seoul Kium Center)

For this program, we approached the District Office first to suggest an after-school care program for elementary school children. It later became a Seoul Kium Center. This was also part of the church's Strategic Plan. Today, five to six teachers care for about 20 children. Parents appreciate that our program treats the children like family, unlike the programs run by schools. Our center is also known as one of the best Kium Centers in Seoul.

Mercy Ministries

Yongsan Household Matching Program (Yongsan Welfare Fund)

Around 30 years ago there was a dire lack of government support for families in the lowest income bracket. They were not in any situation to work and were only provided KRW 40,000 government stipend a month. So our church supported an additional KRW 30,000 for each household. The small but consistent donations to households later grew with the participation of other churches, businesses, and individuals to become the Yongsan Household Matching Program. Today it became Yongsan Welfare Fund. Rather than the church selecting the recipients, the Hannam-dong Community Service Center provides a list at our request each year. Today 36 households are supported with stipends each month.

Participation in Operations of Yongsan Food Bank &Market

Yongsan District supports the homeless and the poor by stocking and providing food like Joseph's grain storage. For the churches in our region, the Food Bank &Market is a major government agency with which we contribute to social service. Our church has been supporting the program regularly and as-needed basis. Yongsan Church-District Council holds charity concerts in the fall to support the Food Bank & Market. This is an opportunity for the churches to grow their presence and influence. The program has grown to rank fifth in the country in scale. I am serving as the chair of operations.

Field Trips for Local Seniors

There are particularly more senior populations in Hannam-dong which means there are more senior centers here than in other towns. But usually what people do at senior centers is simply have meals and sit around. A newspaper company did a survey at the time asking seniors what they would most like to do, and they said sightseeing. So our church boldly planned a field trip that requires much more expense and planning than a simple banquet. Our church was most appreciated by the seniors who went on the trip. Today our church continues to budget funds for the town senior's association banquet.

Charity for the Holidays

We wanted to distribute rice to the needy for the Christmas season but there were limits to handing them out through church members. So we contacted the Community Service Center to identify the needy and hand out the rice for us. This was appreciated by the government workers and neighbors. The reception can be different depending on who is doing the serving. When a missionary directly distributes the rice, the receivers may call it evangelism. But when the town head is asked to share the rice, they see this as the church cooperating in town affairs. This process unexpectedly further promoted the church in town. The sacks of rice brought from the church were divided by the town head, the community center staff, and neighborhood leaders. In subsequent years the district head and representatives also came to share the joy in this town celebration.

Culture Lessons

Hannam-dong is a town in the Itaewon entertainment district. For 33 years since I became the pastor of this church there has never been a good quality private education institution, or *hagwon,* for young people. There is hardly any *hagwon* teaching music other than those teaching the piano. The local elementary school allowed for each student to study one instrument, but many had to commute far to other towns of Yaksu-dong or Gangnam. Our church heard of this situation from the parents and provided violin lessons for free to students who attended the church. This turned out to become Hannam-dong Orchestra and Musical Instrument Lessons on violin, flute, and cello. Today the lessons are given on Sunday afternoons from 1 to 6 pm. Five to ten students gather for each class. This is a very difficult but fulfilling program.

Ministry to Immigrants

Multicultural Café

There have always been multiethnic households in Itaewon. In a Church-District Council meeting the town head mentioned a need for a strategy in response to an increasing number of multiethnic families, so we decided to start a community program. Our church had the experience of operating Sharon's House as a shelter for mothers in the United States. So we initiated to provide a shelter that functions as a café for multiethnic families. The purpose was to provide assistance and healing for people encountering difficulties in cross-cultural settings. In cooperation with the Community Service Center, we meet the families and conducted programs to meet their needs. One program is the Korean language class where people from Nepal, Bangladesh, Mongolia, and ethnic Koreans from China attend. Events like the International Food Festival were organized for multicultural understanding and fellowship. Today the Multicultural Café is run by the International Church

3.3.4.2 International Church

The International Church was started for both Koreans and foreigners residing in Korea. It was originally a church for the Philippines expats, then for an international group, and now it is primarily a missionary group for the Muslims in the region. Pastor Chris who is a US citizen leads with the missionary Kim (name kept anonymous). On the weekends 15 to 16 people gather for service. The church operates the Multicultural Café that is visited by many during the weekdays.

Sharon's House

Sharon's House is led by Director Kim Myeong-bu in Tacoma, USA where the military service people to be stationed at the 8th US Army base in Itaewon were sent. The ministry provides shelter for Korean women married to American servicemen when they need a place to turn. Sharon's House has grown to support not only the women but also the children and the youth in these families. Our church provided assistance at the ministry's establishment, and today we continue to cooperate with financial support.

Overseas Missionaries

The missionaries we send and support are also conducting missional ministry for the overseas communities.

- Park Seon-ho in the Philippines: Vocational training school, housing for students in Myanmar: Housing and vocational training for youth at a cultural center
- Lee Han-seong in Timor Leste: Housing for undergraduate and graduate students at Hannam Jeil Student Housing. Students have returned to hometowns to become teachers, nurses, and judges.
- Cha Heung-ju in Chile: Cooperation with a local church to serve poor households in the community and repair houses.

We also cooperate in missions for the homeless in Mexico, and missions in Mongolia, Russia, Kenya, and Mozambique.

Maeul Community Programs

The Maeul Community Movement was started in recent years in South Korea. Our country's welfare system has changed faster than the speed of societal development. National welfare policies raise citizens' quality of life, but they are also a matter of life and death for some. In the early days, national welfare started as "cultural welfare" such as government-sponsored hobby classes then later grew to become "universal welfare" such as monthly allowances of KRW 200,000 for retirees, free school meals, children's education stipend, and nursing care stipend. But the more the government provided, the greater the need. So the new government welfare policy direction is "maeul welfare." The maeul community can be considered a civil society owned by citizens. The Candlelight Rallies of 2016 may be called a citizens' revolution, meaning the citizens are now able to take the initiative on constructing the social structure. With this policy, the government provides financial support for a project proposed by three or more citizens to solve a practical issue in town. The satisfaction level for this policy has been higher than for any other welfare policy in the past. Now the programs have grown to allow for town communities to organize a maeul project team. A maeul project team is a group that consists of citizens and government officers who together discuss town-wide issues to seek solutions. These policies position citizens as partners with the government rather than consumers, in making a better society.

If churches are today considering what they alone can do for the local community, then they might still be in the older welfare policy framework of cultural welfare. Many churches start cafes hoping neighbors will visit, but many such cafes have already shut down indefinitely. If the congregants want to serve the community they have no other option than to participate in the local maeul project teams and be a maeul activist. Or else the church and the congregation will keep growing apart from the community and become an island. In that sense, maeul welfare is a good opportunity for the church to build relationships with the community. Participating in the local community to raise our own quality of life rather than depending on the government is exactly what the Korean church must do amid change in the 21st century. So the General Assembly of the Presbyterian Church of Korea (Tonghap) (PCK) to which our church belongs made maeul welfare the theme of the 2018 Assembly and promoted maeul ministry nationwide. This spurred much interest and active participation of Korean churches in maeul ministry and missional church.

Maeul Community Programs we are Participating in Today

1. Parent Community Program: “Children who Grow Together”, choir program, guitar lessons for intergenerational groups
2. Neighboring Program: Dream Orchestra (organized the Yongsan District Food Market-Bank Festival), Youth community “In Youths’ Name” (volunteering for seniors living alone, planting flowers and trees by the streets), Fathers’ Choir, “Kids’ Café for Mommy and Baby”
3. Maeul Media Program: The youth community “In Youths’ Name” was selected to get trained for the town media program in 2016. They received KRW 7 million in funding for a 12-week media production training. The goal was to make a town broadcasting station.
4. Cooperative Childcare Program: “Kids’ Café for Mommy and Baby” is a network of mothers in town. About 32 people from 15 households received KRW 5.5 million in funding to operate this program. It is one of the best practices of maeul community projects in Seoul. The community continues to cooperate on childcare on their own initiative.
5. School in the Maeul Program: “Tongtong Book Club” is the School in the Maeul Program initiated by parents of students in Hannam Elementary School. They receive KRW 4.95 million to operate the after-school childcare program where children and parents stay in school after class to read together.
6. Resident Gatherings Association: Twelve of the maeul community projects in Hannam-dong formed a network. They received KRW 7 million to

organize a town conference called "Real Stories of Hannam-dong," provide a public forum, and operate a town exhibition.

7. Hankkum Volunteers: Hankkum Volunteers were organized in March 2016 to register with the Yongsan District Volunteers Center. With the operational funding, about 80 people volunteered for an event called Lunch of Love Program to pack lunches for seniors living alone. It is much appreciated by the local community and has been introduced in television news and newspapers. The volunteering youth can earn 120 hours of social service activity credit to be counted for university admissions. The volunteers also clean the streets and visit nursing homes. The youth volunteers are given a chance to act in the community while discovering their personal career goals for the future. The volunteering also helps the church youth discover a sense of purpose for their education.

Three Principles for Relationship Building between the Church and Local Community

Honoring Local Leaders

The first thing we did to before conducting maeul missions programs was to honor the local community leaders. There is the town head who oversees the town of 30,000 residents, and the district head over 300,000. By honoring these leaders, I wanted our church to also take leadership. For example, for Christmas our church cooperated with the town head to distribute rice to the poor. The "Rice of Love for Christmas" was originally a ministry of the church to the people in and out of church, selected by our church's regional group leaders. Most of the recipients turned out to be church members and it hardly impacted the local community. But having committed to ministry to the local community with the heart of a missionary, I sought out the town head. I introduced myself as the pastor of Hannam Jeil Church and asked for his help with the "Rice of Love for Christmas" program. The town head was actually looking to find support for the poor every year around this time, so he was very happy to find that a church in town came for exactly this task. The next day, the officer in charge of town welfare brought a list of potential recipients categorized by townships and smaller units. They had a rational and objective standard to determine the recipients. A day was set for the event at the church. I asked for the rice to be given out at the town's Community Service Center, but the town head insisted it should be at the church. On that day the center staff came to the church Education Hall to prepare for the event. Local leaders and heads of townships gathered the recipients to conduct the event. The Education Hall was filled with community residents and it became a town celebration. As the town head led the event, he praised the church and the elders and asked for applause for "Hannam Jeil Church, a good church." I was also asked to have a say so I prayed a blessing over the participants, the families, the local leaders, and the residents. After the event, I watched the street full of people each carrying a sack of rice on their head, and heads of townships carrying the rice for others on their motorcycles and bikes. It was quite a sight that moved me to tears. These efforts to honor the local leaders continue today. Field trips for seniors, banquets for local volunteers, *kimchi*-making in preparation for the winter, sharing the church garden in front of our Education Hall as the Maeul Park of Dreams, and allowing the town to use our Education Hall for maeul community gatherings are all such programs. By honoring the local leaders, the church is contributing to the vitalization of the community.

Participating in Local Programs

Participating in local programs is also important. For example, the city of Seoul has a monthly program called Clean Day for citizens to participate in street cleaning. Early in the morning, church members gather to go to the Community Service Center to pick up the brooms, dustpans, and trash bags. The program gets no funding but the town officers and leaders like it because it counts toward their yearly project accomplishments.

In the Covid-19 pandemic, our church initiated the Hannam-dong Pandemic Prevention Crew. The church bought the disinfectants, and the Community Service Center provided the sprays. Every Wednesday we visited restaurants, cafes, stores, and houses asking for the disinfection service. These efforts to help the community do not take much money. The town head calls me the Joker card to mean that I am an indispensable part of the town. Our church could perform these services because we went beyond simple charity work to contribute to community building.

Deferring to Community Needs

This means happily sharing church spaces and facilities when the community needs them. In the fall when the town community service center shares *kimchi* with poor households and needs cars and drivers to distribute them, the church is there to take care of it. For the town Sports Day our church cars are used to transport the residents. The town orchestra, the guitar lessons, and other community resident programs are held in the church Education Hall or café spaces. The Education Hall garden is shared with the community and earned the recognition of the Seoul city government. New flower blossoms for each season are financed by the district office. In the Covid-19 pandemic, our church organized the Pandemic Prevention Crew, and we also made lunch packs for seniors living alone, all in cooperation with the Community Service Center. These cooperations with the public sector are turning our church into a good neighbor.

As a pastor of a local community, I think churches tend to regard the residents as objects of evangelism rather than neighbors to live alongside. For a church to conduct sustainable maeul ministry they should not use community service programs as ways of evangelism but as efforts to be a good neighbor. So I always pray in at any social service gatherings by saying, "If I have one wish, that is for Hannam-dong to be blessed through Hannam Jeil Church." Over the years our town has very much improved culturally and materially. A resident even told me, "Our town has been blessed because of you, pastor, and Hannam Jeil Church."

In this sense, maeul ministry is significant as a new kind of urban community movement.

Challenges in Maeul Ministry

Challenges in the Church

For maeul ministry, I had to persuade the church members and especially the board of elders. It was very difficult to persuade on the need for maeul ministry to Korean church elders captivated by the growth imperative. Nobody opposed giving charity and helping neighbors in need, but when it came down to budgeting, I encountered resistance. The unfortunate reality is that projects initiated with faith are discouraged by the board of elders due to financial limits. Pastors even joke that they'd have all the *hwe* (sushi in Korean) in the world but not the *danghwe* (board of elders). The board is generally supportive of evangelism in town but is opposed to helping the needy. Finding ways to persuade them was one of the major challenges in my ministry. Again, congregants generally agree it is good and right for the church to serve the community. But the problem is, first, that they keep asking if the services resulted in conversion and how much the church membership grew as a result, and eventually the inherent value of service is forgotten. Secondly, if church members, elders, and *gwonsas* are not made leaders in local community programs, they may oppose participation by faulting the leadership, which results in the church being unable to do maeul ministry. Third, the congregants also see the church's attention to community issues as a sign of neglect. Congregants asking to take care of our own first, then worry about the neighbors later can hold back the church from maeul ministry. If the majority of the church members are dissatisfied with the current worship services and visitation ministries, then they will oppose church efforts for the community. Fourth, in our church, over 60% of the congregants reside in other towns today. For these people who come to town only once a week, this is an unfamiliar neighborhood, and naturally, they are not so interested. So to clarify the relationship between our church and Hannam-dong I articulated the mission of Hannam Jeil Church and had the church members recite it like a motto: "Hannam Jeil Church is a faith community gathered with a mission to Hannam-dong." This was very effective. With this missionary motivation, most of the church members have grown to be interested in the area. But it is still difficult for the church members to participate in local matters because of the distance and lack of time during the week. They have their jobs and children to take care of, and they can barely make time to come for Sunday service, let alone Wednesday services and early morning prayers. So we still need more congregants to get involved in the town visitation ministry.

Challenges in the Local Community

Local perception of a church's maeul ministry is not always positive. They are suspicious that the church is interested in community matters because they are looking for ways to evangelize. There was an instance when our church was actually excluded based on this suspicion. Hannam-dong Community Service Center knows our church well, so we have a good working relationship. But the Seoul city government once vehemently opposed our involvement. The city office denied our proposal for the Yongsan District Maeul Community Support Center without giving a reason. We prepared for a long time with the Yongsan District officer in charge, but because the project leader was a pastor the deliberators assumed the project would be used for evangelism. In the end, a Maeul Support Center was placed in Yongsan District. Once, some resident activists complained that churches and ministers who are conducting maeul center programs, getting public funding, and hiring staff are competing for the same sphere of influence. These complaints were laid against our church's nursing home, daycare, and after-school childcare. But we never once heard complaints that we crossed a line on religious proselytization. Yongsan District and the town of Hannam-dong actually appreciate our church's maeul ministry.

Expectations for Church Growth and Difficulty of Evaluation

Christian Schwarz who wrote on natural church development assesses a church on five spheres of worship, evangelism, education, service, and fellowship. Korean churches are assessing ministries in these five spheres and supplementing the weaker parts, but in reality, this is not easy. In church operations, there are also subcommittees on finance, maintenance, and administration. A big part of the finance go to ministers' wage and building maintenance. These financial issues are significant. The indicators of the social credibility of Korean Protestant churches in the survey conducted by the Christian Ethics Movement of Korea are matters like financial transparency, buying and selling of church office, sexual violence, and hereditary succession of pastoral leadership, which are very different from the five traditional roles of the church. Even among Protestant Christians only a little over 60% answer that they trust the Church. Among non-Christians, 34% say they trust the church and 64% do not. The Protestant church is trusted less than the Catholic church or the Buddhists, and the percentage is decreasing every year. The church is not functioning as it should.

In our church, we share a detailed financial report every month. In church officer elections we do not allow them to bring offerings. Our church is also committed to opposing hereditary pastoral succession and has worked to raise awareness of sexual violence in the church. Yet I also recognize limitations to our church's efforts at self-reform; we cannot overcome the foundational desire for growth and revival. An evangelist once said, "Growth is the sign of a good church." Based on this perspective of church growth, there is skepticism that the maeul ministry of a missional church can really grow a church. But for the sustainability of our churches, we cannot neglect maeul ministry.

The Solution in the Threefold Office of Christ

There are many difficulties in maeul ministry. As I kept studying and praying to articulate the relationship between a pastor's ministry, a congregation's faith, and a community's imperative, I arrived at the threefold office of Christ. To believe in Christ is to imitate Christ in life, which means to also imitate the three functions of Christ the Savior. 1) Priest: Just as Jesus was the priest before God and before people we are also called to priesthood. 2) Prophet: This is to fulfill the prophetic office by proclaiming the kingdom of God to the world. 3) King: Just as Jesus came to serve, we are also to be kings of service. Priestly worship, prophetic evangelism, and kingly service are the content of ministry, the faith of Christians, and the reason why the church exists in society. The church's sociocultural value is in being the priest, the prophet, and the king of service for the community. This ministry philosophy became a clear guide for myself and our congregation on how we can live as Christians and relate with the local community.

The children and youth ministry has also transformed into Youth Church for the Community based on the threefold office of Christ. Youth Church is a response to the Sunday School in crisis. The designation as Sunday School with the word "school" in the title was itself problematic. Up until the 1970s and the 1980s the Sunday School kept growing and developing thanks to urbanization. But in the 2000s with the falling birthrate and the new suburban development, the urban population decreased and educational infrastructure deteriorated. As a result, the number of children and youth in inner-city church Sunday Schools kept decreasing. Hannam Elementary School and Bogwang Elementary School near our church today would have to close down if not for the non-Korean students also attending the schools. Congregants who used to live near our church eventually moved out when the promise of town redevelopment did not materialize for 17 years. College entrance rates for graduates from nearby junior high and high schools are so low that once the students graduate from junior high, families tend to move to another town for high schools with better prospects. It is no longer possible to organize multiple classes for one grade level. Twenty years of visiting rural churches for Sunday worship during my summer hiatus tells me that more and more churches no longer have children to operate Sunday Schools. Even if there are children and youth it is difficult to set up separate age-level classes and appoint teachers for each of them, so the Sunday Schools have closed down. But today, the same thing is happening to churches in the cities as well. Hannam Jeil Church is no exception. As the number of children and youth from the local community coming to our Sunday School dramatically decreased, most of the members are the children of congregants attending from another town. There is also the perception that Sunday School participation interferes with the youth's studies when their time would be better used to study for college entrance. So even the children of church leaders attend churches nearer their homes or leave the Sunday School promising they will return to church after they get into college. The Korean church Sunday School is on the road to extinction.

As a solution, our church changed the name of our Sunday School to Youth Church to emphasize the community aspect and reorganized the structure. The children and youth from kindergarten to high school, or even up to young adulthood, are grouped in multi-age groups rather than by age so that they can naturally build multi-age relationships. Our curriculum was also redeveloped based on the threefold office of Christ: priest – worship and pastoral care, prophet – mission and vision, king of service – serving and volunteering. The principle was applied to education to make the curriculum simple and clear: priest – the transformation of knowledge, prophet – the transformation of behavior, king of service – the transformation of character.

In South Korea, four kinds of records contribute to college admission, which are school grades, club activities, volunteering activities, and awards. Youth Church participation helps students be self-motivated to study. After the youth minister's sermon on Sundays, the students gather in groups to share their response to the sermon. As they articulate their thoughts, they are encouraged to be self-motivated while teachers act as facilitators. The contents of each week are given out a week in advance for the students to preview before they come.

Youth Church activities include missions training under the category of prophetic ministry. The Urban Exploration program trains students to find their way through the city on buses and subways and study about specified locations and sites. Three students of different ages are grouped together. Urban Exploration was also conducted in other countries as a vision trip. This program provides experiential learning opportunities that children in other families might enjoy with their parents, so sometimes parents who do not attend church are invited to these activities.

Six hours of volunteering each year is also required in formal education. Our Youth Church requires students to do 120 hours of volunteer work every year. Two hours at the nursing home, two hours of street cleaning, and four hours packing lunch for seniors living alone is required each month, adding up to 96 hours. The rest of the hours can be filled with volunteer activities of choice, so an option could be to form a club that can count as another merit for college entrance.

So Youth Church has helped the participants in their studies and given opportunities for volunteering and club activities. They received scholarships and awards from Yongsan District Office for their volunteer work. With these merits our Youth Church children can be confident when they write a self-introduction or go to interviews for college admission or job application, so the parents and the students are very satisfied. The Youth Church ministry system prepares for the future sustainability of our church.

For Sustainable Maeul Ministry

A Philosophy of Maeul Ministry

In maeul ministry, a church's purpose in a community must be clear. This comes from the ministry philosophy of the pastor. Many pastors are still resistant to maeul ministry thinking it is a liberal social movement unrelated to ministry. The general public holds the same perception. But if the pastor has a clear ministry philosophy, maeul ministry can be a solution for the church's sustainability. I once gave a brief talk on "The Sociocultural Value of the Church for the Local Community" before the Church-District Council and community residents. I wanted to explain why a church would be interested in local community work. I explained the value of the church in three aspects. With the priestly function, the church is always praying for the community. In Korea in the past, every village had a spiritual mechanism such as a shrine for the village deity on which the residents trusted. Now the church is serving the community in the same way. And as a prophet of the region the church seeks out the valleys to fill and mountains to level. In our district nursing home, there were financial mismanagement issues with the previous administrator. Once our church took over the administration the facility earned a good reputation. As so, the church is like a good companion for the community. Finally, the church functions like the king of service who serves without asking for recognition. The pastors who heard my talk appreciated how the public officials now realize the relevance of a church in the community. The sociocultural value of a church relates to Christ's three offices. I persuaded my own congregations with this same basis.

Study of National Welfare Policy

Maeul Ministry Research Center is set up in the General Assembly of the PCK to study the government welfare policies and provide information and education applicable for maeul ministry. The center has the very important role of theological training on maeul ministry and missional church and sharing real instances of implementation in Korea and other countries. For a local church to cooperate with the community it needs to be able to discuss the government welfare policy for the community. In the past, welfare was about financial assistance for poor households and cultural classes targeting housewives. But today in the age of local self-governance welfare came to mean community projects. This was why the Town Office was renamed Community Service Center, and again to Administrative Welfare Center. The welfare policy is changing to provide universal welfare for everyone, and the maeul projects are encouraging citizen participation. The government will continue to invest more in community-initiated projects.

The biggest group in the local community used to be the church. They had the most people and the finances, so they did a lot of work to serve the community. But now South Korea is the tenth most economically developed country. Seniors over 65 are given KRW 300,000 each month as public pension. The government is caring for the citizens like no church can. In the words of Jesus, we must be wise as snakes. The congregants with Christian values must now be an active part of the community to encourage others to live a wholesome life. Churches will be sustainable when they actively participate in these community efforts.

Conclusion: Maeul Ministry is Life-giving Ministry (Interview on Positive and Negative Assessment of Maeul Ministry)

What are some positive elements of maeul ministry?

First, I give credit that maeul ministry is a way for the church to earn recognition in the local community. Some ask how much our church has grown through maeul ministry. They are asking for number of people or the amount of offerings.

But I would ask them this. Does the Korean society envy megachurches? Even associate pastors of megachurches make higher salaries than I do. Does society envy and admire the way pastors become wealthy? Not really. Then a community appreciation for a church might be a better indicator of church growth. The Christian Ethics Movement of Korea conducts surveys on Protestant churches and their social credibility, and the results tell me we should do more maeul ministry. They say 85% of Korean churches have less than 100 members. From the church growth perspective, churches in rural regions should close down. Then that just leaves the megachurches… and that ultimately means the end of the Korean church. So the maeul ministry movement is the way for the church to earn societal recognition, and that is a big merit.

What are your critiques of maeul ministry?

Ministers and church members tend to misunderstand that maeul ministry is project-centered. I actually tend not to refer to maeul ministry specifically in Sunday sermons. As I mentioned before, there is still a lot of misunderstanding about maeul ministry and missional church, though it has improved a lot. People who attend church from further away naturally lack interest in the church's neighborhood. Compared to people who live nearby, pass by the church every day, and attend the Wednesday prayers, Friday prayers, and early morning prayers, others who come from farther away would like more pastoral care. Churches at the heart of a city like ours encounter these realities. But our church is operating the district nursing home, the district daycare, and the city's Kium Center, serving the community like the missionaries did in the past. The church members recognize the need for mission and service. So I am certain that maeul ministry is the answer to sustainability. Based on my 37 years of ministry I take a more active approach to maeul ministry to define our church's function in town as the priest, the prophet, and the king of service. With these functions the church can be the center of the community rather than an island.

Finally, this may be a foolish question,
but how would you define maeul ministry?

It's a very good question. I define maeul ministry by the threefold office of Christ. It is a life-giving movement for not only the town but also the church, the congregants, and Christianity. When a church does ministry to give life to the community, the church can also have hope for sustainability. In that sense, the most local church is the most global church. In the past, churches used to move closer to high-rise apartments for a better chance at growth. But I am against every church becoming mega churches. Small rural churches have their roles, and small urban churches must also exist as members of the community to take up their responsibilities. We must know that we are called to the community. Churches that still open the gates on Sundays only and only to their members will become islands. Churches and pastors must be the center of the community, knowing the community issues and raising residents' quality of life. For this, we must be well-equipped with the theology of the threefold office of Christ and then study the government welfare policies for application. Maeul ministry is life-giving ministry. Just as Jesus became Christ who saves the world, when we minister and teach our faith and act in the community as the priest, the prophet, and the king of service, our church will be the church of the good news of the kingdom of God, and our ministry will be life-giving.

Maeul Ministry Serving the Local Community

Won-bum Chung

Introduction

Kukmin Daily, a Korean newspaper company reported on April 27, 2022 the results of a nationwide survey they conducted on the image of Protestant Christianity. Only 18.1% of the respondents saw the Korean Protestant church as credible. Compared to the "2020 Survey of Social Credibility of the Korean Church" by the Christian Ethics Movement of Korea and the 2021 "Survey of Citizens' Assessment of Government's Covid-19 Prevention Measures" by the Ministry Data Institute on the same question, the credibility fell from 32% in 2020 to 21% in 2021 and 18% in 2022. In the 2022 study, 63.5% of Christians trusted Christianity, and only 8.8% among non-Christians.[1] The results are evidence of how the Korean Protestant church has lost its credibility. How did the Protestant church that initiated the modernization of Korea become what it is today? The two major reasons are that the church has lost its true identity and neglected its public role. And maeul ministry is proposed as the solution. This is so because maeul ministry essentially says that the essence of the church is to participate in the movement of the kingdom of God started by Jesus, and this ministry allows the church to perform its public role.

This essay starts on the basis that maeul ministry is an appropriate response to the Korean church's crisis, and introduces Hannam Jeil church as one of the best cases of a church's maeul ministry. In part 2, I will review the basic concept of the maeul and maeul ministry as described by Oh, Changwoo, the pastor of Hannam Jeil Church, followed by the church's theological basis for maeul ministry in part 3. Part 4 will discuss obstacles to maeul ministry as mentioned by Oh, and part 5 the content of Hannam Jeil Church's maeul ministry. Then I list some accomplishments and remaining tasks for the church's maeul ministry in the final section.

Basic Concept of Maeul and Maeul Ministry

Defining the Maeul

The 2015 Nationwide Maeul Declaration says, "The maeul is a spatial concept where day-to-day life and living space is located, and a social concept where the

[1] KNC, "Kuk-min-ŭn ki-tok-kyo-in-e-ke salm-ŭ-lo tŭ-lŏ-na-nŭn kŭ-li-sŭ-to-ŭi p'yŏn-chi ki-tae-han-ta" [People expect the letter of Christ apparent in Christian lives" (28 April 2022) https://www.kosinnews.com/news/articleView.html?idxno=24455. Accessed 19 March 2023.

environment and culture are shared."[2] The 2018 "Seoul Metropolitan City Ordinance on Support for Maeul Community Making" similarly defines the maeul as a "spatial and social scope in which residents live daily lives and share in economy, culture, and environment." It also defines the maeul community as the "resident self-governing community where the individual residents' freedoms and entitlements are respected and the residents decide on and implement community matters in mutually equal relationships."[3] Pastor Chang-woo Oh does not give a specific definition for the term maeul, but implies the significance of the term by stating "How can one discuss the church's role in local community or maeul ministry with no knowledge of the maeul?"[4] He uses the terms maeul and maeul community interchangeably and simply defines maeul community as "the civil society owned by the citizens."

Defining Maeul Ministry and Background of Implementation

Definition of Maeul Ministry

Chang-woo Oh states that "the church is not a group separate from the community but a member of the community living in the neighborhood." So "maeul ministry is not so different from church ministry; they are one and the same." First, explaining that "maeul ministry is not simply programs of service and evangelism,"[5] he says

> "Maeul ministry means participating in civil society."[6] "Maeul ministry is ministry that builds up people. It is to have people live happily as they participate in local matters and be responsible for the neighbors.... Maeul ministry is the key opportunity for a church to escape its lonely island and recover its essence as the missional church."[7] "Maeul ministry is not a tool for evangelism but a movement to become a good coexisting neighbor."[8] "Maeul ministry means honoring the local leaders." "Maeul ministry is about participating in local programs."[9] "Maeul ministry means caring for the town."[10]

Oh used the phrases "dreaming of a beautiful town with the town" and "make the town dance." Evidently maeul ministry according to Oh is ministry that makes the town happy. As he conducts maeul ministry like so, he also says "maeul ministry should not be the entirety of ministry." That is because church

---

[2] Seongnam Agenda 21 Action Council. *Haeng-pok-ma-ŭl-man-tŭl-ki to-si-a-k'a-te-mi* [Urban Academy for a Happy Town]. 2012. 10-11.
[3]Nationwide Maeul Declaration 2015 https://www.law.go.kr/LSW/ordinInfoP.do?viewCls=ordinInfoP&urlMode=ordinScJoRltInfoR&ordinSeq=1342389&chrClsCd=010202&gubun=KLAW. Accessed 10 March 2023.
[4] Chang-woo Oh, *Han-nam-che-il-kyo-hoe ma-ŭl-mok-hoe* [Maeul ministry of hannam jeil church], Unpublished resource book. 1.
[5] Ibid., 1.
[6] Ibid., 1.
[7] Ibid., 54.
[8] Interview with Chang-woo Oh, 9 March 2023.
[9] Ibid.
[10] Ibid.

members also request spiritual care, and most people become a part of a church through spiritual transformation.[11]

Background of Implementation

Awareness of the Issue of Division between Church and Local Community

Before Oh became the pastor of Hannam Jeil Church he was on his way there to preach. He asked several people in the streets where the church is and even right in front of the church, and nobody had any idea. He was shocked to see how people didn't know where the church is when they were standing right in front of its gate. So the first thing he did when he became the pastor was to break down the church walls. This problem of "the church that became an island in the community" instigated his path of maeul ministry.

Decision to Promote the Church in the Local Community

Once he was shocked to find nobody in the neighborhood knew of the church's existence he committed to make the church known in the area. So he took a sack of rice to the Community Service Center to donate to the poor. He asked the Town Head "I am the new pastor of Hannam Jeil Church. Our church would like to share food with the poor neighbors for Christmas. Please help." The Town Head raises funds to support the poor every winter so he was happy to receive this request. The rice would be shared at the church but selection of recipients and the event operations were taken care of by the town. The Community Service Center officers and Township Heads all came to make the event a neighborhood celebration. The Town Head did not spare good words for pastor Oh and the residents also bean speaking highly of the pastor. This became a good opportunity to promote the church's presence as well as another starting point of pastor Oh's maeul ministry.

The Pastor's Upbringing

Chang-woo Oh experienced Youngnak Presbyterian Church and Euljiro Church in his youth. As a pastoral intern at Youngnak Church he was influenced by pastor Han Kyung-chik's social service work through an orphanage, a woman's shelter, and a nursing home. Oh also operates a nursing home, an after-school care program for elementary students (Kium Center), and a children's daycare, thanks to pastor Han's impact. When Oh was the president of his church youth group, four youth groups of different churches in the vicinity (Chungmu, Hanyang, Euljiro, and Namdaemun Church) gathered to organize a joint sports day and a worship session, naming it CHEN from the first letter of each church. With this experience, when he served as an associate pastor of Munhwa Church, he organized churches of different denominations in the vicinity to put on a worship gathering. Later as the pastor of Hannam Jeil Church he formed Yongsan Church-District Council and the Church-Town Council to lead in

---

[11] Chang-woo Oh. *U-li-kyo-hoe chi-yŏk-sa-hoe sŏm-kim-ŭl mal-han-ta* [On local community service in by our church]. Unpublished resource book. 12.

ecumenical efforts. These ecumenical maeul ministries were nurtured by Oh's upbringing.

Purpose and Principles of Maeul Ministry

Purpose of Maeul Ministry

Oh states that the purpose of his maeul ministry is to change the local community with the gospel and save it. For this purpose, the church and the community must live as a family, and Hannam Jeil Church aims to be a good neighbor indispensable for the town.

Principles of Maeul Ministry

The three principle of Oh's maeul ministry (ministry for the local community) are giving, sharing, and participation. The principle of giving means to give of the body of Christ for the salvation of the world. Sharing means that as stewards of the church that belongs to God, church members must share church facilities with their neighboring residents. And the principle of participation is about participating in the nation's institutions, policies, and maeul community programs.[12] For example, Oh became the first leader of the Resident Self-Governance Council and is participating in the Maeul Community Movement as a member of the Civil Society Advisory Board. He also organized the Church-Town Council and is participating in it. On the relationship between the church and the community he has three principles: 1) Honoring local leaders, 2) Participating in local programs, and 3) Deferring to community needs.

Theological Reflection

First, while pastor Oh defined maeul ministry in many different ways, his definitions come from his practice of maeul ministry so they are highly specific, practical, and realistic. Yet it would have been even better to specify one central definition that represents all others. A possible definition may be, "maeul ministry is a ministry that actualizes the kingdom of God or its values (freedom, equality, flourishing, justice, love, peace, joy, healing, etc.)"[13] or, "Maeul ministry is a ministry that builds a true community by actualizing the values of the kingdom of God (freedom, equality, flourishing, justice, love, peace, joy, healing, etc.)."

Secondly, in Oh's paper on maeul ministry, he could have focused on the necessity and significance of this topic only. Yet he also pointed out how maeul ministry cannot be separate from church ministry and that maeul ministry and spiritual ministry must go hand in hand. This is evident of pastor Oh's balanced ministry philosophy.

---

[12] Chang-woo Oh, *Maeul ministry of hannam jeil church*, 41.

[13] Won-bum Chung. "Ma-ŭl-kong-tong-ch'e-e-sŏ kae-sin-kyo-hoe-ŭi yŏk-hal" [Role of the protestant church in maeul community], Journal *of Religious Studies & Culture*. 19(1) (2022 June), 36.

Third, in pastor Oh's background there are the spiritual experiences of his youth and his ministry experiences in other churches. But the decisive events happened as he became the pastor of Hannam Jeil Church that made him recognize 1) the problem of division between the church and community, and 2) the need to promote the church's existence to the community. Based on our different life experiences we may also try to search for related issues and tasks for our time (or the will of God for our time). The habit of seeking out these issues can provide important turning points in our ministry and life.

Fourth, Oh stated that the purpose of his maeul ministry is to change and save the community through the gospel. I would suggest also adding to the purpose the intention to actualize the (values of) the kingdom of God.

Theological Basis for Maeul Ministry

Ecclesiological Foundation

First, the theological basis of Oh's maeul ministry is the missional church. In missional ecclesiology, the church exists because of God's mission to fulfill God's mission. So mission is not one of the many ministries of the church but the church itself is missional. In other words, the church does not exist for itself but for the local community.[14] Therefore, Oh considers the local community the site of ministry and mission, and the church the center of the community and a good neighbor meeting the needs of the community and not just the congregation. The church pastor should be a neighborhood pastor and a friend serving both the church and the residents. Based on this awareness he served the community, not just the church congregation.[15]

Christological Foundation

The second theological basis of Oh's maeul ministry is the threefold office of Christ. To believe in Christ is to take after Jesus and live as he did. To live like Jesus, we must also take on the role of the priest for the town responsible for the spirituality of the community, the town prophet witnessing to the kingdom of God as we participate in town programs, and the king serving the town as town volunteer.[16] The threefold offices of Christ bring together the church, the Christian, the pastor, and the town. This is Oh's philosophy of maeul ministry and theological grounding.

Theological Reflection

Oh mentioned missional ecclesiology, the philosophy of missional ministry, and the threefold office of Christ as the theological foundations to his maeul ministry. I would like to mention the four theological bases I presented at a talk I gave at the academic forum, "Role of Religion in Maeul Community" by the hosted by

---

[14] Won-bum Chung. *Se-sang sok ha-na-nim-na-la kong-tong-ch'e* [Community of kingdom of god in the world], (Nonsan: Daejanggan, 2021), 117.

[15] Chang-woo Oh. *On local community service in by our church,* 2.

[16] Ibid., 12.

the Chonnam National University Institute of Religion and Culture in May 2022. These points may supplement Oh's theological basis for maeul ministry.[17]

Basis on the Doctrine of God

First, Christian ministry must go beyond church gates to become maeul ministry because God's reign and redemption are universal and cosmic. In other words, God's existence and actions are social and participatory[18] so Christian ministry must also be social and participatory. It follows that the church must move away from local church-centric, growth-oriented ministry to listen to the pains of the socially marginalized and the groans of the created world, restore the broken maeul community, and revive the planetary ecology.

Basis on Christology

The second reason why Christian ministry must be maeul ministry is that Jesus showed the model of ministry by giving life to the maeul community. Jesus' ministry revived the community that was disintegrating under the oppression and exploitation of the Roman Empire and its proxy rulers and turned them into new maeul communities of sharing, cooperation, and mutual care.[19] Richard Horsley stated that the mission of Jesus in Galilee and other towns healed the consequences of the empire's violence and focused on reviving the community spirit and cooperation as they were dividing under the influence of imperialism.[20] So Jesus' ministry was not limited to the synagogues but focused on the restoration of community. Christian ministry must also focus on the restoration of maeul community.

Basis on Ecclesiology

Third, Christian ministry should be maeul ministry because the church exists not for itself but for the world. The church is not a private organization existing for its own benefit but must fulfill its public responsibility to benefit the neighbors and save the world. As Bonhoeffer said, church is only church when it exists for others.[21] The only way a church can maintain its relevance is to fight for the salvation of the world rather than itself. If not, the church becomes a "religious organization" that fights for its own benefit, and stops being for God and for the world.[22] Therefore the church must rightfully be the maeul church that serves the town, and only then will the church become the light of the world.

---

[17] Won-bum Chung, "Role of the protestant church in maeul community," 36-37.
[18] Kenneth Leech, *The Social God*, Eugene, OR: Wipf and Stock, 2003, Korean version translated by Hyun-ki Shin (Seoul: Chungrim, 2009), 24.
[19] Richard A. Horsley, *Jesus and Empire: The Kingdom of God and New World Disorder*, Minneapolis, MN: Fortress Press, 2002, Korean version translated by Joon-woo Kim (Seoul: Korean Institute of the Christian Studies, 2004), 190-210.
[20] Ibid. 208.
[21] ed. John W. de Gruchy, *The Cambridge Companion to Dietrich Bonhoeffer* (Cambridge University Press, 1999), 217.
[22] Larry L. Rasmussen, *Dietrich Bonhoeffer: Reality and Resistance* (Nashville, Tennessee: Abingdon Press, 1972), 21.

Basis on Missiology

Fourth, Christian ministry must be maeul ministry because Christian mission is not the church's mission for its own growth but the mission of God to actualize the kingdom of God in the world. In other words, the subject of mission is not the church but God. Mission is not simply about spreading the gospel to save souls and found churches, but it is all the activities related to sharing the gospel and building the kingdom of God in the world.[23] So if the kingdom of God must be actualized in the world, Christian ministry must essentially start with the maeul, the local community, to work toward this kingdom of God.

Overcoming Obstacles to Maeul Ministry

Internal Factors

The first difficulty Oh encountered in his maeul ministry was the traditional mindset of the church members. Rather than attending to the local community, they were more interested in getting spiritual care from the pastor and the growth of the church. So when Oh took interest in local matters and wanted to do maeul ministry to serve the town and improve it, the congregation responded negatively saying the church and its members should take priority over town matters. To overcome this obstacle Oh tried to instill in them that "Hannam Jeil Church is a faith community gathered with a mission for Hannam-dong." As he emphasized the missionary responsibility most church members eventually acquired an interest in the town.

External Factors

The other difficulty in maeul ministry was the distrust of local officials and residents who were wary that a church's interest and participation in maeul programs made hide evangelical motives. But Oh did not consider community service a tool or strategy for evangelism. Through service out of the love of Christ, the residents and government offices recognize the church's role. The pastor and the church gained opportunities to participate actively in community development.[24]

Theological Reflection

First, pastor Oh identifies internal obstacles as the church members' own view of the church as divided from the world, the church-centric ministry perspective, and the growth orientation. Besides these, there were issues of dualism between body and spirit, individual and society, this world and the world to come, and giving less value to the body, the society, and this world than the spirit, the individual and the world to come. Another issue was individualistic soteriology narrowing down God's redemption history to a matter of personal spiritual salvation, church-centric missiology focusing only on spreading the gospel to

---

[23] Won-bum Chung, *Community of kingdom of god in the world,* 162.

[24] Chang-woo Oh, *Maeul ministry of hannam jeil church*, 3.

save souls and found churches, and individualistic and personalized spirituality applying the Word and faith only to personal and spiritual relationship with God and not to issues of society, politics, economy, and international relations.[25]

Secondly, Oh identified the external obstacle as the residents and community officials who think a church's participation in the community is an evangelism strategy and therefore resist or criticize church involvement. This is a critical point churches must bear in mind as they seek to get involved in community service or welfare. In reality many pastors do consider these involvements the instrument of evangelism. In one recent survey of general citizens, many responded that Protestant churches' community service work did not seem authentic because their purpose was to evangelize. Pastors should take note.

Korean churches continue to devote much effort to community service and evangelism. But why does the size of the congregation keep decreasing? Why does Protestant Christianity rank lowest in social credibility among all religions? We must consider the reasons. Some of them may be that the church is obsessed with church growth, individual church matters, and evangelism at the neglect of others.

After Lesslie Newbigin retired from the mission field and returned to England he lamented the decline and ghettoization of the church. He pointed out that this was because the church gave up its public role and the faith became increasingly personalized and privatized.[26] The Korean church is not much different.

Today the Korean Protestant church must recognize the serious problem of personalization (privatization) of faith, lack of church unity, and the pursuit of church growth. Rather than considering community service a tool of evangelism and the residents the objects of evangelism, and discarding local church-centrism and growth-centrism that cause the church to lose credibility, we must authentically practice the love of God and neighbor and fulfill the church's public responsibility. The church must be the salt and light of the world not just in the private sphere but also in the public sphere.

Content of Maeul Ministry

The content of Hannam Jeil Church's maeul ministry consists of five general types of ministry programs. They are management of commissioned facilities, facility sharing, participation in local charity programs, child-rearing, and ministry to foreign migrants.

Commissioned Management

- District Nursing Home
- District Children's Daycare

---

[25] Won-bum Chung, *Kyo-hoe-ta-un kyo-hoe: ch'am-toen ki-tok-kyo-yŏng-sŏng-ŭi hoe-pok* [Authentic church: recovery of true Christian spirituality], (Seoul: Dongyeon. 2016), 54-61.

[26] Seong-sik Heo, "The Missiological Implications of Lessilie Newbigin's Missional Debates," *Korea Presbyterian Journal of Theology,* 50-2 (2018 June), 221.

- Seoul Kium Center in Hannam-dong

Facility Sharing

- Maeul community: church facilities are open for maeul community gatherings
- Resident Self-Governance Council: church facilities are always available for the council's programs
- International Church: a part of the Education Hall is rented out as worship space for migrant workers
- Community Center (Multicultural Café): Foreign congregants of the International Church use the space to provide shelter and counseling
- Open café space: Ground coffee and tea are available for free to the church and the residents on the first floor of Education Hall
- Dream Maeul Garden: The garden space of the Education Hall that is open to the town.

Participation in Mercy Ministries for Local Community

- Yongsan Household Matching Program: KRW 30,000 support sent to 36 households through the Community Service Center
- Yongsan Food Market-Bank: participating in the operation of the program along with other churches of the Yongsan Church-District Council
- Field Trips for Local Seniors and Seniors in the Church: Treating seniors to a meal out at a restaurant within a two-hour driving distance
- Collaboration with Hannam-dong Community Welfare Council: Packing and distributing lunches to seniors who live alone. The number of volunteers reached over 200 at one time.
- Charity for the holidays: rice distributed for the holidays such as Christmas, Easter, and Thanksgiving

Raising a Child in Town

- Culture Lessons
  - Hannam-dong Orchestra
  - Violine Lessons
  - Flute Lessons
  - Cello Lessons
- Foreign Language Lessons
  - English Class (Every Tuesday, Thursday, Saturday)
- Maeul Community Programs
  - Parent Community Program
  - Neighboring Program
  - Maeul Media Program
  - Cooperative Childcare Program
  - School in the Maeul Program

- Resident Gatherings Association
- Yongsan Youth Support Program
- Hankkum Volunteers

Ministry to Foreign Migrants

- Multicultural Cafe
- International Church
- Sharon's House (Shelter for women in Tacoma, Washington in the United States)

Theological Reflection

According to the resource book "Survey of Ministers' Perception of Maeul Ministry", the types of maeul ministry activities can be categorized into social service, facility usage, community participation, lifestyle and culture, and local economy. According to this categorization Hannam Jeil Church's maeul ministry equally covers all types of activities except the aspect of social economy.

There are several characteristics of Hannam Jeil Church's maeul ministry. 1) It is conducted based on a clear theological basis of missional church and missional ministry. 2) It is incarnational ministry absorbed into the community like salt as the church maintains good relationships with the community residents. 3) The ministry is participatory in that the church accurately discerned the new trends in government social welfare policy to actively participate in the maeul community movement. 4) The maeul ministry is cooperative with the residents, the Community Service Center, the District Office, and the Seoul City Government in social service. 5) The maeul ministry is customized by surveying and finding the needs of the local community. 6) The church is open and welcoming to all. 7) The ministry is holistic in covering social welfare, education, ecology, culture, and community. 8) The ministry is characterized by compassion to the poor and the marginalized such as the seniors living alone and people on the lowest income bracket. 9) The church is adept at organizing efforts such as the Church-Town Council, the Yongsan Church-District Council, Small Church Association, and the Hannam-dong Pandemic Prevention Crew. This enables a more organized and ecumenical service provision.

Accomplishments and Remaining Tasks

Accomplishments

Local Recognition

As Hannam Jeil Church became the community's companion and neighbor meeting community service needs, it earned the recognition of the residents and public offices. The town head, volunteers, and residents appreciate the pastor and the church's care. The residents call the pastor "our pastor", and the district head asks the participants in a local leaders' meeting if they can start with the pastor's brief prayer.[27] Hannam Jeil Church is no doubt a great model of maeul ministry.

Networking between School, Town, and Church

Oh saw the public grant project for the School in the Maeul Program in 2015 and recalled Tongtong Book Club that Hannam Elementary School parents were already conducting with the school. This was the program where parents read textbooks to students after school. Oh met with the parents and suggested they submit a proposal for the grant. Oh became the representative and submitted the proposal which was selected for the grant. The mothers of Tongtong Book Club also organized the "Day of Education for Global Intercultural Understanding". Oh also helped organize the event and established a close supportive network between schools, the town, and the church. Over time these networks can turn into networks of life where people can find meaning in life and try out the church.[28]

Church as Agent of Change in Local Community

Hannam Jeil Church has been responding to community issues, identifying the needs and meeting them through service and support. Naturally the church became a leader in town and the agent of change to make the community happier and improve the resident quality of life.[29]

Remaining Tasks

Establishing Missional Ecclesiology and Missional Ministry Philosophy

To successfully practice maeul ministry the missional ecclesiology and missional ministry philosophy must be clear. Oh has clearly established these to make maeul ministry possible. When the church members first responded negatively the pastor worked to establish missional ecclesiology in them to encourage their united support and participation. For example, he told the church members to recite that "Hannam Jeil Church is a faith community gathered with a mission to Hannam-dong" like a motto. This instance shows the first thing that must be established in practicing maeul ministry. The missional ecclesiology must be established so that the church exists not only for its members but for the world, the town, and the local community. And the holistic missional ministry philosophy also says ministry is not only about caring for the church members but for the community. The minister is also not just for the church and its members but also for the local community. Pastor Oh managed to establish these foundations in the congregation.

---

[27] Chang-woo Oh, *Maeul ministry of hannam jeil church*, 70-71, 81-82.

[28] Ibid., 56.

[29] Ibid., 55, 58.

Assessing Local Community Needs and Studying National Welfare Policies

The second task to practice maeul ministry is to recognize community needs and national welfare policy. Hannam Jeil Church assessed the needs of the local community and studied the national welfare policy well. The church is doing many programs such as handing out packed meals to seniors, after-school care programs for children and youth, and cooperative childcare. These are not initiated by the church alone. They emerged out of communication with the residents, finding out their requests, and through many consultations. The meal delivery program started with the suggestion during a Church-Town Council meeting discussing a response to seniors living and dying alone.

Oh also suggests paying attention to the new national welfare policy of maeul community movement. Today, the citizens take ownership. The civil society can participate in the process of planning to solve town issues. So the church as part of the civil society must participate in the maeul community movement. For the church to take a central role, it must study the national welfare policy.

Theological Reflection

There are eight major tasks of maeul ministry. First, maeul ministry must actualize the kingdom of God in town. The central theme of Jesus' ministry and teachings was the kingdom of God. Jesus cast the vision of the kingdom of God on earth, not just in the afterlife. That is why he prayed, "May your kingdom come, may your will be done on earth as it is in heaven" and taught us to pray likewise. So maeul ministry that is modeled after Jesus' ministry must aim for the kingdom of God to come on earth and in the local community, and live in a completely new lifestyle for flourishing of life, justice, and peace, different from the selfish capitalistic lifestyle of unlimited growth, competition, and ownership.

Second, maeul ministry must be a blessing to the town. The Kingdom of God is the blessed place where God reigns. The kingdom of God basically means that God reigns.[30] The blessed reign of God is an event in the future and at the same time the reality of the present.[31] We wait for the completion of the reign of God in the future but at the same time it is a blessed gift of God that can be experienced in the now. This is a gift of eschatological salvation implying not only the redemption of the body but also the restoration of relationship between God and humanity broken by sin. Therefore to accept the kingdom of God means to enter into true relationship with God. This is given as a gift, and it means to enter into the blessed joy of this kingdom.[32] Therefore maeul ministry that aims for the actualization of the kingdom of God must above all make the church community the community that tastes and enjoys the blessing of salvation, and on that basis, let the blessing of God flow to bless the town.

---

[30] George Eldon Ladd, *The Presence of the Future: The Eschatology of Biblical Realism* (Grand Rapids, Michigan: William B. Eerdmans Publishing Company, 1974), 195.

[31] Glen H. Stassen and David Gushee, *Kingdom Ethics: Following Jesus in Contemporary Context,* Downers Grove, IL: IVP Academic, 2003.

[32] George Eldon Ladd, *The Presence of the Future: The Eschatology of Biblical Realism,* 207-217.

Third, maeul ministry must liberate the people oppressed and exploited by injustice. The kingdom of God is where salvation, in other words, liberation and emancipation, happens. In Isaiah the most important mark of God's reign is God's salvation. That salvation means liberation and emancipation from oppression and injustice, and emancipation from sin, death, state of war and slavery.[33] The words of Jesus at the start of his ministry (Luke 4:18-19) declared that the kingdom of God is the kingdom of liberation and emancipation, and the essence of God's redemptive history is the history of liberation and emancipation. Therefore maeul ministry that actualizes the kingdom of God must work for the liberation and emancipation of people from sin and death, but also the oppression and exploitation and injustice of politics, economy, and society.

Fourth, maeul ministry must first build community in town. God's redemption implies restoration of humanity and the creation as community, so maeul ministry is fundamentally community ministry. Bonhoeffer saw the fall and redemption of creation from community perspective. Creation was the emergence of community, the fall the destruction of community, and redemption the restoration of community.[34] In the same way, God created for man and woman to depend on each other. God desires not the history of individuals but the history of the human community. God does not desire the community to consume the individual, but a community of persons.[35] Therefore a ministry that builds the kingdom of God must not only build up the church but also the town as a community of people living together.

Fifth, maeul ministry must be the ministry of shalom working for justice, love, and healing. As it is said in Romans 14:17, Isaiah 42:1-7, Matthew 23:23, Luke 10:25-37, and Micah 6:8, the kingdom of God is the kingdom of justice, love, healing, and peace. If so, maeul ministry must actively participate in ministries to that make the maeul (the kingdom) of just and peaceful.[36]

Sixth, maeul ministry must serve and care for the poor. The kingdom of God is where those who care for the least can enter (Matthew 25:31-46), and God prioritizes care for the poor. The world has never been so unequal as today. The inequality in South Korea is truly grave. The top 10% owns 66% of all wealth while the bottom 50% owns only 1.8%. The top 10% of South Korea own 96.4% of the country's real estate while the bottom 90% only 3.6%. In our murderous capitalist structure the minority of people win at the expense of the majority. Maeul ministry that works for the kingdom of God must make a new world

---

[33] Glen H. Stassen, David Gushee, *Kingdom Ethics: Following Jesus in Contemporary Context.*

[34] Institute of Public Theology and Church, *Ha-na-nim na-la-wa chi-yŏk-kyo-hoe* [Kingdom of God and local church], (Seoul: Kingdom Books, 2015), 384.

[35] Bonhoeffer, Dietrich. *Sanctorum Communio: A Theological Study of the Sociology of the Church.* Minneapolis, MN: Fortress Press. 1996.

[36] Hoekendijk who understood the mission of God as shalom states that the state of shalom is ultimately humanization. Seung-hyun Chung, "The Missio Dei, the World, and Shalom: The Mission Theology of Johannes Hoekendijk" *Mission and Theology* 24 (2009), 261-262.

where all lives can flourish together (through social economy). The ministry must participate in caring for the poor in obedience to God's command (Deuteronomy 24:19).

Seventh, maeul ministry must work for the restoration of the town's natural environment. The redemption of the kingdom of God is not only about the salvation of human souls, but also the body. This is comprehensive salvation that includes the society and all natural beings (Colossians 1:20). Ulrich Duchrow warned, "between 1850 and 1950 one animal species vanished every year; around 1989 one animal species vanished per day; around the year 2000 one animal species vanished per hour. The recent figures of 2008 speak of one species dying out every 10 minutes. According to the report of the International Panel on Climate Change, the percentage of vanished species is going to be 30% within 50 years."[37] There is also the pollution of the air and water, depletion of natural resources, destruction of the ozone layer, acid rains, and other phenomena. The most serious issue above all is the climate crisis that is causing innumerous weather anomalies. Without solving this issue, the humanity can no longer survive. So maeul ministry that aims for the restoration of all beings must make stewards of creation to restore the natural environment of the town.

Eighth, maeul ministry must work for the blossoming of life-giving and peaceful culture. The kingdom of God abolishes the culture against life and peace. Today the world is rife with culture of death in murder and suicide, extreme poverty, destruction of family and society, terror and war, weapons of mass destruction and nuclear weapons, exploitation of human DNA for cloning, oppression and exploitation. Maeul ministry must actively participate in the movement of the kingdom of God to change the culture of death to one of life and peace that respects the dignity of human life, enables coexistence with others, and allows for the enjoyment of freedom and joy.

Conclusion

Leonard Sweet had said in 2006 that "the churches in Europe have already become museums, the churches in the United States are maintaining the status quo to eventually turn into museums, and the Korean church is becoming churches that maintain the status quo." If he assesses the Korean church again today 16 years from the time, he would diagnose that the Korean church is now heading toward becoming museums.

In this crisis of the church, an important solution is maeul ministry. Maeul ministry is a good prescription for the two causes of the crisis of the Korean Protestant church – the church's loss of its essential identity and its public role. Maeul ministry is about participating in Jesus' movement of the kingdom of God which is the essential element of the church's identity. It is also the ministry that enables the church to appropriately perform its public function in this changing society.

---

[37] Ulrich Duchrow, "The Challenge of Imperial Globalization to Theological Education: Liberation from Violent, Possessive Individualism towards Life in Relationships," IV International WOCATI Congress, 31 May-7 June 2008, Thessaloniki/Greece.

Today the Korean Protestant church is widely mistrusted, which means the church is more often functioning inappropriately. Therefore, for the Korean church to earn the trust of society it must minimize its negative impact and maximize its positive function as a religion for social unity, raising social standards, and social transformation. This is how the Protestant church functioned in the early days of the Korean church. As apparent in the case of Hannam Jeil Church, maeul ministry is allowing the church to perform its positive function very well. May the Korean Protestant church be rebirthed to become a beautiful church that gives hope to Korean society.

Bibliography

Bonhoeffer, Dietrich. *Sanctorum Communio: A Theological Study of the Sociology of the Church.* Minneapolis, MN: Fortress Press, 1996.

Chung, Seung-hyun, "The Missio Dei, the World, and Shalom: The Mission Theology of Johannes Hoekendijk" *Mission and Theology* 24 (2009), 261-262.

Chung, Won-bum. *Kyo-hoe-ta-un kyo-hoe: ch'am-toen ki-tok-kyo-yŏng-sŏng-ŭi hoe-pok* [Authentic church: recovery of true Christian spirituality]. Seoul: Dongyeon, 2016.

_________. "Ma-ŭl-kong-tong-ch'e-e-sŏ kae-sin-kyo-hoe-ŭi yŏk-hal" [Role of the protestant church in maeul community]. Journal *of Religious Studies & Culture.* 19(1) (2022 June).

_________. *Se-sang sok ha-na-nim-na-la kong-tong-ch'e* [Community of kingdom of god in the world]. Nonsan: Daejanggan, 2021.

Duchrow, Ulrich "*The Challenge of Imperial Globalization to Theological Education: Liberation from Violent, Possessive Individualism towards Life in Relationships,*" IV International WOCATI Congress, 31 May-7 June, 2008, Thessaloniki/Greece.

Gruchy, John W. de. ed. *The Cambridge Companion to Dietrich Bonhoeffer.* Cambridge University Press, 1999.

Heo, Seong-sik. "The Missiological Implications of Lessilie Newbigin's Missional Debates." *Korea Presbyterian Journal of Theology* 50-2 (2018 June).

Horsley, Richard A. *Jesus and Empire: The Kingdom of God and New World Disorder.* Minneapolis, MN: Fortress Press, 2002. Korean version translated by Kim, Joon-woo. Seoul: Korean Institute of the Christian Studies, 2004.

Institute of Public Theology and Church, *Ha-na-nim na-la-wa chi-yŏk-kyo-hoe* [Kingdom of God and local church]. Seoul: Kingdom Books, 2015.

KNC, "Kuk-min-ŭn ki-tok-kyo-in-e-ke salm-ŭ-lo tŭ-lŏ-na-nŭn kŭ-li-sŭ-to-ŭi p'yŏn-chi ki-tae-han-ta" [People expect the letter of Christ apparent in Christian lives" (28 April, 2022) https://www.kosinnews.com/news/articleView.html?idxno=24455. Accessed 19 March 2023.

Ladd, George Eldon. *The Presence of the Future: The Eschatology of Biblical Realism.* Grand Rapids. Michigan: William B. Eerdmans Publishing

Company, 1974.

Leech, Kenneth. *The Social God.* Eugene, OR: Wipf and Stock, 2003. Korean version translated by Shin, Hyun-ki. Seoul: Chungrim, 2009.

Nationwide Maeul Declaration, 2015, https://www.law.go.kr/LSW/ordinInfoP.do?viewCls=ordinInfoP&urlMode=ordinScJoRltInfoR&ordinSeq=1342389&chrClsCd=010202&gubun=KLAW. Accessed 19 March 2023.

Oh, Chang-woo, *Han-nam-che-il-kyo-hoe ma-ŭl-mok-hoe* [Maeul ministry of hannam jeil church], Unpublished resource book.

_________. *U-li-kyo-hoe chi-yŏk-sa-hoe sŏm-kim-ŭl mal-han-ta* [On local community service in by our church]. Unpublished resource book.

Rasmussen, Larry L. *Dietrich Bonhoeffer: Reality and Resistance.* Nashville, Tennessee: Abingdon Press, 1972.

Seongnam Agenda 21 Action Council. *Haeng-pok-ma-ŭl-man-tŭl-ki to-si-a-k'a-te-mi* [Urban Academy for a Happy Town], 2012.

Stassen, Glen H. and Gushee, David. *Kingdom Ethics: Following Jesus in Contemporary Context,* Downers Grove, IL: IVP Academic, 2003.

Realizing the Kingdom of God in the World: The Story of Suwonsung Church, Focusing on the Social Missionary System

Gwang-su An and Gi-eop Nam

Ministry of Suwonsung Church

Suwonsung Church was founded on October 31, 1982, by pastor Gwang-su An. The church that started with five households now grew to 4,000 adults and 1,200 children and youth. An defines ministry as "all the tasks related to having non-believers believe in Jesus and having believers grow in faith to raise them as laborers for the kingdom of God in and out of the church."

Evangelism

The highest priority for An has always been saving souls. Jesus also said, "the Son of Man came to seek out and save the lost" (Luke 19:10). In the church's early days, the pastor and his wife went throughout the town to evangelize. Evangelizing for two hours in the morning and two hours in the afternoon every day resulted in adding 50 new church members in one year. Next year, they evangelized with the church members, resulting in 120 more members. In the third year the number increased to 200.

An formed and operated various small groups to make the church more friendly to non-believers, such as groups interested in soccer, hiking, foot volleyball, volleyball, baseball, fishing, gate ball, Korean traditional percussion band, guitar, folksongs, the game of go, billiards, and screen golf. Not a few non-Christians joined for the leisure activities and then came to receive Christ. To lead them to Christ, An preached sermons that anyone could easily understand, and formed discipleship training classes for new believers to teach the basics of Christianity.

Education

A minister is responsible for making people believe in Jesus and helping believers deepen their faith. If evangelism is the birthing of the children of God, then education is nurturing the children of God to live a life worthy of their identity. Pastor An devoted much effort in education.

An formed discipleship training classes for beginner, intermediate, and advanced levels to teach and train the church members. Especially the beginners' classes were conducted by the pastor himself twice a year in spring and fall for 10 weeks each. In these classes, the basic tenets of Christianity were taught to lay a firm foundation of faith in new Christians.

The following is the order of contents in the beginners' discipleship training classes.

1. Does God really exist?
2. How can I be saved?
3. Once saved, how should I live?
4. How should I pray?
5. On church life
6. Why evangelize?
7. Spirit-filled life
8. Fellowship of the saints
9. Let's prepare for Jesus' return

In the beginners' class, they receive communion and go to retreat centers to personally experience carrying a heavy cross. These experiences encourage them to acquire a passionate faith. These beginners' classes were conducted for 37 years to produce 2,900 graduates. These beginners' discipleship training classes were the most important factor that made what Suwonsung Church is today. The ones who graduated from the beginners' class were encouraged to go through the intermediate and advanced classes, then to other Bible study classes conducted by associate pastors to have them mature in faith.

Raising Up Laborers

Once the church members matured in faith through programs such as Fathers' School, Mothers' School, Marriage School, Intercessory Prayer School, and Evangelism School, they were raised to serve the church. Elders, *gwonsas*, and deacons were elected to be responsible for different departments. Since they are well-trained, they are handling their calling capably. For example, for the task of driving three large buses and six medium-sized buses to transport church members on Sundays, 15 volunteers have been serving for over 17 years.

But Suwonsung Church emphasizes the importance of being shining contributors out in the world rather than in the church. A deacon sought out An one day. He was ordained as deacon but he had no time to serve in the church so he wanted to resign. He was the principal of Changhyeon High School in Suwon. An told him, "Deacon, you are the education missionary Suwonsung Church has sent to Changhyeon High School. Don't worry about serving in the church and do your best to share the gospel in Changhyeon High School." After this, the deacon passionately prayed and served the school's students, resulting in 85% of the school's graduates responding that they attend a church.

Another deacon was in the police force. He was the leader of the prayer meeting in his workplace and was passionate about evangelism. At the beginning of the year 30 people met for the workplace prayer meeting. By the end of the year 100 people gathered. This was the result of evangelizing by being a positive influence on others.

Another deacon managed an afterschool private education institution. As more branches were launched in other locations, services were held at each branch and operated with Christian values. God blessed the business so the deacon has built schools worldwide today and supports the education and livelihood of numerous children.

Like so, the pastor has emphasized the importance of raising laborers for the world to create positive change rather than having them serve in the church.

Building the Kingdom of God

God raised the church on earth to save the world. The church is God's instrument to actualize the kingdom of God. Suwonsung Church is devoting much effort to change the world according to God's desire.

Charity Activities

For over 20 years Suwonsung Church has provided breakfast for the homeless every Saturday. In the winter the church also distributes warm inner clothing. Every year for the past 23 years, the church has gathered rice to share with the poor so they would not go hungry.

The mobile bathing service program has been operating for 21 years to help seniors with limited mobility. Volunteers have been helping them bathe, doing their hair, and cleaning their houses.

The Banchan of Love Team has been meeting every Monday to make tasty side dishes and share them with about 100 households. The church has also been operating a Senior Center with the cooperation of the city of Suwon to raise seniors' quality of life. At the center, the Seniors Club is also operated to provide them with work opportunities.

Social Missionary System

The church must not only help and comfort the people who have encountered hardships (social service), but also be responsible for making a just world where hardships are prevented (social action). To contribute to making a more just world, Suwonsung Church has formed a social missionary system. More on this will be explained in a later section.

Ministry Principles of Suwonsung Church

Suwonsung Church has aimed to be a healthy church rather than a growing church. To be a healthy church the pastor established three principles.

Ministry of Peace

The church on earth is a miniature of heaven. The most important value of heaven is *shalom*. So the church on earth must also value peace above all. An has emphasized a few points to maintain peace in the church.

- It is better to have peace with less than the best rather than to have conflict in pursuit of the best:
  There was a time when the pastor was in conflict with the church members due to matters in church construction. The building was built but there was no joy in the church. He realized then that it is better to have peace with less than the best rather than to have conflict in pursuit of the best.

- Fairness in administration: Unfair administration is a key cause of broken peace. If the minister does not operate the church fairly and favors people with personal ties, it disrupts the peace in the church.
- Importance of relationships: Ministry happens through relationships. Even if the pastor can preach like an angel if the relationships are broken the listeners are not blessed. To succeed in relationships the minister must always have the attitude of service. Jesus said he "came not to be served but to serve". When the minister accepts that he is the servant of God and of other people (II Corinthians 4:5) and serves others, the church will be in peace.

Balanced Ministry

For a church to be healthy everything must be in balance. An has emphasized the balance between the Word, prayer, and service. Along with various Bible studies, he encouraged the church to pray through special prayer events such as New Year's Special Early Morning Prayers, Passion Week Evening Prayers, Fall Special Early Morning Prayers, and intercessory prayers. He also encourages people to serve in different departments. In church ministries, there should also be balance among mission, education, and local community service. While outward mission is important, training the next generation in faith is no less important, so he devotes much to the Sunday School and young adult ministry.

An has also emphasized the balance between church, family, and work. He preaches that serving in church should not hinder family life and work life. Suwonsung Church also values balance in age demographics. The church has 1,200 Sunday School children and youth, 500 young adults, and 280 households of young married couples. In all, there are 2,500 church members under age 40. There is also a good balance of 54% women and 46% men. This is evidence of the church's health.

Ministry of Training

There is a saying that a believer is born but a disciple is formed by training. Jesus also called the disciples then trained them before sending them. Gwang-su An saw the necessity of training for the believers to become the chosen soldiers of the cross. After discipleship training the church members go through Fathers' School, Mothers' School, and Marriage School to strengthen the family. Then they are assigned to clean the church restrooms, serve in the kitchen, serve the homeless, and clean the church to train in service. The church is the training ground and the family and the workplaces are battlegrounds, so it is at the church that they should train in service, obedience, and care for others before they can return to their families and workplaces to put their learning into action.

Planting the Values of the Kingdom of God in the World

The central theme of the Bible is the kingdom of God. So the church's main mission is to seek the kingdom of God and God's righteousness on earth. To carry on this mission, Suwonsung Church started the Social Missionary System. The church also consistently conducted ministries to be in solidarity with the victims of disasters. Below is the description of the Social Missionary System and activities in response to the Sewol Ferry Disaster.

The First Social Missionary System in Korea

Purpose

Korean churches have mainly considered only individuals and households as objects of mission. But the society is also an object of mission that must be transformed. In a society full of injustice it is very difficult for individuals and households to live holy lives. Above all, injustice causes great suffering to our neighbors. Therefore society is also the realm that the word of God must completely transform.

But it is realistically impossible for the church to intervene in all social issues and present biblical solutions to transform society. There is the risk of bringing dishonor to God's church. While the church must raise the prophetic voice for large and clear injustices, the church cannot respond to each and every issue. So the solution was to discover, support, and send into the society the people who have the vision for social transformation based on biblical values.

For this purpose, Suwonsung Church began to support social missionaries. The church sought out people who are confident about their salvation and filled with the Holy Spirit, have the desire to transform society, and are spiritually, intellectually, and socially trained for this vision, and have supported them through prayer and resources since 2009. Suwonsung Church was the first to implement this system in the Korean church. Today, several churches with the same goal is operating the social missionary system modelled after our own.

Major Activities

In March 2009 the Social Mission Committee announced the first call and selected the first batch of four people working in various fields. The selected social missionaries are given monthly financial support and invited to share their work with the church twice a year. The first thing our church prioritizes is financial support. Today, we send KRW 500,000 to 600,000 per person per month. Many Christians in their youth become committed to social movements to realize the kingdom of God. But eventually they get married and have children in their early to mid-40s and must stop the activism in order to make ends meet. They are forced to leave the field precisely when they are most experienced and capable. So, our small financial aid is meant to support and encourage their continued social activism. We are also planning programs for the social missionary and the church to cooperate together. With Yoo Mi-ho working in environmental action, Suwonsung Church is planning to transition to become a Green Church, or an environment-friendly church.

Current List of Social Missionaries

The group started out with four missionaries and then grew to seven missionaries today. Here is the current list of social missionaries our church supports.

Name	Organization	Position	Description of Work
Deok-young Kim	Jubilee & Land Justice Association	Director of Jubilee Action Center	Operation Jubilee Bank to practically and materially support young people struggling with debt
Seung-moo Kim	Citizens' Action for Human Rights	Director	Provide counsel for non-regular laborers, counsel and support for church reform, counsel and support for prisoners and other socially marginalized
Seong-hwan Ryu	Migration and Human Rights Education Network	Co-Director	Conduct networking for the protection of the rights of migrants and multicultural families and to foster a multicultural society
Jin-sook Park	Umoja	Director	Umoja is the Swahili term for unity. The organization provides scholarships for children of refugees residing in South Korea. Today, nine Korean families are financing the after-school education of six children in five refugee households (Taekwondo for Harrison and David, piano for Immanuella, violin for Rachel, English literature for Jayden, and half the cost of daycare for Joanna). Facilitate friendship between Korean families and refugee families.
Tae-gyeong Lee	Institute of Land and Liberty	Assistant Director	Various activities to instill in South and North Korea the concept of land as common property
Mi-ho Yoo	Salim Christian Environmental Education Center	Center Director	Conduct environmental and ecological movements for the church based on scripture for the purpose of preserving God's created world.
Jong-deok Choi	Korea Community Education Network for Education and Training	Trainer	Educate and organize the urban poor for their financial independence

Table 3: List of Social Missionaries

Self-Introduction of the Seven Social Missionaries

Deok-young Kim (Director of Jubilee Action Center, Jubilee & Land Justice Association)

Majoring in economics in university I encountered the Christian worldview and became interested in the field of Christian economics. This naturally led to interest in the concept of Jubilee and the Korean society's real estate issues. I pored over publications on Reuben Archer Torrey III and continued interactions with researchers and activists in the Jubilee & Land Justice Association. I realized the importance of Jubilee Action in Korean society and sought ways I could participate as I became a member. Then in 2014, I was called to be a full-time activist.

Because Suwonsung Church is a church that proclaims the Jubilee vision to the Korean church and the Korean society today, I have a great sense of pride and responsibility as a social missionary of Suwonsung Church. The Social Missionary system of Suwonsung Church is based on the true missionary vision to live out the will of God to love our neighbor as ourselves. I am grateful for the church's deep commitment to serving Korean society and I pray that this commitment and system may be widely known to become an important model for many other churches.

Seung-moo Kim (Director of Citizens' Action for Human Rights)

As I meditated before God on the scripture that says true holiness means taking care of orphans and widows, I started to take action for the poorest and the marginalized in Korean society: the homeless. This also led to actions for the migrant laborers, non-regular laborers, and the disabled. Today as I continue this work, I am also serving as the standing Director of the Daegu Civil Society Solidarity Association and the Co-Director of the Nationwide Civil Society Solidarity Association to work toward more structural change in Daegu and nationwide.

As one of the first social missionaries in the first Social Missionary System of the Korean church, I pray to live as the salt that gives taste and prevents corruption, and the light that shines in the darkness. I pray that the Korean church may be the salt and the light of the Korean society.

Seong-hwan Ryu (Co-Director of Migration and Human Rights Education Network)

Since my time in the seminary, I frequented churches that are active on social issues on the urban poor, rural regions, labor, disabilities, and foreigners. I left church ministry in 2005 and started working at the Ansan Migrant Center for migrant and multicultural missions. There, I found the people working in conditions without human rights, welfare, gospel, and missions. I realized that the issues of a multicultural society is not a unique, singular issue but an aspect that permeates all aspects of life and something that the society and the church must cooperate to respond.

Migrants must be considered not as an object of help but as the co-agents of Korean society. For this awareness to be reflected in society's rules and regulations and in the church, our society and church must be improved. Recognizing this to be the work of solidarity and reconciliation in the polarizing Korean society I dared to leap into this work. I work to realize the non-discriminatory kingdom of God in our lives for both foreign migrants and indigenous residents.

I firmly believe that Suwonsung Church's Social Missionary system is the direction of social responsibility for the Korean church. So I deeply sympathize with the system and root for it to be well established in the social mission sphere.

Jin-sook Park (Director of Umoja)

I founded EcoFemme as an organization that supports refugee and migrant women's adaptation to Korean society by nurturing their artistic talent and raising their self-esteem. I served as its director until March 2021. Today, the leadership is handed over to Mia, a refugee woman from Congo who had been the Co-director. Then I started a scholarship foundation Umoja (Unity in Swahili) for refugee children. We are supporting six children in five refugee households. This year, we plan on supporting two more children in two more families.

In addition to alleviating the negative preconceptions on refugees, I produce writings and translations and give lectures for primary and secondary students and the general public. Last year, I enrolled in doctoral studies on social economy at Ewha Womans University to research trends in migrant (refugee) settlement in South Korea in the sphere of social economy. Thanks to consistent support for several years from Suwonsung Church, I could continue my work. I dearly hope that the Social Missionary System of Suwonsung Church spreads widely among Korean churches. This will encourage, comfort, and practically support activists working for the socially oppressed and marginalized in multiple spheres, resulting in even better outcomes and change.

Mi-ho Yoo (Director of Salim Christian Environmental Education Center)

For the last 32 years I have worked on the Christian environmental education movement with the recognition that nature is me, what I do to nature is what I do to myself, and care for nature is care for myself. My new path has been a path of excitement and joy rather than fear since I got hold of a new vision. That vision is to educate and practice until everyone "may have life and have it abundantly" (John 10:10). The calling is to educate and put to practice until all Christians and churches on this land repay the ecological debt stolen from the poor, the future generation, and nature and grow in the relationship and spirituality of *salim.* In recent years, I have been supporting various churches with education programs such as the Environmental Missionary Course, Online Green School, Earth Care Club, and the Ecological Salim Prayer Movement (intercessory prayer for the climate, carbon fasting) for the Decade of Earth Restoration, and by supporting churches to declare themselves Carbon Zero Green Churches and conduct self-assessment toward this goal. On this career path, I have written several publications including *Life-giving Church*

Environmental Education (Dongyeong), *80 Ways to Save the Environment* (Faith and Intellect), *Value Dictionary for Earth Gardener,* and devotional books such as *Presence of God in Trees of the Bible,* and *Christians Responding to the Calling of Creation.*

I am certain that if we take on the appropriate lifestyle of owning less, using less, consuming less, and discarding less to save ourselves from our current crisis, our world will slowly improve. I ask you to walk with me on this path.

Tae-gyeong Lee (Assistant Director of the Institute of Land and Liberty)
I attended Suwonsung Church for a long time since my youth. I have also been a member of the Social and Environmental Missions Committee. As I had been in the movement for the commons since 2005, when I heard of the new Social Missionary System being established in the church I applied to be selected.
Since my younger years, I have sought after a world where human dignity is honored and real liberty and equality are actualized. There are many ways and paths toward this ideal, but I think solving the real estate issue in the Korean society is more urgent than ever. Privatizing unearned revenue from land ownership is causing multiple problems such as income and wealth inequality, misuse and waste of resources, depreciation of the motivation to work, low birth rate, and escalation of social conflict. I have been actively writing and conducting interviews for the Korea Research Institute for Human Settlements since 2005, then I came to the Institute of Land and Liberty in 2018 to work on media production and research.

Jong-deok Choi (Trainer at Korea Community Education Network for Education and Training)
Jesus stood with the poor and the marginalized! So I decided to live like that as well. Not in the form of charity but in the form of community organizing so that they can be self-reliant. That resulted in the organization of a shanty town resident community for weekend farming. I visited the communities to converse with the residents, assess the issues, and find out what can be solved by the residents themselves. The outcome was the organization of Sarangbang Maeul Aid Cooperative (previously Sarangbang Maeul Resident Association). The residents realized that what is impossible alone can be possible together. In 2017, a similar community organization were started in a new town of Donui-dong in Jongno-3ga of Seoul. A new organization is also about to start in the slums of Changsin-dong in Seoul.

Another major task for me is the Self-Supporting Enterprise Movement. This is the work of supporting the low-income residents to become entrepreneurs to found and operate a business for their financial independence and to facilitate networks for solidarity. In 2018, these businesses formed the Korea Self-Support Enterprise Association, and it has been firmly supporting the businesses.

Social mission is not just the calling for the social missionary. All Christians must be social missionaries because they are not just Christians in the church but also as they live and work in society. As a social missionary and a church member of Suwonsung Church, I hope many of my church members participate in social missions.

Figure 14: The first group of social missionaries in 2009 (front row)

Figure 15: Current group of seven social missionaries

Solidarity with Families Affected by Sewol Ferry Disaster

On April 16, 2014, as the entire nation watched, 304 people drowned in the deep seas. There was a period of mourning for the Sewol Ferry Disaster, but things took uneasy turns, with some people denouncing the victims' families who were calling for investigations behind the cause. So, the Social and Environmental Missions Committee of Suwonsung Church started to picket in front of the

Sungkyunkwan University Metro Station in January 2015. The picketing continues today and has reached the 330th mark. The members of Suwonsung Church and local community residents have been participating in this activism.

In addition, Suwonsung Church organized three sessions of talks inviting families of victims, and also visited Ansan to hold services with the families and general citizens and to comfort the families.

April 16th 2017 was the third year anniversary of the Sewol Ferry Disaster and Easter Sunday. Suwonsung Church set up a Sewom Ferry booth in the churchyard to distribute ribbons, badges, and pamphlets to campaign to remember the disaster. 2000 people visited the booth that day.

The church sought to obey the word of Christ to weep with those who weep.

Figure 16: Discussion Meeting with Families of Victims of Sewol Ferry Disaster. 17 June 2018

Scenes from that day are remembered as below.

> The morning of Easter Sunday the church members stopped by the Sewol Ferry booth after service and each took a yellow ribbon spread on the table. Some tied the ribbon at the spot, high schoolers and young adults took extra ribbons to share with their friends, and children tied the ribbons on their bags with their little hands. They all participated in Sewol Ferry ribbon sharing in different ways. On the other side of the booth people signed the petition to demand investigations behind the Sewol Ferry Disaster. Church members waited in a long line in grief and sorrow.

That day, Suwonsung Church distributed over 2000 yellow ribbons. It showed willingness to share in the grief and to stand in solidarity with the families of the victims of the Sewol Ferry Disaster.

Of course, there were people in the church with opposing views. But the pastor persuaded them and helped them understand that the church must weep with those who weep, and that this is not about political ideology but about the value of human life.

Figure 17: Worship conducted while visiting families of victims of Sewol Ferry Disaster in Ansan. 11 May 2017.

Conclusion

Suwonsung Church will continue to seek out trained activists working to root the values of the kingdom of God in society, and to financially support their work. Our church will continue to share in the suffering of our neighbors and respond to their needs.

Figure 18: Handing out ribbons in remembrance of Sewol Ferry Disaster. 16 April 2017

Suwonsung Church: Church Seeking Peace, Balance, and Training[1]

Bright Myeong-seok Lee

Introduction

In this essay I will explore the geographic, historical, and social characteristics of the location of the Suwonsung Church and the relationship between the spiritual leadership and ministry principles of the senior minister at the center of this church's history. I will examine the missionary contributions to the kingdom of God in the church's surrounding community that resulted from applying these ministry principles. For this purpose, I will first examine the life and ministry principles of the church's senior pastor. In addition, I will analyze the historical, geographic, and social characteristics of the church's location. Based on this analysis I will identify essential factors that enabled the church to perform its missional function in the society. I will end by proposing additional points the church may consider to sustainably actualize their discipleship following Jesus Christ.

In this essay I analyzed the life of Gwang-su An, the senior pastor of Suwonsung Church through the life history research method based on several in-depth interviews.[2] Life history research was developed in the 1930s to comprehensively and diachronically study a subject's life and identify the subject's philosophy and value system. Based on the work of Cynthia E. Winston, the life history research method is the most appropriate method to study the 40-year history of the church since its founding as well as its pastor.[3] For this study, the life history is presented in a narrative form. To guard against the risk of subjective bias in this method, I supplemented the in-depth interviews with other sources such as the church bulletins, the book of sermons, and newspaper submissions by the pastor. Other church publications and texts written by church members and assistant ministers for the publication of *The Forty Years of Suwonsung Church* were also collected as data. In addition to examining the historical, geographic, and social characteristics of Suwon I referenced other primary and secondary sources.

---

[1] This paper was adapted from Myeong-seok Lee, "Su-wŏn-sŏng-kyo-hoe, ye-su kŭ-li-sŭ-to-ŭi che-cha-lo kŏl-ŏ-on 40nyŏn-ŭi kil" [Suwonsung Church: 40 years of walking as Jesus Christ's disciple] edited by Suwonsung Church. *Chu-nim-kwa ham-kke kŏl-ŏ-on su-wŏn-sŏng-kyo-hoe 40nyŏn-sa (1982-2022)* [Forty-Year History of Suwonsung Church Walking with the Lord 1982-2022] (Seoul: KIATS, 2023), 31-71.

[2] On life history research I referred to the following: Cynthia E. Winston, "Biography and Life Story Research", In Stephan D. Lapan et. al., Qualitative research: an introduction to methods and designs (San Francisco: John Wile & Sons, 2012), 107-36.

[3] Ibid., 131-33.

Life of the Pastor: Life History Research Method Approach[4]

Suwonsung Church was started on October 31, 1982 by pastor An Gwang-su and five households. Its history reflects the Korean church's history of growth in the 1970s and the 1980s, and the next period of the 1980s to the 1990s. In the history of Christianity in South Korea the geographic context of a new church, the constituent church members, and changes in social context have a great impact on the church that was founded in this location. But above all the most important factor is the pastor as the spiritual leader. Compared to churches in other countries with a longer history, in South Korea the pastor's formative years and spiritual foundations function as the basis for new Korean churches. It is uniquely characteristic of Korean churches that the whole engine of church growth and maturity stands on this foundation of the pastor. Therefore, an examination of the life and spiritual background of the senior pastor of Suwonsung Church is a necessity in studying the church.

Memory of Hometown

A person's hometown is not just a place to reminisce about a person's childhood, but an important factor that gives insight into the foundational character of the person. 585 Deokgye-ri, Hwecheon-myeon, Yangju-gun, Gyeonggi Province holds Gwang-su An's childhood memories. His memories of his hometown have been referenced numerous times in his forty years of preaching. Daeokgye-ri was divided into the upper village and the lower village demarcated by a stream that ran through the middle. Cattle traders for several generations lived in the upper village while the lower village was formed of traditional farmers who valued educating their children. An attributes his opportunity to get an education to his having been born in the lower village. But his ministry career shows that he also inherited the upper village's capacity to discern the changing trends and times. Our hometowns where we spend our childhood have an enormous impact on our lives, like it or not. Pastor An is no exception.

Impression of the Father in Childhood

The person who most impacted pastor Gwang-su An in his childhood was his father and his eldest brother. Pastor An was next to the last of the eight siblings. In the first year of elementary school, he set fire to about half an acre of sheaves of rice. The wind spread the fire to his house, burning a third of the roof. Afraid of getting reprimanded for this accident he hid in the attic and listened to what was going on. He noticed that his eldest brother who was 20 years older than him was searching for him with a stick. Young Gwang-su laid still and listened as he trembled. Then he heard his father say, "He already realizes his mistake. Let him be. Don't you dare lay hand on him." Surprised, he heard his father's voice rebuking his brother. He was so moved by his father's great love that he wept and wailed, then came down from the attic to fall asleep.[5]

---

[4] This section was written based on the in-depth interview of Gwang-su An conducted in the Suwonsung Church pastor's office on November 21 and December 12 of 202a, and January 11, 2022.

[5] In the interview An quickly teared up as he remembered his father in his childhood.

When the boy Gwang-su started sixth grade he followed after his older brothers who had already moved to Seoul and transferred to a school in Seoul. His father would often visit them in their rented rooms. To reach the lodging in Seoul his father had to travel by bus from his rural hometown transferring two or three times. One day, young Gwang-su came home from school and took a nap in his room when he heard his father calling out to him. He went out half asleep to see his father standing at the gate soaked with sweat like he was in a rainstorm, carrying a bushel of rice on his back and carrying clay pots of soybean paste and chili pepper paste in each hand. Seeing his father he felt his father's genuine love and wrote letters to him each week. Such memories of his father's love were so powerful that these anecdotes appear often in An Gwang-su's sermons when he wants to illustrate the love of God.[6]

The deep love of the father he experienced in childhood was projected in his ministry as the image of God who endlessly loves sinful human beings. So his sermons always take an affectionate tone and are gospel-centered in their appropriate characterization of the trinitarian God. In his sermons, there are more images of the God of love always coming to care for the exhausted rather than the fearful God who judges. The members of Suwonsung Church could also easily understand the essence of the gospel through these sermons.

Acquiring Faith in Jesus

The family's oldest brother believed that there should be at least one prosecutor in the family so he had his younger brother Gwang-su transfer to Seoul and sponsored his studies there for seven years. But despite his brother's wish, Gwang-su did not like the image of the prosecutor. Prosecutors seemed like the pawns of the people in power while they also dominated over the weak. So he applied to enter into the Korea Aerospace University. His brother was greatly disappointed that An gave up on becoming a prosecutor so he stopped paying for the tuition. Unable to continue his studies at the university he graduated from high school and returned to his hometown. He had to give up on life in Seoul and returned to his father and the farm. His father did not say a word of reprimand but rather comforted his despairing son.

As young Gwang-su returned home and was helping his father with the farm, he had a decisive experience of faith. He followed his childhood friends to the one church in Deokgye-ri which was Deokgye Church. Pastor Chang-ju Kim in this small rural church provided An with a key turning point. Young Gwang-su asked lots of questions, ones that the rural church pastor could not answer, and in the process came to know Jesus. The pastor struggled to answer this curious young man's questions, but he never lost his smile as he did his best to respond. Perhaps An's own warmth in his ministry was the spiritual characteristic that formed through this experience of encountering the gospel through the affectionate rural church pastor.

---

[6] Gwang-su An, *Salm-ŭi kil-e-sŏ man-nan haeng-pok* [Joy encountered on the path of life], (Seoul: PCK Book, 2016).

Life as a Seminarian

With the recommendation of pastor Deok-ho Kim who succeeded pastor Chang-ju Kim at Deokgye Church, An enrolled into Chongshin University. The church that most impacted him in his seminary years was Daeseong Church in Gimpo which belongs to the Presbyterian Church in Korea (Hapdong) denomination. The church was a considerable size for that time. At this church An served as a pastoral intern to earn special recognition by the senior pastor and the elders. But an unexpected event led Gwang-su An in a completely different direction. It happened at the time of his university graduation. Around seven Daeseong Church members came to celebrate together at the graduation. But at the ceremony, the existing conflict between the professors and the students was on naked display. An was so disappointed by the university that he and two other friends who graduated together continued on the Master of Divinity program at the Presbyterian University and Theological Seminary that belongs to the Presbyterian Church of Korea (Tonghap) denomination. But the elders of Daesong Church were staunchly conservative and greatly disappointed that An made the decision without consulting them.

This event clearly shows An's tendency in his younger days to refuse to let injustice slide without doing something about it. He recalls this event and remembers how he felt like David who said, "I hate the company of evildoers and will not sit with the wicked" (Psalm 26:5). When he sees injustice that goes against the truth he does not stand by but takes action to solve the matter. In my observation, this tendency continued throughout An's lifetime of ministry as the senior pastor.

Throughout An's ministry when he saw people who sought to exercise wrongful authority, he was not only bothered but worked to change the institution so that these things do not happen again. This is the tendency that continued from his youth. This personal characteristic influenced how fairness became a key constitutive element of Suwonsung Church today.

Gwang-su An then served at the PCK (Tonghap)'s Yeongdeungpo Church as the pastoral intern leading the youth ministry and showed outstanding spiritual leadership. The son of the church's pastor who was the biggest troublemaker in the church attended the summer retreat led by An to have a life-changing spiritual encounter. After this, An earned the complete trust of the senior pastor Kim Yong-ho. More students from the youth ministry in this period under An's leadership than in any other period ended up hearing the call to ministry. The senior pastor Yong-ho Kim saw great potential in An and even considered sponsoring his study abroad at his alma mater Columbia Theological Seminary to train him for the long term. Gwang-su An gained much confidence in this period in the possibility of changing lives through the gospel. These experiences as a pastoral intern impacted his ministry as the senior pastor of the Yuljeon Yeongdeung Church he founded where he most prioritized evangelism.

Historical and Geographic Location of Suwonsung Church

The church is a community that confesses the same faith. But it cannot be known apart from the region it is located, the area's unique characteristics and customs, and the residents' particular local culture. In order to accurately assess the characteristics of Suwonsung Church, the next aspect to review is the church's location and the residents who have lived in the neighborhood for generations.

Suwon's Pre-Modern Characteristics

Suwonsung Church is today located in Yuljeon-dong of Jangan District in the city of Suwon.[7] The name Suwon first appears in the historical records in *The History of the Three Kingdoms.* Around 5CE the Goguryeo people who reigned over the land that covers today's Suwon called this place Maehol.[8] According to Cheon So-Young who teaches Korean literature at Suwon University, maehol is the term based on Chinese characters and is synonymous with the Korean words *mul gol* or *mul goeul* (water village).[9] This means Suwon was always closely related to water. From ancient times to the latter Joseon period, Suwon has been associated with various bodies of water or waterways. Not only that, geographically Suwon was a fortress city south of the Han River that surrounded the capital, and was a military base and the center of traffic.

Records of Suwon-gun described the customs of Suwon residents as the following, "They like martial arts and are devoted to farming. People are simple and unpretentious." [10] The description of the people as "simple and unpretentious" is still viable today. Yu Hyeong-won who was a scholar of the Confucian School of Realism in the latter Joseon years also wrote in his *Bangye Surok*, "People of Suwon are devoted to farming and devoted to archery."[11] After the Japanese Invasion of Korea in 1592 and the Manchu Invasion of 1636, defending the capital city of Hanyang became important and Suwon was at a strategic location. That led to the permanent residence of a garrison troop in the city.

---

[7] Yuljeon-dong in Chinese characters means chestnut field. The *Suwon County Records* published in 1899 at the start of modernization contain the timeline, the geography, and administrative structure of Suwon County in Gyeonggi Province, There, the region covering Shngi-chon, Yulheon, Cheoncheon-ri, Taphyeon-dong, Bangchuk-dong, and Yimok-dong, is identified as Yuljeon (栗田). Hwaseong City ed. *Kuk-yŏk su-wŏn-pu(kun) nam-yang-pu(kun)ŭp-chi* [Suwon county and namyang county township] (Seoul: Gyeongin M&B, 2006).; After the Suwon City Ordinance 1607 on January 1, 1990, the old Yuljeon-dong and Cheoncheon-dong have combined to become Yulcheon-dong.

[8] "Su-sŏng-ku pon ko-ku-lyŏ mae-hol-kun kyŏng-tŏk-wang kae-myŏng kŭm su-chu (水城郡 本 高句麗 買忽郡 景德王 改名 今 水州), *Sam-kuk-sa-ki* 삼국사기(三國史記) [Chronicles of the Three States] (第 三十五 卷 雜志 第四 地理 二), https://db.history.go.kr/ancient/level.do?levelId=sg_035_0020_0080 (Accessed 7 March 2024).

[9] Suwon City Website: https://www.suwon.go.kr/sw-www/www05/www05-01/www05-01-01.jsp (Accessed 7 March 2024).

[10] Hwaseong City ed. *Suwon county and namyang county township,* 163, 212.

[11] Quote cited from Joon-hyeok Kim, "*Hwal-sso-ki-lŭl chal-han su-wŏn-sa-lam-tŭl*" [People of suwon who were good at archery]. *Su-wŏn-ŭl a-si-na-yo* [Do you know Suwon], (Suwon: Suwon Cultural Center, 2012), 66-68.

These historical descriptions are not so different from the image of the people of Yuljeon-dong in the early 1980s. Rice paddies and vegetable fields surrounded Yuljeon-dong. As in *The Record of Suwon-gun,* Yuljeon-dong seems like a simple place that smells of earth rather than a place fond of ornamentation. When Suwonsung Church was founded, these historical and cultural sediments served as the foundations.

Marginality and Dynamism of Yuljeon-dong

In modern times, Suwon was located at the point where major roads from the capital to the three southern regions passed through, so it was literally a thoroughfare for transportation and exchange.[12] Materials to be distributed to the rest of the nation were delivered to Suwon Station, and the Gyeongbu Line (laid in 1905, Suyeo Line (laid in 19331), and Suin Line (laid in 1937) all passed through this station. Like the neck that holds up the head and through which the vital nerves pass, Suwon was a very important location where the national transportation network passed.

Unlike the city of Suwon, the town of Yuljeon-dong in Suwon seems less significant. But like the throat hidden under the collar, Yuljeon-dong was a place that connected new people and functioned to support people's preparation for new ventures. Yuljeon-dong has geographic similarities to the town of Galilee where Jesus spent his childhood. Galilee was not a place far apart from the rest of Judea. It was a dynamic town on the Sea of Galilee that functioned as an inland waterway. Jesus actively made use of this transportation infrastructure to efficiently share the gospel throughout his short years of ministry. The disciples who worked with Jesus in Galilee turned out to bring civilizational transportation in Jerusalem, all Judea and Samaria, and to the ends of the earth. It was a small and marginalized, rural-seeming place, but impacted the world.

Likewise, Yuljeon-dong is located in the outskirts of Seoul but is close enough for people to commute. It is also on the margins of Suwon. But through the subway that functioned as the major transportation for regular people in the 1980s and the 1990s, the town could perform a new function for its time. In that sense, Yujeon-dong has much likeness to Galilee whose marginality was able to reveal the dynamism of Jesus' ministry.

Ministry Principles of Suwonsung Church: Evangelism, Education, Raising Up Workers to Build the Kingdom of God

Pastor Gwang-su An sums up his forty years of ministry with the phrase "Have non-believers believe in Jesus and grow the faith of those who believe to raise them up as laborers in and out of the church to build the kingdom of God." This ministry philosophy is focused on the essence of the church rather than the

[12] "Ha-young Yi, Gwansumanrok in late Joseon era recorded on the geography of Suwon "The area is on a crossroad to the three roads to the south, so an event is always spread to all eight provinces." Quote cited from Hyeon-young Hong, "Su-wŏn, sam-nam-ŭi kil-mok" [Suwon, crossroad to three regions in the south], *Su-wŏn-ŭl a-si-na-yo* [Do you know suwon], (Suwon: Suwon Cultural Center, 2012), 38-40.

outward appearance and growth. Rather than the church as a collective or as a form of organization, people are at the center of this ministry philosophy. This is apparent in the pastor's understanding of people. As a pastor, people are not considered instrumental to church growth. His ministry is instead the consequence of his love of the people.

An identifies four most important points in his ministry: evangelism, education, raising laborers, and building the kingdom of God. The four elements will be analyzed below.

Evangelism: Domestic Evangelism and World Mission

According to Gwang-su An, evangelism is the work of finding nonbelievers and bringing them to salvation. Korean church evangelism tend to look like other churches in the denomination. But Suwonsung Church's evangelism involves active participation in wide spheres, and it makes one wonder where the church's interest ends. I distinguish the church's evangelism as domestic evangelism and overseas mission.

Domestic Evangelism: as Salt and Light of the World

Suwonsung Church in its early days generally focused on evangelizing community residents. Pastor and his wife devoted two hours in the morning and two hours in the afternoon every day to evangelism. They focused all their energy on saving souls before they could build a church. Starting with a 70-people evangelism team in 1989, various domestic evangelisms were tried until the early 2000s. For new Christians pastor An started by building the basics of faith through easily understandable preaching. This was based on his unique perspective of sermons since his younger years. The following quote describes his experience.

> When I first believed in Jesus and went to church, for the first year I could not understand anything. I didn't know what salvation was, or how I could be saved. They simply told me to believe, believe in Jesus and I will be saved. But they didn't tell me the details. What does it mean to believe?[13]

This experience caused the pastor to devote himself to communicating the basic message of the gospel in an easy and brief form to the new Christians. And based on this experience congregation was encouraged to evangelize. This led to the unique approach to evangelism taken by Suwonsung Church. Social contact points were made for the nonbelievers to continue fellowship with people of the church community. These were various sports clubs and hobby gatherings. The church members were able to make contact with various people outside the church. The following is an excerpt by G*wonsa* Min Gyeong-ok on her husband Deacon Lee Myeong-bae who came to meet Jesus through the church baseball team.

> On May 7, 2010, the Suwonsung Church Baseball Team visited Wangjin church in Beijing, China for worship and had a friendly match with the baseball team of

---

[13] Interview with pastor Gwang-su An at Suwonsung Church pastor's office (11 November 2022)

> Korean residents in Beijing. The pastor asked me to join but because I couldn't get on the plane by myself I said I would go if my husband could join. At the time my husband had not been attending church. When I asked my husband if he would like to go he gladly said yes, and that is how I could go for the baseball mission trip to China. At the airport lounge, our pastor held my husband's hands tight to ask him to come to church even during the pastor's sabbatical year. That is when I started to see a change in my husband. On the third day of the trip as we had service at Wangjing Korean Church my husband sang the song "Jacob's Blessing" with our team for the first time in his life for the special offering song. He seemed so moved by the affection of the pastor and the baseball team members throughout the trip that the Sunday after we returned, my husband woke up to tell me first that he would go to church. Since that day until the day he passed away he gladly and faithfully attended church.[14]

Deacon Lee Myeong-bae was diagnosed with hyper progressive brain tumor in February 2015 and passed away in February 2016. *Gwonsa* Min recalls, "It is such a relief that my husband met Jesus, was saved, and went to heaven. And it is a miracle that my husband met God through that little baseball gathering." This is the case of Suwonsung Church's sports evangelism leading a non-Christian husband and one household to Christ.

There was one aspect of evangelism that pastor An was committed to and even had a full-time minister in charge of it, and that was Baby School. Baby School became really popular among nonbelieving young parents with newborn babies. According to pastor Yong-seon Cho who served as the education pastor, "When an evangelism team knocks on people's apartment doors to tell them they came to share the gospel, people keep the doors shut. But if they go to hand out information on Baby School people open their doors."[15] Suwonsung Church met the needs of the society by providing support with childrearing when the government support was absent. When the church worked to support the parents of newborns, this naturally led to an opportunity for evangelism. So Baby School was a good combination of evangelism meeting parents' interest in children's education. It became an important part of Suwonsung Church's evangelism efforts to bring people to church and help them acquire membership. This was the evangelism that met the community's needs rather than aspiring for growth while excluding the community, as Kook-il Han criticized about the tendency of the Korean church.[16]

One church may not be able to respond to all social issues. Still, if there is one sphere Suwonsung Church has not been able to respond actively yet and that is the cultural sphere. But since 2022 when the Covid-19 pandemic began to die down, the church has been stepping into culture ministry by organizing worship sessions, concerts that fuse classical genres with Korean traditional music, and art exhibitions.

---

[14] Anecdote by Gwonsa Gyeong-ok Min in "My husband Lee Myung-bae who met Jesus through the Suwonsung Church Baseball Team", from a draft of *Forty-Year History of Suwonsung Church.*

[15] Letter from pastor Yong-seon Cho of Onmuri Church who served as the education pastor of Suwonsung Church, titled "Missing Suwonsung Church."

[16] Kook-il Han. *Sŏn-kyo-chŏk kyo-hoe-ŭi i-lon-kwa sil-che* [Theory and practice of missional church], (Seoul: PUTS Press, 2019), 7.

Overseas Mission: from Yuljeon-dong to the End of the World

Suwonsung Church has been cooperating in foreign missions since its early days. From the early 2000s, the church began to commission missionaries overseas directly. From 2000 to 2020 the church has been selecting missionaries to fully sponsor them, and each year they organized sponsoring events and mission conferences. These events functioned to raise resources and focus attention on missions while facilitating close relationships between the missionaries and the church members.

A look into the missionaries the church has fully sponsored over the years reveals that many of them have been members of the church. This is evidence of Suwonsung Church's accomplishment as a missional church over the past four decades. The roots of this tree can be traced back to laity-centered mission organizations. Suwonsung Church did not decide to send a missionary overseas one day out of the blue. The church community identified potential missionaries from the missional soil of the church over a long period of time, and these missionaries were trained and nurtured through several stages. A laity who commits to full-time missions would enter into seminary to become ordained or go through missionary training to become an overseas missionary for the long term. A lay married couple committed to missions received missionary training and cooperated with a missions organization to be sent overseas. A young man who committed his life to missions attended a missionary training program, met a spouse who would accompany him then became a long-term missionary. There is also a case of a person who became devoted to the mission of the world church as a youth member of the World Council of Churches Central Committee.

The overseas mission of Suwonsung Church spans multiple generations. An took on the responsibility as the Chair of the Committee on Missionary Kids (MK) Ministry for the denomination, which had not received much attention from others. He recognized the importance of caring for the children of missionaries in order to continue missions in the next generation. Today, MK ministry is an important part of Suwonsung Church's overseas mission.

When a layperson commits to missions then enters the mission field without basic missionary training there are significant side effects. To alleviate these issues Suwonsung Church operates a program commissioned by the denomination called Paul Missions University. Paul Missions University provides laity missionary training by missiology professors and missionary professionals according to denominational standards. The training program is contributing to mission mobilization for Suwonsung Church and other local churches and is functioning as the key station at which the laity can acquire basic missionary qualifications.

At least until the Covid-19 pandemic Luke Medical Mission Society sent medical mission teams each year to regions in Asia, Russia, and even Africa. When I was myself a missionary in Ghana, I was moved by the devoted service of Luke Medical Mission Society that came to the field. They took a boat to visit difficult-to-reach rural villages without medical access and returned after providing medical service. I was unspeakably touched, and it remains a precious memory. Since the pandemic Luke Medical Mission Society has been caring for multiethnic families and cooperating with other teams providing haircare and acupuncture treatment.

Overseas mission of Suwonsung Church examined so far still lacks sufficient reflections on the church's missionary imperative. The church is left with the issue of supporting their full-time missionaries after their retirement, the issue of supporting the missionaries with long-term visa overseas, and the welfare of missionary kids.

Missions has been one of the most important and essential callings of the church since the days of the early church. But as Lesslie Newbigin point out, historically the church had conducted missionary programs, but the church itself has not been missional.[17] In the Korean church as well, missions has been understood as one of the many functions a church fulfills or something done by missionary organizations. Suwonsung Church's two decades of overseas missions also reflects these trends. Darrell L. Guder states that mission is the essence of the church by saying that mission defines the church as God's called and sent church of Jesus Christ and the reason for our being.[18] This is why the mission of the church should not be understood as just one function of the church among many.

David J. Bosch said, "Christianity is missionary by its very nature, or it denies its very *raison d'être*."[19] So the church's mission is not simply one of its functions but intrinsic to the church. In addition, it is not the mission of the church but something that God directly does, or the *Missio Dei.* On this foundation lies the imperative of the missional church.

Education: Discipleship Training

While this aspect was mentioned as the second ministry principle by pastor Gwang-su An, this is the aspect on which he was most passionate throughout 40 years of his ministry. He describes education as "teaching children of God to live up to their calling." He devoted greatest care to this aspect, this is evident in his ministry motto "a believer is born but a disciple is trained."

After the fifth anniversary of the church's founding An began the discipleship training classes as part of spiritual formation. Discipleship training classes were started for the church members to learn the Word of God systematically to correctly understand the faith and put them to action so that they can worship, serve, and live a healthy and balanced spiritual life. The first cohort of Beginners' Discipleship Training Class started on June 9, 1987 until July 10 for five weeks, meeting twice a week for ten total sessions. The classes then really took off with the fourth cohort later in December 1987 which lasted until February 1988. There were morning and afternoon classes, which lasted for 12 weeks.[20]

---

[17] Lesslie Newbigin, *The Open Secret: an introduction to the theology of mission.* (Grand Rapids: Eerdmans, 1995), 10.

[18] Darrell L. Guder Darrell and Lois Barrett. *Missional church: A vision for the sending of the church in North America.* Grand Rapids, MI: Wm. B. Eerdmans Publishing, 1998.

[19] David J. Bosch, *Transforming mission: Paradigm shifts in theology of mission.* No. 16. Maryknoll, NY: Orbis books, 2011, 37.

[20] As a university student I was the single person in the evening slot of the fourth batch of the beginners' discipleship class.

> We started with questions like, "How do I know God exists." "What is salvation." "How can I be saved." and "How do I know I am saved". By teaching about these concrete questions I could lead people to believe and receive Jesus and commit to Christianity. In these classes, I could see church members completely transform.[21]

Pastor An's discipleship training classes did not stop at laying the basics of biblical and gospel truths for beginners. He also put the teachings into action himself to show an example as a leader. This is the missionary distinctiveness of Suwonsung Church's discipleship training.

The discipleship training of Suwonsung Church instilled in all its members their identity as disciples. The classes became critical turning points where they learned that they must live as disciples of Christ rather than nominal Christians. The training continued not only in times of peace but also in times of internal conflict. While most of the trainings were conducted for tens or hundreds of people for each cohort, in the early days there was a time when the pastor conducted a four-month class for only one person. The discipleship training started with the belief that a soul has more value than all heaven and earth. Like a grain of wheat falls into the earth and dies to bear much fruit of new life, the discipleship training became a valuable historical fruit of Suwonsung Church.[22] Han Kook-il calls this educational leadership the "church's missionary infrastructure" that actualizes the missional church.[23] Kim Do-il describes Suwonsung Church's education through discipleship training with the image of a farmer who sows good seeds and hopes for fruit, and calls it "Education-in-waiting that gives life to the future generation."[24]

Raising up Workers

Once the congregants were trained as disciples they were raised up as worker to serve the society. The distinctive point is that the senior pastor showed an example through his actions. Deacon Park Hang-soo of Suwonsung Church remembers the pastor's response to the visiting homeless.

> One day a homeless person said to the pastor, "Pastor, your shoes look great." The pastor said "Do you like it? Here, have it." And he took off his shoes on the spot to give them away. Pastor An just stood there on the cold floor in his socks so I quickly brought slippers from my car for him to wear. I was moved to see with my own eyes how he practiced Luke 6:30 "Give to everyone who asks of you." This kept

---

[21] Interview with pastor Gwang-su An at Suwonsung Church pastor's office (11 January, 2022).

[22] I myself have participated in this discipleship training to benefit from it and to cooperate in it.

[23] Kook-il Han, *Theory and practice of missional church,* 279.

[24] Do-il Kim, *Tŏ-pul-ŏ kŏn-kang-ha-ko haeng-pok-han saeng-t'ae-kye-lŭl man-tŭl-ŏ ka-nŭn ka-chŏng-kyo-hoe -ma-ŭl kyo-yuk-kong-tong-ch'e* [Family, church and maeul community making a healthy and happy ecology together], Seoul: Dongyeon, 2018, 296-303.

> on. When somebody told him his tie looked good, he'd give away his tie, and if it's his shoes, he'd give away his shoes.[25]

Gwang-su An emphasizes the need to be a worker not only in the church but also in the workplace. He would say "It is more important to raise people to be workers outside the church to enter into the world and transform it." This spirit of Suwonsung Church goes beyond the dualistic distinction between the sacred and the secular to awaken the church members' calling outside the church.

This is in line with the workplace ministry aspect that started in 1989 at the evangelical Lausanne Movement. At Cape Town, South Africa in October 2010 four thousand Christian leaders from 198 countries gathered for the Third Lausanne Congress on World Evangelization to draft the Cape Town Commitment. It confesses, "In spite of the enormous evangelistic and transformational opportunity of the workplace, where adult Christians have most relationships with non-Christians, few churches have the vision to equip their people to seize this."[26] Bob Doll, the Lausanne Movement Chair (USA) boldly declares, "God has equipped us to be ambassadors so we can meet people in the workplace as God intends."[27] Christians must now be workers not only in the church but out of the church and in their workplaces, taking on their roles and responsibilities.

In the ecumenical movement the spirit of "liturgy after the liturgy" arose already in the 1970s to discuss how a Christian must live in society. According to Ion Bria, eucharistic liturgy is

> Is not an escape into the inner sphere of prayer or a holy turn away from social reality. Rather it requires the believers to conduct "the sacrament of the brother [stranger]" outside the temple and in the public spaces where the cries of the poor and the marginalized can be heard.[28]

According to Bria, the innermost liturgy of the Eucharist is not exclusively for church members. There is a responsibility for Christians to live in the world and in their workplaces with the spirit of liturgy. A Christian is not just a worker who in the church but a social being who must live their Christian calling in the workplace meeting with non-Christians.

Building the Kingdom of God

How Suwonsung Church has practiced God's calling to be salt and light in the local community, and their ministry aims, can be summed up with pastor Gwang-su An's phrase, "building the kingdom of God." One of the distinctive points of

---

[25] Anecdote by the ordained deacon Hyang-su Park in "Friend of the homeless" from a draft of *Forty-Year History of Suwonsung Church.*

[26] Lausanne Movement, The Cape Town Commitment: A Confession of Faith and a Call to Action, 58. https://lausanne.org/wp-content/uploads/2021/10/The-Cape-Town-Commitment-—Pages-20-09-2021.pdf. (Accessed 20 January, 2023).

[27]Lausanne Movement, "Lausanne Global Classroom: Workplace Ministry. Part 01-09" August 28, 2020.
https://www.youtube.com/watch?v=BI3AMJIJ2CE&list=PLYGxDL2dvuo6Z38peuVDGpa46lT6SImQ3 (Accessed 22 November 2022)

[28] Ion Bria, *The Liturgy after the Liturgy* (Geneva: WCC, 1996), 20.

Suwonsung Church is the practice of the Word of God in society. The church functions not only for the health of the church and its members but also to appropriately function in the society where it is located.

This ministry principle is apparent in two forms. The first is the church's social service in which it church helps and comforts the people who have met a robber on their life path, and the second is the church's social action to make the world just so that the robbery does not happen.

Social Service

Suwonsung Church has been doing much to serve the community since 1985. The congregants mainly do Suwonsung Church's social service. Serving the hearing impaired in the church, the sign language class, rice collection, the *banchan* sharing service, service to the homeless, mobile bathing assistant service for the elderly and other programs for seniors, volunteering at Bambat Senior Welfare Center, and volunteering for wedding ceremonies are all avenues of service. They all require the church members' time and energy.

Suwonsung Church congregants do not rest content listening to sermons in church services. Service is a key platform on which they can practice the word of truth in their lives and embody them. When the church members practice the word of God through life and service, just like the food consumed becomes muscles through exercise, the church body also gains muscles that move and bring liveliness to the society they serve. The following is the account of Deacon Jo Man-su who volunteers for the homeless.

> Ever since my close friend died, I became cynical about the world. I got lost in the world, drinking every day. By the time I cleared my head my son was already too addicted to gaming to recover. That was when I heard that our church has a volunteering program for the homeless. I wanted to show my son what the real world is like, so I dragged him to the ministry at church on Saturday. We saw the homeless entering the church. That's when I felt a pang in my heart and heard God speaking to me, "That's your work. You should do it." So next week I went to the homeless volunteer team to join them. It was great. I never felt so proud. Just the act of providing a warm meal to the homeless with my own hands which used to wander, really blessed me. I have been volunteering ever since. I changed and my son changed too. My son could recover from game addiction.[29]

Suwonsung Church's service center is listed as a non-profit organization. This was to allow the youth in the community to come to church and volunteer and have it be credited as community volunteering points for school.[30] As the official service center the Suwonsung Church is known as the church with the best records in community volunteering.

The church is also serving North Korean refugees. Nobody knows how much closer the North and the South will get, but more North Korean refugees and ethnic Koreans in China are settling in South Korean society. In restaurants, we

---

[29] Anecdote by deacon Man-su Cho from a draft of *Forty-Year History of Suwonsung Church.*

[30] Anecdote by Yong-seon Cho "Missing Suwonsung Church" from a draft of *Forty-Year History of Suwonsung Church.*

can meet ethnic Koreans with Yanbian dialect, and North Korean refugees who found jobs have formed communities in the church. The political and military border has divided us, but now it is possible to cross the border if one wants, and even send remittances to the North to contribute to family finances. Approaching them and serving them with expertise is not a task to be pushed for later but an urgent need for today.

Social Action: Social Missionary System

In 2002, Suwonsung Church organized the Social Mission Committee. It was formed to raise the church members' awareness of the church's role to be salt and light of the world. The committee started ministries to the homeless, the elderly, and the migrant laborers. In 2009 professional social activists were selected for the church to cooperate in movements such as labor rights, environmental protection, preservation of God's creation, and the land rights movement. This was the collaboration between the church and the expertise of social missions. Suwonsung Church was the pioneer in the Korean church on this new role for the church.[31]

Comforting and weeping with those who weep in tragedies is one of the things Suwonsung Church has done. On April 16, 2014, the students of Danwon High School in the city of Ansan, not far from Yuljeon-dong, died in the Sewol Ferry Disaster. The families of the victims were invited to the church and the church also visited the families to comfort them. Some of the church members saw these initiatives by the pastor as politically partisan. But the pastor consistently explained the purpose of these events and had them understand this is in obedience to the Gospels. Despite these assertive actions for social participation, Suwonsung Church maintains a firm distance from the political sphere. This is the stance to function as the salt yet guard from losing its taste.

The early church fathers firmly emphasized the need to move beyond listening to the Word to obeying the Word in action. Alan Keider cites the North African Church Father Tertullian's words to mention that the early church community even in their difficult circumstances cared for the orphans and the widows, gave food to the poor, and conducted funerals for the foreigners who had no kin to bury them. Kreider writes that Tertullian taught his community to urge outsiders to see (*vide*) the way they put the love of Christ in action, rather than hear (*aude*) their words or read (*lege*) their writings.[32] Suwonsung Church's social services and social actions are efforts to practice the spirit of the early church community.

---

[31] Yoo-jin Cha, "Sa-hoe-to sŏn-kyo-ŭi tae-sang" [Society is also object of mission], *Hanguk Gidok Gongbo (28 April 2009);* Yo-sep Park, "Tae-hyŏng kyo-hoe-ka si-min-tan-ch'e hwal-tong chi-wŏn-ha-nŭn i-yu" [Why A megachurch supports civil society activism], *News N Joy* (27 May 2017).

[32] Alan Kreider, *The Patience Ferment of the Early Church* (Grand Rapids: Baker, 2016), 60-61.

Ministry Principles of Suwonsung Church

According to the essay by An, Suwonsung Church's ministry has been centered on three principles for the purpose of maintaining church health. The principles are peace, balance, and training. The three principles have supported the church like the three legs of a stool. In this section, I will examine the three ministry principles of Suwonsung Church initiated by the pastor and consider them from the missional church perspective.

Peace

Ministry of Peace became the very first ministry principle after the pastor's self-reflection on the issues that arose with the first attempt at church building construction after its founding.[33] Church buildings that were constructed in subsequent years according to the needs of the time and the functions of the church all have the ministry principle of peace at the bottom of it. Whenever the church membership exceeded the sanctuary capacity the minister and the church members sought to hear God's voice more clearly. The church community's obedience expanded to mission for the local community and for the world.

So after all these years whenever the church sanctuary must go through reconstruction to expand its holding capacity, the church listened to the voices of multiple generations. One example is when the board of elders had already decided on the church reconstruction. When the younger generations voiced opposition the elders took a step back to reexamine the situation and humbly search for God's will. This is according to the first principle of peace: "It is better to have peace with less than the best rather than to have conflict in pursuit of the best." Later the sanctuary reconstruction project changed into the project to construct a new service center building, which laid the foundation for the church to better perform its social function. Especially in the pandemic era when the church could not gather in person, the Service Center was the key location at which the church could serve society in various ways.

Building construction in Suwonsung Chuch is most notable in that they were not accomplished by the pastor urging the church members to give more offerings. The people with large sums of offering for the construction remain remarkably unrecognized. This was the ministerial decision to comfort the church members who do not have the means to offer large sums even if they are willing. So in all construction process of Suwonsung Church there is no trace of church members' names and only the name of the Lord remains.

The church's spatial arrangements also reflect the ministry philosophy and care for the socially marginalized. Spatial arrangement for efficient functioning is essential, but appropriate placement for easy access is also critical in a church building. When one enters Suwonsung Church at the very center, there is space

---

[33] After the first sanctuary was build, there were some uncomfortable disagreements with the congregants on the matter of laying down tiles in the churchyard. Since then, he realized that it is better to have peace in church with the second best rather than arguing with others in pursuit of the best. This was also the experience that made him prioritize peace s the most important ministry principle.

to welcome and inform the new comers. This shows the church's effort to lead each and every soul to the Lord.

Another unique characteristic of the church building is the pastor's office. Whoever has visited the pastor's office would be surprised to see how simple it is. There is only a personal desk and a chair for the pastor to prepare for sermons, no sofa you might find in any other pastor's office. There is a square table and a few chairs for meetings and receiving visitors. There is no trace of authoritativeness, which makes the office feel very comfortable. Whenever one knocks, the pastor cheerfully greets beyond the door. The security system is so old that any traveling salesperson or homeless person can come by, open the door, and step in. In a word, it is a structure with no trace of vain formalities. Because of this openness of the pastor's office, there was even a time when a homeless person's family on the brink of starvation could find help.[34]

A church this size might have a secretary for the pastor, but there is no such position or space for one. An assistant pastor with much ministry experience is in charge of church administration. The senior pastor should rightfully be respected as the church's spiritual leader, but in Suwonsung Church space arrangement there is no indication that the pastor gets special treatment. This is also evident in church parking. No designated parking space is marked for the senior pastor of Suwonsung Church. Nobody's vehicle gets special treatment in the church. This is the trace of the principle of peace.

The board conference room is no exception. The room is arranged so that there is no distinction of seniority among the elders. There is leadership of equality and peace. Similarly, when one steps into the ministers' office, the faces of all the ministers are immediately visible.

Finally, I would mention that nowhere on the façade of Suwonsung Church can one see the mark of the denomination. On this, pastor An states, "What is more important than a church's denomination is whether a church faithfully fulfills its calling and function."[35] By downplaying its denominational identity the church has been emphasizing peace. This primary ministry principle of peace is apparent in how the church uses their space. Perhaps because of this, Suwonsung Church is known to outsiders as a peaceful church.

Balance

Suwonsung Church's ministry principle of balance refers to the balance of Word and prayer on one hand, and service on the other. First, I will examine the meaning of balance explained in the pastor's sermons. Like other Protestant churches, Suwonsung Church's liturgy also revolves around proclaiming the word of God.

When one attends a service in Suwonsung Church, the principle of balance is apparent in the preaching.

The first characteristic of An's sermons is the balance in the message. There is no bias to one side or the other. Analysis of pastor Gwang-su An's sermons

---

[34] Interview with pastor Gwang-su An at Suwonsung Church pastor's office (11 January, 2022).

[35] Ibid.

over the four decades of ministry shows that he chose sermon passages throughout the 66 books of the Bible. This results from the minister's efforts to provide a variety of spiritual food for the flock. The pastor's sermons are based on unchanging scripture, so they do not tilt toward the particular theological direction of the denomination. This may partly be because he went through undergraduate and seminary years at schools of different denominations. In addition, the congregration's openness to the messages complemented the sermons well to maintain the balance and not let the sermons get old. In forty years of ministry there are people who heard the same anecdotes and testimonies multiple times. Many who have been in the church for years can recall and tell the stories even better than the preacher himself. Nevertheless, there is an attraction to his sermons that makes the listeners nod in assent. No matter how often one hears them, the messages quietly seep in and persuade. This is possible due to the element of authenticity in the message. There are traces of the pastor's own life experience, even his utter failures, unadorned and included in the sermons.

Secondly, pastor Gwang-su An's preaching style is comforting to the listeners. This is perhaps because he does not lean to one extreme but bases the messages on appropriate common sense. This is not disquieting leadership displayed by many Korean church ministers in their sermons, but a pastoral leadership that welcomes one with a smile at any time. His sermons also do not require too much of the listeners. So the messages are comfortable to listen to. But his messages have the power to persuade. As he describes himself, he is a minister without even the most commonplace spiritual gift of tongues. Still, his messages can be understood better than many words in the tongue of angels and are memorable after many years. His sermons are generally constructed in easy narratives, so anybody, young and old, men and women, can easily understand. In sum, his sermons are very appropriate for the people of our time.

The third characteristic of pastor Gwang-su An's sermons is that he preaches the gospel message in regular periodic intervals. Throughout forty years of ministry he preached the essential message of the gospel at least once a month so that a new believer can understand. This is perhaps because he met Jesus personally as a young man. So his sermons are simple and clear. And when he mentions sensitive social issues, he is very direct. He is gifted with explaining new things in a way that anyone can understand. Sensitive topics that even scholars have a hard time explaining or unfamiliar theological terms mentioned in sermons are explained to be easily understood. This draws out the agreement of the listeners with various degrees of experience and capacity. Both new Christians and church officers can understand the sermons and make contact with the gospel. This is an element of the ministry of balance.

The fourth characteristic of balance in his sermons is his progressive conservatism. Mid to large-size churches in Korea are generally biased toward conservatism. The Korean church's conservatism has often been used for the wealthy and the vested interests. But pastor An's sermons are always interested in the marginalized. The sermons show the image of wiping the tears of those who weep. This is not just rhetoric; he practices this gospel with his body and his feet, which makes his sermons persuasive. So his messages can be described as progressively conservative.

Overall, the sermons preached in Suwonsung Church achieve an appropriate balance and variety. Especially in the church there is much opportunity to hear sermons preached by assistant pastors. Assistance pastors take turns preaching at Sunday morning services once every month. By providing such preaching opportunities to assistant pastors, Suwonsung Church provides training for ministers, unlike other churches. For the church members, this is also an opportunity to listen to more varieties of sermon topics. From the sermons of young, inexperienced seminarians to the experienced messages of the senior pastor, the varieties of sermons preached out of the life and testimonies of the servants of God provide a rich array of food for the soul.

The ministry of balance is also in the balance between preaching and prayer. The pastor refers to prayer as the hidden and not quite apparent but the most potent element in the church's worship service.[36] There is no doubt that the seeds of tearful prayers of church members sown throughout the forty-year history of the church at Early Morning Prayer Meetings, Wednesday Prayer Meetings, Friday Prayer Meetings, and other designating prayer meetings have reached the heavens to make what Suwonsung Church is today. To a degree, the ministry of prayer is a hidden ministry that is invisible to other people. So while it is hidden, much spiritual energy is produced to make healing and restoration possible. Especially the intercessory prayer ministry is located on the third floor of the church's main building and is a major ministry that has lasted through its 40-year history. Through this history, the church members could share spiritual fellowship with heaven in times of difficulty and receive welcome rain in the dry and desert-like reality. The intercessory prayer team conducts 24-hour prayer relays for families with members who are gravely ill. There was an instance when news came about a missionary overseas who fell sick and in critical condition. The intercessory prayer team's prayer was answered with the miraculous healing of the missionary.

Another critical element in balanced ministry is the role of the praise team and the choir in leading the worshipers. If the preaching is the instrument that stimulates cognition and challenges the listeners, the lyrical ministry of the praise team and the choir affects the emotions and is communal. The praise team of Suwonsung Church is characterized by the members' commitment. This is due to the commitment of the praise leaders with enough talent to enter into full-time praise ministry but chose to take another career. They continue to use their talents serving in the church praise team. In 40 years of church history, along with the senior pastor and his sermons, the praise leaders were central to the growth of Suwonsung Church. According to An, humans cannot understand the vast providence of God, but two of the praise leaders who greatly contributed to the spiritual revival of the church passed away due to sudden illness.

A key element of balanced ministry in Suwonsung Church is horizontal participation in liturgy. Instead of a vertical structure, horizontal collaboration

---

[36] Interview with pastor Gwang-su An at Suwonsung Church pastor's office (11 January, 2022).

and participation of various community members is apparent in the church liturgy. Women's participation in liturgy has been emphasized in Suwonsung Church relatively earlier than in other churches. This was in obedience to the scripture that prohibits discrimination according to gender. In Suwonsung Church congregational prayer and scripture readings are not limited to certain level of church officers. Young adult worship services have their own worship space and independent budgeting so that they can experience responsible church administration before joining the main adult body.

The ministry of balance emphasizing fair administration and the importance of relationships also extends to the balance between church life, family life, and work life. A healthy church is possible when there is an organic relationship between church, family, and workplace, and human relationships are valued. The outcome of highlighting balance in ministry is evident in the numbers. Church members under 40 years old, including the Sunday School, young adults, and young married couples, add up to 2,500, half the entire church membership. This intergenerational balance is one key aspect of the ministry of balance. On gender balance, 54% is women and 46% men which also shows the impact of An's balanced ministry.

Training

Suwonsung Church's Education Hall is much larger than the sanctuary. This reflects the senior pastor's belief that a church's future is unthinkable without faithful investment for the next generation. The Education Hall is significant for the future generation but also critically functions to invite non-Christians into the church. As the city grew, more outsiders moved in. Non-Christian families and young families who moved into Yuljeon-dong looked for a daycare for their children, and many found Suwonsung Church with a great education department and settled in. This means the church's orientation for training also functioned to evangelize to the community residents.

According to An, he could pour himself into the ministry of training because of an unintended administrative error during his seminary years. He had been admitted into the Theology Department of Chongshin University. Then he took a leave of absence for his compulsory military service and returned to find that his major was changed from Theology to Christian Education. He asked about it at the Administrative Office and found out there were too many entrants into the Theology Department, so while some of them were in the military service, they were moved to the Christian Education Department so that the Theology Department could receive more applicants. According to An, the misfortune turned out to be a blessing because he could take many courses on education that he would not have taken as a theology major. His education in psychology, child psychology, lesson planning, and pedagogy were made good use of later when providing systematic Christian education as a senior pastor.[37] As mentioned, these experiences formed the basis for the discipleship training central to his

[37] Interview with pastor Gwang-su An at Suwonsung Church pastor's office (26 November 2021).

ministry. Pastor Gwang-su An turned unexpected events and misfortunes into something positive for himself. Through these events, God's providence beyond human wisdom could impact his life, and this has been one of the most important pillars of his ministry.

Suwonsung Church on Peace, Balance, and Training

As I started this essay, I sought to conduct a life history narrative research on the senior pastor of Suwonsung Church to examine how the pastor's personal life and experience are impacting his ministry direction. The results showed once again that the pastor's life experience was decisive in his ministry. Specifically, his family history and the churches he served formed his character as a minister, which impacted almost every decision he made as the senior pastor of a church. Especially pastor An's dedication to not stand by watching injustice and unfairness but to resolve it with God's justice, was not formed overnight. Nevertheless, his warm and affectionate fatherly persona was rooted in the memory of his own father's infinitely forgiving love. This shows that in studying a church community, examining the life history of the senior pastor is an interpretive key to understanding the church's ministry direction.

In this essay, I also examined the geographical characteristics of Suwonsung Church. The historical context, geographic location, and social context of the church have a greater impact on the church members than expected. This approach had the effect of seeing the past, the present, and the future through a fluoroscope. The dynamism of Yuljeon-dong in Suwon and its marginality that is similar to Galilee were key characteristics that allowed the church planted in this town to expand in multiple directions. In other words, Suwonsung Church's tendency to keep trying new things yet hold on to the gospel's authenticity is not unrelated to the characteristics of the town itself.

Next, I examined how the spiritual leadership and ministry principles at the center of Suwonsung Church are missionally contributing to building the kingdom of God in the local community of the church. The research shows that Suwonsung Church could faithfully function as the salt and light of Yuljeon-dong for the past 40 years partly because of the intimate trust between the well-prepared spiritual leader and the church community. This trust not only led to the church in peace but also enabled the church to appropriately shift the church's aims in response to society's needs. The church community working to hold onto its passion for the gospel in the midst of this change can be summed up in the four ministry elements of "evangelism, education, raising up workers, and building the kingdom of God." These actions were important factors that kept the church healthy. An's trust in people, symbolized by the motto "valuing one soul over all heaven and earth" is well aligned with the purpose of the church to build up the kingdom of God. This harmony in the gospel keeps bringing up the image of the hometown pastor who first shared the gospel with An. The heart-felt commitment of a rural church pastor bore fruit in another region a generation later, spreading the gospel much further.

Finally, since the founding of Suwonsung Church three ministry standards developed based on various ministry attempts and trials and error, and they are peace, balance, and training. These principles allowed the church to maintain its distinct purpose of being in the community while holding onto its function as the body of Christ. They also functioned to provide the church members with gospel resilience. Tracing the ministry principles back to the pastor, we find his childhood perception of his eldest brother who was 20 years his senior. While the image of the generous and kind father risked letting An become too lenient on himself, the image of the oldest brother functioned inside him to keep him awake and weary of human nature. This inner image is enabling Gwang-su An to continue to stay awake in his ministry. These factors have allowed the pastor to guard against the temptation of sinful habits often found in megachurch pastors, and to continue healthy ministry to the end. These inner resources have allowed the pastor to overcome the cowardly desire to let injustice be and to advance God's justice.

Conclusion and Proposal

Personally, as a member of Suwonsung Church for over 36 years, I was spiritually reborn and my faith grew in this church. I was especially privileged to be trained to be a disciple of Jesus Christ and later was ordained and commissioned by this church as a missionary to Africa for about 20 years. Now as a theologian, I examined how Suwonsung Church with 40 40-year history could maintain its health, the cause, and the process. As a researcher, I believe this was possible through the communal faith that values a soul more than heaven and earth, and the effort to imitate Christ.

In recent years factors that critically damage a church's health tend to arise in the period of leadership transition. Suwonsung Church is also in this period of transition. 2023 is the year pastor Gwang-su An retires after 40 years of ministry. Suwonsung Church is faced with the task of pouring new wine into new wineskin. But there is also the dual task of guarding against losing its original, traditional recipe while trying to switch to a new wineskin.

For 40 years under pastor Gwang-su An's leadership, Suwonsung Church accompanied his life. Traces of the pastor can be found throughout the church's history and in the ministries. Now the time has come for a new leader to continue and further develop this ministry. Suwonsung Church has not aimed to become a big church or boasted its membership size, but God has entrusted many responsibilities for the church's surrounding community. Suwonsung Church has been true to its sacred responsibility to weep with those who weep and to empathize with the wounded in the hidden corners of our society. This is the image of obedience and "incarnational discipleship" the world expects from the Korean church.[38]

---

[38] Hee-mo Lim, "Ha-na-nim na-la-lŭl se-u-nŭn han-kuk-kyo-hoe-ŭi sŏng-yuk-sin-chŏk che-cha-to sŏn-kyo" [Incarnational discipleship mission of the Korean church raising the kingdom of god], *Theology of Mission* 63 (2021), 247-49.

Bibliography

An, Gwang-su. *Salm-ŭi kil-e-sŏ man-nan haeng-pok* [Joy encountered on the path of life]. Seoul: PCK Book, 2016.

Bosch, David J. *Transforming mission: Paradigm shifts in theology of mission.* No. 16. Maryknoll, NY: Orbis books, 2011.

Bria, Ion. *The Liturgy after the Liturgy* (Geneva: WCC, 1996). Eerdmans, 1995).

Cha, Yoo-jin. "Sa-hoe-to sŏn-kyo-ŭi tae-sang" [Society is also object of mission]. *Hanguk Gidok Gongbo* (28 April, 2009).

Guder, Darrell L., and Lois Barrett. *Missional church: A vision for the sending of the church in North America.* Grand Rapids, MI: Wm. B. Eerdmans Publishing, 1998.

Han, Kook-ill. *Sŏn-kyo-chŏk kyo-hoe-ŭi i-lon-kwa sil-che* [Theory and practice of missional church]. Seoul: PUTS Press, 2019.

Hong, Hyeon-young, "Su-wŏn, sam-nam-ŭi kil-mok" [Suwon, crossroad to three regions in the south]. *Su-wŏn-ŭl a-si-na-yo* [Do you know suwon]. Suwon: Suwon Cultural Center, 2012.

Hwaseong City ed. *Kuk-yŏk su-wŏn-pu(kun) nam-yang-pu(kun)ŭp-chi* [Suwon county and namyang county township]. Seoul: Gyeongin M&B, 2006.

Kim. Do-il. *Tŏ-pul-ŏ kŏn-kang-ha-ko haeng-pok-han saeng-t'ae-kye-lŭl man-tŭl-ŏ ka-nŭn ka-chŏng-kyo-hoe -ma-ŭl kyo-yuk-kong-tong-ch'e* [Family, church and maeul community making a healthy and happy ecology together]. Seoul: Dongyeon, 2018.

Kim, Joon-hyeok. "*Hwal-sso-ki-lŭl chal-han su-wŏn-sa-lam-tŭl*" [People of suwon who were good at archery]. *Su-wŏn-ŭl a-si-na-yo* [Do you know Suwon]. Suwon: Suwon Cultural Center, 2012.

Kreider, Alan. *The Patience Ferment of the Early Church* (Grand Rapids: Baker, 2016).

Lausanne Movement. "Lausanne Global Classroom: Workplace Ministry. Part 01-09." August 28, 2020. https://www.youtube.com/watch?v=BI3AMJIJ2CE&list=PLYGxDL2dvuo6Z38peuVDGpa46lT6SImQ3 (Accessed 22 November 2022).

Lausanne Movement. "The Cape Town Commitment: A Confession of Faith and a Call to Action." 58. https://lausanne.org/wp-content/uploads/2021/10/The-Cape-Town-Commitment-—Pages-20-09-2021.pdf (Accessed 10 January 2023)

Lee, Bright Myeong-seok, "Su-wŏn-sŏng-kyo-hoe, ye-su kŭ-li-sŭ-to-ŭi che-cha-lo kŏl-ŏ-on 40nyŏn-ŭi kil" [Suwonsung Church: 40 years of walking as Jesus Christ's disciple], edited by Suwonsung Church. *Chu-nim-kwa ham-kke kŏl-ŏ-on su-wŏn-sŏng-kyo-hoe 40nyŏn-sa (1982-2022)* [Forty-Year History of Suwonsung Church Walking with the Lord 1982-2022].(Seoul: KIATS, 2023, 31-71.

Lim Hee-mo, "Ha-na-nim na-la-lŭl se-u-nŭn han-kuk-kyo-hoe-ŭi sŏng-yuk-sin-chŏk che-cha-to sŏn-kyo" [Incarnational discipleship mission of the Korean church raising the kingdom of god]. *Theology of Mission* 63 (2021), 247-49.

Newbigin, Lesslie. *The Open Secret: an introduction to the theology of mission* (Grand Rapids: Wm. B. Eerdmans Publishing, 1995).

Park, Yo-sep. "Tae-hyŏng kyo-hoe-ka si-min-tan-ch'e hwal-tong chi-wŏn-ha-nŭn i-yu" [Why A megachurch supports civil society activism]. *News N Joy* (27 May, 2017).

"Su-sŏng-ku pon ko-ku-lyŏ mae-hol-kun kyŏng-tŏk-wang kae-myŏng kŭm su-chu (水城郡 本 高句麗 買忽郡 景德王 改名 今 水州). *Sam-kuk-sa-ki* 삼국사기(三國史記) [Chronicles of the Three States] (第 三十五 卷 雜志 第四 地理 二) https://db.history.go.kr/ancient/level.do?levelId=sg_035_0020_0080: (Accessed 7 March 2024).

Suwonsung Church ed. *Chu-nim-kwa ham-kke kŏl-ŏ-on su-wŏn-sŏng-kyo-hoe 40nyŏn-sa (1982-2022)* [Forty-Year History of Suwonsung Church Walking with the Lord 1982-2022] (Seoul: KIATS, 2023).

Winston, Cynthia E. "Biography and Life Story Research." In Stephan D. Lapan et. al., *Qualitative research: an introduction to methods and designs* (San Francisco: John Wile & Sons, 2012).

Interview with pastor Gwang-su An at Suwonsung Church pastor's office (26 November 2021)

Interview with pastor Gwang-su An at Suwonsung Church pastor's office (11 January 2022)

Missiological Reflection on Local Evangelization Programs of Jeju Love Mission Society

Kook-il Han and Sung-hwan Suh

Introduction

Jeju-do is an island with a beautiful natural environment surrounded by a clear blue ocean. With its dense forests and intriguing geological formations, the Korean island has uniquely exotic scenery, making it a popular tourist destination for Koreans and foreigners. But unlike its beautiful outer appearance, Jeju-do is an island with a tragic history. It has a long history of exploitation by outsiders and was excluded from the economic, educational, and cultural development of the mainland. In this reality, the natives of Jeju had to work in the seas and on land endlessly to survive. Pastor Yi Gi-pung first came in 1908 to share the gospel on this island. 110 years have passed, but missionary activity in Jeju-do is still more difficult than in other regions. According to the National Statistics Office, the number of people in Jeju-do who identified as Protestants made up about 10%.[1] This is an improvement from a decade earlier, but compared to the rate of growth of other religions, the speed of evangelization is relatively slow. What is the reason for this?

The Korean church's ecology is formed by denominationalism and local church-centrism. That is why it is very difficult for local churches to join and cooperate. Perhaps the Korean church that grew after the 1970s is very similar to the capitalist market system that rapidly grew in Korean society during the same period. We are more familiar with competition for lone survival rather than unity and cooperation. When we focus on our church's survival and growth, it is difficult to turn our attention to matters outside the church in society and the world. The result is that most ministers and Christians' attention is emersed in their own church matters. The increasing number of ministers even as the number of congregants decreases makes the situation even more dire. It is time to break the paradigm dominated by denominationalism and local church-centrism.

Churches that focused on their own growth since the 1970s must now turn their missionary attention to community evangelization. We must turn our religious attention from the church to the actualization of the kingdom of God in the community, the larger society, and the world. This is possible through the churches, ministers, and congregants' voluntary fellowship and solidarity. Jeju Love Mission Society I will introduce in this essay was formed as an interdenominational mission society for the evangelization of Jeju-do. Jeju Love Mission Society's[2] purpose is to be faithful to church ministry while also aiming for the larger goal of evangelization of Jeju-do.

---

[1] Jeju Gidok Shinmun Issue 576, 2017 February 11, 1.

[2] Hereafter, JLMS.

JLMS starts with the need to understand the unique elements of Jeju-do with its unique history, culture, tradition, and tendencies that are different from other regions in Korea. Based on this understanding various missional agendas and strategies were formed. Programs of JLMS over the past 20 years will be diagnosed and analyzed through missiology to find their significance, then action principles will be drawn in the hopes that similar activities may be adopted in other regions as well.

To study the history and programs of JLMS from a missiological perspective I will advance the discussion on the following points. These points were also used as a list of questions to conduct interviews with JLMS members. First, what sparked the beginning of (your participation in) JLMS, and what is the society's aim? Second, what are the characteristics of JLMS? Third, How did JLMS's main activities (fellowship, studies, missions programs, spiritual pilgrimage) benefit and support the participating ministers and churches? Fourth, how have various forms of study groups resulted in a positive impact? Fifth, what was the impetus and engine that sustained JLMS for 20 years? Sixth, what are the leadership characteristics of the people who have directed JLMS? Are there any regrets in recalling the 20-year activities of JLMS? Eighth, what are the priority principles and factors to consider if JLMS is to be founded in another region?

Beginning of JLMS: History of Jeju-do and Religious and Cultural Characteristics

JLMS was launched in 2002 as a Protestant interdenominational gathering for the evangelization of Jeju. On the island, there are a few large Protestant churches but most are small in scale. This alone shows how difficult it is to conduct missions in Jeju-do. When I attended the first JLMS gathering I heard the young ministers sharing how it is difficult for them to make a living for their own family. Nevertheless, I saw in their young faces the spirit I never saw anywhere else. From the first encounter, I realized that JLMS is no regular gathering.

Pastor Sung-hwan Suh who played the main role in starting JLMS aptly reflects on the mistakes of Jeju mission in the past and systematically presents alternative strategies in his paper, "Jeju Mission, Yesterday, Today, and Tomorrow." Despite over a century of Jeju mission, the island is the least evangelized in the country. Suh examines each reason to point out the problems of the Protestant mission.[3] According to Suh, other religions, Buddhism, Soka Gakkai, and Catholicism were accepted by the Jeju residents and settled to grow in Jeju-do, but Protestantism remains an outsider's religion. Why has Protestantism not been successful with its mission in Jeju-do? He explains the reasons from a few perspectives, which I find appropriate to mention before I launch into the main topic.

---

[3] Section 2 is a summary of the book by Sung-hwan Suh, *Che-chu-sŏn-kyo 100nyŏn, ŏ-che-wa o-nŭl nae-il – pi-p'an-chŏk sŏng-ch'al-kwa tae-an-mo-saek* [100 Years of Jeju Mission, Yesterday, Today, and Tomorrow Critical Reflection and Exploration of Strategies], (Seoul: Yeyoung Communication, 2008).

First, Protestantism has not deeply participated in the pains Jeju residents experienced in history and in their harsh natural environment. Especially compared to the Catholic church, the Protestant mission never deeply intervened in the distinct troubles of Jeju.

Second, as the 19th-century Protestant missions began in Korea the entire society benefited from Western modernization, especially in education. But Jeju-do did not receive the benefits of the new civilization that came with the Protestnat mission. Education mission through mission schools, or medical mission through hospitals were never conducted in Jeju-do. This is evidence that the church did not fulfill its social responsibility for Jeju and remained absorbed in the private sphere or in their own local churches.

Third, the Jeju Protestant Christian stance on the national tragedy of foreign occupation was ambivalent and passive. Nationwide, churches directly and indirectly led and participated in the March First Movement and the general Independence Movement but Protestantism in Jeju-do kept a spectator's distance on the state of the nation. This irresponsible and apathetic stance gave the learned elites a negative impression of Protestant Christianity.

Fourth, the Protestant stance on the April Third Massacre and the Democracy Movement was also very passive. When the Catholic Church actively led and participated in these movements, Protestant churches hardly convened assemblies or prayer meetings on the issues. Protestant churches' anti-social and ahistorical stance were apathetic to the pains and wounds of Jeju residents, and the churches could not exist as true agents of reconciliation.

Fifth, on interactions with other religions and cultural transformation, Protestantism has approached matters from a very narrow and fundamentalist stance. For the Jeju residents, Protestantism was experienced as an exclusionary outsider's religion. Folk religion dominates every Jeju resident's soul and lifestyle, and ancestral rites and *gwendang* (kinship) culture form close-knit local communities. In this context, Protestantism's valuation of the local church above all and narrow orthodoxy prevented the church from entering deep into the lives of the residents and kept it on the margins.

Sixth, the above fact is related to the fundamental issues in Protestantism's missiology and missionary policies. The problem is with attempting unilateral missionary strategies to convert the Jeju residents without accurately understanding the island's context. Rather than the church impacting the society the society has impacted the church – the *gwendang* culture that should be overcome has seeped into churches to let a few people with power determine whether a new Christian can settle in a church.

The six issues mentioned appropriately analyze why Protestantism has not seen the fruit of its mission despite a century of history in Jeju, compared to Catholicism or other religions.

In sum, 1) Protestantism could not deeply participate in the pains of Jeju residents, 2) it was not established as the responsible and practicable religion for the Jeju society, 3) it was exclusionary to the sentiments and interests of the residents evident in folk religion, and 4) Protestantism remains an external religion that never succeeded in approaching the residents nor settling in the society. According to this analysis, on top of basic faith and passion, there is also a need for the Protestant churches' united efforts to reflect on the faults in their missionary history and discuss strategies to overcome them if they are to do mission in Jeju.

Missiological Reflection on JLMS

Characteristics and Roles of JLMS as a Mission Society

Unlike Western churches with a long tradition of Christianity, the Korean church is new and has different structures and characteristics. In the West, the local church may be weak but the denominational assembly has the institutional power and the financial means to support the local church. But the Korean church completely relies on individual churches' capacity, so if the local church fails, then the presbytery and the assembly both follow suit. Therefore, in mission it is necessary to strengthen the local churches at the frontlines and sustain their passion, interests, and dynamism for missions.

The strengths and limitations of local churches in Korea are crystal clear. Churches are extremely dynamic in that they practice the catholicity of the church at the frontlines, but they are also mired in denominationalism and absorbed in local church matters. Their interests do not go beyond matters of individual church members or the self-centered motivations of the church or the denomination. So the local churches tend to have a narrow understanding of the church's vocation and are not considering the universal values of the reign of God such as freedom, peace, fairness, justice, healing, and reconciliation that the catholic church must practice in the world. Churches are so absorbed in their own matters that they cannot participate in the *oecoumene*, or the mission of God. In this situation, the ministerial attention must be expanded beyond the sphere of the local church to evangelization of the local community through the missional church and ministry perspective. In the 1970s and the 1980s decade of growth, theories on church growth were popular. In the following era, there is a need for solidarity and cooperation of churches for regional evangelization. In this situation, the following are the two missiological reasons why the characteristics of JLMS are notable.

In the history of mission, there had been movements to reform the church from the inside or to form distinct specialized organizations outside the church. An example of the former may be German Pietism's "ecclesiola in ecclesia" that formed various small groups to breathe life into the church. The latter are the mission societies that operate outside the church as a joint effort of multiple churches.[4] The two movements influence each other. The missions of the

---

[4] A. F. Wals, *The cross-cultural process in Christian history* (Maryknoll, New York: Orbis Books, 2002), 16-17; F. J. Verstraelen (ed.), *Missiology An Ecumenical Introduction* (Grand Rapids, Michigan: Wm. B. Eerdmans, 1995), 238-239.

medieval Catholic Church and the post-Reformation Protestant Churches were started by these movements.[5]

The missiologist Ralph D. Winter stated in his "The Two Structures of God's Redemptive Mission" how the church and mission societies are distinct in their function and are mutually complementary.[6] His thesis is that for the continuation of Christian missions, both the church and the mission society must exist. This is based on the continuous existence of the two structures throughout the 2000-year Christian history. Winter concludes that for an appropriate mission, one structure should not be dominated or absorbed into the other but exist independently to complement each other. On the distinct functions and roles of the churches and mission societies, Winter uses the term modality for the church as the faith community and sodality for mission societies such as monasteries. According to this distinction, the denominations and local churches are in the form of modality while the different men's and women's missions associations in the church are in the form of sodality. Winter assesses that in the Medieval Roman Catholic Church modality and sodality existed in synthesis, where church reform and missionary movements were possible as the vitality of the sodality could nourish modality.

Winter stated that the Protestant missionary movement could progress vigorously due to structural developments in solidarity. It is necessary for modality with human resources and financial support to combine with mission societies' systematic missionary expertise.[7] Assuming the need for mutual cooperation between modality and sodality, in the mission field of Jeju-do the two structures of the local church and the mission society can help the churches overcome their limitations, grow their missionary capacity, and expand their practice through unity and cooperation.

Wolfgang Huber, the Chairperson of the Council of the Evangelical Church in Germany, distinguished the existing forms of the church into four – local community, initiative group, parish church, and united council – in his work *Kirche*.[8] The local community (local church) is the smallest unit of the church that organizes Sunday services and liturgy and conducts education, pastoral counseling, and social services. Then there are "Initiative Gruppe" or initiative groups that are also under the umbrella of the catholic church but are beyond the local church community and have distinct purposes and characteristics. The initiative groups awaken the local church's sense of responsibility for mission, service, and culture by challenging and complementing the churches. Another form of the church is the united council. Of course, there are local church councils such as presbyteries within the church structure, but they generally take

---

[5] D. J. Bosch, *Witness to the World*, Translated into Korean by Jeon Jae-ok (Seoul: Duranno, 1995), 136-140, 158-160.

[6] The following is a summary of Ralph Winter's writing: Ralph Winter, "The Two Structures of God's Redemptive Mission," *Missiology* 2.1 (1974), 121-139.

[7] For more on this topic, see: Lausanne Occasional Paper No. 24. "Cooperating in World Evangelization: A Handbook on Church/Para-Church Relationships" 1983.

[8] W. Huber, *Kirche*, Translated into Korean by Lee Shin-geon (Seoul: Korea Theological Study Institute, 1990), 42-47.

care of administrative matters and cannot provide missionary motivation. Ecumenical unity programs can mobilize missionary resources in cooperation with local churches according to societal needs and demands. They gather local churches' missionary capacity to be used on the larger scale rather than overlapping among themselves at the local level. Especially in the Korean church where the local church is the most powerful, such regional church councils are critical.

The united council of churches or initiative groups both raise the capacity of local churches and can function beyond the limitations of the churches to unite and cooperate for a higher missionary purpose. These forms aptly explain JLMS. JLMS was formed to vitalize local churches and evangelize Jeju-do in ways the churches cannot, and in that sense, functions as both an initiative group and a united council. JLMS which unites local churches has increased the missionary expertise and capacity of the churches for the evangelization of Jeju. Specifically JLMS has conducted prayer meetings, fellowships, and various study groups for ministers, and has progressed as a grassroots ecumenical movement. Now I will explain the activities of the society in further detail below.

Fellowship of Churches and Ministers

In the difficult missionary context of Jeju, if ministers remained separate in their own churches it would have been difficult to sustain ministry for the long time, no matter how lofty their sense of vocation. JLMS has supported the ministers through fellowship gatherings to guard against isolation, loneliness, and burnout. It has provided opportunities for renewal and active participation in mission. Fellowship is a necessary element for healthy ministry for the laity and the ministers.

In the gospels Jesus' ministry is described in three terms, kerygma (including didache), diakonia, and koinonia. Kerygma is the proclamation of the good news of the kingdom of God, diakonia is the works of service to actualize the kingdom of God, and koinonia is the act of fellowship in boundary-crossing love of God. These three types of activities are not separate from each other and are not distinct in different situations but are organically connected.

The use of the term koinonia in the New Testament was primarily for the fellowship of the saints, fellowship among churches, or the fellowship of the Trinity. In other words, the term's usage seems limited to the fellowship of the Christian community. In ecumenical theology, koinonia is used to explain fellowship and unity activities among different denominations. In the New Testament and especially the Gospels, Jesus is recorded to have willingly interacted with the people with whom the Jewish leaders would not have associated. Jesus had fellowship to the point that he was known as "a glutton and a drunkard." Bosch identifies Jesus' boundary-crossing fellowship as the beginning of missionary activity.[9] Christianity is clearly the religion that crosses boundaries. Not only in the Gospels but also in Acts and the epistles the process of gospel expansion is described as the crossing of boundaries between the Jews and the Gentiles. It is evident that koinonia in mission means God's transcendent

---

[9] D. J. Bosch, *Witness to the World*, 71-72.

love that extends over the church fences to cross the boundary lines between Christians and non-Christians.

In the Korean church that emphasizes evangelism, kerygma is prioritized among the three above concepts. But deeper study of the Gospels show that Jesus' missionary activities are based on koinonia. Scriptures show that Jesus came not simply as a teacher or an evangelist but above all as someone who crosses innumerable boundaries to make all humanity one in Christ. This ministry of Jesus crosses all lines of exclusion and discrimination between people to accept all people called to be children of God.[10]

JLMS could be sustained thanks to the affectionate fellowship of the members. The Society was formed for unity and cooperation among ministers. The Society continues to convene meetings in regular intervals for local church ministers to support each other through fellowship. Its members describe the Society as voluntary gatherings where they can meet for conversation, study, and leisure to support and comfort each other to sustain their ministry.

The fellowship in JLMS is actualized in sporting activities. At the regular gatherings, they not only pray and study together but also play soccer to form deeper friendships. Soccer becomes the medium with which they can have fellowships with people outside the church. This means the fellowship is performing a missionary function, and the fellowship is itself missional. For example, the JLMS ministers networked with the Jeju National University student soccer club to organize the soccer tournament. This allowed contact with university students in Jeju that one local church would not have been able to organize.[11]

Fellowship is a foundational element in missions and the church. One of the most urgent problems of ministers is burnout. The cause may be multiple, but isolation, loneliness, and limited individual capacity are some of the biggest factors. Jeju-do is a very arid environment for missions. As mentioned, the evangelization rate in Jeju is the lowest in the nation. It is very difficult to evangelize to the local residents. In this context, if ministers are isolated, despite

---

[10] Pastor Jong-myung Lee of Songak Methodist Church in Asan practiced maeul ministry by dwelling in the community and serving them for almost thirty year, but at first he did not think to cooperate with other churches in the region. Then he found that while his church was getting recognition the pastor himself was spiritual bunt out. As he met with other local church pastors regularly to relieve stress and study the Bible together he experienced spiritual renewal. Now he looks forward to forming a resident community of retired pastors across denominations. It is difficult to sustain healthy ministry alone. He personally experienced the truth of the African proverb: "If you want to go fast, go alone, if you want to go far, go together.".

[11] To make contact with non-Christians in the university they had been organizing the Collegiate Soccer Tournament sponsored by JLMS. The tournament was organized twice last year were 400 students in 18 teams participated. The teams were connected to local churches so the churches can continue to serve them. It took much resource and thorough preparation and the participants were well-served and the event well-coordinated. For now, JLMS is focusing on college students, but they are praying to conduct such events for secondary, primary, and preschool children as well if resource allows.

their firm sense of vocation they will eventually experience burnout. Regular gatherings of ministers and their spouses for fellowship, sports, study, and prayer are important for them to overcome these situations.

The fellowship in JLMS allows participating ministers to encourage and comfort each other and supports them to continue local church ministry. It provides opportunities for continued learning to deepen and expand their theology. The Society supports physical and spiritual health through prayer and physical activities.

Efforts toward Sustained Growth and Change

Theology provides an important basis and perspective for ministers to critically reflect on the present ministry situation and establish appropriate ministry strategies. There is still a tendency in the Korean church to regard ministry practice and theology as oppositional and to relatively neglect theology. This is due to ignorance of the conscious and unconscious impact of theology on ministry. All ministers whether they are aware or not are impacted by a certain theology. In the process of scripture interpretation and all aspects related to ministry – ecclesiology, ministry philosophy, worldview, perspective on the laity, ministerial identity – theology is at the bottom. Therefore, ministers need continued theological education to reflect on their current ministry and correctly regard the current issues in society and respond to them. Continuous theological education applies not only in seminary but is necessary for healthy and vital ministry after graduation. So JLMS considers theological studies an important activity that connects the gap between theology and practice and supports healthy church growth.

The study groups called Shinhak Madang (theology space) are organized in three broad types: one-day seminar, intensive seminar that lasts over four days, and special lectures in the form of storytelling. They are each named Jeju Love Shinhak Madang One-Day Seminar, Jeju Love Theology Forum, and Jeju Love Storytelling Madang.

Jeju Love Shinhak Madang One-Day Seminar: The seminars are organized four times a year, every other month on Mondays, inviting renowned scholars. They are open to all ministers in Jeju-do. The ministers planning to participate in the one-day seminar must participate in the five-to-eight-week preparatory seminar. These preparatory gatherings are conducted on Monday mornings each week (prayer meeting from 10 to 11 am, seminar from 11 am to 12 pm). These gatherings are called Jeju Love Monday Shinhak Madang. The official One-Day Seminars are planned in two sessions, one in the morning and another in the afternoon, including a joint luncheon for fellowship.

Jeju Love Theology Forum: The theology forums are organized twice a year, each session lasting four or five days for intensive study on a select topic. The event takes the form of lectures, seminars, and forums, and is accompanied by spiritual training. The participants must be ministers in Jeju-do and must have studied the selected topic at the Jeju Love Monday Shinhak Madang organized by JLMS.

Jeju Love Storytelling Madang: These events are organized as study sessions and special lectures inviting experts in theology, humanities, and Jeju-do's distinct history, culture, and traditions.

The interviews with ministers participating in the study groups reveal how these programs have contributed to their ministries. Through these studies, the JLMS members can activate their theological and missional imagination, build their inner courage and strength to sustain their mission and ministry in the harsh mission field of Jeju, and gain insights and ideas for healthy ministry. Compared to seminary education that revolves around the professors, the participants initiate studies in JLMS in response to the needs in practical ministry situations. Even when speakers are invited the sessions are conducted as dialogues with participants to enable the learning to take root in the field. These opportunities support continued theological reflections even after seminary. The scope of study is not limited to theology but also covers various spheres of liberal arts. They discuss the history, culture, and traditions of Jeju, especially the distinct cultures such as *gwendang* and ancestral rites to approach matters missionally. Ministers risk falling into narrow thought processes when isolated in their ministries. These study groups are opportunities for them to look beyond, assess the issues of the society, and understand their ministry field. They lead the ministers to a theological conversion.

Missional Church Movement

Since the 1963 International Mission Conference in Mexico City themed "witness in six continents, every region inhabited by people is recognized as a mission field. If Jeju-do is recognized as a mission field, the island can be approached missionally by examining various factors than when approached simply as church ministry. If JLMS aims for unity and cooperation of local churches for the evangelization of Jeju-do, then what are the aims of the member churches? As mentioned above, JLMS considers the entire island the mission field. This means the local churches also recognize their surrounding locale as the mission field and approach them accordingly. They call this initiative the missional church movement for the community. Missional ecclesiology overcomes the narrow ecclesiology of the Korean church and practices ministry that participates in the mission of God, who is already working in the community and in the world.

The maeul, or the town, is identified as the sphere of ministry with the recognition that principles of the kingdom of God must be first and foremost practiced in the local community. The local community is the primary mission field of the local church. To approach the local community missionally means to go beyond the existing ministry paradigm with its highest goal of numerical church growth. Today, the local church must focus its mission on ways to coexist and walk with the local community. If the existing ministry focuses on the local church's survival and growth, maeul ministry expands the focus to the town. Maeul ministry is a movement that enables local churches to actualize and live out their salvation within the Christian value system, rather than understanding the kingdom of the kingdom of God in abstract terms only, as they live among the town residents.[12]

Missional churches have three general characteristics. The first is the connection to the community-building movement. Missional churches can contribute to local community building that works to restore the communities that were broken during the 1970s industrialization and urbanization. Above all, the experience of communality which is an essential value of the church should be provided outside the church and in the local community as well. The ethical standards of the church are resources that can overcome individualism and egoism, and church members' voluntary commitment and service can function to vitalize the local community. The second factor of the missional church is that it has the most contribution toward local community development. People with various gifts and professional expertise are concentrated in the church along with material resources. Christians' voluntary commitment and service based on their spirituality are great resources of the church that can be employed for community development and welfare. The church can actualize the kingdom of God by contributing to regional development to practice its public responsibility. The third aspect is that missional churches lead in the rediscovery of local traditions and cultures.[13] Churches must have greater love for their surrounding community and society than anyone else. Therefore, missional churches understand the region's history and traditions, identify the cultural characteristics to preserve and develop them, and promote their relevance to contemporary society.

In sum, missional churches go beyond the church, the building, or the institution to the local community for vigorous fellowship. They accept the various social issues as missionary agendas and respond to local needs. Therefore, missional churches do not belong to the church members but are churches for the local community. Their ministers are also the ministers for the community. The church practices its vocation by becoming the madang, or the community space, and existing among the residents to share the blessings it has received.

The member churches of JLMS do not aspire toward numerical growth of their individual churches as in the 1970s but aim to become maeul churches that fellowship with the local town residents and take action for the community. In terms of missionary strategy, it is also necessary to shift from the come-structure that waits for the community to come to church, to the go-structure in which the church goes to the community. Overcoming the separation from the local community, churches must work toward "mission in fellowship" rather than a "mission without fellowship." One of the mission activities of JLMS is to start churches in regions without one. This is practiced based on missional ecclesiology. The minister sent out the start of a church must first live as a local

---

[12] On this topic, refer to Kook-il Han, *Sŏn-kyo-chŏk kyo-hoe-ŭi i-lon-kwa sil-che* [Theory and practice of missional church], (Seoul: PUTS Press, 2019).

[13] A good case is the ministry of Jeju Gujwa Jeil Church. The ministry started with a local children's center then grew to other children's education service programs. Through these programs town adults also became interested. The town has developed to become a social service, culture, and learning community.

resident and form neighborly relationships, then attempt organic church planting strategies.

The missionary statement "Together Towards Life" declared at the Busan WCC Assembly emphasized the importance of local churches in mission and ecumenical movement.[14] Local churches are growing weak not only in Korea but all over the world. In this situation, the ecumenical movement with its theology and various practices must contribute to building up and vitalizing the church. In that sense, the ecumenical movement needs much effort to go beyond the milieu of a minority of experts in theology and practice but must actively converse with local churches.

The ecumenical movement that cannot put down roots in the local churches is powerless in reality. In the process of agenda setting as well, the issues and needs relevant to local communities and churches, and not just the grand narratives and issues of the global scope must be accepted as ecumenical agenda if the movement is to expand.[15] If in the 20th century, the global churches led the ecumenical movement and the localities were places where the agendas were implemented, the 21st century requires a reversal of the paradigm where the local leads and the global responds.[16] There is a need for a post-institutional and post-technical expertise character appropriate for our century in which the movement's universality and accessibility allow the participation of all local churches.[17]

Local Ecumenism:
Grassroots Missionary Cooperation for Evangelization of Jeju

Despite the need and the legitimacy of the ecumenical movement, it has unfortunately been unable to put down roots on the local church level but is staying on the level of scholarly discourse and activists in ecumenical institutions. Korea has very conservative tendencies, so the ecumenical movement known to be relatively progressive remains on the margins. In the Korean church the ecumenical movement must in the future be spread and

---

[14] Kenneth R. Ross, et al, ed. Ecumenical Missiology, Translated by Korea Ecumenical Society (Seoul: CLSK, 2018), 536-575.

[15] Sung-hwan Suh, "Che-chu-chi-yŏk e-k'yu-me-ni-k'al un-tong i-ya-ki," [The story of ecumenical movement in Jeju] *Nongchongwa Mokhwe* 48 (2010 Winter), 97-104.

[16] Sung-won Park, *Saeng-myŏng-ŭi mul-kyŏl-ŭl tta-la kil-ŭl kŏt-ta – na-ŭi e-k'yu-me-ni-k'al yŏ-chŏng* [Walking along the waterway of life – my ecumenical journey (Gyeongbuk: Living Waterway, 2014), 120-126.

[17] Kook-il Han, "Chi-yŏk-kyo-hoe-wa chi-yŏk-e-k'yu-me-ni-chŭm", [Local church and local ecumenism] *Nongchongwa Mokhwe* 77 (2018 Spring), 20-30; The following are some cases of local ecumenical movement. Pastor Jeong-woo Nam of Haneul Dameun Church became a part of Daegu Church-District Council to have his ministry attention expand to the entire city of Daegu. Nine churches in Huam-dong in Seoul have been coopeating for over 25 years for local evangelization. Seongam Church in Eunpyeong District in Seoul have gathered 18 churches to jointly provide healing mission programs for local secondary school teachers and principals. Saerom Church in Bucheon is a small church but it has cooperated with other local churches to operate a night eatery for the local youth every Friday.

vitalized by based on local community initiative. The existing institutionalized ecumenical movement seems to have encountered its limits. In the new churches, as in South Korea, the ecumenical movement can only be vitalized if it has the assent and support of the local churches.

JLMS is a local ecumenical movement on the level of local churches. It began organically as a fellowship of ministers gathering for the evangelization of Jeju-do, and has progressed into different types of meetings. It is not a top-down ecumenical movement initiated and operated by an institution, but a model of indigenously initiated, bottom-up ecumenical movement.

Today in 2022 JLMS consists of about 50 member churches and their ministers. But 20 years ago it started as a small church ministers' prayer meeting. Their biggest issue was not being able to find education ministers for children and youth, for which the churches met to seek joint solutions.[18]

JLMS progressed to organize various types of studies, sporting events, and domestic and foreign pilgrimage trips. Through these gatherings the ministers could expand their theological horizon and learn Jeju's history, culture, and traditions to understand the ministry field, as well as study the distinct characteristics of Jeju that hinders mission to discuss solutions. In the Korean church ministry schedules are too packed to allow continued scholarly reflections after seminary. If a minister's theological thinking does not progress, the churches inevitably stagnate. JLMS was aware of this fact, which led them to study various theological topics after a period of ministry practice, and together search out alternative solutions for evangelization of Jeju in response to the distinct issues and problems that arise in the field.

If theology forms the ministry philosophy, then spirituality energizes ministry. The Society conducts spiritual pilgrimages by visiting various places in Korea and in other countries.[19] Ministerial gatherings include woman ministers, and ministers' spouses [most of them women] also meet regularly for fellowship and prayer. These gatherings of interdenominational churches and ministers for prayer, fellowship, and study have catalyzed the local ecumenical movement in the region.

Leadership of JLMS

Leadership is the capacity to transmit a person's goal to another, sharing a sense of purpose and inviting others to participate.[20] The sharing of a leader's vision and goal and putting them into practice are made possible through the leader's leadership. Types of leadership are closely related to the times and situations.[21] In the age of economic development, strong authoritative leadership was

---

[18] Interview with pastor Sung-hwan Suh (Sunday 11 April 2022, 10:30 am)

[19] Some of the field trips have been to Ulreung-do Island, Mosegol Spiritual Community, and Garakjae Spiritual Retreat Center in Korea. They have also visited historical sites of Protestant Reformation and spiritual communities in German, France, Switzerland, and the Czech Republic.

[20] Sang-bok Kim, *Mok-hoe-cha-ŭi li-tŏ-sip* [Minister's Leadership] (Seoul: Emmaus, 1997), 77-78.

[21] Eddie Gibbs, *Leadership Next*, Translated by Lee Min-ho (Seoul: Qumran Publishing House, 2010), 35, 46-48.

effective.[22] But today in a democratic society with a strong sense of individual agency a more creative, innovative, flexible, and inclusive leadership is required to overcome today's issues.

In the Korean church with a short history lacking firm traditions and cultures, the capacity and function of the minister make the biggest impact. Especially to acquire the kind of leadership that does not stay within the church but draws out cooperation with the local community and churches, there must be the element of missional ministry leadership. Below, I list a few characteristics of missional ministry leadership.[23]

The first is authentic leadership. The dictionary definition of authenticity is the quality of being genuine and not false. Authenticity is necessary for human relationships and restoration of trust, but also to draw out assent in the leader's vision and thoughts and the willingness to participate in it. In traditional leadership, the minister's capacity was more highly valued than their character and personality. But today church and society are interested in the person of the minister.

Authentic leadership arises out of the minister's demeanor and intention rather than their role and function. The minister's personal characteristics, in other words, their spirituality, critically impact their ministry. What actually motivates a gathering's attendants to trust in the leader is the leader's faith, character, and demeanor that arise from the heart.[24] For a leader to be trusted their being is more important than their doing. In that sense, the spirituality of the minister is more important than their skills and giftings. For appropriate ministerial capacity, healthy spirituality is a prerequisite.[25]

Secondly, pioneering and creative leadership is required. In the Western church with a long history and tradition the church institution and organization, rather than the minister's personal capacity, can sustain the church. European churches have stable parish systems inherited from their Christian society, so the leadership capacity of individual ministers has less impact on local churches.

In the Korean church with a weaker institutional capacity, the pioneering spirit of a missionary is necessary. The Korean church's growth and revival relied on the leadership of ministers who stepped into untrodden paths, the pioneers who saw what others could not see, and the practitioners who did not fear loss and put new initiatives into practice. From the bottom up, this pioneering spirit based on faith in God became the Korean missionary movement.

Third, the leadership of dialogue and accompaniment arising out of flexibility and inclusiveness is necessary. In the age of growth, the model of leadership was charismatic leadership. Here, charisma means the minister's authority and initiative-taking capacity. In most instances of church growth, the minister's

---

22 Young-gi Hong, *Han-kuk ch'o-tae-hyŏng kyo-hoe-wa k'a-li-sŭ-ma li-tŏ-sip* [Korean Mega Churches and Charismatic Leadership] (Seoul: Church Growth Institute, 2001).

23 The four characteristics of leadership has been summarized from Kook-il Han, *Theory and practice of missional church*, 363-396.

24 Eddie Gibbs, *Leadership Next*, 190.

25 Seong-choon Oh, *Sin-hak. yŏng-sŏng. mok-hoe* [Theology, spirituality, ministry] (Seoul: PUTS Press, 1997), 338-41.

vision and capacity to implement the vision were critical. The minister led on the front lines and all communication flowed from the top to the bottom.

Today, leadership is based on mutuality in which the leader can persuade the participants to assent to the leader's thoughts and share them with others. The minister may have valuable insights but they also need communication skills to share the thoughts with the followers. For better communication, a degree of flexibility in which differences can be respected and accepted is necessary. Rather than delivering one's thoughts on-way, discovering the members' hidden talents, capacity, and potential and providing motivation and opportunity to develop and exercise them is the kind of leadership that accompanies the followers side by side.[26]

The fourth is the leadership that serves and honors others. In missional ministry, the minister functions to support the laity.[27] This leadership of mutual communication does not lead at the front but supports the church members from behind so that they can take sight of the direction in which they should go and become agents of the ministry.

When one wants to stand at the center of a community it makes others remain on the margins. The result is the center-periphery structure of community relationships where the person at the center leads and the people on the periphery passively follow. But a true leader does not stand at the center but supports others to take the center stage. A community requires various types of leadership so all constituents can actively participate as agents.

Such leadership is not authoritative or vertical. Like the words of Jesus, such leadership is practiced by humbling oneself and becoming a servant of others (Mark 10:42-45). The authority of the leader of the missional ministry is respected not by authoritativeness but by loving service, and such leadership has an impact on the church members and the local community.

In studying JLMS researching how its leadership progressed over 20 years has been of interest. Based on interviews with participating ministers, I could find individual and communal leadership characteristics that have led the Society.

On the individual level, the leadership of pastor Suh Sung-hwan who first organized the Society and centrally managed the Society's operations played a key role. This was the common assessment of all the interview participants. Small churches in Jeju-do could launch the Society thanks to the pivotal role of Sung-hwan Suh. What are the characteristics of Suh's leadership? From the interviews I could identify the characteristics as persuasive leadership that does not impose but earns the participants' assent through conversations; inclusiveness and flexibility in avoiding judgment against differences but respecting and accepting them as they are; leadership of accompaniment that

---

[26] Michael Moritz studied the leadership of the the legendary manager of the Manchester United Football Club in England to find that Ferguson's leadership was not impositional but motivating and accompanying. He brought out the last 5% of potential that the athletes had not been aware of themselves. *Joongang Ilbo (*27 February 2016, p.18).

[27] On theology of the laity refer to R. P. Stevens, *The Abolition of the Laity* (Carlisle, Cumbria: Send the Light, 2000).

walks side by side rather than leading at the front; understated leadership that honors others rather than claiming one's due; and leadership of willing service without being authoritative even when he is the senior member. These characteristics have the power to move people. Various types of study groups could be sustained every week for 20 years thanks to Suh's passionate and scholarly thinking, providing creative ideas and directions.[28] Suh himself states that what he tries to remember when he meets with people is to truly pay respects, accept the differences rather than disregarding them, and to recognize and serve others.[29]

On the community's leadership characteristics, there is familial and affectionate relationship building. They respect each other and treat everyone equally regardless of age and seniority, rather than forming authoritative and hierarchical relationships. Above all, the participation is not imposed but voluntary; there is a sense of companionship on the same path, and they build close, supportive relationships, encouraging each other in an unstrained and liberating atmosphere. In accompanying pastor Sung-hwan Suh the participants have taken on his leadership characteristics and are reflecting back the energy to continue the gatherings.

Through the exceptional leadership of an individual and the familial leadership of the community, JLMS could provide not only the strength to sustain ministry in the difficult mission field of Jeju-do, but also see individual ministers mature and the churches experience revival.

Accomplishments and Limitations of JLMS in the Words of JLMS Members

One visible accomplishment of JLMS is the cooperative education program. This was also the specific reason why the Society was convened. There is no seminary in Jeju-do and it was difficult to find pastoral interns for the education departments, so it was difficult to train the younger generations in the faith and to operate the Sunday School. Various different solutions such as the short-term missionary system were suggested, but none of them succeeded. JLMS member churches themselves sought solutions by cooperating with urban churches to receive financial assistance to provide training for the ministers' spouses and had them serve as pastoral interns for the education departments. This program greatly supported the Christian education of children and youth in Jeju-do where Sunday School operations is difficult.

Another accomplishment is church planting in unchurched regions. In Jeju there are still many towns without a church. Two towns were selected for JLMS to send out ministers. They were not to start by founding churches but to settle in the towns as second-career farmers. As they become primarily known as a

---

[28] This section is a summary of my phone interviews with nine members JLMS. Date and Time: 9 April 2022, 10:40 am. Participants: Nam-su Ko (Paju Bit Church), Pan-su Ku, Hyo-geun Kim (Hanrim Church), Ho-young Ryu (Seongsan Church), Sung-hwan Suh (Sarang Soomgeyol Church), Gwang-deok An (Banya Church), Hye-suk Jang (Jeju Gujwa Jeil Church), Jong-won Jae (Dongnam Church), Ho-min Hwang (Jeju Gujwa Jeil Church).

[29] Interview with pastor Sung-hwan Suh (11 April 2022, 10:30 am)

necessary resident in town who also happens to be a minister, they can earn the trust of the residents before they can start a church. Among the two towns, the efforts in one town failed while the other town (Sanbangsan) resulted in church planting which is progressing well today.

JLMS also managed to construct the missionary infrastructure for the island. In missions it is important to till the ground before sowing seeds. JLMS provides an opportunity for contact with non-Christians in the university. For example, they regularly organize the University Student Soccer Tournament sponsored by JLMS. One year 400 students in 18 teams participated. Considering the difficulties meeting young college students in churches today, these events are undoubtedly encouraging for missions. These are important activities that build the missionary foundations for the evangelization of Jeju-do.[30]

Among the visible accomplishments, the interviewees confess that "the existence of JLMS for 20 years has been the greatest accomplishment."[31] It is astonishing that the Monday meetings never once went into recess for 20 years even though this is a voluntary meeting. This is due to how the ministers have received encouragement, comfort, and motivation to sustain their ministry amid difficult situations.

Most of the member churches of JLMS are small. Not a small number of ministers fail to sustain church ministry and leave the island. The Jeju society is unresponsive to missions, the minister and their family's sense of isolation and loneliness on the island, and the unchanging ministry environment ultimately cause the minister to burn out and cease.

In this arid missionary landscape, JLMS provides comfort, encouragement, and courage to continue ministry through affectionate fellowship to water their ministry. Interviews with participants show that JLMS member ministers have sustained ministry for over a decade compared to the two-and-a-half-year average years of ministry. The sustained studies and seminars have also matured the minister and the church. This is a valuable experience and accomplishment of JLMS found in no other ministers serving on the mainland.

As for the limitations of JLMS, because of free and loose relationships built in the Society,' there may be a lack of a sense of responsibility and programs lack strong driving initiative. With the passage of time and the need for generational transition, there is also the task of contacting and responding to new younger ministers to pass on the tradition and spirit of JLMS. Another limitation is that JLMS has been operating for ministers only and has not made space for laity participation. Expanding the reach of JLMS to include the laity is the remaining task.

Conclusion

There are mainly two ways a person can live through life. One is the passive stance, where difficult situations are avoided and external circumstances are blamed. The other is the assertive stance, in which one tries to overcome the

---

[30] Sung-hwan Suh, "The story of ecumenical movement in Jeju" 95-97.

[31] Interview with pastor Jong-won Jae (9 April 2022, 10:40 am)

difficulties and change the situation creatively. JLMS holds valuable stories of ministers who stuck to their churches and continued their missionary activities in the most challenging setting of Jeju-do, thanks to unity and cooperation with others. It is difficult to find anywhere else such voluntary society of local churches that sustained its dynamism for two decades. JLMS did not despair in the island's parochial nature and limitations but rather responded by reframing them as communality.

JLMS provides many insights and hope for the Korean church that cannot discard denominationalism and obsession with local church growth. In the difficult church and mission context where it was difficult even to find a pastoral intern for the education department, the young ministers and their small churches' prophetic imagination and willingness to experiment, the courage to pioneer the kingdom of God, and their lofty sense of vocation and perseverance despite financial hardships, and the way they stand in solidarity with one another, provides new hope for the Korean church. The lesson of JLMS for us is that in missions and ministry, the most critical factor is not the place but the people. The message is that together, we can overcome all obstacles. What sustained JLMS for 30 years was the higher perspective on Jeju-do, Korean society, and the world, as well as the faithful and persevering ministry in small churches. Not many people besides the member churches and ministers. But as someone who observed the Society through its two decades, I hope missionary movements like JLMS get started in other regions in Korea. The theory and practice of the Society's experience should be urgently shared in the world's mission fields.

Interview Questionnaire

1. How long have you participated in JLMS and what led you to participate?
2. What do you think are the characteristics of JLMS?
3. How have you benefited from or been supported by JLMS? (Jeju mission, individual minister, local church)
4. How have you benefited from study groups?
5. What do you think are the impetus and the engine that sustained JLMS for 20 years?
6. What are the characteristics of the leadership that had directed JLMS?
7. What are the fruits and limitations of JLMS?
8. If one is to start a gathering like JLMS in another region, what are the necessary factors?

Bibliography

Bosch, D. J. *Witness to the World,* Translated into Korean by Jeon Jae-ok. Seoul: Duranno, 1995.

Gibbs, Eddie. *Leadership Next.* Translated by Lee Min-ho. Seoul: Qumran Publishing House, 2010).

Jeju Gidok Shinmun. Issue 576, 2017 February 11.1.

Han, Kook-il. "Chi-yŏk-kyo-hoe-wa chi-yŏk-e-k'yu-me-ni-chŭm" [Local church and local ecumenism]. *Nongchongwa Mokhwe* 77, 2018 Spring, 20-30.

_________. *Sŏn-kyo-chŏk kyo-hoe-ŭi i-lon-kwa sil-che* [Theory and practice of missional church]. Seoul: PUTS Press, 2019.

Hong, Young-gi. *Han-kuk ch'o-tae-hyŏng kyo-hoe-wa k'a-li-sŭ-ma li-tŏ-sip* [Korean Mega Churches and Charismatic Leadership]. Seoul: Church Growth Institute, 2001.

Huber, W. *Kirche,* Translated into Korean by Lee Shin-geon. Seoul: Korea Theological Study Institute, 1990.

Kim, Sang-bok. *Mok-hoe-cha-ŭi li-tŏ-sip* [Minister's Leadership]. Seoul: Emmaus, 1997.

Lausanne Occasional Paper No. 24. "Cooperating in World Evangelization: A Handbook on Church/Para-Church Relationships." 1983.

Oh, Seong-choon. *Sin-hak. yŏng-sŏng. mok-hoe* [Theology, spirituality, ministry]. Seoul: PUTS Press, 1997,

Ross, Kenneth R., et al (ed.). *Ecumenical Missiology, Translated by Korea Ecumenical Society* (Seoul: CLSK, 2018)

Stevens, R. P. *The Abolition of the Laity.* Carlisle, Cumbria: Send the Light, 2000.

Suh, Sung-hwan. "Che-chu-chi-yŏk e-k'yu-me-ni-k'al un-tong i-ya-ki," [The story of ecumenical movement in Jeju] *Nongchongwa Mokhwe* 48, 2010 Winter. 97-104.

________. *Che-chu-sŏn-kyo 100nyŏn, ŏ-che-wa o-nŭl nae-il – pi-p'an-chŏk sŏng-ch'al-kwa tae-an-mo-saek* [100 Years of Jeju Mission, Yesterday, Today, and Tomorrow Critical Reflection and Exploration of Strategies]. Seoul: Yeyoung Communication, 2008.

________, *Saeng-myŏng-ŭi mul-kyŏl-ŭl tta-la kil-ŭl kŏt-ta – na-ŭi e-k'yu-me-ni-k'al yŏ-chŏng* [Walking along the waterway of life – my ecumenical journey]. Gyeongbuk: Living Waterway, 2014.

Verstraelen, F. J. Verstraelen (ed.). *Missiology An Ecumenical Introduction.* Grand Rapids, Michigan: Wm. B. Eerdmans, 1995. 238-239.

Walls, A. F. *The cross-cultural process in Christian history* (Maryknoll, New York: Orbis Books, 2002), 16-17.

Winter, Ralph, "The Two Structures of God's Redemptive Mission." *Missiology* 2.1, 1974.

Maeul Ministry: Cases and Theological Reflections – Urban Churches

Contributors

Gwang-su An studied Christian Education at Chongshin University, then continued at Presbyterian University and Theological Seminary and the Graduate School of Administration at Kyonggi University. As the Senior Pastor of Suwonsung Church, he served as the Committee Chair of Missionary Kids Ministry and the Stated Clerk for the Judicial Commission for the General Assembly of the Presbyterian Church of Korea, as well as the Moderator of Gyeonggi Presbytery and the General Secretary of Christian Conference of Suwon. He is also serving as the Chair of the Board of Suwon-Hwaseong Chapter of Korea Food for the Hungry International, the Chair of the Board of the Ministers' Council for Bereaved Families, the Chair of the Board of Family, Church, and Maeul Institute, the Chair of the Board of Hana Hospice Center, and the Chair of the Board of Gyeonggi Bible Institute.

Hung-young Baek graduated from Presbyterian University and Theological Seminary (M.Div., M.A. in Christian Education) and has been co-pastoring with In-sung Hwang at Gongmyung Church since January 2018. He has written books and spoken on family worship for the past ten years.

Eun-ha Cho studied Theology (Th.B.) and Christian Education (Th.M., Ph.D.) at Yonsei University and worked as an Adjunct Professor at the United Graduate School of Theology at Yonsei University. Currently she is a Professor of Christian Education at Mokwon University Department of Theology. She served as the President of Korean Society of Christian Religious Education, the Chair of Education Committee of Life Hope Christian Suicide Prevention Center, the General Secretary of the Korea Association of Accredited Theological Schools, a member of the Advisory Committee of Salim Christian Environmental Education Center, and the Co-Director of Family, Church, and Maeul Institute.

Joo-hee Cho studied at Presbyterian University and Theological Seminary (M. Div.) and got his doctoral degree (D. Min.) at Fuller Theological Seminary. Today he is the Installed Pastor of Seongam Church, a Co-Chief Executive Officer of Christian Ethics Movement Korea, a member of the Board of Seoul Jangsin University, and a member of the Board of Eunpyeong District Social Welfare Council.

Won-bum Chung, after graduating from Presbyterian University and Theological Seminary (Th.B., M.Div., Th.M., Th.D.), worked as a professor at Daejeon Theological University for 35 years until retirement. He also served as a Visiting Professor at Columbia Theological Seminary, Union Theological Seminary, and Anabaptist Mennonite Biblical Seminary, the Chair of the Korean Association for Christian Ethics, Chair of the Council of Research Institutes for the Presbyterian Church of Korea (PCK Tonghap), the Chair of the Peace Mission Guideline Publication Committee, and the Principal of Oikos Summer (Winter) School. Currently, he is the Cooperating Minister of Sekwang Church, a Board Member of

St. Francis Peace Center Foundation, the Director of the Church and Society Research Center, the Representative of Shalom Restoration Corporation, the Director of Korea Christian Coaching Academy, and a member of the Executive Committee of Korean Church Life Theology Forum.

Kook-Il Han studied Christian Education, Theology, and Church History (B.A, M. Div., Th.M.) at Presbyterian University and Theological Seminary (PUTS), then got his doctorate at Heidelberg University (Dr. Theol.) on missiology. He served as President of the Korean Society of Mission Studies, taught at Youngnam Theological University and Seminary and at PUTS as a Professor of Missiology until retirement in 2020. Today he is the Director of Workplace Mission Research Center for the Presbyterian Church of Korea, and the Co-Director of Family, Church, and Maeul Research Center.

Hong-eyoyl Hwang studied at Sogang University (B.A.), Presbyterian University and Theological Seminary (M.Div., Th.M.), and Birmingham University in England (Ph.D.). He was the Director of Research at Korean People's Peace Missions Research and the Professor of Missiology at Busan Presbyterian University (BPU). Since retirement, he has been the Co-Chair of the Council of Research Institutes for the Presbyterian Church of Korea, the President of the Korean Society of Mission Studies, the Director of the Institute for World Missions at BPU, and the Director of Missional Church Maeul Ministry Institute.

In-sung Hwang majored in biology and chemistry at Seoul National University. After spending time as a lay minister in England, he completed his studies at Presbyterian University and Theological Seminary (M.Div, Th.M, Ph.D). Today, he is the Clerk of the Family, Church, and Maeul Institute, the *Chaekbogo Gage* Bookshop owner, and a co-pastor of Gongmyung Church.

Hong-sun Kim studied at Mokwon University and continued to study social welfare administration at the Graduate School of Social Welfare at Silla University. He got a Th.M. in Church History at the United Graduate School of Theology at Yonsei University, then started church ministry in a rural town (which became today's Sejong City) in 1985. He returned to Myungsung Methodist Church in Ansan in 2001 and, for 23 years since, has been doing Maeul Ministry for the church to be in and with the local community. He is a neighborhood pastor who owes much to his congregation and local residents.

Bright Myeong-seok Lee studied at Sungkyunkwan University (B. Eng), Chongshin Theological Seminary (M.Div.) and at Presbyterian University and Theological Seminary for transfer of ordination and at its Graduate School of World Mission (ThM). Then he acquired his Ph.D. under the supervision of Professor Andrew F. Walls at Akrofi-Christaller Institute. From 1994 to 2002 he did ministry for migrant laborers and also worked as the Director and the General Manager of C3TV. In 2002 he was commissioned as the Presbyterian Church of Korea's ecumenical missionary to Ghana where he served for 20 years. Today he is a professor at ACTS (Asian Center for Theological Studies and Mission) International

Graduate School, the General Secretary of the International Association for Mission Studies (IAMS), a member of the Executive Committee of AMRIConnect (Association for Mission Researchers and Institution), the Co-Director of Korea IAMS Fellowship, and a Cooperating Minister of Suwonsung Church.

Byung-ohk Lee, after studying at Presbyterian University and Theological Seminary (PUTS), got his Ph.D. under the supervision of Craig Van Gelder – one of the pioneers of the missional church movement – at Luther Seminary in the United States. Today, he is a Professor of Missiology at PUTS and the Director of the Institute of Shalom Theology for South and North Korea. His research interests are in missional church and leadership, cross-cultural missions, and missional reformation of denominational structure.

Won-don Lee, since graduating from Presbyterian University and Theological Seminary (M.Div.), has been serving as the Senior Pastor of Bucheon Saerom Church for 37 years. He is the Director of Yakdae-dong Exciting Library, a Special Advisor to the Commission on the Decade of Life Ministry for the Presbyterian Church of Korea (PCK) General Assembly, and a member of the Board of PCK Maeul Ministry Network.

Gi-eop Nam studied political science and diplomacy at Sunggyunkwan University and got his doctorate at the same institution on the thoughts of Henry George, who pioneered the concept of common land ownership. He has lectured at Sunggkyunkwan University and Seoul National University. He is devoted to the study and practise of real-estate reform based on land justice and jubilee year as the model of the kingdom of God. His published works include Just Nation, Apartment Democracy, Jubilee (coauthored), *Restitution of Unearned Income: Theory of Real Estate System,* and many other books and articles. Currently, he is the director of the Institute of Land and Liberty, and the head of the social and environmental mission department of Suwonsung Church.

Chang-woo Oh graduated from Presbyterian University and Theological Seminary (B.A., M.Div.) and researched on the contact point between church and society in the local community at Fuller Theological Seminary (D.Min.). He has been the Senior Pastor of Hannam Jeil Church on Itaewon Street of Seoul for the past 38 years. He is serving as the Chief of Hannam-dong Silver Volunteers, the Head of the Steering Committee of Yongsan District Food Bank & Market, the Chair of the Board of Korea Jubilee Foundation Coop, the Chair of the Board of Korea Christian Ministry Support Network that trains young ministers, and the Chair of the Board of Poomda Maeul Community. In the Presbyterian Church of Korea (PCK) General Assembly, he is also the Chair of the Migrant Laborer Support Committee, the Chair of the Workplace Mission Committee, and a member of the Education Curriculum Committee. In the past, he served as the Moderator of West Seoul Presbytery, the Chair of Yongsan Church-District Council, and the Chair of the Laity Training Commission for the PCK General Assembly.

Seong-won Park graduated from Hanyang University (B.A.), Presbyterian University and Theological Seminary (M.Div., Th.M.), San Francisco Theological Seminary (D.Min.), and the University of Bern (Dr. theol.), then served as a professor at Seoul Jangsin University, an executive secretary of the theology department of the World Communion of Reformed Churches (WCRC), the senior pastor of Busanjin Church, the executive secretary of Cooperation and Witness Department of the WCRC, a Board Member of Ecumenical Advocacy Alliance, a Professor of theology at Youngnam Theological University and Seminary, and a member of the Central Committee of the World Council of Churches. Currently, he serves as the president of Gyeongan Graduate University and the moderator of OIKOTREE Global Movement.

Young-sang Ro studied at Seoul National University and Presbyterian University and Theological Seminary (M. Div., Th.M., Th.D.). His doctorate was in Christian ethics. He served as the president of Honam Theological University and Seminary, the dean of Theological Seminary of Presbyterian University and Theological Seminary, the president of Korea Association of Christian Studies, the president of Korea Association of Accredited Theological Schools, the chair of the board of Soongsil Cyber University, and the director of the Presbyterian Church of Korea Research Center. Today, he is the president of Korea Habor Evangelism & World Concern, the president of Bible Academy, and the deputy chair of the Private Education Ethics Council.

Sung-hwan Suh studied at Presbyterian University and Theological Seminary (B.A., M.Div.) and at the United Graduate School of Theology at Yonsei University (Th.M. in Systematic Theology). He was commissioned as a missionary of the Presbyterian Church of Korea (Tonghap) as the Cooperating Missionary of the Evangelical-Lutheran Church in Württemberg and served as the Installed Pastor of Nambu Region Korean Church of Germany. Upon returning to South Korea, he served as the Installed Pastor of Jeju Seongan Church, then founded and pastored Sarang Soomgyeol Church on Jeju Island for 21 years until his honorary retirement. In March 2002, he and an interdenominational group of pastors organized Jeju Love Mission Society (JLMS), and he served as its founding president. He continues to participate as a member of JLMS today.

Rebekah Hwajhin Lee (translator) holds a BA from Cornell University, an MDiv from Princeton Theological Seminary, and a PhD in Education from Seoul National University where she studied global education cooperation focusing on development education, global citizenship, and the work of faith-based institutions. She currently teaches at Korea National University of Education and works as a Korean-to-English translator, bringing her expertise in education, theology, and sustainability to both roles.